IMMORTALITY

THE OTHER
SIDE OF DEATH

D0888078

IMMORTALITY
THE OTHER SIDE OF DEATH

Gary R. Habermas
J. P. Moreland

THOMAS NELSON PUBLISHERS
Nashville

Published in Nashville, Tennessee, by Thomas Nelson, Inc., and distributed in Canada by Lawson Falle, Ltd., Cambridge, Ontario.

Unless otherwise noted, Scripture quotations are from the NEW KING JAMES VERSION of the Bible. Copyright © 1979, 1980, 1982, Thomas Nelson, Inc., Publishers.

Scripture quotations noted NASB are from THE NEW AMERICAN STANDARD BIBLE, Copyright © 1960, 1962, 1963, 1968, 1971, 1972, 1973, 1975, 1977 by The Lockman Foundation and are used by permission.

Scripture quotations noted NIV are from The Holy Bible: NEW INTERNATIONAL VERSION. Copyright © 1978 by the New York International Bible Society. Used by permission of Zondervan Bible Publishers.

Library of Congress Cataloging-in-Publication Data

Habermas, Gary R.
   Immortality : the other side of death / Gary R. Habermas, J.P. Moreland.
   Includes bibliographical references.
   ISBN 0-8407-7677-2 (pbk.)
   1. Future life—Christianity. I. Moreland, James Porter, 1948– . II. Title.
BT902.H27 1992
236'.22—dc20
                92–8039
                CIP

Printed in the United States of America
1 2 3 4 5 6 7 - 96 95 94 93 92

With much love, to our wives,
Debbie and Hope,

two Christian saints who
"desire a better country, that is
a heavenly one. Therefore God
is not ashamed to be called their God;
for He has prepared a city for them."
(Heb. 11:16 NASB)

Contents

Beyond Life's "Certainties"

Conventional wisdom has it that there are only two certainties to life: death and taxes. However, there is one main difference between them: You can cheat on your taxes. But the grim reaper will not be denied. All of us will die. This is a book for people who will die. But it is not only about death. It also concerns life, here and beyond.

Have you ever thought about your own death? Most likely, you have. But there is a good chance that you have not dwelt on it for very long. Death is not a subject that usually brings us pleasure or comfort.

Our cultural attitude toward death has been largely shaped by hospitals and mass media. Our main exposure to death is in the movies or on television, where death is one step removed from reality. In the real world, though, most people die in a hospital surrounded by health-care professionals.

Contrast this with the way people used to experience death. Paintings as recently as one hundred years ago often depict the dying person at home, surrounded by friends, making his final peace in community with others. The family would often help prepare the body for burial, and children were routinely exposed to death. We today are out of touch with death; we do not face it like most of those who passed before us.

When we do think about death, we're likely to raise various questions: Is there really such a thing as life after death? And if so, must I merely take its reality by faith or perhaps on the basis of something like the Bible? Are there good reasons for believing in life after death? What is the afterlife like? What happens to me the moment I leave my body? How can I see, talk, and do other things if there is a disembodied state immediately following death? Is reincarnation true? Is there really such a place as heaven? If so, what is it like? Is there a hell, and how can such a place be reconciled with a loving God? If there is a life hereafter, how can my belief in such a reality affect my life here on earth?

In this book, we will explore answers to these questions as well as other related issues. The chapters are divided into three main sections. Section 1 takes up the question of whether life after death is real and what rationale or evidence supports its reality. The second section explores what the afterlife is really like. In the last section, we seek to show how immortality in the hereafter can have real value in how we live here and now.

Two final words before we embark on our journey. You should know that we, the authors, are Christians. We think there are some excellent reasons to accept the Bible and its orthodox interpretation as true. Nevertheless, we do not assume the truth of Christianity or the Bible in Part 1 (we do make that assumption in Parts 2 and 3, though not without presenting some supporting evidence). This should not be taken to mean that we believe faith is the *only* support for these beliefs. There are many good reasons to accept orthodox Christianity, and we ask you to seek out these reasons in some of our other books and the many sources we cite.[1] We sincerely hope you will interact with our reasoning there and in this volume too.

Second, as you read *Immortality,* you will notice citations to numerous endnotes. Just because these notes occur at the end of the book does not mean they are unimportant. We hope you will refer to them to gather the names of sources that could help you pursue subjects of interest. These endnotes also contain more technical treatments of certain points for those of you with more philosophical or theological training. Of course, if you prefer, you can bypass these notes without jeopardizing your ability to engage in this fascinating journey through death and beyond with us.

Each of us contributed material according to our own expertise and interest. J.P. Moreland wrote Chapter 1. He also wrote the chapters on dualism (2-3), the intermediate state (7), hell (11), and end-of-life ethical decisions (14). Gary Habermas penned the chapters on the resurrection of Jesus (4, 9), near-death experiences (5-6), reincarnation (8), heaven (10), the top-down perspective on life (12), and the fear of death (13). Throughout the entire process, we carefully reviewed each other's work so that what you hold represents a true coauthorship.

We recognize that the material in this book may seem somewhat technical to you. We also know that it will probably take some effort to work through it. This is especially true for Chapters 1-3, which you could skip and read later if you find them too difficult to wade through at first. But don't lose heart! We live in a TV generation that expects instant success and simple packaging. Some issues are of such importance and of such a nature that they are distorted and their richness lost if we oversimplify them. We spend hours learning how to perform a hobby, invest money wisely, or fix something in our homes. And usually, this is time well spent. How much more should we be willing to invest mental effort to learn why we believe what we do about life's most important questions? So we invite you to read on with an open heart, a critical mind, and a persevering spirit. We believe the journey will be well worth the effort.

PART 1

The Evidence for Immortality

Chapter 1

Some Reasons to Believe

My (Moreland's) grandfather died when I was in seminary. I received the news just after finishing a class where we had studied the second coming of Christ, life after death, heaven, and hell. But the course had seemed unreal and dry. The lectures and exams had focused on comparing different views about the topics and examining their biblical support. So when the phone call came about my grandfather's death, I was unprepared.

On the way to Missouri to attend his funeral, I was flooded with thoughts and feelings. I thought of the times we had hunted geese together. But now he was gone. And his laugh when he won a game of cards. But I would hear it no more. There were the porch swings he built at his lumber yard. None would come from his hands again. As my plane headed north to Kansas City, the finality of death filled my heart. I cried like a child.

I will never forget looking at his body in the coffin. His lifeless form only resembled the man I had loved. He was much more than this body, which he had seemed to own for a time. I wondered, *What was life like for him now? Is there really such a thing as life after death? When it comes right down to it, why do I believe in life after death anyway? Is such a belief reasonable, or do I merely have to accept it by blind faith?*

This last question was especially important to me. I have known people who believe things just because they help them, but these people have apparently cared little about whether their beliefs were true or reasonable. But deep down, I believe no one really wants to be a fool and draw comfort from a belief that turns out to be a mere placebo—a false belief that gives comfort simply because it is believed. As the ancient Greek philosopher Aristotle pointed out, all of us, by our very nature, desire to know things. We want to know what is true and false, and we want to know if we are rationally justified in our beliefs. We acknowledge that a person is foolish to buy a house, change jobs, or get married without giving any thought to whether those decisions are wise and reasonable. How much more should we seek to be reasonable when it comes to life's most fundamental issues: God, our own nature, values, and life beyond.

So in the next six chapters, we will investigate some of the reasons it is rational to believe in life after death. In this chapter we will begin by focusing on a potpourri of arguments that have been offered in support of this belief. But before we look at these, we need to take a brief look at the concept of rationality itself and how it applies to matters of death and immortality.

When Is Belief Reasonable?

When we say something is rational to believe as true, what do we mean? What does it take for a belief to be rational? We do not need to explore or establish a full-blown theory of rationality here.[1] However, two aspects of rationality are important for us in this context.

The first aspect concerns degrees of rationality.[2] Not all beliefs are equally reasonable. Some are very, very reasonable ($7+5=12$); some are very, very unreasonable (George Bush is a Martian); and others fall somewhere between these extremes.

Consider any belief: say, the belief that it will rain today, or that there is life after death, or that dogs are mammals. Let's designate such a belief with the letter p. There are three attitudes we could take toward p: we could believe p is true; we could believe p is false, for shorthand's sake call it not-p; or we could withhold belief altogether. If we withheld a conclusion regarding some belief p, we judge that the belief is counterbalanced; in other words, the rational support for p and for not-p would be equal and it would be irrational to believe in either the truth or falsity of p. Instead, we should suspend judgment.

With this in mind, let's consider the following ranking of belief states:

less reasonable to believe	State 0: Counterbalanced
↓	State 1: Probable
	State 2: In the Clear
more reasonable to believe	State 3: Beyond Reasonable Doubt

If a belief p is *counterbalanced*, say the belief that my kids will go swimming today, then neither p nor not-p has any positive rational status for me. If a belief p is *probable*, then believing p is more reasonable than believing not-p, but it may be as good or even more reasonable to withhold belief and suspend judgment.

Sometimes we have enough evidence for some belief to make accepting the belief more reasonable than thinking the belief is false. But our evidence may be slim so that the wisest position may be not to commit ourselves either way, but to suspend judgment and wait for more evidence.

Stronger still is a belief that is *in the clear:* You are not more justified in withholding p than in believing p, but it may be as reasonable to withhold as to believe p. In a case like this, the evidence for a belief is stronger than the evidence against it. But more important, the evidence is good enough that the wisest thing is no longer suspending judgment. Now the evidence implies that you have two options that are equally reasonable: accepting the belief or continuing to suspend judgment. When a belief is merely probable, you should still suspend judgment. But when a belief is in the clear, committing yourself to the belief is no more or less reasonable than suspending judgment. Either way, you would not be acting irrationally.

Even stronger is a belief that is *beyond reasonable doubt:* You are more justified in believing *p* than in withholding *p*. In this case, the evidence for *p* is so strong that not only would it be unreasonable to believe that *p* is false; it would also be unreasonable to withhold judgment and ask for more evidence.

It may be helpful to illustrate these states of rationality with respect to the belief that life after death is true. If we claim that such a belief is *probable,* then we claim that belief in life after death is more reasonable than the belief there is no life after death, but it may be more reasonable to suspend judgment and not believe either way. The evidence is just not good enough to justify a commitment to either stance.

If we claim that belief in life after death is *in the clear,* then we claim that believing in life after death is better than believing there is no life after death and, furthermore, suspending judgment on the question is not more reasonable than believing in an afterlife.

Finally, if we claim that belief in life after death is *beyond reasonable doubt,* then we claim that believing is more reasonable than denying it or withholding judgment.

How should we view belief in life after death? You will have to make up your own mind on that question. But given the contemporary bent toward naturalism (only the natural world exists; that God, the soul, objective values, and life after death are irrational, perhaps outdated notions), if belief in life after death were even probable or in the clear, that would be an improvement for most people.

But in our opinion, the belief that immortality is true is beyond reasonable doubt, and we will show you several reasons why we hold this position. But keep in mind the fact that if you do not believe our arguments warrant this strong a position, you would be unwise to jump immediately to the conclusion that belief in immortality is positively irrational. For it may be that this belief is probable or in the clear, which is still a rather strong position in a society drawn to naturalism.

A second feature of rationality is this: Often, a particular belief is a part of a larger system of beliefs, and it gains rational support from its role in that system. In cases like these, it is less rational to accept the belief if it is evaluated on its own, apart from its supporting web of beliefs, assuming, of course, that the system itself is reasonable.

For example, suppose the Kansas City Royals were just beaten 10-0 by a minor league team. This may leave us wondering whether to believe the Royals are a very good team. If we come to a conclusion on the basis of this one game alone, then it may be unreasonable for us to believe that they are a great team.

But, suppose we have a lot of other background beliefs about the Royals: For example, they have a great pitching staff, a high team batting average, a consistent winning record, and a poor attitude toward playing minor league teams. Given this broad system of background beliefs, it would now be reasonable for us to hold that they are a very good team, even though this position would not be reasonable in light of just one game. In general, therefore, a belief can be less rational if considered alone, but it can grow in rationality if it is part of and supported by a system of beliefs, which is itself rational.

What does this have to do with life after death? We are going to evaluate belief in the hereafter without assuming the truth of a system of beliefs in which life after death is embedded. This may seem artificial to you. Questions about life after death arise most naturally in conjunction with questions about the existence of God and the truth of a specific religion.[3] Part of the support for belief in an afterlife comes from the rationality of theism.

According to theism, especially Judeo-Christian theism, the material universe is not all there is. There is a personal Creator God who exists even though he is a spirit and is invisible. God made humans in his image, and human beings consist of both body and soul. Further, God loves his creation, especially human beings, and he has planted in their hearts a desire to live in relationship with him forever.

So even if one judged that belief in immortality was not very rational considered on its own, it could still be beyond reasonable doubt when the evidential force of the rationality of, say, Christian theism is thrown into the equation.[4]

Why, then, are we looking at the rationality of belief in life after death apart from general considerations of the rationality of theism? Even though our approach is not the usual one, still, many people (even Christians) wonder whether or not there is any evidence for certain theological notions apart from the support they get from theism in general, or Christian theism in particular. So if a good case can be made for life after death independent of theism, then such a case will tend to confirm theism and, as we will show, Christian theism as well.

In our following examination of the reasonableness of belief in the afterlife, we will not assume that God exists or that Christianity is true. The only exception we will make will be in our exploration of an initial set of arguments that do appeal to God for support. Now let's press on.

Arguments Based on God's Existence

When most of us wonder about life after death, we find ourselves thinking about God as well. This attitude is quite natural and proper, for while it is possible to believe in God without believing in life after death (and vice versa), the two notions do fit together in a rational, mutually reinforcing way. In fact, if we grant the existence of a theistic God, especially the God of Christian theism, then belief in immortality is overwhelmingly probable, beyond a reasonable doubt. Consider the arguments.

Kinship with the Divine

Take the argument from kinship with the divine.[5] It has at least three forms. First, humans are made in the image of God and are like God in many ways: We can transcend our bodies by thinking, loving, feeling, and willing. One of the ways we resemble God is in possessing a form of immortality.

Unfortunately, this argument is not a good one. According to theism, only God possesses a natural immortality in himself. Everything else, including the human body and human soul, is sustained in existence by God. Immortality is not a natural aspect of what we are—instead, it flows from what God does in our behalf. He holds us (and the entire universe) in existence.

On the other hand, the kinship-with-the-divine type of argument might be used in another way. God is a pure, unchanging spirit and is suited for life in a place like heaven (more accurately, heaven is a suitable place for a being like God). Humans are like God in this respect. The apostle Paul, for example, claims that we are strangers and sojourners on this earth and our real citizenship is in heaven (Phil. 3:20). Perhaps we are like God in this respect. We were meant to live a type of life suited for a heavenly mode of existence.

This idea is certainly reasonable and plausible. Most of us have experienced periodic longings for a different world, and these longings may be indicators of our kinship with the divine in this sense.

There is yet a third way our kinship with God might be used to argue for life after death. If we are made in God's image, we have an incredible degree of intrinsic value as persons. From this notion, the following moral principle seems reasonable: It is wrong, all things being equal, to annihilate or extinguish something with intrinsic value, especially of the sort possessed by God and those made in his image. Put more simply, it is wrong to dispense with the indispensable.

Consider things with lesser intrinsic value than humans, say a work of art. All things being equal, it is wrong to destroy a work of art and take it out of existence, because, among other things, the universe loses something of value. Similarly, it would be wrong for anyone, even God, to annihilate a creature made in God's image, for such an act would remove the value sustained in being by that creature's existence, and it would treat the person as a mere means to an end (say, of getting rid of him) instead of as an end in himself.

This argument was stated nicely by philosopher Geddes MacGregor:

> If there is a Creator God who is infinitely benevolent as well as the source of all values, then he must be committed to the conservation of values. The

highest values we know are experiences of the fulfillment of ideal purposes by individual persons. The existence of these values depends upon persons. God must, therefore, be the conserver of persons. Every argument for theism is an argument for the preservation of all persons whose extinction would seem to entail a failure on God's part in his benevolent purpose.[6]

If this argument is a good one, and we think it is, then it poses some intriguing conclusions concerning the existence of hell, which we will take up in Chapter 8.

Justice

A second major argument flows from our sense of *justice*.[7] It is obvious that in this life goods and evils, rewards and punishments, are not evenly distributed. Inequities abound. Good people often live miserable lives, and evil people often prosper. If God is infinitely just, as theism affirms, he must rectify these injustices. Because that rectification does not take place in this life, it must take place in the life to come.

This argument has some force, but it is inconclusive for at least two reasons. It would not apply to those who have not suffered serious inequities in this life (if there are such people!). Further, it does not prove that the afterlife is unending. Perhaps life's inequities could be balanced in a finite period of life after death.

Divine Love

This third argument goes like this: As infinite, pure love, God intends the highest good for his creatures. Man has been made for communion with God, and the highest good would be for that communion between finite lovers and the infinite lover to be endless. Further, God has placed in our hearts a desire for eternity, and it would be cruel for him to frustrate that desire. The same love that moved him to create in the first place, that keeps him from deliberately and cruelly withdrawing his presence from us during our earthly life, and that moved him to seek to save us from destruction, that same love is what guarantees our eternal, face-to-face communion with God for eternity.

Revelation

This fourth argument makes the simple observation that, in the Bible, God has revealed his intentions that all people will live forever in some form or other, and God does not lie.

For those who accept the Bible as propositional revelation and who accept traditional, orthodox interpretations of biblical passages regarding the afterlife, this argument is persuasive.

Although these arguments are based on theism, if theism *is* rational they hold a lot of weight.[8] In fact, some philosophers and theologians have argued that the only reason for believing in life after death is that it follows from a prior belief in theism. But we will argue that this position in itself is too strong. We will give evidence for life after death that does not depend upon a prior acceptance of theism in general or Christian theism in particular.

On the other hand, it is certainly true that if belief in the theistic God, especially the Christian God, is rational, then it is rational to believe in life after death. In light of this, it is hard to understand the motivation of those who claim to be Christian theologians and who claim to believe in God, but who, nevertheless, deny any form of personal life after death.[9]

Arguments from the Unity of the Self

Quite a number of thinkers have argued that there is something about the very nature of the human self that implies or supports life after death.[10] The most prominent of these arguments has been the argument based on the simplicity of the soul.[11] Advocates of this approach include Plato, G.M.E. McTaggart, and Augustus Strong, to name a few.

Before we look at some different ways of formulating this argument, a word of clarification is in order. According to classic, Christian theology, God alone possesses natural immortality in himself (cf. 1 Tim. 6:16).[12] He is a self-existent being and everything else depends upon God, not only for coming into existence, but for continuing in existence. Nevertheless, a standard, orthodox way of understanding life after death within a Christian framework is as follows: Human beings are properly and normally to be construed as a unity of material human bodies and immaterial substantial souls. Upon death, a person enters into a temporary disembodied state that is less than complete, and receives a new resurrected body at the general resurrection. The important point is that this view includes a picture of being human that supports life after death. Part of that picture is the truth of substance dualism, roughly the idea that humans have immaterial souls that can have properties, remain the same through change, survive and maintain its identity with itself even if the body is destroyed, and that makes the body a *human* body. In Chapters 2 and 3, we will investigate the truth of substance dualism. For now, let us assume the existence of a soul and ask whether there is something about the soul's nature that entails or supports belief in life after death.

The Soul's Simplicity

A common argument involves the simplicity of the soul. *Simplicity* in this case means that the soul has no parts; it is not a complex entity that can lose parts and still remain a soul. For example, a human being can lose an arm or leg and still be human. A soul has no parts as human bodies do, therefore, all a soul can lose is *all* it is. The argument looks like this:

(1) There are two ways for something to be destroyed: annihilation (something simply pops out of existence, as it were, all at once) and through separation and loss of parts.

(2) Science does not give examples of annihilation. Rather, physical objects are destroyed through the loss of their parts as they leave or rearrange to form new things. For example, a chair ceases to be when its legs, seat, and back are torn apart and shredded. In general, our experience does not give us examples of annihilation. Thus, the most reasonable way to understand a case of ceasing-to-be is to treat it as an example of disassociation of parts.

(3) Physical objects are complex entities in that they are complex wholes composed of a number of different parts. The soul, being an immaterial, spiritual substance, is a basic, simple entity—that is, it is not a heap or complex of parts as a chair or computer is.[13]

(4) Therefore, the soul is immortal, because there is no good reason to believe it can be annihilated or can lose parts.

How should we evaluate this argument? Premise 1 seems reasonable enough. It accounts for the vast majority, and perhaps all, of the cases of ceasing to exist that we encounter in daily life, so let us agree to accept it.

Similarly, let us agree to accept premise 2. In science, one of the main points of advocating the existence of atoms is to explain change in terms of the separation and recombination of those atoms.[14] For example, when a piece of paper is burned up, this change is viewed as a chemical rearrangement of the atoms that make up the paper. They rearrange and combine with oxygen in the process of burning, and they form new chemical compounds. True, the soul is not a material object as are most of the standard objects of scientific investigation, but for the sake of argument we can reasonably understand our general experience of coming-to-be and passing away to be consistent with science.

The main problem with the argument is found in premise 3. The argument assumes the soul is a simple, noncomplex entity, but there are good reasons for rejecting this assumption. It is true that ordinary physical objects (e.g., tables) are not simple, but complex. One reason for this is that these objects are extended throughout a region of space. Consider a round, five-inch disk. The left half of the disk cannot be identical to the right half, or else the disk would not have *two* halves! In general, physical objects must be complex, because they must have different parts to occupy different points of space throughout the region they occupy.

On the other hand, some people have thought that the soul is simple because it is not a spatially extended entity. Now, the soul is in fact fully present throughout the body and completely "in" each part of the body. But the "in" is not a spatial concept. Water is spatially "in" a glass. However, even though my thoughts are "in" my mind, my mind is not a container like a bucket with thoughts spatially inside it. It makes no sense to ask if my thought of lunch is closer to my left ear than my right one! In the same way, my soul is "in" my body in some sense, but my body is not a spatial container for my soul. If you cut off my hand, you do not cut off part of my soul.

Thus, while it is true that all spatially extended things are non-simple (i.e., composed of parts), it is not true that all non-spatially extended things, such as the soul, are simple. In fact, we can reject the soul's simplicity on different grounds. For instance, the soul is capable of having desires, beliefs, thoughts, sensations of color, sound, and so forth. A thought of love is not the same thing as a sensation of red. Further, the soul contains various capacities that differ from each other—a vast array of intellectual, emotional, and volitional capacities. These capacities are contained within the soul itself, and they differ from each other. Thus, the soul contains internal differences, which means it could not be simple.

Therefore, the argument from simplicity does not work. However, there is a second, and closely related argument that is better. Though the soul may not be a simple entity, it does seem to possess a *different* and *deeper* type of unity than do ordinary physical objects and other types of things like the physical body. This characteristic leads us to the argument from the *unity of the soul*.

The Soul's Unity

Things in the world manifest different degrees of unity. There are various types of wholes that have parts united with each other to form those wholes and whose parts are united together to a greater or lesser degree of intimacy.[15] Here are four examples that go from lesser to greater unity: a heap of salt; a car; a living organism like an amoeba; and the self with its thoughts, feelings, and so forth.

The heap of salt is one, single thing in a very weak sense: Its parts are homogeneous (each part, in this case a grain of salt, is just like the other parts), and they are related to each other in a loose, spatial way (each grain of salt is close to each other grain).

The car has a set of heterogeneous parts (e.g., the door and the carburetor are different from each other), and they are united in more than a mere spatial way. The parts of a car work together in a mechanical manner to produce motion.

The various parts of a living organism, like an amoeba, are deeply united to each other to form an organic whole that has a higher degree of unity than that of a mere machine. For example, the various parts of an organism relate to one another in a variety of complicated ways: They get their identity from the system of which they are a part (e.g., the heart is that which functions to pump blood), and ultimately, the organism as a whole (the whole is prior to the parts) and its parts cease to exist as functional units when they are severed from the organism (a severed hand is a hand in name only).

Now a number of thinkers, such as G.M.E. McTaggart and Peter Kreeft, have argued that the soul has a *different* and *deeper* unity than things like heaps of salt, machines, living organisms like an amoeba, and even the physical body.[16] The argument can be summarized in this manner. When we reflect upon ourselves, certain things become evident to us. First, we know that we *have* a body but are not the same thing as our body. Also, even though my self contains a plurality of contents—different thoughts, pains, feelings, desires, sensory experiences, episodes of willing—I am not identical to a bundle of those contents, nor am I a combination of those contents. My thoughts, feelings, and so on could not exist without me. And the reality of me could not be due to a certain combination of the contents that compose me. I am not a heap or combination of anything. Instead, I am a *center* of consciousness, an irreducible *I*, an *ego* that has my various mental contents but is different from them and more basic than they. I could exist without any one of them, but they could not exist without me.

Now, since I have a different, deeper unity than that of my body or my experiences taken as a mere collection or combination, then it is certainly possible, indeed there is some presumption in favor of the notion, that *I* survive death.

What can be said in favor of this argument? For one thing, when we reflect upon ourselves, it is surely evident to us that we are not a mere combination of entities, but rather a unified self, a center of subjectivity.

Some philosophers disagree with this claim, arguing that we are a "multitude of selves."[17] But we do not see any good reason to accept their claim.

When I experience various things at the same time—a feeling of pain, a sweet smell, a sensation of red—if I consider whether or not I am actually having these experiences, I know for certain that I am. Similarly, if I consider whether or not I am the same, single center of consciousness that has my various experiences, I am certain that I am the single center of consciousness that has them all. The burden of proof is clearly on someone who tries to turn me into a combination of things, and no sufficient reason has been given for overturning what I already know to be true by simple reflection on my own mental life. The critic must give me more reasons to believe that I am not a unified, single self than I have for believing what is already evident to me. He has not done so.[18]

These basic intuitions about the unity and singularity of my self can be illustrated with a thought experiment.[19] Suppose it becomes possible someday to perform a brain operation upon a person in such a way that exactly half of his brain is transplanted into each of two different brainless bodies. The person operated on, we'll call Sally. Let's imagine that the left hemisphere of her brain is placed in body 1, and the right hemisphere of her brain goes into body 2.

Suppose further that, upon recovery, each of the two previously brainless bodies manifest the same character traits and have the same memories as Sally did. The transplants, therefore, would have created two new persons, but Sally cannot be identical to both of them because one thing cannot be the same as two things. It may be that Sally ceased to exist, and the two other entities are two totally new people. Or it may be that Sally survived and is now identical to the brain-filled body 1, so that only one new person—the brain-filled body 2—came into being as a result of the operation.

Either way, we learn two things from the example. First, a person is not identical to her body or to her memories and character traits. Remember, persons *have* these things, they are not *identical to* them or to a collection of them. You see, bodies 1 and 2 may each have Sally's memories and character traits and an equal share of her brain, but they cannot both be Sally. Therefore, the fact that Sally is a person must amount to more than just being a brain with memories and character traits.

The second lesson is this: Persons are not capable of partial identity and survival as are physical objects. If you break a table in half and use each half to build two new tables, it makes sense to say that the original table partially survives and is partly present in each of the new tables.[20] But in our brain operation example, the following four options are the only possible ways to understand what happened:[21] 1) Sally ceases to be and two new persons come to be; 2) Sally survives and is identical to body 1, and a new person, body 2, comes to be; 3) Sally survives and is identical to body 2, and a new person, body 1, comes to be; 4) Sally partially survives in bodies 1 and 2. Although option 4 may make sense of physical objects like tables, it is not a reasonable option with regard to persons.

To see why option 4 is not a good one, consider another experiment offered by philosopher Bernard Williams.[22] Suppose a mad surgeon captures you and announces that he is going to transplant the left hemisphere of your brain into one body and the right hemisphere into another body. After surgery, he is going to torture one of the resultant persons and reward the other one with a gift of a million dollars. You can choose which of the two persons, A or B, will be tortured and which will be rewarded. It is clear that whichever way you choose, your choice would be a risk. Perhaps you will cease to exist and be neither A nor B. But it is also possible that you will be either A or B. However, one thing does not seem possible—your being partially A and partially B. For in that case you would have reason to approach the surgery with both a feeling of joyous expectation and horrified dread! Why? After the operation you would simultaneously experience torture and reward because you yourself would partially be A and partially be B! But it is hard to make sense of such a mixed anticipation because *there will be no person after the surgery who will experience such a mixed fate.* Partial survival, at least when it comes to persons, does not seem to make sense. No sense can be given to the notion that a person is partly in that body and partly in this one. Persons are deep unities, not mere collections or combinations of things that admit of partial survival like physical objects.

Our basic awareness of ourselves, as illustrated in the two thought experiments above, indicates that we as persons have a different and far deeper unity than do physical objects. Further, our unity of consciousness rules out the notion that we are a mere collection or combination of more basic things.

Now this argument does not prove, beyond a shadow of doubt, that the person survives the death of his body. But the argument does open up the possibility of survival, because the unity of the self is different from the unity of the body. Moreover, the argument lends some support to survival after the death of the body because the unity of the self is deeper than that of the body. Taken by itself, this argument may not be sufficient to place belief in life after death beyond reasonable doubt, but when it is made part of an overall case for life after death, it does give some support to that case.

Before we move to another argument for life after death, one more objection to the argument from the unity of the self should be considered. It may be true that the type of unity the self possesses is greater than that of a mere collection or combination of things as we find in a physical object. And it may be that the self could not cease to be by a gradual, quantitative loss of parts, as is the case when a table ceases to be by gradual loss of parts. But there is another way for something to cease to be: by gradually diminishing in a qualitative way. This objection was forcefully made by the great German philosopher Immanuel Kant.[23]

Kant's argument is that, while the soul may not be a collection of parts extended in space (therefore, not have extended quantity), it still has intensive quantity and, like a sound, it can gradually lose more and more existence until it fades out of existence altogether.

Is Kant's objection sound? We don't think so. As Roderick Chisholm points out:

> [Kant] thought that some things could have *more* existence than others. It is as though he thought that there is a path between being and nonbeing, so that one day you may set out from nonbeing and head in the direction toward being with the result that the farther you go in that direction the more being you will have. But surely there is *no* mean between being and nonbeing. If something *is* on a certain path, then that something *is*. Or if it *isn't* yet, then it can't be on the path between being and nonbeing. Of course things can be more or less endowed. But things cannot be more or less endowed with respect to being. What is poorly endowed *is* poorly endowed and, therefore, *is*.[24]

In cases like a sound gradually fading away or a mind gradually losing consciousness or some other faculties, what is really going on is the alteration of something that exists, not its gradually ceasing to be. Something can gradually be altered in the properties it possesses—you can gradually lose your hearing—but something cannot be gradually altered with respect to existence. That is all or nothing.

Consider a pain's diminishing. There is a difference between a thing's diminishing in its intensity and a thing's diminishing in its being. A pain may diminish in its intensity, but that is not the same thing as its diminishing in its being a pain or in its being real. A pain is simply altered, or rather the person who has the pain is altered. But the pain remains a pain as long as it exists.

The Argument from Desire

A different argument for life after death has been called the argument from desire. Briefly put, it looks like this:

(1) The desire for life after death is a natural desire.

(2) Every natural desire corresponds to some real state of affairs that can fulfill it.

(3) Therefore, the desire for life after death corresponds to some real state of affairs—namely life after death—that fulfills it.

Let's consider two elaborations of this basic argument by two of its most famous advocates—Thomas Aquinas and C.S. Lewis. We will begin with Aquinas.[25]

According to Aquinas, things in the world have natures that define what those things are. Fido is in the class of dogs because he possesses dogness. Beatrice is in the class of humans because she possesses humanness. Dogness and humanness are the natures of Fido and Beatrice, respectively. Now a thing has a set of natural tendencies, aspirations, and desires—conscious or unconscious—grounded in its nature. Dogs have a natural tendency to bark; humans have a natural tendency to acquire knowledge and use language.

Now, Aquinas continues, a thing has a natural tendency to maintain itself in existence in a manner natural and appropriate to the kind of thing it is. Furthermore, among the things that have knowledge, desires naturally arise according to the type of knowledge possessed. An apple does not possess knowledge. On the other hand various mammals, such as dogs, possess sensory knowledge; they have sensory experiences of particular things immediately present before them. And humans have intellectual knowledge; they can contemplate general ideas, such as the class of dogs, triangles, or even existence itself.

When we apply these different kinds of knowledge to the knowledge of existence, animals only know existence here and now because that is the only notion of existence of which they can have a particular sensory awareness. But humans are intellectual creatures and, as such, have an intellectual understanding of everlasting life. Since natural desires ensue upon, or flow from, the knowledge possessed by a living thing, then humans have a natural desire for everlasting life.

Finally, according to Aquinas, natural desires are not in vain. For every natural desire there is a real state of affairs that has the potential to respond to or fulfill that desire. Therefore, there is such a thing as everlasting life.

Now let's look at C.S. Lewis's form of the argument from desire.[26] He claims that it is not necessarily egoistic to desire our own good and hope for happiness; indeed, it can be quite appropriate. This is because there are different kinds of rewards, and some are proper because they have a natural connection with the things we do to earn them. Money is not the natural reward for love (one is mercenary to marry for money) because money is foreign to the desires that ought to accompany love. By contrast, victory is a natural reward for battle. It is a proper reward because it is not tacked onto the activity for which the reward is given, but rather victory is the consummation of the activity itself.

A third case is a schoolboy enjoying Greek poetry. In the beginning, he works at grammar as a mercenary (to get good grades, avoid punishment, etc.) because he has no idea what the enjoyment of Greek poetry would be like. The reward he will get (enjoying Greek poetry) will, in fact, be the proper reward for his activities, but he does not know that at the beginning.

Christians are like the schoolboy. Those who have attained heaven or who mature as believers desire everlasting communion with God as a proper reward for the consummation of our efforts on earth. But when we begin the Christian life, we often obey God for other reasons (to please others, out of fear of punishment, and so on).

Now, according to Lewis, we all desire heaven, although that desire can be hidden from us. Sometimes we desire lesser, finite goods (such as beauty), but these are symbols of and pointers to the transtemporal, transfinite good that is our real destiny. The desire for heaven is a desire that no natural happiness will satisfy.

Furthermore, our natural desires are indicators of what the world is like. If we have a natural desire for something, then that thing must exist. We may desire food and not get it, but we would not be hungry in a world where food and eating did not exist. Again, a man may love a woman and not win her, but falling in love would not occur in a sexless world. By the same token, someone may desire heaven and not obtain it, but such a desire would not occur in a world where heaven was not real. Therefore, life after death must be real.

As you might imagine, the argument from desire has had its critics. First, some claim that the desire for heaven is just an example of ethical egoism: the view that an act or desire is right if and only if it is in the person's own self-interest. But Lewis's argument appears to answer this objection. Some desires are proper for humans, and seeking to meet them is part of what we ought to do, part of what it is supposed to mean to be human in the first place. Additionally, one could desire heaven for other reasons besides self-interest. We might desire it because it is simply right to seek the type of life heaven offers and avoid the life awaiting us in hell. Finally, the desire for heaven can be an expression of the fact that I view myself as an end in myself. Since I see myself as a creature of intrinsic value, my desire for heaven is a way of treating myself as a person of value, as an end in myself. So this first objection lacks sufficient punch to knock out the argument from desire.

A second objection is this: We simply don't desire heaven, or at least many people do not. But this objection does not appear decisive either. We could reply that abnormal people do not desire what they ought to. For instance, anorexic people lose their desire for food, which is self-destructive. We could also argue that people who desire finite goods are really desiring in them, or at least in addition to them, an eternal good. But we must admit that both of these points, while plausible, are nevertheless controversial. In support of the first point, we could note that the vast majority of people throughout history have desired an afterlife of some type. Even those who have claimed not to desire it have found themselves with such a desire in unguarded moments, especially when close to death. Regarding the second point, we could make a case that finite goods leave us unsatisfied. No matter how many finite goods we accumulate, we still have a longing for something more, something that, in fact, only eternity with God and his followers could satisfy. But neither of our responses are conclusive against this criticism, though they do place it in some doubt.

A third criticism against the argument from desire is that even if there are such things as natural desires, and even if we have a desire for heaven, the desire is not a natural one but a learned one. But this objection is problematic also. The widespread endurance of the desire—it seems present wherever humans live, regardless of the period in history or the culture—lends support to the idea that it is natural. Furthermore, a case could be made that the loss of the desire is a learned response, perhaps a defense mechanism of repression or suppression. But again, our answer does not provide a conclusive, knockout punch.

A fourth criticism points out that there is no natural desire for heaven for the simple reason that there are no natural desires because there are no natures (e.g., a human nature) to have them. This criticism raises a plethora of difficult issues that are well beyond the scope of this book. But suffice it to say that if the notion of a nature, in this case *human* nature, is a reasonable one, then this objection loses its force, and a number of philosophers and theologians have believed that natures exist.[27]

A final criticism is the claim that even if there are natural desires, they are, in fact, sometimes frustrated. There is no necessary connection between a desire and what the world is like.[28] Our response to this objection could go something like this: There is, in fact, a very large correlation between what appear to be natural desires and the existence of objects that could potentially satisfy them. Think of what human life would be like if, in the majority of cases, nothing existed that answered to the basic, natural desires humans have. Therefore, it is wrong to say that no evidence exists to show that our natural desires are in vain. In fact, the majority of human experience indicates that this principle is true. Our natural desires are, in fact, good indicators that objects really exist to satisfy those desires.

Where does this leave us? In our opinion, the argument from desire has value, but it is inconclusive. The criticisms we just listed indicate that the argument has problems, and one would not be foolish in rejecting it. On the other hand, one would not be irrational to accept it either, for the argument is plausible and answers do exist for the criticisms listed above. The value of the argument from desire will come down to one's assessment of the strength of the criticisms of the argument vs. the argument itself and the responses to those criticisms.

Where Do We Go from Here?

So far, we have seen that a number of considerations provide initial evidence for life after death: the truth of theism (especially Christian theism), the nature and deep unity of the self, and the natural desire for everlasting life with God.

On the other hand, the arguments against life after death, which we will deal with more fully as our case unfolds, usually boil down to four points.

First, the evidence *for* life after death is not conclusive, and, since the burden of proof is on the one who believes in life after death, agnosticism or unbelief is the appropriate rational stance until such proof is offered and evaluated.

Second, the concept of an afterlife is somehow incoherent or unintelligible. For example, something cannot be a person or be recognized as such without a body; therefore, a disembodied state—which is what many claim the afterlife to be—is incoherent.

Third, without a soul of some kind, an afterlife where I am literally the same person who survives in the eternal state as I was on earth is impossible. And since our mental functions are so dependent upon our brains, the soul could not exist without the body and, in fact, there probably isn't a soul to begin with anyway.

Fourth, a common-sense approach to the question objects to an afterlife, based on the stark realism of death, accented by the presence of a body that doesn't move or respond, the casket, and the cold, impersonal grave. Dead people simply appear to be senseless. This objection seems to exert much emotional influence in causing us to question life after death.

The second and third criticisms, which are often expressions of a naturalistic or physicalistic worldview (everything that exists is made of matter and its modifications), we will deal with in later chapters. The first criticism can be answered by assessing the cumulative evidence for life after death presented in Chapters 1 through 6. For now, we must admit that the evidence in this chapter is inconclusive. But that does not mean it is value-less. If the theistic God exists, then belief in an afterlife is the most reason-able position to take. Furthermore, the nature of the self and of human desire provide evidence that an afterlife is possible. How much evidential support they provide is a hard question to answer, but as part of an overall case for life after death, these phenomena do play a positive role.

Chapter 2

Body and Soul

In Chapter 1, we saw some reasons for believing that life after death is real and not merely wishful thinking. Still, death is such a dramatic, disruptive event that we may wonder if anyone could really survive it. An answer to this question is significantly related to what is called the mind/body problem and the existence of the soul.[1] Is a human being just composed of matter—a body, a brain, and a central nervous system—or does a person also have an immaterial component called a mind or soul? Physicalists claim we are only material beings; dualists claim we are composed of both body and soul. This is a fundamental difference.

If we are simply material beings, then when our bodies die, *we* die because we *are* our bodies, nothing more, nothing less.[2] On the other hand, if dualism is true, then we are both bodies and souls. In this case, with the destruction of the former, it could be true that we continue to exist in a disembodied state indefinitely, or according to Christianity, while awaiting a new, resurrected body.

When we see the interrelationship between belief in life after death and belief in the soul, we are in a position to understand one of the main reasons our modern culture has lost belief in life after death: We largely disbelieve in the soul, and those who still believe in such an entity often think that such a belief must be based on blind faith or an appeal to revelation alone. Few recognize that a serious rational case can be made for dualism.

Why has there been a decline in belief in the soul's existence? No doubt the answer to that question would involve a number of factors, but renowned philosopher John Hick has put his finger on two main ones:

> This considerable decline within society as a whole, accompanied by a lesser decline within the churches, of the belief in personal immortality clearly reflects the assumption within our culture that we should only believe in what we experience, plus what the accredited sciences certify to us.[3]

As Hick points out, if we define experience narrowly, then we adopt the standpoint of strict empiricism—the idea that something can be a proper object of knowledge if and only if it can be verified with one or more of the five senses.[4] Seeing is believing, and since the soul appears to be embar-

20

rassingly invisible, then we must remain agnostic about its existence. A slide of the brain can be made for an overhead projector, but a slide of the mind would be hard to come by.

Hick singles out a second factor contributing to a decline in belief in the soul and an afterlife: scientism. According to scientism, science is the measure of all things. A belief is true and reasonable only if it can be tested scientifically—observed, measured, quantified, and so forth.[5] But here again, the soul does not appear to be an entity that the so-called ideal sciences, physics and chemistry, can quantify and measure.

But in spite of the cultural bias toward empiricism and scientism, we believe a very strong case can be made for dualism.[6] In this chapter we will present a case for dualism in contrast to physicalism. If dualism is true, then life after the death of the body is at least possible, and more likely than if dualism were false. We will also look at arguments that show that substance dualism is preferable to property dualism (to be defined below).

But before we move on, we would like you to understand the limits of our discussion so two extremes can be avoided. It is easy when philosophical issues are addressed to believe that no one has a right to draw any philosophical conclusions unless one is a professional philosopher familiar with all, or at least most, of the technical details on either side of the matters discussed. It is also easy to simplify an issue in such a way that it is caricatured and distorted. The latter responsibility rests with us as we (the authors) seek to set forth the pertinent issues and arguments. The former matter rests with you, the reader and judge of this book.

A strong case can be made for dualism, and we are going to present such a case in a brief way and in terms hopefully accessible to nonspecialists in philosophy. We want you to understand that counterarguments exist for each of the points we will make. But you should also realize that dualists have offered adequate rejoinders to those counterarguments. We do not have the space here to share all the details of this exchange, but we believe the arguments to follow, while simply presented, are capable of a much more technical defense. We will touch on a few of these counterarguments and dualist responses in the endnotes and there offer you resources for further study. But our primary goal here is to provide a good case for dualism so you can have access to all the most important support for this position.

In the next chapter, we will look at some of the main criticisms of dualism, as well as some reasons for thinking that the soul can survive the destruction of its body. But for now, we want to outline the main types of arguments that can be offered in defense of dualism. However, before you can be in a position to appreciate the strength of these arguments, you need to first consider some preliminary issues, which form the background for the rest of this chapter.

First Things First

The Mind/Body Problem

In more technical treatments, it would be important for us to make distinctions between the mind, soul, spirit, ego, and self. But for our purposes, we will use these concepts interchangeably.[7] Our main concern here is to focus on the mind/body problem and defend the claim that, in addition to a body, brain, and central nervous system, a human being has an immaterial component as well. The mind/body (or immaterial/material) problem focuses on two main issues: Is a human made of only one component—say, matter—or is a human made of two components—matter and mind? If the answer is two components, do mind and matter interact? And if so, how does that interaction take place?

In this chapter, we will only look at the first question. The problem of the interaction between mind and matter will be discussed briefly in the next chapter when we consider criticisms of dualism.

Currently, there are two main positions taken on the mind/body problem:[8]

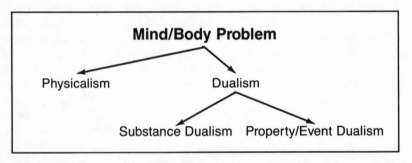

The two main views are physicalism and dualism. The former claims that a human being is completely physical, whereas the latter maintains that a human being is both physical and mental.

Dualism comes in two major varieties: substance dualism and property/event dualism. Physicalism comes in different varieties as well, but we will not explore them here. Our present purpose is to compare the different views listed in the chart above. We will begin by clarifying the nature of substances, properties, and events. This material may seem somewhat technical and far afield to you. We ask that you bear with us. As we move ahead, looking at the evidence for and against immortality, these definitions and distinctions will become enormously important. Just as an adequate understanding of any discipline or argument has its key terms, definitions, and distinctions, so does one of the most significant issues of our lives: the possibility and type of life beyond the grave. We don't want to treat this issue lightly or slop through it. So we urge you to tread this ground with us and to follow carefully and thoughtfully. In the end, you will not be disappointed.

Key Concepts

A *substance* is an entity like an apple, an acorn, a leaf, a carbon atom, a dog, or an angel. Substances have a number of important characteristics.[9] First, substances are particular, individual things. A substance, like a particular acorn, cannot be in more than one place at the same time.

Second, a substance is a continuant—it can change by gaining new properties and losing old ones, yet it remains the same thing throughout the change. A leaf can go from green to red, yet the leaf itself is the same entity before, during, and after the change. In general, substances can change in some of their properties and yet remain the same substance. That very leaf that was green is the same leaf that is now red.[10]

Third, substances are basic, fundamental existents. They are not *in* other things or *had by* other things. My dog Fido is not in or had by something more basic than himself. Rather, properties (and parts) are in substances that have them. For example, Fido has the property of brownness and the property of weighing twenty-five pounds. These properties are in the substance called Fido.

Fourth, substances are unities of parts, properties, and capacities (dispositions, tendencies, potentialities). Fido has a number of properties like the ones already listed. He also has a number of parts—four legs, some teeth, two eyes. Further, he has some capacities or potentialities that are not always actual. For example, he has the capacity to bark even when he is silent. As a substance, Fido is a unity of all the properties, parts, and capacities had by him.

Finally, a substance has causal powers. It can do things in the world. A dog can bark; a leaf can hit the ground. Substances can cause things to happen.

In addition to substances, there are also entities that exist called *properties.*[11] A property is an existent reality, examples of which are brownness, triangularity, hardness, wisdom, painfulness. As with substances, properties have a number of important features.

One feature is that a property is a universal that can be in more than one thing at the same time. Redness can be in a flag, a coat, and an apple at once. The very same redness can be the color of several particular things all at the same time.

Another feature of properties is their immutability. When a leaf goes from green to red, the *leaf* changes by losing an old property and gaining a new one. But the property of redness does not change and become the property of greenness. Properties can come and go, but they do not change in their internal constitution or nature.

Moreover, properties can, or perhaps must, be in or had by other things more basic than themselves.[12] Properties are in the things that have them.

For example, redness is in the apple. The apple has the redness. One does not find redness existing all by itself. In general, when we are talking about a property, it makes sense to ask the question "What is it that has that property?" That question is not appropriate for substances, for they are among the things that have the properties. Substances have properties; properties are had by substances.

Finally, there are entities in the world called *events*. Examples of events are a flash of lightning, the dropping of a ball, the having of a thought, the change of a leaf, and the continued possession of sweetness by an apple (this would be a series of events). Events are states or changes of states of substances. An event is the coming or going of a property in a substance at a particular time, or the continued possession of a property by a substance throughout a time.[13] "This shirt's being green now" and "This acorn's changing shape then" are both examples of events.

Options Regarding the Mind/Body Problem

Keeping these critical distinctions in mind, we can now move on to consider in more detail the different mind/body views. Let's look at physicalism first.

According to physicalism, a human being is merely a physical entity. The only things that exist are physical substances, properties, and events. When it comes to humans, the physical substance is the material body, especially the parts called the brain and central nervous system. The physical substance called the brain has physical properties, such as a certain weight, volume, size, electrical activity, chemical composition, and so forth.

There are also physical events that occur in the brain. For example, the brain contains a number of elongated cells that carry various impulses. These cells are called neurons. Various neurons make contact with other neurons through connections or points of contact called synapses. C-fibers are certain types of neurons that innervate the skin (supply the skin with nerves) and carry pain impulses. So when someone has an occasion of pain or an occurrence of a thought, physicalists hold that these are merely physical events—events where certain C-fibers are firing or certain electrical and chemical events are happening in the brain and central nervous system.

Thus, physicalists believe that we are merely a physical substance (a brain and central nervous system plus a body) that has physical properties and in which occur physical events. My conscious mental life of thoughts, emotions, and pain are nothing but physical events in my brain and nervous system. The neurophysiologist can, in principle, describe these events solely in terms of C-fibers, neurons, and the chemical and physical properties of the brain. For the physicalist, I am merely a functioning brain and central nervous system enclosed in a physical body. I am a material substance, a creature made of matter—nothing more, nothing less.

What is matter? There is no clear definition of matter, and the fact of the matter is that we know precious little about what matter actually is.[14] But examples of matter are not hard to come by. Material objects are things like computers, carbon atoms, and billiard balls.

Material properties are the properties that one finds listed in chemistry or physics books. They are properties such as hardness; occupying and moving through space; having a certain shape; possessing certain chemical, electrical, magnetic, and gravitational properties; having density and weight; and being breakable, malleable, and elastic. A physical event would be the possession, coming, or going of one or more of these properties by a physical substance (or among physical substances).

Another very crucial observation to make about material substances, properties, and events is this: *No material thing presupposes or has reference to consciousness for it to exist or be characterized.* You will search in vain through a physics or chemistry textbook to find consciousness included in any description of matter.[15] A completely physical description of the world would not include any terms that make reference to or characterize the existence and nature of consciousness. Assume that matter is actually like what our chemistry and physics books tell us it is. Now imagine that there is no God and picture a universe in which no conscious, living beings had evolved. In such an imaginary world, there would be no consciousness anywhere in the universe. However, in this imaginary world, matter would still exist and be what scientists tell us it is. Carbon atoms would still be carbon atoms, electrons would still have negative charge. An electron is still an electron regardless of whether or not conscious minds exist in the world. This is what we mean when we say that the existence and nature of matter are independent of the existence of consciousness.

Dualists disagree with physicalists. According to them, mental entities are real. As with matter, it is hard to give a *definition* of mental entities.[16] But *examples* of mental entities are easy to supply. First, there are various kinds of *sensations:* experiences of colors, sounds, smells, tastes, textures, pains, and itches. Sensations are individual things that occur at particular times. I can have a sensation of red after looking in a certain direction or by closing my eyes and daydreaming. An experience of pain will arise at a certain time, say, after I am stuck with a pin.

Further, sensations are natural kinds of things that have, as their very essence, the felt quality or sensory property that makes them what they are. Part of the very essence of a pain is the felt quality it has; part of the very essence of a red sensation is the presentation of a particular shade of color to my consciousness. Sensations are not identical to things outside a person's body—for instance, a feeling of pain is not the same thing as being stuck with a pin and shouting, "Ouch!" Sensations are essentially characterized by a certain conscious feel, and thus, they presuppose consciousness for their existence and description. If there were no conscious beings, there would be no sensations.

Second, there are things called *propositional attitudes:* having a certain mental attitude toward a proposition that is part of a that-clause. For example, one can hope, desire, fear, dread, wish, think, believe that *P,* where *P* may be the proposition "The Royals are a great baseball team." Propositional attitudes include at least two components. First, there is the attitude itself. Hopes, fears, dreads, wishes, thoughts, etc. are all different attitudes, different states of consciousness, and they are all different from each other based on their conscious feel. A hope is a different form of consciousness from an episode of fear. A hope that it will rain is different from a fear that it will rain. What's the difference? A hope has a very different conscious feel from a fear.

Second, they all have a content or a meaning embedded in the propositional attitude—namely, the propositional content of my consciousness while I am having the propositional attitude. My hope that *P* differs from my hope that *Q* because *P* and *Q* are different propositions or meanings in my consciousness. If there were no conscious selves, there would be no propositional attitudes. My hope that it will rain is different from my hope that taxes will be cut. The contents of these two hopes have quite different meanings. (We leave it to the reader to decide which hope is more likely to happen!)

Third, there are *acts of will* or *purposings.* What is a purposing? If, unknown to me, my arm is tied down and I still try to raise it, then the purposing is the "trying to bring about" the event of raising my arm. Intentional actions are episodes of volition by conscious selves wherein and whereby they do various actions. They are acts of will performed by conscious selves.

To summarize, dualists argue that sensations, propositional attitudes, and purposings are all examples of mental entities.

In addition to these differences between physicalists and dualists, there is also an intramural debate between *property dualists* and *substance dualists.*

Property dualists believe there are some physical substances that have only physical properties: For example, a billiard ball is hard and round. They also maintain that there are no mental substances. On the other hand, they contend there is one material substance that has both physical *and* mental properties—the brain. When I experience a pain, there is a certain physical property possessed by the brain (a C-fiber stimulation with chemical and electrical properties) and there is a certain mental property possessed by the brain (the pain itself with its felt quality). The brain is the possessor of all mental properties. I am not a mental self that *has* my thoughts and experiences. Rather, I am a brain and a series or bundle of successive experiences themselves.

Moreover, property dualists claim that, just as wetness is a real property that supervenes over a water molecule, so mental properties supervene upon brain states. This view has an implication for life after death. When a water molecule is destroyed, the property of wetness that molecule *had* ceases to exist. Similarly, when the brain is destroyed, the conscious properties and events *had by* the brain cease to exist.

According to those property dualists who believe in eternal life, the main hope is this: When you die, you become extinct, but at the resurrection of the dead, God recreates you all over again out of nothing. This view has its problems, which we will explain in Chapter 7. But one obvious problem is that if God recreates a human at the resurrection, how is it that the recreated human is identical to me, if I became extinct? When a group of water molecules breaks down into hydrogen and oxygen gas, the wetness of the water ceases to exist. Similarly, if my conscious is just a property of the brain, then at death I myself cease to exist. When Christ returns, there is no real resurrection, since there is nothing there to raise. God recreates me all over again because I have been extinct for a while. But what is it about this new recreated person that makes the person *me?* This new person does not have the same soul or the same body as I do now. So it is hard to understand how this new recreated person can be identical to the person who died and became extinct years earlier. In any case, this is what property dualism looks like.[17]

In contrast with property dualism, substance dualism holds that the brain is a physical substance that has physical properties and the mind or soul is a mental substance that has mental properties. When I am in pain, the brain has certain physical properties (electrical, chemical), and the soul or self has certain mental properties (the conscious awareness of pain). The soul is the possessor of its experiences. It stands behind, over, and above them and remains the same throughout my life. The soul and the brain can interact with each other, but they are different substances with different properties. Since the soul is not to be identified with any part of the brain or with any particular mental experience, then the soul may be able to survive the destruction of the body.

The Nature of Identity

It is time to turn to a topic that will explain our strategy for defending dualism: the nature of identity.[18] The eighteenth-century philosopher/ theologian Joseph Butler once remarked that everything is itself and not something else. This simple truth has profound implications.[19]

Suppose you want to know whether J.P. Moreland is Eileen Spiek's youngest son. If J.P. Moreland is identical to Eileen Spiek's youngest son (everything true of one is true of the other), then in reality, we are talking about one single thing: J.P. Moreland, who *is* Eileen Spiek's youngest son. However, if even one small thing is true of J.P. Moreland and *not* true of Eileen Spiek's youngest son, then these are two entirely different people. Furthermore, J.P. Moreland is identical to himself and not different from himself. So if J.P. Moreland is *not* identical to Eileen Spiek's youngest son, then in reality we must be talking about two things, not one.

This illustration suggests a truth about the nature of identity known as Leibniz' Law of the Indiscernibility of Identicals: For any entities x and y, if x and y are identical (they are really the same thing, there is only one thing you are talking about, not two), then any truth that applies to x will apply to y as well. This suggests a test for identity: If you could find one thing true of x not true of y, or vice versa, then x cannot be identical to (be the same thing as) y. Further, if you could find one thing that could *possibly* be true of x and not y (or vice versa), even if it isn't actually true, then x cannot be identical to y.[20]

For example, if J.P. Moreland is five feet eight inches tall, but Eileen Spiek's youngest son is six feet tall, then they are not the same thing. Further, if J.P. Moreland is five feet eight and Eileen Spiek's youngest son is five feet eight, but it would be possible for J.P. to be five feet nine while Eileen's youngest son was five feet ten, then they are not the same thing either.

What does this have to do with the mind/body problem? Simply this: Physicalists are committed to the claim that alleged mental entities are really identical to physical entities, such as brain states, properties of the brain, overt bodily behavior, and dispositions to behave (for example pain is just the tendency to shout, "Ouch!" when stuck by a pin, instead of pain being a certain mental feel). If physicalism is true, then everything true of the brain (and its properties, states, and dispositions) is true of the mind (and its properties, states, and dispositions) and vice versa. If we can find one thing true, or even possibly true of the mind and not of the brain, or vice versa, then dualism is established. The mind is not the brain.

We will present a number of arguments that try to show that something is true of the mind and not the brain, or vice versa, and thus, the mind cannot be identical to the brain. But if they are not identical, physicalism is false and, taking dualism to be the only other option, dualism would be true.

Keep in mind that the relation of identity is different from any other relation, for example, the relation of causation or constant connection. It may be that brain events cause mental events or vice versa: Having certain electrical activity in the brain may cause me to experience a pain; having an intention to raise my arm may cause bodily events. It may be that for every mental activity, a neurophysiologist can find a physical activity in the brain with which it is correlated. But just because A causes B (or vice versa), or just because A and B are constantly correlated with each other, that does not mean that A *is identical to* B. Something is trilateral if and only if it is triangular. But trilaterality (the property of having three sides) is not identical to triangularity (the property of having three angles), even though they are constantly conjoined.

Therefore, and this is critical, physicalism cannot be established on the basis that mental states and brain states are causally related or constantly conjoined with each other in an embodied person. *Physicalism needs iden-*

tity to make its case, and if something is true, or possibly true of a mental substance, property, or event that is not true or possibly true of a physical substance, property, or event, then physicalism is false.

Can a case for dualism be made? Most definitely, and we will show you how. In fact, we will go beyond that. We will first list some arguments that give equal support to both property and substance dualism over physicalism. Then we will look at some arguments that show the superiority of substance dualism over both physicalism and property dualism.

In Support of Dualism

Mental vs. Physical

Mental events are feelings of pain, episodes of thoughts, or having sensory experiences. Physical events are happenings in the brain and central nervous system that can be described exhaustively using terms from chemistry and physics. However, physical events and their properties do not have the same features as do mental events and their properties. My thoughts, feelings of pain, or sensory experiences do not have any weight; they are not located anywhere in space (my thought of lunch cannot be closer to my right ear than my left one); they are not composed of chemicals; they do not have electrical properties. On the other hand, the brain events associated with my thoughts, etc.—indeed, material things in general—*do* have these features.

An experiment will help you see the difference. Picture a pink elephant in your mind. Now close your eyes and look at the image. In your mind, you will see a pink property (a sense datum or a sensory way of experiencing). There will be no pink elephant outside you, but there will be a pink image of one in your mind. However, there will be no pink entity in your brain; no neurophysiologist could open your brain and see a pink entity while you are having the sense image. The sensory event has a property—pink—that no brain event has. Therefore, they cannot be identical. The sense image is a mental entity, not a physical one.

Self-Presenting Properties

In addition, consider the following argument:[21]

(1) No physical properties are self-presenting.
(2) All mental properties are self-presenting.
(3) Therefore, no mental properties are physical properties.

Mental properties—such as feeling sad, experiencing red, having a thought that three is an odd number—are self-presenting. They present themselves directly to the knowing subject. They are psychological attributes that are directly present to a subject because that subject simply has them immediately in her field of consciousness. There are two pieces of evidence for the claim that mental properties are self-presenting while physical properties are not: I can have private access to my mental properties and not my physical ones, and I can know my mental properties incorrigibly but not my physical ones.

First, let us look at the issue of *private access.* I have private access to my own mental life. I am in a privileged position to know what I am thinking and sensing. Whatever ways you have for finding out if I am presently sensing a red after-image (by analyzing my brain states or by looking at my behavior, say, my shouting "red" after looking at the flag), those ways are available to me too. But there is a way of knowing I am having a red after-image that is not available to anyone else—my own immediate awareness of my own mental life. I am in a position to know my own mental life in a way unavailable to anyone else.

But that is not the case for any physical property, including my brain and its various states. Physical objects, including my brain, are public objects and no one is in a privileged position regarding them. A neurophysiologist can know more about my brain than I do, but he cannot know more about my mental life. I have private, privileged access to my mental life because it contains self-presenting properties. Physical properties, however, are not self-presenting.[22]

Furthermore, not only do I have private access to my mental states, but I can know them *incorrigibly.* If something is incorrigible to a knowing subject, then that subject is incapable of being mistaken about that thing.

Suppose I am experiencing what I take to be a green rug. It is possible that the rug is not there, or that the light is poor and the rug is really gray. But it does not seem possible for me to be mistaken that I seem to see something green, that I am having a green sensation. The former claim is about a physical object (the rug); the latter claim is about a mental state within me—my seeming to see something green, my having a green sensory experience.

Again, I can be wrong if I think that a chair is in the next room. But I cannot be wrong about the fact that I at least *think* the chair is there. The former claim is about a physical object (the chair); the latter is about a mental state within me—a thought that I am currently having. In general, claims about physical states, including claims about my brain and its properties/states, can be mistaken. But if I am being attentive, I can know my sensory states (the ways I am being appeared to, the current sensory experiences I am having) and my episodes of thought (that I am having such and such thought right now).[23]

To summarize then, physical states/properties are not self-presenting, but mental states/properties are, as evidenced by the twin phenomena of private access and incorrigibility. Thus, physical states/properties are not identical to mental states/properties.[24]

The Subjective Nature of Experience

The subjective character of experience is hard to capture in physicalist terms.[25] The simple fact of consciousness, constituted by the subjective feel or texture of experience itself, is a serious difficulty for physicalists. To see this, consider the following example.

Suppose a deaf scientist became the world's leading expert on the neurology of hearing. It would be possible for him to know and describe everything there is to the physical aspects of hearing. Nothing physical would be left out of his description. However, something *would* still be left out: the experience of what it is like to be a human who hears. "The notion of *having something as an object of experience* is not, *prima facie*, a physical notion; it does not figure in any physical science. *Having something as an object of experience* is the same as the subjective feel or the *what it is like* of experience."[26]

Subjective states of experience are real. I experience sounds, tastes, colors, thoughts, and pains, and they are essentially characterized by their subjective nature. But, as Thomas Nagel points out, this fact raises a critical problem for physicalism:

> If physicalism is to be defended, the phenomenological features [the felt quality or experiential texture of experiences that make them the kinds of things they are, e.g., the painfulness of pain, the sounds, colors, odors of sensory experiences] must themselves be given a physical account. But when we examine their subjective character it seems that such a result is impossible. The reason is that every subjective phenomenon is essentially connected with a single point of view, and it seems inevitable that an objective, physical theory will abandon that point of view.[27]

To summarize: The subjective texture of our conscious mental experiences—the feeling of pain, the experience of sound, the awareness of color—are different from anything that is simply physical. If the world were only made of matter, these subjective aspects of consciousness would not exist. But they *do* exist! So there must be more to the world than matter.

Secondary Qualities

Secondary qualities are qualities such as colors, tastes, sounds, smells, and textures. Primary qualities are qualities that are thought to be among the properties that characterize matter—weight, shape, size, solidity, motion. Physicalism seems to imply that secondary qualities do not exist in the external world. For example, we are led to believe that color is really nothing but a wavelength of light. So in general, physicalism reduces secondary qualities to nothing but primary qualities. We are left with a picture of matter bereft of secondary qualities.

But the world of our common-sense experience is replete with second-ary qualities. Thus, such qualities must exist, but where? Some dualists contend that if secondary qualities do not exist in the external world as properties of matter, they must exist as mental entities in the conscious minds of experiencers themselves. Frank Jackson has put the point this way:

> It is a commonplace that there is an apparent clash between the picture Science gives of the world around us and the picture our senses give us. We *sense* the world as made up of coloured, materially continuous, macro-scopic, stable objects; Science and, in particular, Physics, tells us that the material world is constituted of clouds of minute, colourless, highly-mobile particles. . . . Science forces us to acknowledge that physical or material things are not coloured. . . . This will enable us to conclude that sense-data are all mental, for they are coloured.[28]

In other words, many dualists argue that science may do away with secondary qualities in the physical realm, but since we know they do exist—we see them—they must exist in our minds as mental entities.

Intentionality

Some have argued that the mark of the mental is something called inten-tionality. Intentionality is the mind's ofness or aboutness. Mental states point beyond themselves to other things. Every mental state I have is of or about something—a hope that Smith will come, a sensation of the apple, a thought that the painting is beautiful. Mental states can even be about things that do not exist: a fear of a goblin or a love for Zeus.

Now intentionality is not a property or relation of anything physical. Physical objects can stand in various physical relations with other physi-cal objects. One physical thing can be to the left of, larger than, harder than, the same shape as, or the thing causing the motion of an-other physical object. But one physical object is not of or about another one.

When I am near a podium, I can relate to it in many ways: I can be two feet from it, taller than it, and my body can bump into it. These are all examples of physical relations I sustain to the podium. But in addition to these, I can be a conscious subject that has the podium as an object of various states of consciousness I direct toward it. I can have a thought about it, a desire for it (perhaps I want one like it), I can experience a sensation of it, and so forth. These are all mental states and they have intentionality (ofness, aboutness) in common.

Hence, mental states possess intentionality, while physical states do not. Mental states are not physical states.[29]

In Support of Substance Dualism

The arguments we have just gone through favor dualism over physicalism and, therefore, also make the claim of life after death more viable. But we can further show that among the dualistic views (substance and property dualism), substance dualism should be preferred. So the arguments that follow support this form of dualism over and against property dualism and physicalism.

Before we consider these arguments, however, it may be helpful to review the differences between substance and property dualism. Remember, the main differences between a substance and a property are that a substance (1) is the possessor of its properties, and (2) it can remain the same through change, where it gains new properties and loses old ones. By contrast, properties are *had by* substances, and they are replaced in a substance when it changes. If a leaf is green, then orange, then yellow, the leaf undergoes a succession of replacements in which it has, in a series, three distinct attributes.

How does this relate to the mind/body problem? If substance dualism is true, I am a self, a soul that *has* my mental experiences.[30] I can hear a sound and feel a pain at the same time, or I can experience the sound and, later, the pain. Either way, *I* am the thing that has the mental events and properties. They come and go, but *I* remain the same because the self is the thing standing beyond and under my mental properties as their possessor and unifier.

If property dualism is true, there is no mental self that has my mental life, my series of mental experiences. The brain is the real possessor of that mental life, and the brain itself is not conscious. Rather, the brain has a series of conscious experiences. If I simultaneously experience a sound and a pain, the mental "self" is just the bundle or conjunction of the experiences themselves. If I "experience" them successively, then the mental "self" is just a series of separate, discreet mental events/experiences that come and go and replace one another through time. The "soul" is just a bundle of mental events/properties at a time and a series of mental events/properties through time. There is no mental substance that stands under them as their possessor.

How does this relate to eternal life? Since a substance is not identical to its properties, then it can exist as they come and go. A leaf can exist as green without being red and later as red without being green. The leaf as substance does not owe its existence to its (accidental) properties; its properties owe their existence to the substance that has them. That does not mean that the leaf can survive if all its properties or physical parts disappear, but it can survive the loss of some of them.

On the other hand, when a property or event is had by a substance, then if the substance is destroyed, so are the demonstrated properties or events within it. When H_2O is destroyed, the wetness of the water is gone. If the brain is destroyed in death, the mental properties are destroyed. Thus, property dualism labors to justify life after death in a way not necessary for substance dualism. With this in mind, the following arguments are designed to show that substance dualism is superior to both physicalism and property dualism.

Our Basic Awareness of the Self

When we pay attention to our own consciousness, we can become aware of a very basic fact presented to us: We are aware of our own self (ego, I, center of consciousness) as being distinct from our bodies and from any particular mental experience we have. I simply have a basic, direct awareness of the fact that I am not identical to my body or my mental events; rather, I am the self that *has* a body and a conscious mental life.

An experiment may help convince you of this. Right now I am looking at a chair in my office. As I walk toward the chair, I experience a series of what are called phenomenological objects or chair representations. That is, I have several different chair experiences that replace one another in rapid succession. As I approach the chair, my chair sensations change shape and grow bigger. Further, because of the lighting of my study, my chair experiences change color slightly. Now, the chair doesn't change in size, shape, or color; but my chair experiences do.

I am, of course, aware of all the different experiences of the chair during the fifteen seconds it takes me to walk across my study. But if I pay attention, I am also aware of two more things. First, I do not simply experience a series of sense-images of a chair. Rather, through self-awareness, I also experience the fact that it is I myself who has each chair experience. Each chair sensation produced at each angle of perspective has a perceiver who is I. An "I" accompanies each sense experience to produce a series of awarenesses—"I am experiencing a chair sense image now."

I am also aware of the basic fact that the same self that is currently having a fairly large chair experience (as my eyes come to within twelve inches of the chair) is the very same self as the one who had all of the other chair experiences preceding this current one. In other words, through self-awareness, I am aware of the fact that I am an enduring I who was and is (and will be) present as the owner of all the experiences in the series.

These two facts—I am the owner of my experiences, and I am an enduring self who exists as the same possessor of all my experiences through time—show that I am not identical to my experiences. I am the thing that has them. In short, I am a mental substance. Only a single, enduring self can relate and unify experiences, a fact that property dualists and physicalists cannot adequately account for or explain away.[31]

More than Third Person

A complete physicalist description of the world would be one in which everything would be exhaustively described from a third-person point of view in terms of objects, properties, processes, and their spatiotemporal locations. For example, a description of an apple in a room would go something like this: "There exists an object three feet from the south wall and two feet from the east wall, and that object has the property of being red, round, sweet, and so on."

The first-person point of view is the vantage point that I use to describe the world from my own perspective. Expressions of a first person point of view utilize what are called indexicals—words like "I", "here", "now", "there", "then". Here and now are where and when I am; there and then are where and when I am not. Indexicals refer to me, myself. "I" is the most basic indexical, and it refers to my self that I know by acquaintance with my own consciousness in acts of self-awareness. I am immediately aware of my own self, and I know who "I" refers to when I use it: It refers to me as the owner of my body and mental states.

According to physicalism, there are no irreducible, privileged first-person perspectives. Everything can be exhaustively described in an object language from a third-person perspective. A physicalist description of me would say, "There exists a body at a certain location that is five feet eight inches tall, weighs 160 pounds," and so forth. The property dualist would add a description of the properties possessed by that body, such as the body is feeling pain, thinking about lunch, and can remember being in Grandview, Missouri, in 1965.

But no amount of third-person descriptions captures my own subjective, first-person acquaintance of my own self in acts of self-awareness. In fact, for any third-person description of me, it would always be an open question as to whether the person described in third-person terms was the same person as I am. I do not know my self *because* I know some third-person description of a set of mental and physical properties and I also know that a certain person satisfies that description. I know myself as a self immediately through being acquainted with my own self in an act of self-awareness. I can express that self-awareness by using the term *I*.

I refers to my own substantial soul. It does not refer to any mental property or bundle of mental properties I am having, nor does it refer to anybody described from a third-person perspective. *I* is a term that refers to something that exists, and *I* does not refer to any object or set of properties described from a third-person point of view. Rather, *I* refers to my own self with which I am directly acquainted and which, through acts of self-awareness, I know to be the substantial possessor of my mental states and my body.[32]

Personal Identity Through Change

Imagine a wooden table that had all its parts removed one by one and replaced with metal parts. Now suppose someone took the original wooden parts and made a new table. Which one would be the original table—the metal one or the wooden one? The answer seems to be clear.

The original table would be the wooden one. Why? Because if something is made out of stuff called parts, then it cannot remain identical to itself if it gains new parts and loses old ones. If a table here and now is going to be the very same table as one that was here, say an hour ago, this table must be made out of the same stuff as the one an hour ago. If not, then they are different tables. In general, physical objects cannot remain literally the same if they gain new parts and lose old ones.

But now a question arises regarding persons: Am I literally the same self that I was a moment ago? An hour ago? Seven years ago? I am constantly losing parts. Each moment I lose hundreds of thousands of skin cells, hair, and other microscopic parts. In fact, every seven years my cells are almost entirely replaced. Do I maintain literal, absolute sameness through change? The same difficulty arises for property dualism. I can also gain and lose mental properties. Pains, thoughts, and sensations come and go, my ability to have memories can be lost through amnesia, and so forth. Can I gain and lose mental properties and be literally the same person?

Substance dualists argue that persons do maintain absolute identity through change, because they have, in addition to their bodies and current mental experiences or mental capacities (say, the capacity to remember a childhood event), a soul that remains constant through change. Personal identity is constituted by sameness of soul, not sameness of body or mental abilities, such as memory.[33]

Physicalists and property dualists have no alternative but to hold that personal identity through change is not absolute. Usually they argue that persons are really ancestral chains of successive, momentary "selves" (called person-stages) that are connected with one another in some way. At each moment a new self exists (since the organism is constantly in flux, gaining new parts and mental experiences and losing old parts and mental experiences), and this self resembles the self prior to and after it.

The relation of resemblance between selves, plus the fact that later selves have the same memories as earlier selves and the body of each self traces a continuous path through space when the whole chain of selves is put together, constitutes a relative sense of identity. At this moment I merely resemble a self that existed a moment ago: My body resembles that body, my memories resemble the memories of that earlier self, my body was reached by the body of the earlier self through a continuous spatial path.

So substance dualists hold to a literal, absolute sense of personal identity, and physicalists and property dualists hold to a loose, relative sense of personal identity that amounts to a stream of successive selves held together by resemblance between each self in the stream—similarity of memory or brain, similarity of character traits, and/or spatial continuity. But this perspective creates certain problems for physicalism and property dualism.

First, the fact that I can have a memory that an earlier self had presupposes that I am the same person as that alleged earlier self. Memory presupposes personal identity, it does not constitute it. The same can be said for the other traits listed above.

Second, in self-awareness, I seem to be aware of the fact that I am literally the same self that continues to exist throughout my life and that unites my stream of consciousness into one stream that is mine. How can a physicalist or property dualist explain this basic awareness?

Third, why should "I" ever fear the future, say, going to the dentist next week? When it gets here, "I" will not be present; rather, another self who looks like me (or has my memories) will be there, but "I" will have ceased to exist. The same issue arises with any emotion or attitude related to the future.

Fourth, why should anyone be punished? The self who did the crime in the past is not literally the same self who is present at the time of punishment.

Physicalism and property dualism seem to require a radical readjustment of these basic, common-sense notions because these notions presuppose a literal, absolute sense of sameness through change, and this makes sense only if the soul is a substance that is a continuant (something that remains the same through change). If the intuitions expressed in points one through four above are reasonable—and we maintain they are—then this provides further evidence for substance dualism.

Free Will, Morality, Responsibility, and Punishment

When we use the term *free will,* we mean what is called libertarian freedom: Given choices A and B, I can literally choose to do either one. No circumstances exist that are sufficient to determine my choice. My choice is up to me, and if I do A or B, I could have done otherwise. I act as an agent who is the ultimate originator of my own actions.

If physicalism is true, then human free will does not exist. Instead, determinism is true.[34] If I am just a physical system, there is nothing in me that has the capacity to freely choose to do something. Material systems, at least large-scale ones, change over time in deterministic fashion according to the initial conditions of the system and the laws of chemistry and physics. A pot of water will reach a certain temperature at a given time in a way determined by the amount of water, the input of heat, and the laws of heat transfer.

Now, when it comes to morality, it is hard to make sense of moral obligation and responsibility if determinism is true. They seem to presuppose freedom of the will. If I "ought" to do something, it seems to be necessary to suppose that I *can* do it. No one would say that I ought to jump to the top of a fifty-floor building and save a baby, or that I ought to stop the American Civil War in 1992, because I do not have the ability to do either. If physicalism is true, I do not have any genuine ability to choose my actions.

It is safe to say that physicalism requires a radical revision of our common-sense notions of freedom, moral obligation, responsibility, and punishment. On the other hand, if these common-sense notions are true, physicalism is false.[35]

The same problem besets property dualism. There are two ways for property dualists to handle human actions. First, some property dualists are *epiphenomenalists*. Richard Taylor explains epiphenomenalism in this way: "A person is a living physical body having a mind, the mind consisting, however, of nothing but a more or less continuous series of conscious or unconscious states and events . . . which are the effects but never the causes of bodily activity."[36] Put another way, when matter reaches a certain organizational complexity and structure, as is the case with the human brain, then matter produces mental states like fire produces smoke, or the structure of hydrogen and oxygen in water produces wetness. The mind is to the body as smoke is to fire. Smoke is different from fire (to keep the analogy going, the physicalist would identify the smoke with the fire or the functioning of the fire), but fire causes smoke, not vice versa. The mind is a by-product of the brain, which causes nothing; the mind merely "rides" on top of the events in the brain. Hence, epiphenomenalism rejects free will, since it denies that mental states cause anything.

A second way that property dualists handle human action is through a notion called *state-state causation*.[37] To understand state-state causation, consider a brick that breaks a glass. The cause in this case is not the brick itself (which is a substance), but the brick's being in a certain state—a state of motion. The effect is the glass being in a certain state—breaking. Thus, one state or event (an event is another name for a temporal state)—the moving of a brick—causes another state to occur—the breaking of the glass.

When one billiard ball causes another one to move, it is the moving of the first ball that causes the moving of the second ball. In general, then, state-state causation involves a state of one thing's existing as an efficient cause that is prior to an effect, which is the production of a state in another thing.

Agent causation is required for libertarian freedom of the will; substance dualists embrace this view. One example of agent causation is a typical case of a human action: my raising my arm. When I raise my arm, I, as a substance, simply act by spontaneously exercising my causal powers. *I* raise my arm; I freely and spontaneously exercise the powers within my substantial soul and simply act. No set of conditions exists within me that is sufficient to determine that I raise my arm.

In agent causation, substances are the cause; in state-state causation, a state within a substance is the cause. According to state-state causation, when I raise my arm, there is some state within me that causally necessitates or determines that I raise my arm, for example, a state of desiring that my arm go up or a state of willing that my arm go up.

Unfortunately for property dualists, state-state causation is deterministic. Why? For one thing, there is no room for an agent, an ego, an "I" to intervene and contribute to my actions. I do not produce the action of raising my arm; rather, a state of desiring to raise an arm is sufficient to produce the effect. There is no room for my own self, as opposed to the mental states within me, to act.

For another thing, all the mental states within me (my states of desiring, willing, hoping) are states that were deterministically caused by prior mental and physical states. "I" become a stream of states/events in a causal chain. Each member of the chain determines that the next member occur.

In summary then, property dualism denies libertarian freedom, because it adopts either epiphenomenalism or state-state causation. Thus, property dualism, no less than physicalism, is false, given the truth of free will, moral ability, moral responsibility, and punishment. Our common-sense notions about moral ability, responsibility, and punishment are almost self-evident. We all operate toward one another on the assumption that they are true (and these common-sense notions assume free will). However, if physicalism or property dualism are true, we will have to abandon and revise our common-sense notions of moral ability, responsibility, and punishment because free will is ruled out. One wonders if such a revision is worth the price. These common-sense notions seem more reasonable than physicalism or property dualism. If anything should be abandoned, it is the latter, not the former.

Self-Refuting Positions

A number of philosophers have argued that physicalism and property dualism must be false because they imply determinism and determinism is self-refuting. Speaking of the determinist, J.R. Lucas says,

> If what he says is true, he says it merely as the result of his heredity and environment, and of nothing else. He does not hold his determinist views because they are true, but because he has such-and-such stimuli; that is, not because the *structure* of the universe is such-and-such but only because the configuration of only part of the universe, together with the structure of the determinist's brain, is such as to produce that result. . . . Determinism, therefore, cannot be true, because if it was, we should not take the determinists' arguments as being really arguments, but as being only conditioned reflexes. Their statements should not be regarded as really claiming to be true, but only as seeking to cause us to respond in some way desired by them.[38]

H.P. Owen adds:

Determinism is self-stultifying. If my mental processes are totally determined, I am totally determined either to accept or to reject determinism.

But if the sole reason for my believing or not believing X is that I am causally determined to believe it, I have no ground for holding that my judgment
is true or false.[39]

Others have pointed out that property dualism suffers at the hands of
this argument no less than does strict physicalism. Note A.C. Ewing's
comments:

If epiphenomenalism is true, it follows that nobody can be justified in believing it. On the epiphenomenalist view, what causes a belief is always a
change in the brain and never the apprehension of any reason for holding it.
So if epiphenomenalism is true, neither it nor anything else can ever be
believed for any good reasons whatever.[40]

When we explore the nature of self-refutation and couple that with rationality itself and its preconditions, we discover yet more reasons to reject
physicalism and property dualism.

First, let's look at self-refutation. A statement is about a subject matter.
"All electrons have negative charge" is about the subject matter called
electrons. Some statements refer to themselves; they include themselves in
their own field of reference. "All English sentences are short" refers to all
English sentences whatsoever, including that very sentence itself. Now
sometimes a statement refers to itself, and it fails to satisfy its own criteria
of rational acceptability or truthfulness. "I cannot say a word of English,"
"I do not exist," "There are no truths," "I am rational in thinking that
there is no rationality" are all self-refuting. They refer to themselves and
they falsify themselves. Self-refuting statements are necessarily false—
they cannot possibly be true.

Physicalism and property dualism are self-refuting. They undercut the
necessary preconditions for rationality itself in order for them to even be
possible. In other words, they make rationality itself impossible. People
who claim to know that physicalism or property dualism are true, or to
embrace them for good reasons, if they claim that they choose to believe in
them because of good reasons, then their claims are self-refuting. At least
three factors must be assumed if there are to be genuine rational agents
who exhibit rationality. All three are ruled out by physicalism; only the
last two are inconsistent with property dualism.

First, humans must have genuine *intentionality;* they must be capable of
having thoughts and sensory awarenesses *of* or *about* the things they claim
to know. For example, one must be able to see or have rational insight into
the flow of an argument if one is going to claim that a conclusion follows
from a set of premises. We can simply see that if you have (1) If P, then Q,
and (2) P, therefore, you also have (3) Q. This requires an *awareness of* the
logical structure of the syllogism itself.

As we saw earlier in this chapter, intentionality is a property of mental

states, not physical ones. Thus, this first feature of rationality is incompatible with physicalism, though it is compatible with property dualism. Intentionality is not a physical property, but it could be claimed that it is a
mental property of the brain.

Second, in order to rationally think through a chain of reasoning such
that one sees the inferential connections in the chain, one would have to be
the same self present at the beginning of the thought process as the one
present at the end. As Immanuel Kant argued long ago, the process of
thought requires a genuine enduring "I."

In the syllogism above, if there is one self who reflects on premise (1),
namely, "If P, then Q", a second self who reflects on premise (2), namely,
"P", and a third self who reflects on the concluding statement (3), namely,
"Q", then there is literally no enduring self who thinks *through* the argument and *draws* the conclusion. As H.D. Lewis noted, "One thing seems
certain, namely that there must be someone or something at the centre of
such experiences to hold the terms and relations together in one stream of
consciousness."[41]

But we have already seen that physicalism and property dualism deny a
literal, enduring I, and substitute for it a series of selves. Thus, they are at
odds with this necessary condition for rationality.

Finally, rationality seems to presuppose an agent view of the self and
genuine libertarian freedom of the will. There are rational "oughts."
Given certain evidence, I "ought" to believe certain things. I am intellectually responsible for drawing certain conclusions, given certain pieces of
evidence. If I do not choose that conclusion, I am irrational. But "ought"
implies "can." If I ought to believe something, then I must have the ability
to choose to believe it or not believe it. If one is to be rational, one must be
free to choose her beliefs in order to be reasonable. Often, I deliberate
about what I am going to believe, or I deliberate about the evidence for
something. But such deliberations make sense only if I assume that what I
am going to do or believe is "up to me"—that I am free to choose and,
thus, I am responsible for irrationality if I choose inappropriately. But we
have already seen that physicalism and property dualism rule out libertarian freedom.

Therefore, physicalism and property dualism rule out the possibility of
rationality. It is self-refuting to *argue* that one *ought* to *choose* physicalism
or property dualism on the *basis* of the fact that one *should see* that the
evidence is *good* for physicalism or property dualism. Thus, substance
dualism is the best view of the self and is most consistent with the preconditions of rationality.

A Look Ahead

Today, there are powerful social forces that deny the existence of the
soul and claim that belief in the soul is merely a matter of blind faith. But

this chapter has tried to show that this is not true! In fact, a very strong case can be made for the soul's existence, and we have surveyed part of that case in this chapter.

In the next chapter we will look at criticisms of dualism. We will also see how the soul's existence fits into the case for life after death. Such issues cannot be left to blind faith, even though it requires a good deal of effort to learn to defend the existence of the soul. If you have worked through this chapter, you are to be congratulated. We realize it may have been tough going for you. But we hope this chapter and the next will put you in a position to develop *rational* connections between the soul's existence and its survival of the body's death. Such connections are worth the price! So let's press on.

Chapter 3

Dualism and Eternal Life

Recently, the evening news advertised a segment entitled "Battle of the Brains." As I waited for the program to begin, I expected to see men bumping their heads together (people seem to be tiring of arm wrestling), or perhaps, a fraternity fight where chicken brains were thrown at each other. Unfortunately, neither was shown. Instead, the news story covered a high school math contest. It was no battle of *brains*. Instead, it was a contest of *minds*. So pervasive is our implicit identification of the mind with the brain, that we unconsciously speak and act as though the mind were just a complex computer made of material components.

In the last chapter, we saw good reasons for rejecting the mind-brain identity perspective and, instead, embracing dualism in general and substance dualism in particular. We are not merely creatures of matter; we have souls as well. But because of the cultural bias we have toward physical and empirical reality, you may still not be entirely convinced that the soul is real. You may wonder what kinds of objections have been raised against dualism. Further, you may still be somewhat skeptical that eternal life is really related to the existence of the soul. How does a case for the soul enhance the rationality of belief in eternal life?

In this chapter, we want to look at these issues. But before we do, we should mention one thing. In our view, the burden of proof is on the one who denies dualism, not on the dualist, in spite of the current cultural bias. Why do we claim this? Recall the point we made in Chapter 2 about the incorrigibility of our mental states. If we are having a green sensation or a thought, then we are in a position to know these things with certainty. Our mental states are self-presenting. Now, we know from simple introspection that we are mental selves that remain the same through change, act freely, and have a body that we are not identical to. In light of this knowledge, the burden of proof is on any view that tries to defeat dualism. Having said this, however, we will still briefly evaluate some of the more frequent arguments raised against dualism.[1] Then we will turn our attention to explaining how dualism supports belief in eternal life.

43

Arguments Against Dualism

Mind/Body Interaction

Physicalists claim that on a dualist view of a human being, mind and body are so different that it seems impossible to explain how and where the two different entities interact. How could a soul, totally lacking in any physical properties, cause things to happen to the body or vice versa? How can the soul move the arm? How can a pin-stick in the finger cause pain in the soul?

This objection assumes that if we do not know *how* A causes B, then it is not reasonable to believe *that* A causes B, especially if A and B are different. But this assumption is a poor one. We often know that one thing causes another without having any idea how that happens, even when the cause and effect are different. As C.D. Broad argued long ago:

> One would like to know just how unlike two events may be before it becomes impossible to admit the existence of a causal relation between them. No one hesitates to hold that draughts and colds in the head are causally connected, although the two are extremely unlike each other. If the unlikeness of draughts and colds in the head does not prevent one from admitting a causal connection between the two, why should the unlikeness of volitions and voluntary [bodily] movements prevent one from holding that they are causally connected?[2]

There are several cases where we know that one thing causes another even though we do not know how causation works and even though the causes are different from the effects.[3] Even from a nontheistic perspective, it is not inconceivable to believe it possible for God, if he exists, to create the world or to act in that world, even though God and the material universe are very different. A magnetic field can move a tack; gravity can act on a planet millions of miles away; protons exert a repulsive force on each other. In these examples, we know *that* one thing can causally interact with another thing, even though we have no idea *how* that interaction takes place. Some interactions are simply taken as basic and ultimate. Furthermore, in each case the causes would seem to have a different nature from their effects—forces and fields versus solid, spatially located, particle-like entities.[4]

In the case of mind and body, we are constantly aware of causation between them. Episodes in the body or brain (being stuck with a pin, having a head injury) can cause things in the soul (a feeling of pain, loss of memory), and the soul can cause things to happen in the body (worry can cause ulcers; I can freely and intentionally raise my arm). We have such overwhelming evidence *that* causal interaction takes place, there is no sufficient reason to doubt it.

Furthermore, it may even be that a "how" question regarding the interaction between mind and body cannot even arise. A question about how A causally interacts with B is a request for a description of the intervening mechanism between A and B. You can ask how turning on the key starts your car because there is an intermediate electrical system between your key and your car's running engine that is the means by which turning on your key accomplishes an act of starting your car. Your "how" question is a request to describe that intermediate mechanism. But the interaction between mind and body may be, and most likely is, direct and immediate. There *is* no intervening mechanism and thus a "how" question describing that mechanism is misplaced at best, meaningless at worst. It has no application to the phenomenon under investigation.

The objection we are currently examining is often just an expression of physicalist bias.[5] Because the physicalist cannot understand how dualism fits into his view of the world, he rejects it. But this assumes the truth of physicalism, which is what dualism questions. We conclude, therefore, that this objection does not carry sufficient weight to abandon a dualist understanding of the interaction of mind and body.[6]

Science and Scientism

We live in an age where science is thought by many to be the sole and supreme paradigm of truth and rationality. There are many advocates of this perspective, scientism—namely the view that a belief is true and reasonable if and only if it is scientifically testable or entailed by a widely held scientific theory. If scientism is correct, then dualism must be abandoned, the objection goes, because the soul is an outdated, unscientific notion.

But, however widely scientism may be held, it is a cultural myth that is patently absurd and false for at least three reasons.[7] First, scientism is self-refuting. Scientism is a statement *of* philosophy *about* science; it is not a statement of science itself. And as a philosophical statement, it claims there are no true or rational philosophical statements because they cannot be scientifically tested, nor are they necessary implications of a scientific theory. So if scientism is true, no nonscientific statements can be true or rational, including the thesis of scientism itself. If science is the test for every truth claim, then science cannot test itself for truth. As Jenny Teichman has observed:

Can science and scientists themselves decide whether or not science is the only form of real knowledge? Science, as Neitzsche remarked, does not investigate itself, but the rest of the world. Although a scientist, like anyone else, might well hold philosophical theories which can be rationally defended as philosophy, science *per se* does not deal with questions like What is science? What is knowledge? And it is far from obvious that the methods of science are themselves appropriate for objectively examining the claim that those very methods are valid and extendable paradigms which other enquiries should emulate.[8]

Second, science cannot justify the necessary assumptions that must be made if science itself is going to be practiced. Science cannot be done in thin air. It requires the truth of certain philosophical assumptions if science is even going to get off the runway. For example, if orderliness is an illusion, if the external world is unknowable, if our intellect and five senses are unreliable tools for gathering truth about the world, if various values such as "be objective and report data honestly" are unfounded, if nature is not basically uniform, if numbers and truth do not exist, if the laws of logic are inapplicable to reality, if skepticism is true . . . then science is impossible.

Now each of these assumptions has been challenged, and rational alternatives offered. The task of defending or criticizing the assumptions of science is one of the tasks of philosophy. Since scientism rules out philosophy, then it also eliminates a defense of the presuppositions of science and leaves science dying in an intellectual wasteland. In this way scientism shows itself to be a foe of science, not a friend.

Finally, scientism fails to account for something that we all know to be a fact. Scientism notwithstanding, there are numerous examples of rational debate and truth in areas outside of science: ethics, political science, philosophy, law, history, literature, art, mathematics, theology, and so on.

Therefore, scientism is false. Science is not the sole arbiter of reality. So even if we grant that the truth of dualism must be settled outside of science, that does not count against it. In fact, dualism and science are in the same boat, intellectually speaking. Each requires *philosophical* justification before it can be accepted. In the previous chapter, we argued that dualism does have good philosophical justification, so scientism as an objection fails.[9] Furthermore, we will see in Chapter 5 that empirical, scientific evidence that supports dualism does exist.

Dualism vs. Naturalistic Evolutionary Theory

One of the driving forces behind Charles Darwin's exposition of evolution was materialism regarding the mind/body problem. As Howard E. Gruber explains:

[T]he idea of either a Planful or an Intervening Providence taking part in the day-to-day operations of the universe was, in effect, a competing theory [to Darwin's version of evolution]. If one believed that there was a God who had originally designed the world exactly as it has come to be, the theory of evolution through natural selection could be seen as superfluous. Likewise, if one believed in a God who intervened from time to time to create some of the organisms, organs, or functions found in the living world, Darwin's theory could be seen as superfluous. Any introduction of intelligent planning or decision-making reduces natural selection from the position of a necessary and universal principle to a mere possibility.[10]

In other words, if the soul exists, it would be beyond the scope of evolutionary theory, and this would threaten the theory's plausibility.[11] So the soul's existence has been rejected in light of the acceptance of a naturalistic form of evolution. Here are some recent examples of this argument: According to Paul Churchland:

> The important point about the standard evolutionary story is that the human species and all of its features are the wholly physical outcome of a purely physical process. . . . If this is the correct account of our origins, then there seems neither need, nor room, to fit any nonphysical substances or properties into our theoretical account of ourselves. We are creatures of matter. And we should learn to live with that fact.[12]

Likewise, D.M. Armstrong asserts,

> It is not a particularly difficult notion that, when the nervous system reaches a certain level of complexity, it should develop new properties. Nor would there be anything particularly difficult in the notion that when the nervous system reaches a certain level of complexity it should affect something that was already in existence in a new way. But is is a quite different matter to hold that the nervous system should have the power to create something else, of a quite different nature from itself, and create it out of no materials.[13]

Arthur Peacocke agrees:

> I find it very hard to see why that functional property [i.e., consciousness] coded in a certain complex physical structure requires a new entity to be invoked, of an entirely different kind, to appear on the scene to ensure its emergence. How could something substantial, some substance or some other entity different in kind from that which has been evolved so far, suddenly come in to the evolutionary, temporal sequence?[14]

In sum, this objection claims the following: Since we are merely the result of an entirely physical process (the processes of evolutionary theory), which works on wholly physical materials, we are wholly physical beings.

If this objection is merely an expression of scientism, then it is false for the reasons we have already given. On the other hand, if it is simply an expression of the adequacy of naturalistic evolutionary theory to explain the nature of man, it is clearly question begging.

It goes like this: (1) If we are merely the result of naturalistic, evolutionary processes, then physicalism is true. (2) We are merely the result of naturalistic, evolutionary processes. (3) Therefore, physicalism is true.

But why should we accept premise 2? Dualists do not. They argue: If we are merely the result of naturalistic, evolutionary processes, then physicalism is true. But physicalism is not true. Therefore, it is not the case that we are merely the result of naturalistic, evolutionary processes.[15]

In other words, the evolutionary argument begs the question against the dualist. The real issue is the evidence for and against dualism. If the evidence is good, then the dualists' response should be embraced. We have seen good reasons for taking dualism to be true. This means not only that the evolutionary argument fails but also that there will never be a complete scientific account of the nature and origin of mankind.[16]

Artificial Intelligence

This objection builds on the assumption that advances in artificial intelligence research, computer technology, and computational theory indicate that the mind is to the brain as software is to hardware. In other words, computers can, or will be able to, do all the thinking, talking, and so forth that humans do. Computers add, subtract, interact, and so on, but we do not postulate a mind or soul in a computer to explain these abilities. Similarly, human beings can be adequately explained as complex computers without postulating an immaterial entity as a part of what gives them the abilities they have.

This critique of dualism makes a fundamental error. It equates artificial intelligence, of which computers are examples, with intelligence itself. This is a mistake. Computers are designed by intelligent minds to imitate mental states. But computers do not think, see, hear, feel, love, or have any consciousness at all. Computers do not think through a logical syllogism and draw a conclusion. They simply have on and off switches built into circuits by designers that allow them to imitate such intellectual activities.

In order to see the difference between intelligence and artificial intelligence, we need to be clear on what physicalist advocates of artificial intelligence are claiming here. In the standard sense, typical intellectual activities include thinking, believing, or grasping a propositional content or a semantic meaning in one's mind.

For example, one grasps the meaning of the sentence "All whales are mammals" by having the semantic meaning of the sentence and a mental entity called a proposition (which is distinct from the physical markings, called a sentence, used to express that meaning) in one's mind. One then understands the meaning of another sentence "All sperm whales are whales," and then, intentionally and by means of rational insight, draws the conclusion "All sperm whales are mammals." The notions of "semantic meaning", "proposition", "understanding," "thinking," "rational insight," "drawing a conclusion," are, *prima facie,* mentalist, dualist notions.

Now the physicalist advocate of an artificial intelligence model of human beings (called advocates of strong AI) believes that these mental, semantic notions *are identical* to computer operations that are completely physical in nature. Computers receive input, manipulate symbols (understood as merely physical entities, such as physical scratchings or sounds, electrical impulses) according to certain rules, give output, and advance to a new matching state ready to receive new input. For example, a computer "adds" when it receives the input "2+2" by undergoing a set of machine operations, resulting in the output (e.g., on a screen) "4."[17]

Now, you should recall from Chapter 2 that if A is identical to B, then *there is no possible situation where you can have A without B or vice versa.* If we can find a case where all of the artificial intelligence operations are present (the reception of certain inputs, syntactical manipulation of symbols, and the production of certain outputs) but we do not have real intelligence (the semantic understanding necessary for real thinking), then we will have shown that intelligence, which the dualist claims to be a feature of mind, cannot be reduced to and identified with artificial intelligence. Is there such a case? Yes, there is.

John Searle has offered the following situation known as the Chinese Room:[18]

> Imagine that you are locked in a room, and in this room are several baskets full of Chinese symbols. Imagine that you (like me) do not understand a word of Chinese, but that you are given a rule book in English for manipulating the Chinese symbols. The rules specify the manipulations of symbols purely formally, in terms of their syntax, not their semantics. So the rule might say: 'Take a squiggle-squiggle out of basket number one and put it next to a squoggle-squoggle sign from basket number two.' Now suppose that some other Chinese symbols are passed into the room, and that you are given further rules for passing back Chinese symbols out of the room. Suppose that unknown to you the symbols passed into the room are called 'questions' by the people outside the room, and the symbols you pass back out of the room are called 'answers to the questions.' Suppose, furthermore, that the programmers are so good at designing the programs and that you are so good at manipulating the symbols, that very soon your answers are indistinguishable from those of a native Chinese speaker. There you are locked in your room shuffling your Chinese symbols and passing out Chinese symbols in response to incoming Chinese symbols.
>
> Now the point of the story is simply this: By virtue of implementing a formal computer program from the point of view of an outside observer, you behave exactly as if you understood Chinese, but all the same you don't understand a word of Chinese.

The Chinese room with the person inside would simulate a computer to an outside person. For a person outside, the room receives input and gives output in a way that makes it appear that the room understands Chinese.

But of course, all the room does is *imitate* mental understanding, it does not *possess* it.

Computers are just like the Chinese room. They imitate mental operations, but they do not really exemplify them. Computers and their programs are not minds, because they fail to have consciousness, intentionality, and understanding of real semantic contents. Computers merely imitate minds; thus, this objection fails.[19]

Ockham's Razor

Ockham's Razor tells us that we should not multiply entities beyond what is needed to explain something. Given two explanations of the same thing, we should prefer the one that is simpler—the one that uses the fewest number of entities to explain the thing in question. Now physicalism is simpler than dualism because it postulates only one type of entity (matter) to explain a human being instead of two (matter and mind). Thus, in keeping with the requirements of Ockham's Razor, we should prefer physicalism to dualism.

There are two main problems with the application of Ockham's Razor to the mind/body problem.[20] First, if Ockham's Razor is understood to be the fairly conventionalist principle that an explanation of a phenomenon should only include elements within it necessary to explain that phenomenon, then the principle is uncontroversial and even supports dualism. You see, the dualist cites several phenomena (see Chapter 2) for which physicalism as a theory is inadequate, and she postulates dualism as the most adequate explanation for these phenomena. Dualists can agree that one should not postulate dualism needlessly, but they insist that dualism is, in fact, needed to honestly and fairly explain important features of human beings. The real debate, then, is not about Ockham's Razor, but about the relative merits of dualism vs. physicalism.

Second, if Ockham's Razor is used to place a burden of proof on the dualist, then the following applies: In light of the self-presenting nature of my mental states—my knowledge of them is often incorrigible and I have private access to them, neither of which is true for physical states—I am more certain that I have a soul than that I have a body. So the burden of proof is on the physicalist who wants to dispute this evidence.

Although other objections can be raised against dualism, these are some of the major ones and none of them is sufficient to refute dualism.[21] We conclude, therefore, that dualism in general, and substance dualism in particular, are rationally justified, true beliefs about human beings.[22] Now we need to consider the importance of dualism for belief in eternal life.

Substance Dualism and the Case for Eternal Life

Substance dualism lends support to belief in life after death for at least four reasons.

First, substance dualism makes eternal life more *plausible* than does physicalism. If physicalism were true, then with the death of the body, the person would become extinct. The only way eternal life could be possible would be for God to recreate an individual out of nothing at the final resurrection. But this view is very hard to square with a fair reading of the Bible, and it provides no indication of life after death apart from some form of special revelation from God. We have tried to see if we can discover reasons for such a belief apart from special revelation, and we believe we have done this to some degree so far. Besides, as we have argued, if substance dualism is true, the soul is an immaterial substance in its own right, and the destruction of the body does not necessarily entail the destruction of the soul.

Second, substance dualism makes survival in an afterlife *intelligible*. When we ponder eternal life, we are interested in a survival where I am literally the same person who survives death and exists in the afterlife. We are not interested in becoming extinct at death and having a double recreated who looks like us or has our memories or character traits. What we want to know is whether *I myself* will live on after the death of my body.[23]

The substance dualist has a way of making sense out of my literal survival of death. The person who lives in the afterlife will be the same person as I am now, because that person will have my soul. Sameness of soul is what constitutes personal identity through change, even death. I am the same person I was at childhood and who will be in the afterlife because the very same soul will exist at all those times.

As we saw in the last chapter, physicalism and property dualism cannot account for this literal sameness through change. Thus, compared to substance dualism, these views fail to clarify personal identity issues that surround our beliefs about eternal life. More will be said about this in Chapter 7.

Third, the nature of the human soul *lends more support to* the notion of eternal life than merely making it possible and intelligible. Throughout the history of the church, the classic understanding of living things has included the doctrine that animals, as well as humans, have souls. Christians have maintained this because the Bible teaches that animals have souls (Gen. 1:30, Rev. 8:9). Furthermore, Christians have believed that animals are not merely automatons, capable of exhaustive description in terms of the laws of chemistry and physics. Rather, animals are living things with a principle of life in them (an animal soul), and they have sensory awarenesses, feel pain, and enjoy a certain form of sentient life.

Even though the church has been quite clear about the existence of animal souls, there has been no consensus about the existence of animals in the afterlife, some Christians favoring the idea, some arguing against it, some remaining agnostic.[24] Thus, the mere presence of dualism regarding animals has not been sufficient, by itself, to carry clear conviction regarding animal immortality. An important reason for this ambivalence is that,

while the church has always held that animals have souls, it has also taught
that animal souls are different in nature from human souls and that there is
something about human souls that makes them better candidates for eternal life than animal souls.

Thomas Aquinas advanced this type of argument in the thirteenth century.[25] To fully evaluate his argument would require a detailed treatment
of his metaphysics, which is not possible here. But his case is worth
pondering.

Aquinas argued, reasonably enough, that animal souls function in clear
dependence on the animal body. For example, animals' functions are tied
to sensory experiences and these, in turn, depend upon the sense organs of
sight, smell, and so on. However, the human soul gives evidence of being
self-subsistent, of existing in its own right apart from the body. Why?
Aquinas' main premise seems to be this: Because certain functions of the
human soul appear to be independent of the body, therefore, the existence
of the human soul can be independent of the body. The human soul has
certain abilities that rise above a dependence upon a specific body organ,
and the exercise of these abilities requires that the human soul have a foothold in being all its own, independent of the body.

For example, the human soul can engage in abstract reflection about
broad concepts that do not depend upon any specific sense organ. Some of
these concepts would be existence in general, truth, causation, mathematics, and morality. An animal, on the other hand, can sense a specific shade
of red, but it cannot contemplate redness or color in general, much less the
notion of a property or existence. These latter abilities require the soul to
transcend the body. Moreover, the human soul has freedom and that requires the soul to act independently of the body in the sense that the conditions in the body are insufficient to cause the self to act in a certain way. If
the self is free, it must be self-subsistent in order to be a free self-mover.
Thus, these features of the human soul give some indication that the human soul can survive apart from the body.

Aquinas' argument does lend some support to belief in the survival of
the human soul after the death of the body. But how much support is hard
to say, so his argument is inconclusive by itself. The most we can say is that
it contributes to the case for life after death.

There is a fourth contribution of dualism to belief in eternal life: *Dualism supports belief in a transcendent realm of reality.* Dualism breaks the
stranglehold of scientism and physicalism and supports belief in God and a
transcendent dimension of reality. The main reason modern people do not
believe in eternal life is that they explicitly or implicitly embrace the
worldview of scientism: The sensible, spatiotemporal, physical world that
science investigates is all there is to reality. Dualism refutes that worldview because the soul is not an entity that can be embraced by scientism.

The existence of at least one nonphysical, nonempirical reality opens up
the door for the claim that there is an entire transcendent domain of reality.

Also, as the evolutionary argument against dualism showed, the existence of the soul cannot be explained by natural processes. Thus, the existence of the soul provides some evidence for the existence of an immaterial God who created it.[26] Something cannot come from nothing, and an immaterial soul cannot come from mere matter.

Because dualism supports theism, we have more reason to accept at least some of the arguments for eternal life that depend on the existence of God.[27] (These were mentioned in Chapter 1.) Dualism provides evidence for a transcendent realm of reality and for the existence of God. Eternal life is at home in a worldview that embraces both these notions, but it is alien in a worldview that denies a transcendent realm of being and the existence of God.

Where does this bring us? In the first three chapters, we have examined a number of philosophical arguments that provide a good, cumulative case for belief in eternal life. True, this case is not completely conclusive (proven), but it is not negligible either. In our view, the case for eternal life would be significantly weakened if the arguments of these first three chapters were unreasonable or void of supporting evidence. But because neither is true, the case for eternal life has some sturdy legs to stand on.

But we do not need to leave the matter here. Apart from philosophical arguments for eternal life, there are also arguments that are more empirical in nature. The next three chapters will deal with this evidence, beginning with the bodily resurrection of the historical Jesus.

Chapter 4

The Resurrection of Jesus

If all we had were philosophical reasons for accepting life after death, we would have enough to believe. But what if we had empirical evidence as well? What if we had evidence based on historical and scientific research that verified what philosophy showed was rational? What if we could find events that occurred in our world that showed that life beyond the grave was true? In fact, what if we could find at least one person who survived death and returned to tell us and show us what immortality was really like? We would likely find this fascinating, incredible, perhaps scary, hopefully comforting. Whatever our response, we would not likely ignore it. We would want to know what it is so we could evaluate it in light of our individual situations. After all, if there is life in the hereafter, we will all find out sooner or later. How much better it would be to find out sooner!

In this chapter, we will begin to explore the empirical evidence for life after death. And we will start with the most solid and dramatic of the historical strands of evidence: the bodily resurrection of Jesus of Nazareth from the grave.

Setting the Stage

In Mark 16:1–8 we read perhaps the earliest Gospel account of the women who went to the tomb on the very first Easter morning. Intending to finish the job of anointing Jesus' body for burial, it is clear that the last thing they expected to see was an empty tomb. They had seen Jesus' body buried there with their own eyes.

But what really must have shocked them was having an angel tell them that Jesus was not there but was risen from the dead. They were also told that the resurrected Jesus would actually appear to his disciples. No wonder they reacted in fear and silence, trembling in their perplexity.

Looking back to that event, most of us do not truly take the time to comprehend the mindset of the women as they left the tomb that morning. Sure, they had the word of the angel that Jesus was alive, but their reaction reveals that they were far from convinced.

What went through their minds as they fled from the tomb? Did they think it unlikely that such a seemingly supernatural event had happened?

Could it have been that they were just seeing things? Did it occur to them that someone may have taken the body, as Mary Magdalene thought later?

Initially, we will try to look through their eyes and watch the evidence mount. Why did they, and later the disciples, finally come to be such strong believers in the resurrection of Jesus? What did they learn over the next few weeks that convinced them? We will look at this evidence through four sets of arguments, each of which views the case for Jesus' resurrection from a different angle. The first two sets are general overviews, while the last two are more specialized.

The first group of arguments will deal with the sorts of naturalistic alternative schemes that even occurred to the disciples when they heard the women's news: Did something besides an actual resurrection explain the facts even better? Similar alternatives are still proposed today. This area of argumentation is vast, so we will have to treat it briefly while trying to handle it adequately and fairly.

From there we will shift to our second set of arguments: Are there positive reasons to think that Jesus did rise from the dead? After that, we will delve into one especially potent argument for Jesus' resurrection. Lastly, we want to respond in a more specialized manner to skeptics who prod more deeply.

Naturalistic Theories

The Major Options

If someone claims a supernatural event occurred, often someone else will pose an alternative scenario that substitutes only natural causes for that event. Such naturalistic proposals reached their heyday in the nineteenth century, but they had much earlier roots. In regard to the New Testament, naturalistic explanations are recorded in response to affirmations that were made about Jesus' resurrection. In fact, believers themselves voiced most of these earlier objections.

Mary Magdalene wondered aloud if the gardener had taken Jesus' body away (John 20:10–15). Matthew says that the Jewish leaders expressed a similar objection—namely, that the disciples stole Jesus' body (Matt. 28:11–15).

The Roman governor Pilate hinted at another possibility when Joseph of Arimathea requested Jesus' body: Perhaps Jesus had not yet died (Mark 15:42–45). Later, when facing what appeared to be the risen Jesus, the disciples questioned whether they were seeing things: Maybe Jesus was a ghostly spirit or even an hallucination (Luke 24:37). We also read that the disciples entertained another suspicion. When they first heard the women's story concerning the empty tomb, they interpreted it as nothing but an empty tale or gossip *(leeros;* Luke 24:10–11). Perhaps this explanation was an early forerunner to the more full-blown suggestion that the entire Christian scenario was only a legend.

At any rate, the formulation of naturalistic theories is not a recent phenomenon. This approach has been around since the inception of Christianity, where alternative explanations have occurred to both believers and unbelievers alike.

We will walk you through some legitimate responses to these challenges, but first we want to make two points. First, by way of reminder, we will have to be brief in order to remain within the parameters of this chapter and the scope of this book.[1] Second, in refuting these theories, we will try to use only those data that can themselves be reasonably established as factual. For example, we will not assume that the New Testament is divinely inspired, or even very trustworthy, in order to establish our points. Rather, we will present data that virtually all critical scholars who address this subject, whatever their school of thought, also accept. This, we believe, puts our case on a firm basis.

We will provide a brief, nonexhaustive list of the minimal data relevant to our present discussion. These facts can be supported individually, and most scholars (even many skeptical ones) generally recognize them as historical. Our summary includes at least eleven separate facts, with a twelfth allowed by many.[2]

Jesus died due to the rigors of crucifixion and was later buried. As a direct result, his disciples doubted and despaired because Jesus' death challenged their hopes. Although not as widely accepted, many scholars argue forcefully that the tomb in which Jesus was buried was discovered to be empty just a few days later.

These data further show (and almost all critical scholars agree) that the disciples had real experiences that they believed were actual appearances of the risen Jesus. Because of these experiences, the disciples were transformed from doubters who were fearful of identifying with Jesus to bold proclaimers of his death and resurrection who were even willing to die for the truth of these events. This gospel message was the very center of preaching in the early church and was even proclaimed in Jerusalem, the city where Jesus had died and was buried shortly before.

As a result of this apostolic preaching, the Christian church was established, with Sunday—the day Jesus had risen—as the primary day of worship. James, who had previously been a skeptical unbeliever, was converted to the faith and transformed when he also believed he saw the resurrected Jesus. A few years later, Paul, a leader in the persecution of the church, was also converted and thoroughly changed by a real experience that he believed to be an appearance of the risen Jesus.

These facts are crucial for our present investigation of Jesus' resurrection. With the exception of the empty tomb (which is still attested by numerous good arguments) virtually all critical scholars who have studied this subject agree concerning the historicity of these events. As such, any conclusion concerning the facticity of the resurrection should properly account for these data, which will also play a vital part in our own study, as well.

TWELVE HISTORICAL FACTS

(1) Jesus died due to the rigors of crucifixion.

(2) Jesus was buried.

(3) His disciples doubted and despaired because Jesus' death challenged their hopes.

(4) The tomb in which Jesus had been buried was discovered to be empty just a few days later.

(5) The disciples had real experiences that they believed were actual appearances of the risen Jesus.

(6) The disciples were transformed and were even willing to die for the truth of these events.

(7) This gospel message was the very center of preaching in the early church.

(8) The gospel was even proclaimed in Jerusalem, the city where Jesus had died.

(9) The Christian church was firmly established by these disciples.

(10) The primary day of worship was Sunday—the day Jesus was reported to have risen.

(11) James, Jesus' previously skeptical brother, was converted when he believed he saw the resurrected Jesus.

(12) Paul, a leader in the persecution of the church, was also converted by a real experience which he believed to be the risen Jesus.

Body stolen?

Is it likely that someone took the body of Jesus and that this accounts for the belief in his resurrection? Theories based on a positive answer to this question have always fallen on hard times, which probably explains why they have almost always been rejected by serious scholars in the last two centuries. Their problems are legion. For example, if Jesus' disciples took the body, why were they willing to die for their conviction that he had actually been raised from the dead by God? Also, how could we explain the disciples' deep certainty, not only that the resurrection had occurred, but also that this event was the very *center* of their faith, the foundation on which their own eternal life was based? The stolen-body theories have never been able to address these issues satisfactorily since they assume that the disciples had perpetrated the "crime" themselves.

There are other very serious difficulties also. After the crucifixion, the disciples were paralyzed by fear and despair. They were not even in the necessary frame of mind to plot the stealing of Jesus' body. And even assuming they stole the body, why have we never heard of one of them later recanting? Why were there no defections from the faith? Would they not be prime candidates for such? With what we witnessed in recent history during Watergate and the Iran-Contra Scandal, can we reasonably suppose that the disciples could have totally covered up their lie?

Further, how would such a plot have convinced Jesus' brother James to become a believer? Even worse, what would have motivated Paul to "sell out" to his former "ministry," when he thought he was doing God's will by persecuting Christians? From his viewpoint, why would he risk the damnation of his own soul by converting to what he perceived as anti-Jewish beliefs?

For reasons such as these, even skeptical scholars have almost unanimously rejected these proposals and have admitted that, whatever else might be said, the disciples at least believed that Jesus had appeared to them after his death.

So could someone else other than the disciples, perhaps even an unknown individual, have "done the dirty work" at the tomb and stolen the body? Mary Magdalene suspected this when she spoke with the "gardener."

But this explanation is even weaker than the former one. *Even if it were true,* it leaves the most crucial puzzle pieces unexplained. Posit any thief you want. No matter his or her identity or motive, the thief hypothesis does not even get to first base explaining the nature of the disciples' experiences, which are the key to the entire resurrection question. What did the disciples see, feel, touch, hear, and speak to? They became convinced it was the risen Jesus, the one who had died and been buried only days before.

But further, like the earlier form of the fraud thesis, this version also has major problems explaining the conversions of both James and Paul. Aren't we really stretching credulity even more by supposing that these two critics would be so duped by such a scheme?

Aside from all this, however, there is not a shred of evidence for supposing that anyone else actually stole Jesus' body. So it may be an interesting claim, but it is groundless.

At best, it only tries to account for the empty tomb. Therefore, very little of the known data is explained by this supposition alone. The remainder of the case for the resurrection goes unresolved. As a result, *another* critical thesis needs to be developed *in addition* to this one in order to do the job. And if another hypothesis is needed, then that one had better be developed first, because it is required for the most crucial portions of the Christian message: the apostles' experiences and corresponding transformations. So really, no other criticisms are needed to topple the thief theory since it fails miserably in its attempt to explain the resurrection itself.[3]

Swoon?

What about Pilate? Didn't he wonder if Jesus was ever dead in the first place? And if he, being so close to the site of Jesus' crucifixion, raised such a doubt, why can't we? Perhaps Jesus did not die on the cross. Maybe he fainted, only to revive later in the coolness of his rock tomb.

The swoon thesis suffers from numerous medical problems, including the nature of crucifixion. Even though a direct cause of death may not be apparent, the prevailing medical opinion is that death by crucifixion is essentially death by asphyxiation. Hanging in the low position on the cross induces the victim's muscles around the lungs to constrict, eventually making it impossible to exhale. But the individual is not able to keep pulling himself up indefinitely in order to breathe. So, once a victim has been hanging in the low position for any extended length of time without pushing himself up, he is dead. A Roman soldier or bystander could easily tell when such had occurred in Jesus' case. An autopsy was not needed. Moreover, Jesus could have also died from complications due to hypovolemic shock and heart failure.[4]

Additionally, the nature of the chest or side wound Jesus received, which reportedly induced a flow of blood and water (John 19:34–35),[5] is another major evidence of death. By far the most common medical conclusion is that this outward phenomenon caused by a Roman lance indicates that the weapon pierced Jesus' chest cavity, through his pericardium (which contains a small amount of water) and into his heart, thereby insuring his death if it had not yet occurred due to the other factors.[6] After analyzing the factors leading to Jesus' death, a team composed of a physician, a medical technician, and a pastor (William Edwards, Wesley Gabel, and Floyd Hosmer) concluded, "Accordingly, interpretations based on the assumption that Jesus did not die on the cross appear to be at odds with modern medical knowledge."[7]

Another death-inducing technique used by the Roman soldiers was the common practice of *crucifragium,* or the breaking of the victim's ankles, in order to hasten death by asphyxiation. This is illustrated by the skeleton of a first-century crucifixion victim named Yohanon.[8] While the New Testament record reports that Jesus did not suffer this fate (John 19:31–33), the spear wound was a *replacement* for breaking his ankles; it insured his death just as effectively. So if one questions the historicity of the side wound, he would be faced with the likelihood of *crucifragium,* which was a very commonly applied death-causing procedure. So at least one of these techniques (reported in the same biblical text) would have been used—and indeed was—to guarantee Jesus' demise.[9]

Apart from this data, the major refutation of the swoon theory comes from a famous critique by nineteenth-century liberal theologian David Strauss, who argued that this was a self-defeating hypothesis:

It is impossible that a being who had stolen half-dead out of the sepulchre, who crept about weak and ill, wanting medical treatment, who required bandaging, strengthening and indulgence, and who still at last yielded to his sufferings, could have given to the disciples the impression that he was a Conqueror over death and the grave, the Prince of Life, an impression which lay at the bottom of their future ministry. Such a resuscitation could only have weakened the impression which he had made upon them in life and in death, at the most could only have changed their sorrow into enthusiasm, have elevated their reverence into worship.[10]

Strauss is right. By any estimation, Jesus would have been in very serious condition—bleeding, limping, sweating, and bent over—obviously in need of a doctor's care. But then how could anyone have mistaken this Jesus as the resurrected Lord of life? Such a sight would actually have served to *weaken* any such conclusion. Hence, the swoon theory is false. It fails to explain the very fact it sought most to address: the well-established conclusion that the disciples believed that Jesus was the "Conqueror over death" and the "Prince of life" (Acts 2:24, 3:15).

As if this were not enough, the swoon theory dies for still other reasons. It cannot account for the impetus for James's conversion, as well as for Paul's dramatic reversal of worldviews. No wonder this thesis passed out of scholarly popularity long ago.[11]

Hallucinations?

Perhaps some will think, maybe as the disciples initially did long ago, that the apparent post-resurrection appearances of Jesus were really hallucinations.[12] While this view was the most popular one about a hundred years ago, it probably suffers from the largest number of problems of any of the naturalistic theories. Accordingly, like the others, it is rarely cited even by contemporary critical scholars. Why? Let us show you.

We will begin by pointing out that hallucinations are essentially private events. Unlike the common cold, where one person's sneeze can be another's downfall, hallucinations are not contagious or collective.[13] As one psychologist puts it:

Hallucinations are individual occurrences. By their very nature only one person can see a given hallucination at a time. They certainly are not something which can be seen by a group of people. Neither is it possible that one person could somehow induce an hallucination in somebody else. Since an hallucination exists only in this subjective, personal sense, it is obvious that others cannot witness it.[14]

Therefore, the groups who reportedly saw Jesus at one time are a serious roadblock to any hallucination hypothesis.[15]

There are yet other problems with such a thesis. For example, the disciples' state of mind after the death of Jesus—characterized by fear, doubt, and despair—militates against the personal expectation and positive emotion required in the experience of hallucinations.

A very serious problem in proving the hallucination theory concerns the variety of persons, places, and times of Jesus' appearances. He did not simply appear in the same way, at the same time, and to the same people. Rather, he showed himself to a group of women outside on a sunny morning; to two men on a long walk and later indoors; to the combined disciples and apostles more than once; to five hundred people at one time, presumably outdoors; to the disciples on a Galilean mountain; to several disciples on a seashore; and to his followers outside Jerusalem.[16] That these different individuals in each of these various circumstances would all be candidates for hallucinations really stretches the limits of credulity.

And what about the empty tomb? Hallucination theories do not even try to deal with it. Or what about James the skeptic? What evidence indicates that he was a candidate for hallucinations? And what about Paul—did he also long to see the risen Jesus so that his mind invented such a picture?

These are just some of the problems for this hypothesis.[17] So it is no surprise that so few contemporary scholars espouse this theory and most are critical of it,[18] including the influential German theologian Wolfhart Pannenberg who said, "These explanations have failed, to date."[19]

Legends?

Lastly, there are those who charge what the disciples initially implied concerning the report of the women—that their testimony was a groundless tale or legend. How do we know that the reports of Jesus' resurrection and appearances were not really mythical embellishments that grew over time?

Our initial two responses will simply be stated here and defended later in this chapter, when we explore in detail the early Christian witness to Jesus' resurrection and appearances. The evidence shows that we have reports of Jesus' appearances that are close to the events they describe, and reported by or based on eyewitnesses. Since this is the case, legends cannot be the basis for the initial accounts of these appearances, since they are traceable to the witnesses' *original experiences* themselves. In other words, whatever else might be said about the testimony of the early eyewitnesses, their absolute conviction that they actually saw Jesus is not justifiably explained in terms of nonhistorical legends or myths.

Furthermore, these witnesses were totally convinced that the resurrection message was the very center of their faith, a message that was preached even under threat of persecution and death. The legend theory cannot adequately account for this *specific* conviction or the willingness to die for because these two facts reveal how sure and careful the witnesses were in their acceptance of the resurrection's veracity.

And like the other naturalistic theories, additional problems are common with the legend view. In spite of what was sometimes reported at the end of the nineteenth century, there is an insufficient basis from parallels in ancient mythology to explain the Christian gospel message.[20] In fact, not one clear case of any alleged resurrection teaching appears in any pagan text before the late second century A.D., almost one hundred years *after* the New Testament was written.

Moreover, what is to be done with the facts in favor of the empty tomb?[21] The mythological theories do not explain those, therefore, another explanation would have to be supplied.

Furthermore, are we to suppose that James and, later, Paul, were converted by some teaching taken from the nonhistorical mystery personages?

As with the other naturalistic hypotheses, the legend theory has also taken a deserved beating, even by critical scholars. After viewing the important evidence from 1 Corinthians 15:4–9 alone, Pannenberg concluded: "Under such circumstances it is an idle venture to make parallels in the history of religions responsible for the *emergence* of the primitive Christian message about Jesus' resurrection."[22]

Four Final Critiques

We have just covered the chief naturalistic theories, and each has been disproven by the factual data. However, we have refuted these theories only by citing facts that are individually demonstrable and accepted as historical by virtually all critical scholars who deal with this subject. We did not draw on the vast array of material available in the Bible itself. Nor did we cite all the available historical and philosophical reasons for rejecting these views. And yet, even with our brief criticisms, we marshalled enough evidence to reject the major naturalistic explanations.[23]

But we would like to hammer four more nails in the naturalist's coffin. Each of these further considerations is not necessarily an independent reason against all naturalistic theses, but each one does seal their coffin ever more tightly. The first nail begins with David Hume.

Many intellectuals have been profoundly affected by the ideas of Scottish philosopher David Hume (1711–1776), who basically charged that miracles are opposed by both the laws of nature and man's uniform experience of these laws.[24] In other words, the evidence for a miracle claim can always be questioned since it is based mainly on the reliability of eyewitness testimony that cannot be counted on as strongly as our knowledge and experience of natural laws.

Hume's essay was probably the most influential treatise to those in the last century who thought that naturalistic theories needed to be developed in the first place to account for miracle stories. In this way Hume's ideas served as a backdrop for the nineteenth-century popularization of these alternative theories.

However, in spite of Hume's popularity in certain circles, his suppositions on this subject were based on faulty reasoning, as numerous scholars have shown. He committed informal logical fallacies, as well as other internal inconsistencies. For example, he improperly ruled out the possibility of miracles before the facts could even be investigated. Since miracles almost certainly cannot occur, there's no reason to investigate the so-called evidence for a miracle. There could be no valid evidence in support of such a claim. This led to his chief weakness: Hume failed to even try to ascertain if there already was sufficient evidence to conclude that an historical event such as the resurrection of Jesus had happened, performed at that moment by superior force beyond that of the laws of nature. In other words, the question is not the strength of the laws of nature, but whether there is sufficient evidence to show that, *in a particular case,* a miracle claim is justified due to the exercise of a greater power.

Hence, Hume did not actually attempt to support a particular naturalistic theory against the resurrection. Rather, he and his supporters assumed that the best psychological or physical explanation, even if it is unlikely, is more believable than a miracle. So even if one has to go to extremes in answering a miracle-claim, it is still more likely that this alternative is correct than is a miracle.

Let's think about this for a moment. We could agree with Hume that nonmiraculous events are more common than miraculous ones. But if we held that *no* evidence can *ever* be sufficient to establish an event such as the resurrection, we would be rejecting miracle claims *a priori,* out of hand, before we checked out any possible supporting facts. Is this really reasonable or responsible? We don't think so. On the other hand, if evidence for such an event were allowed and checked, we think the evidence for the resurrection is superior to any naturalistic explanation.

Or let's look at another problem. Why should miracles be rejected because of the regularity of the laws of nature? *General* evidence for these laws does not necessarily contradict *particular* evidence for a miracle. The former only states what is usually (or even almost always) the case, while the latter asserts that there just may be some exceptions. Each type of evidence has its own realm of application, and there is no necessary conflict between them.

Further, we could grant to Hume that it may be preferable on occasion to accept a naturalistic explanation over a supernaturalistic one. But this is a far cry from accepting a *series* of improbable natural events in order to explain all of the data for a miracle claim, such as what would have to occur to account for the resurrection of Jesus. Supposing that only *one* spontaneous event transpired is not the same as inventing an entire string of unlikely natural explanations so as to explain the empty tomb, the various appearances of the transformed body of Jesus, or life changes like Paul's. A miracle is preferable to an ad hoc series of explanations whose only goal is to do anything to avoid the supernatural.

But even these points do not end Hume's problems. In the case of Jesus, the resurrection did not happen in a vacuum; it was not a lone "anomaly" in his life. Jesus also made a number of unique claims about himself and his mission. Additional elements such as these, that coincide with his resurrection, allow us to argue that there is a pattern here. His life cannot be accounted for in naturalistic terms. His unique claims, actions, personality, and life-style, together with his miracles and the fulfilling of Old Testament predictions, all combine to create a scenario that disproves naturalistic explanations.[25]

Lastly, if we have reason to think that this is a theistic universe, we have yet another avenue from which to argue that the resurrection was not some freak event of nature. In fact, such an event would best be explained by the action of God.

To be sure, there are a number of other crucially important issues concerning Hume and those who have updated his thesis that we cannot cover here, but these have been adequately handled elsewhere.[26] Indeed, Hume's case against miracles has been so thoroughly critiqued that one contemporary scholar has drawn this telling conclusion: "I believe it is now generally recognized that Hume overstates his case. We cannot *a priori* rule out the possibility of miracles or of rational belief in miracles. . . . It looks, then, as if Hume's argument against miracles . . . fails."[27]

A second nail concerning the naturalistic theories themselves is that not one of them, *even if true,* can explain even the minimal number of facts that critical scholars accept as historical, let alone the remainder of the biblical data. In other words, at least two naturalistic hypotheses are needed to just begin doing the job. But combining two improbable theories will not produce a probable explanation. It will actually increase the degree of improbability. It's like putting leaky buckets inside of each other, hoping each one will help stop up the leaks in the others. All you will get is a watery mess.

The third nail is that each of the naturalistic hypotheses, which was advocated by nineteenth-century liberal scholars, was also disproven by these scholars. They refuted each other's theories, thereby leaving no viable alternatives. For example, we have already explained how David Strauss delivered the historical death blow to the swoon theory held by Karl Venturini, Heinrich Paulus, and others. On the other hand, while Strauss popularized the hallucination theory, Friedrich Schleiermacher and Paulus pointed out errors in it.[28] The major decimation of the hallucination theory came later in the century at the hands of Theodor Keim.[29] The fraud theories had long before been dismissed by liberal scholars,[30] while the legend theories, popular later in the century, were disproven by later critical research.[31] So these scholars demolished each other's theories, thereby burying the major naturalistic attempts to account for Jesus' resurrection by the late 1800s.

The fourth nail in the naturalistic coffin is this: While nineteenth-century liberals decimated each other's views individually, chiefly by shooting their wounded, twentieth-century critical scholars have joined the fray by generally rejecting these theories as well. These contemporary scholars have judged that the entire lot of naturalistic theories is incapable of explaining the known data. This contemporary approach is characteristic of twentieth-century thought in general, across partisan lines of opinion.

For instance, Karl Barth mentioned a number of these hypotheses and pointed out how each one suffers from many inconsistencies. He then concluded that "to-day we rightly turn up our nose at this," further noting that "these explanations . . . have now gone out of currency."[32] After likewise listing a number of these theses, New Testament scholar Raymond Brown similarly observes that twentieth-century critical scholars have rejected them. He adds that contemporary thinkers ignore these alternative views and any new renditions of them as well, even treating them as unrespectable.[33] Beyond the ranks of Barth and Brown, you can find theologians as diverse as Paul Tillich, Gunther Bornkamm, Joachim Jeremias, John A.T. Robinson, Wolfhart Pannenberg, Ulrich Wilckens, Pinchas Lapide, and A.M. Hunter—all of whom have turned away from accepting naturalistic explanations of Jesus' resurrection.[34] Most of these scholars detect many of the same problems as do other researchers, both liberal and conservative. That even such critical scholars have rejected these naturalistic theories is a final epitaph on their failure, not simply because intellectuals think these theories are mistaken, as significant as that is, but because they have agreed that the problems with these theories are insurmountable.

Thus these four considerations, coupled with the initial and crucial truth that the minimal amount of factual data alone is still sufficient to disprove the naturalistic theories proposed against the resurrection of Jesus, are more than is needed to allow us to consider that Jesus' resurrection may be a true historical miracle. The failure of Hume's basic reasoning and the fact that no single alternative thesis is sufficient to explain the details surrounding Jesus' resurrection are also important factors. Finally, the nineteenth-century counter-critiques and the twentieth-century wholesale critical rejection of such theories are significant and final reminders of the myriad of problems involved in trying to discount the facticity of the resurrection.

Evidence for the Resurrection

Now the case for the resurrection of Jesus does not simply rest on the failure of any naturalistic theory to account for the known data. There are also many positive evidences that confirm the actual historical nature of this event. Nine of these evidences will be listed here, each of which is based on our earlier list of facts that are both confirmed by the known data and that are generally admitted to be historical by virtually all scholars who study this topic. The lone exception is the empty tomb, which is nonetheless strongly attested by the evidence[35] and is still accepted by most scholars.

Nine strands of evidence

The strongest evidence for the resurrection of Jesus is provided by (1) the *disciples' experiences,* which they believed to be actual appearances of the risen Jesus. This is especially so since the reports of these early eyewitnesses cannot be explained by naturalistic theories and because the evidence points to actual appearances. Another strong evidence includes (2) the *transformation of the disciples* into bold witnesses who were even willing to die for their faith in Jesus' resurrection.

Additional evidence includes (3) the historical facts that support the *empty tomb* and (4) the resurrection's being the very *center of the apostolic message.* The resurrection wasn't only believed, but it was also the disciples' pivotal affirmation. This would seem to require more introspection and assurance for the factual claims themselves. Further, the disciples proclaimed this message precisely in the city of Jesus' death, Jerusalem itself, and in repeated confrontations with the authorities. In fact, (5) the *Jewish leaders were not able to disprove their message,* in spite of having both the motive and the means to do so if it was possible.

(6) The very existence of the *Christian church,* (7) featuring *Sunday* as the primary, fixed day of worship instead of the Hebrew Sabbath, needs historical causes as well. The earliest believers were Jews. Accepting such monumental changes in their pattern of worship would have been taboo without sound warrant. Additionally, the astounding spread of the Christian faith around the Mediterranean region is without cause if Jesus had not come back to life.

Two additional and very powerful facts are that two skeptics, (8) *James,* the brother of Jesus, and (9) *Paul,* became believers after personally experiencing what they believed were actual appearances of the risen Jesus. New Testament scholar Reginald Fuller goes as far as to conclude that even if Jesus' appearance to James was not recorded by Paul (1 Cor. 15:7), such an incident would have to be postulated anyway in order to account for James's conversion from skepticism and his subsequent promotion to a high position of authority in the early church. The same could be said even more emphatically concerning Paul, the early Christian persecutor.[36]

When we combine these nine evidences with the failure of the naturalistic theories to adequately explain the data, they provide a strong case for the historicity of Jesus' resurrection from the dead. Even critical scholars who do not accept the inspiration of Scripture recognize the minimal factual basis behind these evidences, which further indicates the strength of our case.

So when the early and eyewitness experiences of the disciples, James, and Paul are weighed in conjunction with their corresponding transformations and the centrality of their message, the historical resurrection is shown to be the best explanation for the facts, particularly in light of the failure of the naturalistic theories.[37] Therefore, we conclude that the resurrection is an historical event. As former Oxford University church historian William Wand has said about the empty tomb alone: "All the strictly historical evidence we have is in favor of it, and those scholars who reject it ought to recognize that they do so on some other ground than that of scientific history."[38]

Some Important Testimony to Jesus' Appearances

Now let's zero in on one biblical text which, by itself, presents what is perhaps the single most powerful argument for Jesus' resurrection.[39] Throughout the New Testament, numerous oral traditions that were preached or taught in the early church were later written down in the text.

Essentially, all scholars agree that Paul in 1 Corinthians 15:3ff recorded an ancient creed(s) concerning Jesus' death, resurrection, and appearances that is actually much earlier than the book in which it is recorded. We know this for a number of reasons. His usage of the technical terms *delivered* and *received* traditionally indicate the imparting of oral tradition (cf. 1 Cor. 11:23). Further pointers include the text's parallelism and somewhat stylized content, the use of proper names for Cephas and James, the presence of non-Pauline words, and the possibility of the text's being orally transmitted in Aramaic originally. Still more reasons for the presence of traditional material include the Aramaic name Cephas (1 Cor. 15:5; see the parallel in Luke 24:34), the threefold use of *and that* (which is similar to Aramaic and Mishnaic Hebrew means of narration), and the two references to the Scripture's being fulfilled.[40]

Regarding the date of this creed, critical scholars generally agree that it has an exceptionally early origin. Joachim Jeremias refers to it as "the earliest tradition of all."[41] Ulrich Wilckens proclaims that it "indubitably goes back to the oldest phase of all in the history of primitive Christianity."[42] As a matter of fact, most of the scholars who date Paul's reception of this tradition place it from two to eight years after Jesus' crucifixion, or from about A.D. 32–38.[43]

Why do they think this creed should be dated so early? The majority hold that Paul probably received this material three years after his conversion, during his trip to Jerusalem to visit Peter and James, who are each included in the list of appearances (1 Cor. 15:5, 7; Gal. 1:18–19).[44] As Dodd states, "At that time he stayed with Peter for a fortnight, and we may presume they did not spend all the time talking about the weather."[45]

To help confirm this scenario, Paul's use of *historeo* in Galatians 1:18 in reference to his visit with Peter may indicate an investigative inquiry. William Farmer argues that the use of this term in this text signifies Paul's acting as an examiner or observer of Peter.[46] Furthermore, in the immediate context both before and after Paul's description of this trip to Jerusalem, his topic is the nature of the gospel (Gal. 1:11–17; 2:1–10), with the second reference specifically referring to his checking the content of his message with the other apostles fourteen years later.[47]

In summary, then, we can list at least four important indications that the *content* of the gospel confession in 1 Corinthians 15:3ff (if not the actual words themselves) is actually apostolic in nature. First, Paul recorded very early material that he himself received, recounting the eyewitness appearances of Jesus to the disciples, apostles, and others (vv. 5–7). He also probably obtained the list directly from Peter and James. Second, Paul himself is the eyewitness and apostolic source behind Jesus' appearance to him as recorded in verse 8. Third, Paul declares that the appearance reports are of apostolic origin and that the apostles themselves were currently teaching the same message concerning Jesus' resurrection appearances (vv. 9–11, 14, 15). And fourth, Paul specifically corroborated his teaching on the nature of the gospel (which included the resurrection, vv. 1–4) with the apostolic leadership at Jerusalem and found that the content of his message was accurate (Gal. 1:11—2:10).

These are potent reasons for concluding that this creedal data reported by Paul is authoritative and apostolic. As far as we (Habermas and Moreland) know, no contemporary, reputable scholar has argued that Paul was completely mistaken at all four of these junctures. Thus, this testimony presents a powerful basis for any discussion of the foundations of the Christian gospel. And critical scholars almost unanimously recognize its importance in this regard as well.

German historian Hans von Campenhausen insists, "This account meets all the demands of historical reliability that could possibly be made of such a text."[48] Jewish scholar Pinchas Lapide contends that this creed "may be considered as a statement of eyewitnesses."[49] And C.H. Dodd adds that this material is so close to the original source that anyone who would maintain the position that Paul was mistaken regarding the apostolic nature of the gospel message must bear the burden of proof.[50] Consequently, Paul's testimony in 1 Corinthians 15:3ff. is an invaluable report of the original eyewitnesses' experiences. The data help to piece together what they actually perceived.

Most critical scholars who have studied these facts have concluded that the disciples' experiences were definitely visual in nature, for no other conclusion satisfies all the data. Historian Michael Grant even attests that an investigation can actually "prove" that the earliest witnesses were convinced they had seen the risen Jesus.[51] Carl Braaten explains that contemporary skeptics even agree with the conclusion that, at least for the early believers, the Easter appearances were real events in space and time.[52]

Fuller classifies the disciples' belief in the risen Jesus as "one of the indisputable facts of history." He also states that we can be sure that the disciples had some sort of visionary experiences and that this "is a fact upon which both believer and unbeliever may agree."[53]

Pannenberg agrees: "Few scholars, even few rather critical scholars, doubt that there had been visionary experiences."[54] But since the hypothesis of hallucinations (or other subjective theories) fails badly in its attempt to explain the data, as we have already observed, the facts certainly favor the view that the original disciples experienced appearances of the risen Jesus.

In other words, the core elements of the disciples' experiences indicate that they witnessed actual appearances of the risen Jesus. And there is extensive agreement among contemporary theologians on just this conclusion: Jesus appeared to his disciples, and not just as a spirit.[55] Of course, and we wish to *carefully emphasize* this: This is not true simply because scholars say so, but because *the facts dictate this conclusion*. So, while the agreement among scholars is helpful, the most important consideration is that the *factual data demonstrate* that Jesus objectively appeared to his disciples after his death.

Now, even if one doubts our conclusion about the actual date and specific location of the creedal material in 1 Corinthians 15:3ff, there still exists an excellent case for this data's being early and apostolic in nature and, therefore, authoritative and reliable. So our argument is very strong.

We conclude, then, that this pre-Pauline report in 1 Corinthians 15 of Jesus' resurrection appearances and the attendant information clearly link the eyewitness content of the gospel with its later proclamation, and the evidence shows that the earliest Christians actually saw the risen Jesus, both individually and in groups.

Just the Minimal Facts, Please

In spite of the broad, almost unanimous realization among most reputable critical scholars who study this subject that each of the dozen facts discussed in this chapter is historical, what if our list of facts was challenged by some skeptics? In fact, what if some of these facts became disputable, even highly doubtful? What kind of case would be left? Let's find out.

Let's limit ourselves to just five of our twelve minimal facts: (1) Jesus' death by crucifixion; (2) the earliest disciples' experiences that they thought were appearances of the risen Jesus; (3) their subsequent transformations to the point of even being willing to die for their faith; (4) the resurrection as the very center of early apostolic preaching; and (5) the conversion and resulting transformation of Paul. We will briefly consider each one and see how well-established the resurrection is even when the historical evidence presented is only bare bones.

The *death of Jesus* due to the rigors of crucifixion is corroborated by the nature of crucifixion (including the prominence of asphyxiation), medical research on the location of the spear wound, the early creed in 1 Corinthians 15:3ff, and Strauss' famous critique of the swoon theory. Numerous other sources of information on Jesus' death are provided in the Gospels, other early New Testament creeds (such as 1 Cor. 11:23–26; Phil. 2:8), early non-New Testament Christian writings (such as Clement of Rome's *Corinthians* 24, 49), and non-Christian sources from a few decades later (see Tacitus' *Annals* 15:44).[56]

The fact of the *disciples' experiences,* which they believed to be actual appearances of the risen Jesus, is best evidenced by the report of early, eyewitness testimony in 1 Corinthians 15:3ff. These events occurred to individuals as well as to groups. Critical scholars have found other portions of trustworthy information in several other accounts from both the New Testament and outside it.[57] Hence, it is little wonder that these same scholars accept the death of Jesus and the disciples' experiences as the two most widely recognized factual events from the life of Jesus and afterward.

That Jesus' resurrection appearances led to the *transformation of the apostles* is the witness of the New Testament as a whole. Before the crucifixion the apostles fled in fear, denying Jesus.[58] But because of Jesus' resurrection appearances, their entire lives were radically changed, even to the point of being willing to suffer death for their testimony.[59] But we should not miss the forest for the trees here: The entire New Testament is a witness to this transformation as the disciples evangelized, taught Christian theology and ethics, and founded local churches. Extrabiblical sources, both Christian and non-Christian, also record the fact of the disciples' transformation.[60]

The evidence for Jesus' resurrection as the very *center of the early apostolic preaching* is in the early texts themselves. Paul declares that Jesus' resurrection is the capstone upon which all other doctrines are based; apart from this event, there would be no distinctive Christian theology (1 Cor. 15:12–20). This centrality goes back to Jesus himself, who explained to his disciples that their entire mission of preaching the gospel started with his death and resurrection (Luke 24:44–48). And as the church was born, this message was the heart of her proclamation.[61] In fact, it is fair to say that throughout basically every level of New Testament tradition we learn that the resurrection is the foundation for major doctrinal and practical precepts.[62] It remained central in the early post-New Testament church as well.[63] Fuller pointedly states, "The resurrection of Jesus from the dead was the central claim of the church's proclamation. There was no period when this was not so."[64]

Lastly, *Paul's conversion and transformation* based on an event that he believed was an appearance of the risen Jesus is confirmed chiefly by his own testimony. He explains that he had been a zealous Pharisee ("a Hebrew of Hebrews") and a persecutor of the church (1 Cor. 15:9; Gal. 1:23; Phil. 3:4–6). He had authority to imprison and kill believers (Gal. 1:13). But then he met the risen Jesus (1 Cor. 9:1, 15:8; cf. Gal. 1:15).

Luke, in three separate passages, provides the most details concerning Jesus' appearance to Paul.[65] Paul's corresponding transformation is not only indicated by specific statements that relate the degree of his commitment—being willing to die for his Christian beliefs[66]—but perhaps even more so by his theological and ethical dedication to his calling, which is exhibited throughout all of his travels and writings. Moreover, naturalistic theories do not apply to Jesus' appearance to Paul,[67] and critical scholars often defend the historicity of these events.[68]

Therefore, we contend that even this greatly reduced number of demonstrable facts can provide a powerful (though brief) defense of Jesus' resurrection. These five historical facts are decisive enough to disprove each of the naturalistic theories, and they provide some of the strongest evidences for the actual appearances of the risen Jesus. Therefore, the known historical facts accepted by even critical scholars further verify the resurrection appearances of Jesus and lay to rest naturalistic alternative schemes.[69]

In addition, virtually all contemporary scholars who study this subject, even over a broad theological spectrum and across interdisciplinary lines, generally admit that these five facts are knowable history. This does not guarantee the truth of these facts, but it is another indication of their evidential strength.

So how might skeptics respond to this evidence? They could reply that it is tainted because of "discrepancies" in the New Testament texts, or because of the general "unreliability," "legendary character," or "cloudiness" of Scripture. But not only are such assertions problematic on grounds not discussed here, they all run into one major roadblock that we have discussed: The resurrection can be historically demonstrated *even when only the minimum number of critically admitted historical facts are used.* In other words, the objection that there may be scriptural difficulties in areas *other than* these five facts *does not change* the truthfulness of *these* five facts. And these five facts are all we need to build an adequate case.

An extremely common skeptical response today is that "something" actually happened, but that its exact nature is unknown and must stay that way. Another often similar reaction is that Jesus lives on through his teachings, but not literally. However, these responses do *not* even answer the questions. They are untenable because the *minimum number of historically ascertainable facts are adequate* to demonstrate what *did* happen: Jesus actually appeared alive to his followers after his death.

In short, instead of simply raising questions about what they believe we *cannot* know concerning the New Testament accounts, critics should concentrate on what even they admit *can* be known about these texts. The minimally known factual basis is ample enough to show that Jesus' resurrection is by far the best historical explanation of the data. While skeptics may still have questions concerning other issues in the New Testament, the minimal historical facts are adequate in themselves to show that the same Jesus who died by crucifixion later appeared to his followers.

For the issue of life after death, Jesus' resurrection means not only that life after death is possible, but that at least one person has experienced it and given us some indication of what it is like. Have others tasted the hereafter too? Have others returned to tell us if it is real and what it may be like? We are now prepared to find out.

Chapter 5

Near-Death Experiences

For almost twenty years, hundreds of thousands of people interested in the subject of life after death have been captivated by near-death experiences. Numerous bestselling books and a profusion of movies on the topic are simply two indications of this popularity. In fact, in recent years, two of the top money-making films—*Ghost* and *Flatliners*—focused on life beyond the grave.

Beginning just before the publication of Raymond Moody's book *Life After Life*,[1] the bulk of the attention has focused on some of the common phenomena associated with near-death experiences: the sense that one is dead, looking down on one's body, traveling down a tunnel or dark passageway, seeing a light, meeting other persons or supernatural beings, participating in a life review, seeing beautiful scenery, reentering one's body, and experiencing feelings of peace, including losing the fear of death.

Are these experiences only subjective? Are they perhaps the results of brains that oppose the idea of death? Is there any way to know if these episodes are more than subjective and personal? Are any of them true to objective reality? What evidence, if any, can be marshalled in their support? Can these occurrences be tested in any way? Do many of these reports conflict with a Christian worldview?

These are some of the many questions we will investigate in this chapter and the next. First we will deal with the question of evidence, then we will turn to the remaining questions.

Before we move ahead, we need to make an important distinction between clinical (or reversible) death and biological (or irreversible) death. In clinical death, external life signs such as consciousness, pulse, and breathing are absent.[2] In such cases, biological death virtually always results if no steps are taken to reverse the process. Biological death, on the other hand, is not affected by any amount of attention, for it is physically irreversible.[3] Many scholars, such as Moody, add a category between these two—the absence of brain wave activity (indicated by a "flat" EEG reading).[4] But most near-death reports are from those who were close to clinical death.

At first, the early publications dealing with these experiences were usually popular. They reported the claims of those who came close to death and survived and often used some rather fantastic stories to support their "findings." This made it easy for many critics to complain that anecdotal accounts of dying persons who report similar experiences are inadmissible as scientific data. They also correctly argued that these experiences lacked the required evidence that would verify the factual nature of life after death. Indeed, other hypotheses were put forward, showing how easily these experiences could be accounted for apart from the existence of a hereafter.

But studies since that time have become much more empirical and scientific. These more recent data have effectively challenged such alternative explanations and, therefore, presented strong evidence for at least a minimalistic view of life after death. By a "minimalistic view of life after death" we mean life in the initial moments after death, not some detailed version of heavenly life or even necessarily eternal life. In other words, near-death experiences, at best, generally only make reference to life a few minutes or hours after death (although we will indicate some exceptions to this later). So while we cannot proceed beyond the evidence, even a minimal life beyond death remains crucially important, since this would still be a major blow to those who deny the afterlife. So let's consider the evidence.

Corroborated Reports

The evidence for near-death experiences[5] includes corroborated reports and some limited scientific means of testing and systematizing them. We will begin by enumerating four different types of evidence that emerge from these studies.[6]

Almost Dead

First, many cases have been gathered in which dying persons were able to view individuals, events, or circumstances around them, or even in other places, with amazing accuracy after coming close to dying or being pronounced clinically dead. Some of the descriptions were of occurrences that happened even while the patients were comatose. In other words, these subjects reported independently corroborated data that would not normally have been in the range of their senses even if they were fully conscious at the time.

Many of these reports were investigated by using rather ingenious controls and quantifying the data. Through this research it was discovered that many of these individuals reported details they could not have known or witnessed by any normal means.

In one case, a young girl, Katie, had almost drowned in a pool. After her emergency room resuscitation, a CAT scan showed massive brain swelling, and her doctor had an artificial lung machine attached to her to keep her breathing. He gave her a 10 percent chance of living. But three days later she totally recovered and relayed an amazing story. She accurately described the physical characteristics of the doctors involved in her resuscitation, details of the hospital rooms she was taken into, and reported particulars of the specific medical procedures used on her, even though she was "profoundly comatose," with her eyes closed, during the entire time.

As if all of this was not enough, Katie claimed to have met "Jesus and the heavenly Father" and an angel named Elizabeth. She also "followed" her family home during the time her body was comatose in the hospital and remembered seeing specific minutiae such as the selections for the evening meal prepared by her mother, how her father was reacting to her accident, and which toys her brother and sister were playing with at the time.

Her doctor investigated these claims, from his personal presence in the hospital emergency room and the procedures he used, to the testimony of the nurses, and to the whereabouts of Katie's family when she watched them at home. The family members were astounded at her descriptions of their clothing, where they were positioned in the house, and the food served at dinner. All the information she gave checked out.[7] She was able to see and report details of what was happening to her and around her in the hospital as well as what occurred in her home while her body lay in another location.

Another case concerns five-year-old Rick. He suffered from meningitis and was rushed to the hospital in an ambulance. As his body was whisked away, he decided to "stay behind." When he did, he was able to watch different family members and their grief-stricken reactions to his emergency. In one situation he watched his father weeping as he entered the car to take the family to the hospital. Then Rick rushed to the hospital, "arriving" ahead of the ambulance, and watched hospital personnel move a girl about twelve years old out of the room he was to occupy.

Again, the details of his report were correct. Rick's family was astounded by the richness of the particulars he had witnessed, especially when these incidents occurred away from the vicinity of his body. The incredibility of the event was magnified when they recalled that Rick was comatose before he was taken in the ambulance, and he stayed that way for several days afterward.[8]

Another young lady, who was in a hospital and near death, experienced herself leaving her body and visiting her relatives in another room. There she witnessed her brother-in-law saying he was going to wait and see if she was going to "kick the bucket" or not. Later, after her recovery, she confronted and shocked her relative by repeating his words to him![9]

Other particularly interesting cases involve blind persons. A chemist, for example, after being blinded a year earlier in an accident, correctly reported the visual details surrounding his near-death experience. Other individuals who had been blind for years (and were even tested for blindness again afterward) accurately described the design and colors of clothing and jewelry worn by those around them when they almost died.[10]

These cases are not rare; they are unexpectedly common.

After the Heart Stops

Second, a number of near-death experiences have been reported during confirmed heart stoppage. The evidence from this sort of incident is not as strong as in the absence of measurable brain activity; the central nervous system could still effect a NDE while the heart is dying. If the brain had stopped functioning, the patient's report of the experience apparently could not be due to normal means alone. However, one must take NDEs during heart stoppage seriously, especially if several sources can verify the information and the heart had stopped for an extended period of time. According to the Russian scientist Negovskii, "Considerable experimental material . . . indicates that 5-6 minutes is the maximum duration of the state of clinical death which the brain cortex of an adult organism can survive with subsequent recovery of all its functions."[11] If the heart has stopped beating for longer than that, the details of a NDE during that time are more credible.

For instance, an eleven-year-old boy suffered a cardiac arrest while in a hospital and had no heartbeat for at least twenty minutes. During this time he found himself watching his body from the ceiling, as well as observing the actions and discussions of the doctors and nurses below him. After his recovery, he accurately reported the medical procedures used on him, the locations and colors of the instruments in the emergency room, the genders of the medical personnel, and even reproduced their discussions.[12]

In another instance, an eight-year-old girl who was swimming in a pool got her hair caught in the drain and almost drowned. It took forty-five minutes of CPR to get her heart beating again. In the meantime, she said that she floated out of her body and visited heaven. Additionally, in spite of her condition, she was able to totally and correctly recount the details from the time the paramedics arrived in her yard through the work performed later in the hospital emergency room. So her report was not a brief recollection, but a blow-by-blow account of the long process of emergency treatment she received.[13]

Again, these sorts of incidents are not rare. Cardiologist Michael Sabom details three other cases where, after heart stoppage, patients were later quite able to detail items such as the layout of the hospital room, precise observations about the instruments in the room (and usually some of the readings on the dials themselves), the various procedures applied to them, including several particulars that were "odd" or uncommon practices.[14] Sabom even devised a procedure by which he could check the accuracy of these reports (see below).

Likewise, Maurice Rawlings, another cardiologist, delineates two other similar cases. In the first, there had not been a heartbeat for a long (but unspecified) time, and it was accompanied by dilated pupils and the absence of a pulse. An EKG later confirmed the lack of heartbeat. Later, the patient correctly identified Rawlings's suit coat and tie colors, as well as details of other individuals who had been involved in the resuscitation. But while all of this was going on, the patient was in the first day of a four-day coma. The second example Rawlings gives concerns a patient who properly reported similar details, even though that patient had no heartbeat or apparent consciousness.[15]

After the Brain Stops

Third, some near-death experiences have even been reported while the individual actually registered an absence of brain waves. The largest sample of this nature was gathered by distinguished cardiologist Fred Schoonmaker. He drew from an eighteen-year study of 1,400 near-death experiences. Included in his analysis were the cases of about fifty-five patients whose experiences occurred while flat EEG readings were recorded, sometimes for periods as long as thirty minutes to three hours! Further, the pattern of these experiences fits those of other researchers, and many of the patients reported incidents that were also corroborated by others.[16]

It is fascinating to consider, therefore, that some of the most vivid memories in the lives of these people happened while their brains registered no known activity.

Now it is conceivable that the EEG may not measure all brain activity; there may still be some residual action in the brain. However, presently the absence of any EEG brain wave function is the best and the most widely accepted indication that the brain is not functioning. And flat brain waves on the EEG, when present for long periods, are the chief contemporary definition of the nature of death.[17] So ordinarily, life *during* such times appears to be powerful evidence that human consciousness may, in fact, exist after death. And we have such evidence. Sometimes independent corroboration of near-death experiences and the absence of brain wave readings are both present. Even though there was no brain activity, certain individuals have reported details that were independently verified by others.

As a specific example, a woman who had both a flat EEG reading and no vital signs had been declared dead. But she spontaneously revived about three and one-half hours later. In fact, she regained consciousness and lifted the sheet off of her face as she was being taken to the morgue by an orderly! Then she reported that she had floated over her body during the resuscitation attempts. She precisely described not only the procedures that were used in her attempted rescue but also the number of persons who came into the hospital room, what they said (she even repeated a joke told to relieve the tension), and perhaps most interestingly, she described the designs on the doctors' ties!

All of these claims were carefully checked with the medical records and the doctors present. It was determined that her entire description was correct, even though her EEG reading had been flat during that entire time.[18]

They Saw Friends and Love Ones They Didn't Know Had Died

A fourth kind of corroborated report is provided by cases in which an individual, after a near-death experience, tells of having just seen and visited with a loved one whom he affirms was also deceased. In some of the more evidential cases, no one present had known that the loved one was dead—neither the one who was near death nor, in some cases, anyone immediately involved. Strangely enough, the result is sometimes that the experiencer is so convinced that he met the other person that his entire attitude toward death is altered to a sense of peace, well-being, and even a desire to be with the loved one. Then later, it is discovered that the other individual had truly died, sometimes at that very hour.

An often-cited and well-publicized example is told by Natalie Kalmus of the Technicolor Motion Picture Corporation concerning her sister's death. As her sister Eleanor lay dying, she began calling out the names of loved ones who had died beforehand, but whom she was now seeing. Then she saw a cousin named Ruth and asked, "What's she doing there?" Ruth had died unexpectedly the week before and, because of her condition, Eleanor had not been told. Then just before she died, "Suddenly her arms stretched out . . . 'I'm going up,' she murmured."[19]

Another case has even more evidential value. A woman who was near death perceived herself leaving her body and viewed the hospital room, the doctor shaking his head, and her distraught husband. Then she believed that she went to heaven and saw an angel, along with a familiar young man. She exclaimed, "Why, Tom, I didn't know you were up here!" Tom responded that he had just arrived too. But the angel told the woman that she would be returning to earth, which disappointed her because, as she later reported, heaven was "the most beautiful, peaceful, wondrous place—far beyond anything she had ever dreamed." Then she found herself back on the hospital bed with the doctor looking over her. Later that night, her husband got a call informing him that their friend Tom had died in an auto accident.[20]

Then there's the incident of seven-year-old Cory and his fight with leukemia. In a near-death vision, Cory told his mother that he had visited a "crystal castle," where he met one of her old high school boyfriends who had died after being crippled in an auto accident. Phone calls to some friends confirmed that the old boyfriend had indeed died the exact same day that Cory had the vision. In another instance, Cory also reported that one of his best friends from the hospital had also died. His mother thought this was unlikely, since they had just recently seen the boy. But when they went to the hospital the next day for chemotherapy, they were told that the friend had died unexpectedly the previous night.[21]

Sometimes individuals recount meeting deceased persons whom they never knew. A forty-eight-year-old man had a heart attack in Rawlings's office. The EKG registered no heartbeat. In several subsequent near-death episodes, the man reported going to hell repeatedly.

Precisely during one of these incidents, he became a Christian. Then in one of his subsequent experiences, this man found himself in a gorge full of beautiful colors, lush vegetation, and light. There he met both his stepmother and his mother. The latter had died when he was only fifteen months old. His father had remarried soon after her death, and the son had never even seen a photo of his mother. After hearing of his latest near-death experience, his aunt visited a few weeks later and brought a picture where his mother was posing with a number of other people. The man had no difficulty picking his mother out of the group, which astounded his father.[22]

In another example, a girl had a near-death experience during heart surgery and said she met her brother, even though she didn't have one. Her father, very much moved by her testimony, told her that she did, in fact, have a brother, but that he had died before she was born.[23]

One of the most moving, as well as evidential accounts of this nature, involves a family who experienced a fiery car wreck. The mother died at the scene, and her two sons were taken to different hospitals. While Kubler-Ross sat at the bedside of the youngest child, he came out of his coma during a commonly observed "clear moment." Although in considerable pain, the child was quiet and at peace.

The doctor asked him how he felt. The little boy responded, "Yes, everything is all right now. Mommy and Peter are already waiting for me." Then, with a contented little smile, he lapsed back into his coma and died. But he had not been told that the other members of his family had already expired. Then as Kubler-Ross walked past the nursing station, she was told that a call had just come in from the other hospital telling them that Peter, the older brother, had died just minutes earlier.[24]

Unlike the other types of cases, this fourth category, by its very nature, provides data concerning those who have *already* died. At times these deaths had occurred some time before, although this was not always known.[25] After investigating cases like this all over the world, Kubler-Ross came to the same remarkable conclusion:

> In all the years that I have quietly collected data . . . every single child who mentioned that someone was waiting for them mentioned a person who had actually preceded them in death, even if by only a few moments. And yet none of these children had been informed of the recent death of the relatives by us at any time.[26]

In these four categories of data, we have seen highly evidenced near-death reports, as well as other accurate details being given during the lengthy absence of heartbeat (including flat EKGs), corroboration during flat brain wave readings (EEG), and accounts of deceased loved ones being met, whose deaths were not known by those present. It would appear that each of these types of cases contributes something special to our argument for an afterlife. But we can't rest here. We still have some critical issues to consider.

Systematizing the Findings

Are near-death episodes just single, unrelated experiences, or is there some rhyme or reason to their occurrence? A number of researchers have gone far beyond the initial, somewhat anecdotal, accounts gathered in the past. Numerous studies have quantified the data and devised some rather ingenious ways to check results. These systematic studies lend further credibility to the claim that near-death experiences are not freak, haphazard events.

Karlis Osis and Erlendur Haraldsson, both psychologists, were among the first to scientifically document the results of near-death visions and experiences. Sending carefully constructed questionnaires to literally thousands of medical doctors and nurses, they categorized minute data on over 1,000 reported incidents, more than half of them from India, with the remainder from the United States. In a carefully detailed volume, they explained their research and presented massive amounts of information through charts, graphs, and tables. They addressed crucial issues, such as the chief features of near-death experiences, the characteristics and especially the medical status of the patients who experienced them, and the mood elevation in these persons prior to death.[27]

From all of this material, Osis and Haraldsson were able to authoritatively address concerns such as the affect of medicinal drugs or high fever on patients who were near death. The presence of unconsciousness, diseases, or hallucinogenic possibilities were also carefully factored into their study.

Another psychologist, Kenneth Ring, also attempted to quantify the results of near-death research, concentrating more on the systematization of results similar to those popularized by Raymond Moody.[28] Ring's major contribution in this volume is probably the creation of an extremely detailed "interview schedule" and questionnaire.[29] From these research instruments, he gathered such features as the different stages of the near-death experience; the various sorts of causes; how close the individual was to actually dying; correlates; and qualitative considerations. Many charts also spell out these findings. Ring was also one of the first to focus attention on the effects of the experience on the patients themselves.

Cardiologist Michael Sabom also wished to place the more popularized near-death phenomena on a firm scientific footing. He was one of the first to attempt to precisely document cases of corroborated citings by the persons reporting the experiences. But not only was he interested in any possible substantiation but he even devised a rather ingenious means to check nonexperiencers in order to ascertain the possibilities of mimicking the same types of corroboration.

He organized the interviewing of 25 control patients whose backgrounds were quite similar to near-death experiencers. All 25 were "seasoned cardiac patients," most having had heart attacks and/or heart surgery of one kind or another. So these patients had had ample opportunities to observe instruments, various procedures, as well as having watched televised examples of relevant techniques. Each of the 25 persons was asked to imagine observing a medical team resuscitating an individual whose heart had stopped beating.

Yet, while two of the 25 control patients claimed to have no relevant knowledge of the subject, 20 of the 23 who attempted a description made one or more major errors in their reporting. Of the three who made no errors, none gave more than a limited description. This was a far greater percentage of errors than was found in the reports of those who had reported similar details from their near-death experience.

Sabom also included extremely detailed charts that contained particulars, such as various personal minutiae from each of his cases, the intervals between the crisis event and the interview, the estimated time of unconsciousness, the results of other near-death experiences by the same person, descriptions of "transcendental" (or otherworldly) elements reported by each, and the number of overall characteristics of each.[30]

Melvin Morse, a pediatrician, devised two methods by which crucial data could be further checked. He also used control groups on each occasion, this time to ascertain if one actually had to be near death in order to have one of these experiences, and if natural conditions (such as drugs, lack of oxygen, hallucinations, stress, or patient knowledge) could successfully account for these near-death experiences. Morse also gave particular attention to reporting corroborative cases.[31]

Each of these researchers and many others have also been interested in whether naturalistic explanations can adequately account for the data.[32] We will look at these explanations in the next chapter. But from the kind of scientific and psychological testing that has been done, we see that we can place greater confidence in the evidential value of near-death experiences. These experiences cannot be ignored or slightly regarded. They play an important role in establishing support for life after death.

Evidence from Brain Physiology

Contemporary studies in brain research are also yielding some helpful data supporting dualism and perhaps even life beyond the grave.

Wilder Penfield, often acclaimed the father of modern neurosurgery, "mapped" the brain during surgery by electrically probing the appropriate areas while the patient was fully conscious. He was able to do this by using only a local anesthetic because the brain itself feels no pain. By probing these areas, Penfield could cause the patient to move his arms or legs, turn his head or eyes, talk, or swallow. But interestingly, the patient would "invariably" respond by saying, "I didn't do that. You did." Or sometimes, if the right arm was moved, the individual would reach over with his left arm in order to stop his right from moving.[33]

Yet, no matter how much probing Penfield did, even in the cerebral cortex (where the highest level of human consciousness is located), he testified: "There is no place . . . where electrical stimulation will cause a patient to believe or to decide." This was quite a blow to Penfield's materialism. For if materialism is true, all the "neuronal action within the brain must account for all the mind does."[34] Penfield could not establish this. If anything, his research contradicted it.

Recent brain research has done much to validate Penfield's findings. In the 1960s, Roger Sperry and his associates researched the differences between the right and left hemispheres of the brain. They discovered that the mind has a causal power independent of brain activity. This led Sperry to the conclusion that materialism was false. Yet, while he recognizes that the mind is separate from the brain, Sperry does not believe in life after death. Still, he notes the recent shift in neuroscience, in which many scientists think that the latest research indicates scientific evidence for an independent mind.[35]

Sir John Eccles, a distinguished neurobiologist, has also thrown his academic weight into this debate.[36] Agreeing that materialism is unable to explain the scientific data, Eccles states, "We do have mental events before they are converted into brain events. The monist materialist thinks that the mental events are simply derivative of aspects of the nerve endings. But there is no evidence for this whatsoever." For these reasons, he adds, "I hope very much that we are recovering from the long deep depression of materialistic monism."[37]

Other scholars have agreed with these results. A German neurophysiologist, Hans Kornhuber, and his associates demonstrated that the way we think changes the neuronal activity of the brain. "His experiments reveal that simply by thinking one can will action that is not initiated by external stimuli."[38]

Neurophysiologist Richard M. Restak was another who abandoned the mind/brain identity theory due to his own research and that of scientists such as Kornhuber. Restak realized that, since willed action cannot be localized in a particular brain area, this introduces a radical means of understanding the interrelation between mind and brain. He even concluded that these results in brain research are as influential in his own area as Einstein's were in physics.[39]

Moreover, in a ten-year test, scientist B. Libet demonstrated that there was a delay between an electrical impulse's being applied to the skin, its reaching the cerebral cortex, and the self-conscious perception by the person. This research strongly suggests that the self is more than just neuronal machinery that reacts to the stimuli as it receives them.[40]

In fact, Wood argues that all of this data "is so remarkable that many brain scientists have been compelled to postulate the existence of an immaterial mind, even though they may not embrace a belief in an after-life."[41] Most of the scientists above have even abandoned their materialistic views because of these data. So, speaking for many, Penfield concluded: "For my own part, after years of striving to explain the mind on the basis of brain action alone, I have come to the conclusion that it is simpler (and far easier to be logical) if one adopts the hypothesis that our being does consist of two fundamental elements."[42]

So how is all of this data relevant to near-death research? First, it provides further support for dualism, which lends credence to the reality of an afterlife. Even Penfield recognized this implication: "But, when the nature of the energy that activates the mind is discovered (as I believe it will be), the time may yet come when scientists will be able to make a valid approach to a study of the nature of a spirit other than that of man."[43]

Second, it may even have led to the discovery of the physical link to near-death experiences. Ironically, Penfield may have been the one to connect brain physiology with near-death studies. In some of his operations, he electrically stimulated the Sylvian fissure in the right temporal lobe of the brain. When he did, the patient would say, "I'm leaving my body now." Several patients reported, "I'm half in and half out." They also described phenomena like that experienced in the near-death studies, such as music, life review, and seeing God or deceased friends.[44] Morse thinks that the "seat" for near-death experiences has now been discovered. He says, "By locating the area for NDEs within the brain, we have anatomy to back up the psychological experience. *We know where the circuit board is.*"[45]

In general, if Penfield's data are correct, we have two broad possibilities: (1) This brain mechanism is a "mimic" that can potentially explain in natural terms a number of the near-death incidents, or (2) it is a physical "gateway" to our mind and its future. The first option would explain the phenomena subjectively, while the latter would hail Penfield's research as Morse does—as the discovery of the "trigger" of the soul. The first approach would be forced to explain corroborated reports, such as those presented in this chapter, in natural terms; the second would reject a purely naturalistic account.

Which option is correct? That will be the focus of the next chapter.

Where We've Been

Before pressing ahead, let's get a handle on where we've been. We worked through four categories of evidence for near-death experiences.

Each type relied on the presence of corroborative reports in the face of various conditions: death-threatening circumstances, the extended absence of heartbeat (including EKG), flat EEG (brain wave) readings, and meetings with dead loved ones. We saw the potency of this evidence, at least for a minimalistic concept of life after death. In fact, even the first category of verified reports (often of a rather spectacular variety) in the presence of clinical (or reversible) death, which is sometimes thought to be the weakest type of evidence, is still excellent confirmation since they cannot be adequately explained on a purely naturalistic basis and because they indicate consciousness beyond at least the initial states of death.

Therefore, while irreversible (biological) death had obviously not occurred in the first category of cases, known bodily functions could not explain these experiences, and clinical death had sometimes already occurred. When flat brain wave or heart readings, or confirmed visits with deceased loved ones are also present, the evidential factor of NDEs goes up considerably. The fact that these people were, in some nonphysical sense, active and aware with no known physical cause present is strong enough evidence to indicate a probable case for the initial stages of life after death.

We want to be careful at this point. This minimalistic life does not provide sufficient data for a detailed heavenly existence. So the presence of irreversible death is not required in order to establish the lesser point being made here. Our claim is that if the brain is not functioning (or is otherwise unable to account for the corroborated phenomena in view) and consciousness is still evidenced during that time, then this is the definition of minimalistic life that exists *at that moment after death*.

Therefore, if verified consciousness is both separate from and extends beyond brain activity, there is no reason to think that, just because there is no irreversible death, one can somehow magically account for this life by naturalistic means. Since these intellectual faculties exist independently of brain activity (even when the brain has ceased for a time), there is no viable reason to assume that the permanent cessation of brain activity would adversely affect personal consciousness. In short, normal bodily activity does not explain these data, which actually provide significant evidence for at least minimal consciousness beyond death.

How have naturalists responded to this research? In an older article in the journal *The Humanist,* John Beloff argued that the data in favor of life after death was already significant enough that even humanists should admit an afterlife and attempt to interpret it in naturalistic terms. Beloff declared that the evidence indicates a "dualistic world where mind or spirit has an existence separate from the world of material things." He also conceded that this could "present a challenge to Humanism as profound in its own way as that which Darwinian Evolution did to Christianity a century ago." Therefore, naturalists "cannot afford to close our minds . . . to the possibility of some kind of survival."[46]

Since that time, in a 1981 meeting of the American Psychological Association, a panel discussed the nature and origin of near-death experiences. Only one of the panelists, UCLA psychologist Ronald Siegel, believed that these could be explained totally by natural means. He favored hallucinations as the true cause. Yet, Siegel was challenged later by a fellow panel member, cardiologist Michael Sabom, who asked how the hallucination hypothesis could explain his as yet unpublished corroborative accounts of near-death experiences. Siegel responded by saying that he was unable to answer this data. The other panel members likewise agreed with Sabom that near-death research points to and provides evidence for a spiritual realm and/or life after death.[47]

More recently, eminent atheistic philosopher A.J. Ayer actually had a near-death experience. Recovering from a return bout with pneumonia, he was placed in a hospital in intensive care, then sometime after suffered heart stoppage for a period of four minutes. Ayer explains that he had a "very vivid" experience during his crisis: "[I was] confronted by a red light, exceedingly bright, and also very painful even when I turned away from it. I was aware that this light was responsible for the government of the universe." However, "I also had the motive of finding a way to extinguish the painful light." He added that two other creatures, who were said to be in charge of space, were also present.[48]

The episode caused even Ayer to do a bit of musing about the likelihood of an afterlife. He says that the experience "could well have been delusive," but it might also have had a truthful element as well. Then Ayer confesses: "On the face of it, these experiences, on the assumption that the last one [that of a friend] was veridical, are rather strong evidence that death does not put an end to consciousness." Then he discusses what form of an afterlife may await us, and pronounces that he is "attracted" to the theory that such might involve "the elongation of our experiences," perhaps with the opportunity to learn. Yet, Ayer states that such a belief would not necessarily entail the belief in God. He ends his report by saying that his convictions that there is no afterlife "slightly weakened." Still, and rather sadly, he acknowledges that his death "is due fairly soon" and says that he hopes there will be no afterlife. Ayer's last two sentences continue to affirm to all his friends that "there is no god."[49]

Perhaps these developments signal a new shift in attitude on this subject. Beloff's exhortation to humanists to make room for the belief in an afterlife is a seldom-heard plea. The American Psychological Association panel provided more insights concerning the growing discussion on this subject even in such professional circles,[50] as well as the inability of naturalistic hypotheses to explain near-death experiences. Ayer's experience was fascinating in its content and conclusions regarding the evidence for life after death on the part of someone as opposed as he has been for decades to such metaphysical concepts. His continuing and self-assured rejection of God's existence after standing before a light "responsible for the government of the universe" is also baffling.

Regardless of whether the tide of skepticism about the afterlife is turning or not, the chief issue concerns the validity of this evidence. We now turn to those questions and challenges.

Chapter 6

NDEs: Questions and Objections

Near-death experiences, or NDEs as they are often called, are intriguing and even inspiring. Many want to believe they tell us something about a life beyond. We the authors think they do tell us something about a life beyond, and we believe they give us some insight into that life. But many people have argued otherwise. Some have suggested that NDEs are purely subjective, explainable in terms of drugs, hallucinations, or other natural causes. Other people have maintained that even if NDEs do have some objective reality, they are incompatible with Christian theism.

Who is right? What position is true? We want to face these issues head-on in this chapter. We will begin by considering some basic questions related to NDEs, then we will move on and deal with worldview concerns and objections.

Basic Questions

How widespread are the reports of near-death experiences? Are they very common?

From the research, it is clear that NDEs are extremely widespread.

In 1982, a Gallup survey reported that 15 percent of the respondents claimed to have been close to death and had something to tell about it—a figure that could have translated to 23 million Americans. Approximately one-third of these people described some sort of "mystical" experience, with characteristics often like those in classic near-death reports. George Gallup, Jr., was so surprised at the large number of claimants that he polled audiences a second and then a third time. But the results were largely the same each time.[1]

In addition, literally thousands of near-death testimonies have been cited in near-death literature, such as the sources we mentioned in the last chapter. The reports we used were largely written by professional philosophers, psychologists, and medical doctors. Their scholarship, of course, does not guarantee truthfulness or soundness of argument, but the careful and interdisciplinary nature of their work and similar research is a testimony to the extensive amount of work that has been done, as well as the number of NDE cases available.

Of the large number of persons who have been near death, how many report near-death experiences? How many persons remember nothing from their brush with death?

This is a difficult issue because many studies concerned those who *reported* these episodes rather than those who did not. Still, a few researchers did compile figures on larger samples that involved both experiencers and nonexperiencers.

Rawlings reports that about 20 percent of resuscitated patients volunteer their perceived memories.[2] However, that may be a general estimate, since Rawlings does not provide precise data regarding his research. Rawlings's fraction is smaller than that of others who kept a careful tally. Sabom indicates that 43 percent of his prospective interviews indicated a post-crisis experience.[3] Ring states that 48 percent of his cases were similar to the classic "core experience."[4] The largest sampling, however, comes from Schoonmaker's eighteen-year study of 2,300 near-death cases, of which 60 percent reported NDEs.[5] So the three studies here that provide detailed figures place the number of experiencers at 43-60 percent of those in their samples.

Why did perhaps 50 percent or more of those who came close to dying not recall a NDE?

No one knows exactly why some persons have near-death experiences and others do not. It has been suggested that such incidents perhaps even occurred but are later forgotten,[6] maybe due to the nature of the crisis itself, or from the administration of anesthetics or other drugs, or from any frightening or negative aspects to the episode.

But Morse points out that even positive experiences are sometimes forgotten afterward. This happened to a ten year old named Chris, who, after a beautiful heavenly vision, could not recall what had happened just a few months later. Although much younger, Mark apparently underwent a near-death incident at the age of nine months during a cardiac arrest that involved forty minutes of resuscitation efforts. Mark first mentioned this episode when he was three. But when his trachea tube was removed two years later, he began to forget the experience, even though he had reported a beautiful memory as he "ran through fields with God."[7]

Is it likely that all unremembered NDEs are forgotten?[8]

However this question is answered, it is clear that a number of patients who have reported more than one encounter with death have had at least one near-death experience while having no other episodes on other occasions. In fact, while Sabom lists 33 cases of persons having more than one crisis event in their lives, only eight of these reported more than one experience. Thus, 25 patients had no other experiences at all, in spite of there being five circumstances where the individuals had five to ten close calls each.[9]

So, whatever conclusion we draw here, there appear to be no objective grounds for distinguishing between those who have experiences when close to death and those who, for whatever reasons, do not. Additionally, we must not lose sight of the fact that the corroborative cases that *were* reported still have to be explained.

How widely do near-death experiences differ from one another?

The answer depends on how you define the terms. A commonly defined, "complete" incident might involve the perception of one's death, peace, the reported separation from one's body, observing nearby physical conditions, entering a dark tunnel or void, a life review, seeing a light, entering another world, seeing others, and returning to one's body. But there is *no* certain, fixed definition of what a NDE should be like.[10]

Comparing Ring's statistical results with Sabom's is certainly interesting. For Ring, the perception of peace was the most dominant characteristic (60 percent), followed by perceived bodily separation (37 percent), darkness (23 percent), seeing the light (16 percent), and entering the light (10 percent).[11] Sabom, with twice as many experiential components, or categories, went from peace, bodily separation, and the return to the body (each at 100 percent), to the perception of one's death (92 percent), entering another world (54 percent), observing nearby physical conditions (53 percent), seeing others (48 percent), seeing the light (28 percent), darkness (23 percent), and the life review (3 percent).[12] There are similarities and differences between these two surveys,[13] but for whatever reasons, the general resemblances are still close enough to notice.

Must someone be close to death in order to have a NDE?

On this question, researchers differ and even appear to change their minds. For instance, some researchers have reported that one does not have to be close to death before NDEs can occur. Some have claimed that drugs can cause NDEs or even that they can occur spontaneously. Moody retells the case of an individual who left his body just *before* an impending car accident.[14] He goes on to say that

> Many people have told me of out-of-body experiences which took place spontaneously. The persons involved were not 'dead' or even ill or in jeopardy. Further, in most cases these experiences were not being sought in any way. They came as complete surprises.[15]

But years later, in the Foreword to Morse's book, Moody reported that Morse and his research team have proven that a person actually needs to be near death to have a near-death experience. . . . The team was able to determine that one does need to cross that threshold before glimpsing the other side.[16]

What did these investigators discover? Why did they come to this conclusion?

Morse and his researchers selected two groups of children. The "control group consisted of 121 children who were critically ill, but not near death." Ranging from three to sixteen years of age, they had serious diseases and were hospitalized in intensive care, but they were estimated to have less than a five percent chance of actually dying.

Another group, called the study group, was made up of a dozen children who probably would have died or at least been severely handicapped without intervention from modern medicine. Having a various assortment of diseases, each of these children had had at least one cardiac arrest.

At the conclusion of the study, the researchers observed that none of the 121 children in the *control* group "had anything resembling a near-death experience." However, eight of the twelve children in the *study* group had these experiences. So Morse concluded, "The study showed that near-death experiences are seen in the great majority of critically ill children and clearly have some association with the dying process."[17]

While Morse's research is intriguing and may certainly be on the right track, is his conclusion warranted? We think that to base such a conclusion on one study may be a case of weak induction. Just because 121 seriously ill children did not have near-death experiences, does this mean that no one will have one unless they are close to dying? Furthermore, what about the testimonies of those who claim to have had just such an experience, such as the one noted above? Are these not exceptions? As we said, he could well be correct at this point, but maybe we should keep the possibilities open for now.

We could address many other questions concerning NDEs, but these are some of the most basic ones. Now we will turn to issues concerning how NDEs are interpreted within different systems of thought.

Worldview Concerns

Multiple Interpretations

One intriguing subject has to do with how near-death patients interpret their experiences. Many claim to encounter an incredible light,[18] which they often identify as a specific person. Other individuals not associated with light are also seen in both pre-death visions and near-death experiences. And contrary to the impression you may get when hearing popular reports, persons identified as friends and relatives are seen much more frequently than religious figures are.[19]

But when religious figures are reported, Christians often identify them as God or Jesus, Jews often as angels, and a large number of Hindus in the study by Osis and Haraldsson identified these figures as Shiva, Rama, Krishna, angels, or other religious messengers.[20] Taken at face value, these differing identifications raise an intriguing question: Should we conclude that each of these beings was actually seen by the experiencers? Did Christians really see Jesus? Did Jews see angels? Did Hindus see Krishna? We already argued in Chapter 5 that previously deceased loved ones have frequently been reported by near-death experiencers. How can we say that those dead individuals really were seen but these religious figures were not?

First of all, researchers have checked and verified the reliability of those who reported seeing loved ones who were dead, unknown to those involved. But no such evidence is available for verifying the real appearances of these religious persons. In fact, how would these near-death patients know the identity of the religious personages *even if* they did see them? Obviously, previous acquaintance plus corroborated testimony, as with the dead loved ones, separates these reports from the religious ones that lack both evidence of identity and previous familiarity.

Second of all, in light of this lack of any preceding acquaintance with the religious person in question and the theological (as well as other) intellectual commitments of the patient, it makes sense that the identification of the figure will come from the patient's own background. For reasons such as these, we will argue that whenever something of a religious nature is claimed but not evidenced, the more important factor in terms of interpretation consists of one's previous beliefs. Not surprisingly, Osis and Haraldsson's cross-cultural research backs up this contention in several ways.

For instance, no American claimed to have seen Shiva, Rama, or Krishna.[21] Americans also reported more than five times as many deceased figures as religious ones (66 percent to 12 percent, respectively). But Hindus, conversely, saw almost twice as many religious figures as deceased ones (48 percent to 28 percent, respectively). Moreover, social factors seem to be at work with regard to the sex of those who are observed. While Americans perceived 61 percent female figures, Indians claimed only 23 percent. Even the Indian women reported twice as many male figures as female ones, all of which makes it tempting to claim that this is perhaps due to the apparently lower status of women in Indian culture.[22]

Similarly, William Wainwright has argued in an important essay that, of the different cross-cultural sorts of religious experience, sensory reports (such as seeing or hearing certain phenomena) tend to be the most dependent on outside factors.[23] But none of this disallows the possibility of some true religious element's being involved. After all, distorted experience is still experience.

It would appear, then, that previous religious, cultural, and sociological beliefs affect the wide differences in NDE interpretations, including the way figures are identified. For example, Osis and Haraldsson think that the "inhibition" to see female figures contributes heavily to the lower number of deceased women reported among Indian patients.[24]

Another vantage point from which to view the importance of personal interpretation is how the near-death patient responds to the experience afterward. While one patient might construe the episode as encouraging one sort of faith, another could well interpret it in an opposite direction. Now this does *not* mean that the individuals involved never change their beliefs due to the experience, for this happens, as we will see. *Neither* does it mean that there cannot be *good reasons* why one interpretation is better than others. But our point here concerns the differing *meanings* that are found in the experiences upon later reflection.[25]

So there are important reasons that certain factors of interpretation comment more on a person's beliefs, society, and culture than they do on the facts themselves. This is one of the reasons it is important to have evidence for our conclusions. Where we have no evidence (as with the identity of the religious figures whose presence is claimed), we have grounds to question the claims.

No Judgment?

It has been widely reported that even atheists and other admitted non-Christian near-death experiencers describe a beautiful, heaven-like environment. But why is there no mention of judgment, of punishment for wrongs? Our responses will come from several angles.

Admittedly, the vast majority of reports involve blissful experiences.[26] But a number of persons have also claimed they were in hell-like environments. These near-death reports were largely popularized by Rawlings,[27] who theorizes that many of those who do not remember their near-death experience may actually be repressing painful hell encounters. He provides examples where several of his patients who had recently claimed to have been in hell, usually terror-stricken, later forgot the whole incident.[28] This scenario has been disputed (but not denied) by Ring.[29] Other researchers have also reported hell cases, but in lesser numbers and not always of the same sort.[30]

However, to reverse the issue totally, why should the average near-death experiencer, Christian or not, have gone to hell at all? If he was not biologically (irreversibly) dead, we could argue that the reason he did not see hell was simply because he had not finally died.[31] In the New Testament book, Hebrews, we are told that people die *once,* then judgment follows (9:27). So if they have not finally died, they do not experience judgment.

Additionally, drawing from the frequent near-death reports that there is a line of demarcation or barrier beyond which a person may not pass and still return to the body,[32] Rawlings argues that there could well be a "sorting ground" or meeting place after death that separates a person from his final destination.[33] Along these lines, we could conclude that positive experiences by dying persons do not always have to be interpreted as trips to heaven. They could simply have been a quite natural reaction to a new environment, or the immediate relief from a disease- or an injury-racked body, or a temporary meeting place after death.

Interpretations of one's experiences are notoriously tricky things. Interpretations of even everyday episodes sometimes vary widely from person to person. This by no means indicates that things don't really happen as they appear, only that we should be very careful about reporting them and especially our opinions *about* them.

Again, this has been confirmed regarding near-death experiences. In a scholarly, historical study of near-death experiences of ages past, Carol Zaleski concludes that the interpretations of them often reflected popular concepts of the afterlife held at that time, which is just what we see today.[34]

Therefore, we hold that NDEs cannot be used to describe (or interpret) details concerning heaven or hell. Interpretation regarding heaven and hell and the identity of religious persons cannot be verified (on this side of the grave, at least).[35] Of course, as we have shown, many other aspects of NDEs can and have been examined and verified as objective and reliable.

Satanic Counterfeits?

Sometimes Christians raise the question "Could these near-death experiences be some sort of satanic performance for the purpose of misleading people about the afterlife? After all, isn't it enough for us to have biblical testimony on the subject of what lies beyond the grave?"[36]

It is definitely possible that certain aspects of these NDE studies are caught up with spiritual realities that are occultic in nature. When dealing with thousands of testimonies and many researchers, personal beliefs and practices are not always obvious. There will certainly be non-Christian beliefs present in samples this large and while dealing with this sort of subject. We do not want to underemphasize this point.

Furthermore, several analysts, including some Christians, have pointed out specific occultic connections with individual near-death researchers, including more overt involvement with the spirit world.[37] In the literature we have reviewed, we think there is no question that occultic elements are sometimes present. We believe that Satan can even disguise himself as an angel of light (2 Cor. 11:14), appearing harmless and inviting.

But this does not mean that all near-death experiences are occultic and unbiblical. As Anderson notes, this conclusion does not follow because counterfeit experiences presuppose genuine ones. Just as you can't have fake money without real money, so you can't have fake NDEs without real ones. You can't counterfeit what doesn't exist. Besides, some NDEs fit a biblical pattern.[38] Further, even if the spirit world is involved in some of these circumstances, it still means that naturalism is mistaken and that there really is a world with which life after death is compatible.

Although this next point cannot be defended here, it is also at least possible that near-death phenomena are reported in Scripture. Stephen had a pre-death vision (Acts 7:55–56). Some think that the experience Paul describes in 2 Corinthians 12:1–5 occurred to him after he was stoned at Lystra and left for dead (Acts 14:19).[39] In Jesus' story about the death of the poor man Lazarus, his post-death experience has similarities with some of the NDEs we have discussed (Luke 16:22). For that matter, the scenario in Luke 16:22–24 about the death of the rich man may remind us of some hellish near-death experiences.

Also, going to be with Christ is precisely what the Bible says will happen to the Christian after death.[40] So if believers experience this after having a very close call with death, why should we object on biblical grounds? We don't think there are good reasons to hold that believers at death are turned over to Satan and his whims (cf. Ps. 23:4).[41]

We conclude, then, that there is no doubt occultic tendencies can and do play an important role in this topic. And it is crucial that we obey the often-repeated biblical commands to avoid contact with the occult.[42] There is no biblical room for exceptions here.

At the same time, it doesn't follow that all near-death experiences are satanic counterfeits. Some even appear to follow biblical expectations. At any rate, there is nothing inherently occultic about NDEs. Dying is a natural event and does not automatically involve aspects of the occult, as some other activities do. Therefore, each NDE needs to be viewed according to its own merits.

To be sure, there are a number of worldview concerns that are relevant when we discuss the nature of near-death experiences.[43] We addressed three of these issues here. However, while our discussion helps place interpretational guidelines around this subject, it does not expose anything that challenges the essential facticity and genuineness of at least some of these experiences.

Critical Objections

Could NDEs be explained by medical causes such as drugs or by psychological reasons such as hallucinations, natural abilities, biases, or fakery? This question raises crucial issues that need to be addressed. So let's do that now.

Medical Questions

What are the possibilities that drugs, either medicinal or otherwise, could cause or significantly contribute to NDEs?[44] While there is no doubt that drugs can cause all sorts of side effects, including perhaps certain aspects of these experiences, there are a number of solid reasons why such medical causes do not explain the major data.

Several researchers have documented a plethora of cases where either no drugs, or at least those that would not effect NDEs, were administered to patients. Moreover, in the large sample studied by Osis and Haraldsson, there was only a very low percentage of cases where drugs could have been relevant. Of the 425 patients with medical data, 61 percent received no drugs, while another 19 percent were given drugs that have no effect on consciousness. So the author concluded, "Thus, 80 percent of the terminal patients who had had apparition experiences during their illnesses were not affected by drugs. This means that only one-fifth were considered to have been influenced by the medication."[45]

In order to check this hypothesis himself, Morse organized and interviewed "thirty-seven children who had been treated with almost every kind of mind-altering medication known to pharmacology." He discovered that not one of them "had anything resembling a NDE."[46] Besides, many other researchers have reported numerous cases where no medication whatsoever was administered to the individual who had a NDE.[47] So even if a connection could be shown between NDEs and medicinal agents, many other near-death reports would have to be explained by another hypothesis.

A similar objection to the validity of near-death reports has focused on medically-induced hallucinations, which might account for some near-death visions.[48] In answer to this counterexplanation, Osis and Haraldsson actually devised an "hallucinogenic index" obtained by factoring high fever of over 103 degrees, drugs that affect the mind, past medical history, and diseases such as brain disorders (or injury) or uremia. This index is even higher than necessary, for the factors that were counted *may* cause hallucinations, but don't always. Thus, because indices such as stroke, for instance, *could* cause these conditions, they were counted. Nonetheless, these factors affected only 38 percent of the cases tested, with the remaining 62 percent being free of them. Quite incredibly, Osis and Haraldsson found that hallucinatory factors even tended to *reduce* rather than generate near-death phenomena.[49]

And in Morse's group of 37 children, the very sorts of medications that sometimes do cause hallucinations still did not cause any near-death incidents. One girl who was even *helped* to hallucinate still did not have any episodes that resembled NDEs.[50] When you add to all this that some researchers have noted that patients who have had both hallucinations and NDEs can clearly distinguish the difference,[51] you are left with an hallucination hypothesis riddled with mortal wounds.

The truth is that none of the medical conditions offered as explanations for NDEs are capable of accounting for the various sorts of corroboration we outlined in the last chapter. Even if a link between drugs and NDEs could be demonstrated in a few cases, their influence cannot account for all such experiences. NDEs are more than subjective sensations. The evidence indicates that near-death experiencers have objectively perceived something beyond themselves, something that exists outside and independent of them.

But what about other medical conditions, such as the presence of high fever,[52] cerebral anoxia (lack of oxygen to the brain), endorphin release (a natural substance in the brain that can produce "highs" or mimic certain drugs), or temporal lobe stimulation or seizure (when this area of the brain is affected by either process, producing various sensations)? Could they explain all NDEs? No. For example, Osis and Haraldsson specifically checked 442 patients in their study for high fevers. They found that 58 percent of those who saw apparitions had normal temperatures and another 34 percent had fevers below 103 degrees. Only 8 percent had fevers over 103 degrees. So fevers, even high ones, do not account for most NDEs.[53]

Schoonmaker reported that the blood oxygen level was measured at the time of his patients' cardiac arrests, and near-death experiencers had sufficient oxygen present for normal brain functioning.[54] In Morse's research, the medical records relative to the lack of oxygen in the blood gasses were consulted. None of the experiencers had any more oxygen deprivation than did those in the control group who did not report these incidents at all.[55]

With regard to temporal lobe seizure, epilepsy is not a common condition in near-death experiencers.[56] But the chief response to these alleged explanations, once again, is their inability to explain the corroborative reports of NDEs, especially the accountings of patients outside of their bodies, especially in remote locations, and their knowledge of deceased loved ones that they had no way of knowing were dead.

Psychological Questions

What about psychological factors such as hallucinations not caused by medical factors,[57] depersonalization (a reaction to life-threatening danger in terms of personal detachment from a situation), wishful thinking, dreams, or other altered states of consciousness like those sometimes achieved in various sorts of isolation conditions? These cannot account for all NDEs either.

As much as can be judged from the relevant data, these factors do not closely approximate many of the central elements of NDEs. In fact, some of the results are exact opposites. For example, depersonalization is a negative phenomenon that shrinks mental abilities, while NDEs are positive, exhibiting a profound heightening effect on one's experience.[58]

But even granting that there are similarities between certain psychological experiences and NDEs, similarities do not prove identical causes, which is what psychological explanations must do in order to count against the objective validity of NDEs. But it's hard to demonstrate this. Similar effects do not necessitate identical causes. Such must be proved on a case-by-case basis, not simply supposed. And no such proof has been given for linking the causes of psychological factors to all the characteristics of NDEs. But even if we allow the unproven linkage to account for some NDE characteristics, it cannot explain all of them. Psychological experiences are subjective in nature, therefore, they do not explain the *objective* factors substantiated by NDE researchers—the kind of factors mentioned in the last chapter. So we must look elsewhere if we are to find a valid counterexplanation for all NDEs.

Other Naturalistic Proposals

Whereas medical and psychological proposals chiefly address subjective factors, some critics have suggested more natural hypotheses to account for NDEs, including their more objective elements. Could the near-death experiencers have collected the data they reported in more normal ways? Or could they have fabricated the data, consciously or unconsciously? Or could the researchers be at fault? Perhaps their biases have influenced their studies?[59] Let's see if these responses fare any better.

Could the patient have gathered the reported data normally, from his own senses, in spite of the chaotic conditions around him? Since death is a process, maybe the eyes or ears picked up information even while the body was failing.[60] On the surface, at least, this appears to be the toughest objection we have handled so far, but it, too, fails to account for the very details it aims to explain.

For example, the first type of evidential data presented in the last chapter was characterized by substantial amounts of corroboration while the individual was very close to death. Each of the described instances involved persons who properly viewed events, usually over quite a distance, which they could *not* have physically observed. Katie watched and reported minute particulars about what her family members were doing at home while she was comatose in the hospital. Rick correctly viewed his family members at home and details in the hospital while his body was elsewhere in an ambulance. More than one person looked in on loved ones in another part of the hospital and accurately described their positions and language. Blind individuals reported many accurate particulars about people and events around them, including the designs and colors of their jewelry and clothes. And what about those who correctly reported seeing other loved ones of whose death they had no knowledge? Each of these examples provides many insuperable difficulties for those who think that the persons who were so near death somehow still observed details such as these naturally.

Could shortcomings in the research methods or the biases of the researchers or patients account for the data? Anderson raises tough issues, such as there being no way to get "behind" the reports of the researchers to check the patients themselves, the lack of "rigorous scientific experiment," and the need to rely on the memories of the patients.[61]

We readily acknowledge that NDEs are often kept private, they usually cannot be predicted ahead of time, researchers must generally rely on retrospective interviews, and the patients' memories. However, it does *not* follow that these conditions must *always* apply, or that, as a result, the research is tainted.

For instance, one way to get behind the privacy of the reports published in books and articles is to conduct one's own research. As difficult as this may seem, it is certainly possible. I (Habermas) know firsthand. Over a fifteen-year period, I personally investigated and interviewed (or heard others interview) dozens of persons who reported NDEs. Several of these individuals provided corroborative testimony (like that we presented in the last chapter), which I checked out and confirmed with the relevant reports and persons involved. You could do the same, and we believe you would arrive at similar findings as the other researchers have. Evidential cases will often turn up in the course of such an investigation.

Although rigorous tests are generally not possible with near-death patients, Sabom's research with a control group and Morse's tests with his own control groups were enlightening. Furthermore, the careful quantification and reporting in numerous charts and tables by Osis and Haraldsson, Ring, and Sabom are invaluable research tools. So critic Douglas Lackey is simply incorrect when he objected, well after all of this research was published, that:

> Moody and the other collectors of near-death experiences do not report how many near-death experiences they collected and what percentage of these reports mentioned the dark tunnel, the bright light, and the faces of dead relatives. Perhaps only a small percentage of people near death have these experiences, in which case the similarity of the experiences proves nothing.[62]

So the point is that, given the conditions that limit NDE research, the amount of testing and quantification that has been done is incredible.

While researchers must rely on the interview process and a patient's memories, perhaps the best way to insure as much accuracy as possible is to interview the subject very soon after the NDE. This can help keep embellishment to a minimum. And of the evidential examples that we reported in the last chapter, several of the persons were interviewed immediately after the crisis experience.[63] In Sabom's research, 30 of the 116 cases (26 percent) were investigated within one month (or less) of the crisis, six of these on the very first day.[64]

Interestingly enough, even in the studies by both Sabom and Osis and Haraldsson, there was no significant statistical difference in content between the reports of those patients who were interviewed quickly after their near-death experience and those who were interviewed even much later.[65] Osis and Haraldsson even cross-checked the possibility of hidden biases in their own research data, checking the methods themselves, and possible biases in the respondents and patients. But they found no significant bias, especially anything that would have distorted the actual phenomena themselves.[66]

Therefore, alleged biases in research methods, researchers, or patients have not changed any major finding in near-death studies. Even the sheer number and variety of careful NDE researchers, when coupled with their generally complementary results, mitigates further against potential bias and its impact on their findings. Partialities are always possible, and may often be present in some form, but there appear to be sufficient checks and balances here to alleviate any major problems.[67] And one can always attempt the same research to check out matters firsthand.

We might also point out that NDE researchers are not the only ones who have to depend on memories, interviews, and so on to gather information. Historians also rely on the same type of interviews, research, and dependence on memories. Strict scientific testing is not an option for either NDE researchers or historians, but that does not mean their findings are tainted.

Some critics have proposed fabrication, either conscious or unconscious, as a plausible explanation for NDEs. Among the natural options, this one is the weakest. Sabom carefully considers this proposal, then enumerates several problems with it.[68] We will mention several of his criticisms as well as others.

For starters, the near-death experiencer often has nothing to gain by answering the researcher's questions and frequently does not even know that the researcher is interested in his experience, thinking that the inquiry is simply a part of the medical process. Furthermore, the similar patterns of NDEs could not be best accounted for this way, at least in the beginning, before the data were popularized. The patterns themselves do not, of course, prove the NDEs to be genuine, but they are an aspect of NDEs that are very difficult to explain on the fabrication hypothesis.

Also, several authors have pointed out the aspect of radical life changes in those who have reported NDEs and in the researchers themselves.[69] The fabrication theory does not adequately handle this phenomenon either.

Another problem surfaces with the many patients who had multiple encounters with death *without* recalling any NDEs.[70] Why would they not fabricate more examples? Or for that matter, why were so many of the experiences so plain in the first place? We might expect much more elaboration in fictitious accounts, but such is rarely present.

Another often-overlooked factor, although it is rather subjective, is the down-to-earth honesty of those "everyday people" involved. Why would they lie about something so strange and personal?

Then, too, while the corroborated cases could involve some fabrication, the large number of persons who would have to be involved in many of the reported instances militates strongly against that possibility. In fact, the thousands of persons who would have to be involved at all may be one of the tougher criticisms of the fabrication hypothesis.

Finally, there's always this antidote: We can carry out some research personally. This way, the process of verification can be tested firsthand and privately.

A Not-So-Natural Theory

What about posing a "not-so-natural" hypothesis—telepathy or some other form of ESP? Could drawing from the minds of living persons credibly explain corroborative near-death experiences? We don't think so.

To begin with, the supposition involved here often presupposes the so-called "super ESP" hypothesis, or some related idea, that these powers both permeate and can explain countless phenomena that are now misunderstood. But a major problem with the grandiose portion of this thesis is that it is unproven. Therefore, it is a shot in the dark, and not a very good one at that. But even supposing some form of ESP actually exists, it still does not account for all NDEs. Here's why.

Take the suggestion that corroborative information could have been received by telepathy from a living person (or by some similar means). That still does not account for enough of the crucial features of these evidential near-death cases, such as those we described in the last chapter. For example, is telepathy the best explanation for Katie's knowledge of "everyday" details concerning her family at home—the specific food being served for dinner, the toys her siblings were playing with, where in the house the people were located, and so on? Even harder to explain, could telepathy account for the blind persons who correctly described the colors and styles of clothes and jewelry? Are we to suppose that such mundane items were even being thought about during an emergency? Similarly, did the patients with heart stoppage "pick up" the same ordinary information about the specific colors of suit coats, ties, and other articles of clothing?[71]

Consider also that near-death experiencers frequently report and describe these items from the vantage point of the ceiling. This positioning is unexplained by telepathic contact with another person, yet Sabom's control sample confirmed the truth of the data.

But it gets even tougher from here. How can persons report *any* kind of information when their brains are not functioning, as with those who had a flat EEG? Learning mundane information about the room and clothes is one thing, but doing that when one's brain is not operating is another matter altogether. How would that be possible?

Lastly, and one of the most difficult categories to explain, is the conviction of being with other loved ones who have died, whose deaths were previously unknown to the patient or even to those in the room with him. In particular, telepathy does not seem able to resolve the conviction that the dead person is doing fine, neither can it handle the peaceful desire of the patient to be with the deceased.[72] In other words, if the near-death experiencer had somehow learned of the loved one's demise from a living individual, any such mental information would necessarily include the fact of the loved one's death and presumably a negative emotional reaction from the one who knew the information. After all, their death likely would not generate positive thoughts. But then this situation would not account for the patient's conviction that the deceased was peaceful and content, or the patient's willingness to join the deceased loved one. So the most likely cause for the information about dead loved ones is the deceased person himself. At least in this sense, this information yields post-death data.[73]

But let's ask ourselves an important question: How many of us would react positively if we were suddenly notified of the death of a loved one? Most likely none of us would. Yet, near-death patients who claim to discover such tidings from the newly deceased loved one respond positively, not negatively. They are not shocked or sorrowful, but at peace and happy, often wishing to *join* the deceased loved one!

Let's extend our generosity. Let's arbitrarily suppose for argument's sake that ESP involvement somehow overcame some of these seemingly insuperable difficulties and established itself. That still would not help the thesis. The ultimate clincher is that it by no means disproves the existence of an afterlife.[74] If an individual's ESP exists after the death of the body, this would simply be another way to argue that we experience an afterlife. After all, the NDE includes the person's own private memories and knowledge of self—as when the patient happily greets the loved one whom he immediately recognizes, or is still concerned about family members who are "left behind." So even if someone could authenticate ESP after death as a causal thesis, it would simply *provide details concerning our personalities in that state*—it would not refute life after death.

So we conclude that alternative hypotheses do not successfully explain the NDE in natural terms, especially in its corroborative aspects. Even combinations of these theories do not cancel the best NDE data. Medical, psychological, and other natural or not-so-natural proposals of various sorts all fall short of the needed explanatory goal. Therefore, our task now is to inquire whether NDEs provide strong evidence for an afterlife.

Evidence for Life After Death

The answer to the evidential value of NDEs for an afterlife is best developed in response to one final objection. Some critics have pointed out that NDEs are exactly that—*near* death. Therefore, since the person is not irreversibly dead, her experiences may still be explained by some residual brain activity. That is, the physical body could still be the cause of NDEs. Thus, we cannot rely on them as evidence for life *after* death.[75]

In order to fully respond to this objection, we need to deal with three critical, inherent issues: (1) the extent to which the definitions of death have been satisfied by NDEs; (2) whether any residual activity in the body can still account for the corroboration of NDEs; (3) if there is any decent evidence here for life after death.

In the last chapter, we defined the three major concepts of death, including clinical (or the cessation of vital life signs) and biological (irreversible physical death). Between these two lies the other major concept: the absence of brain wave activity (EEG).[76] So now our four main types of evidence outlined in Chapter 5 can be divided in the following chart, according to which evidence addresses the criteria required by each of the three definitions of death:

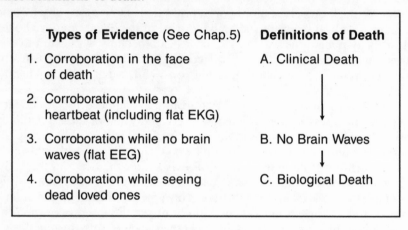

Types of Evidence (See Chap.5)   **Definitions of Death**

1. Corroboration in the face of death   A. Clinical Death

2. Corroboration while no heartbeat (including flat EKG)

3. Corroboration while no brain waves (flat EEG)   B. No Brain Waves

4. Corroboration while seeing dead loved ones   C. Biological Death

Now we will turn to each of the three inherent issues involved in the objection above, and address each by referring to the chart.

Regarding the first issue (the extent to which the definitions of death have been satisfied), from everything we have said in the last two chapters, it should be clear that there is confirmed life after clinical death (definition A above). Many documented cases exist where there were no life signs such as pulse and respiration, yet an incredible number of facts were reported and corroborated, evidencing some type of continuing consciousness during and beyond this time (evidence 1 above). There are also a number of cases where heart stoppage had occurred, sometimes for very long periods of time, as well as in the presence of confirming reports (evidence 2). These indicate that life after clinical death is a fact.

NDEs have also been reported, although not as commonly, where there was a distinct absence of brain wave activity (EEG), sometimes for a duration of thirty minutes to three hours, during which time the patient reported experiences that were corroborated (evidence 3). While the ideal criterion for brain death (definition B) often requires longer periods of EEG inactivity in order to pronounce the person biologically dead (definition C), we want to make a different point here. Even when the brain is inactive for shorter periods of time (one-half hour to three hours is certainly significant) and corroborated consciousness continues, NDEs under such conditions very probably cannot be accounted for by the physical body. So the occurrence of strict biological death is unnecessary to establish the presence of life after death, since we already have evidence for perception apart from brain activity *during those moments.* This is our earlier definition of *minimal* life after death.

In addition, we have corroborated near-death reports of previously unknown data concerning loved ones who had already died (evidence 4). We have argued that the best thesis here is that the information was supplied by the deceased loved one; no other supposition accounts for all the details. But if this is so, then even the criteria for biological death (definition C) have been satisfied by the evident consciousness of the deceased loved ones, in light of their "post-death experiences." This phenomenon is not dependent on the near-death experiencer's (or anyone else's) brain function.

So it would seem that we have our answer to the first portion of the objection posed above. Corroborated NDEs have been reported while *each* of the definitions of death has been met. The criteria for clinical death have frequently been fulfilled. The absence of brain waves has also been observed, even for fairly long periods of time, indicating the probable absence of brain activity *during those specific times.* And while final brain death obviously has not been measured relative to the one who returned with the NDE (since it would constitute irreversible biological death!), biological death in the broader sense (including the final cessation of brain activity) is satisfied by the near-death reports of previously deceased loved ones.

The second issue raised was, can any residual bodily activity account for these NDEs? Not at all. First, and most obviously, it cannot explain the cases where there were flat EEGs or experiences with deceased loved ones. And second, residual bodily activity cannot even handle evidence types 1 and 2 from the chart above. As we showed, natural processes cannot account for these corroborative instances that occurred in the face of death, including those with heart stoppage. In fact, even if the patient had been *fully conscious* at the time of the NDE, many of the reports could not be explained on the basis of bodily activity. This is especially true of those cases involving blind persons and those that took place some distance from the location of the patient's body. So whether there was the possibility of residual bodily activity or not in evidence types 1 and 2, it still cannot account for the bulk of the examples we presented in Chapter 5.

This brings us to the third inherent issue: Is there evidence for life after death here? It would be difficult to avoid the conclusion that NDEs provide a strong case at least for a minimalistic view of life after the initial moments (or hours) after death. Of course, the data from deceased loved ones (evidence 4) would lead us to an opinion even somewhat stronger than the minimalistic perspective. We have shown that consciousness exists during and after all three concepts of death. Furthermore, even though residual bodily activity is not present in some examples of corroboration (evidences 3 and 4), it doesn't even appear that such activity can account for most of the cases presented in any of the four types of evidence outlined in Chapter 5. Chart 2 presents a visual picture of this conclusion:

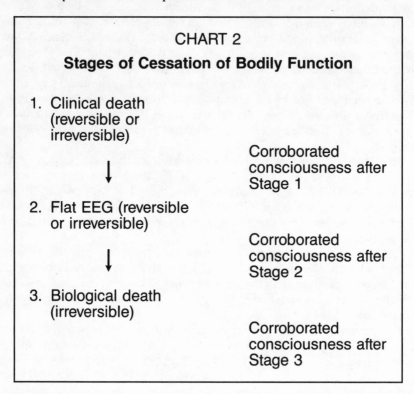

CHART 2

Stages of Cessation of Bodily Function

1. Clinical death
   (reversible or
   irreversible)

   ↓   Corroborated
                                  consciousness after
                                  Stage 1

2. Flat EEG (reversible
   or irreversible)

   ↓   Corroborated
                                  consciousness after
                                  Stage 2

3. Biological death
   (irreversible)

                                  Corroborated
                                  consciousness after
                                  Stage 3

While the evidence presented here does not constitute proof or total certainty, it does provide rather strong evidence for life after the death of the body (including the brain). How far beyond death this life extends is still an unanswered question, but that an afterlife exists is not. Now life after death should not be defined as some mystical dimension; in its simplest (or minimalistic) form, it only indicates the presence of conscious life beyond the death of the physical body. Since human consciousness does not depend on the central nervous system (or other bodily activity), NDEs are evidence of at least a short period of life after death. Verifiable consciousness during periods when brain readings are nonexistent and shared experiences with loved ones who have previously died (sometimes long before) together indicate longer periods of life beyond death.

Perhaps a word needs to be said concerning the type of consciousness revealed through NDEs. The individual retains his own knowledge of self, as well as his own private memories (such as those revealed in the joyful reunions with deceased loved ones and in the remembrance of one's family left behind), but all this is retained in the absence of one's functioning physical body. These details of one's ongoing personality (identified earlier as the "enduring I") are yet a further, empirical indication of the dualistic position argued in Chapters 2 and 3.[77] To this we have now added extensive empirical evidence for life after death, both from Jesus' resurrection and from NDEs.

Life beyond the grave exists beyond a reasonable doubt. We survive our bodies. But for how long? What is life after death like? What else can we know about the hereafter? We can know more than you may think. Let's press on.

PART 2

The Nature of Immortality

Chapter 7

Life in Between:
The State Between Death and
Eternity

As we have seen, NDEs provide us with some fascinating information about what life is like while a person is dying and right after that person has passed on. But what about after those initial moments? What is life farther beyond death's door really like? Is it different for various people? Do good, moral people experience something different from bad, immoral people? Do those of different religious persuasions have afterlives that coincide with their particular beliefs? What is the hereafter really like?

Depending on their beliefs, people give different answers to these questions. Buddhists would not answer them the same as Mormons would, and atheists would give a different scenario from theists. However, the issue is not what one believes the afterlife is like. After all, believing something, even if the belief is sincere, does not make the belief true. The real issue is this: Is there a true, real picture of the afterlife, and what evidence supports that picture?

We are convinced that the evidence surveyed here—as well as a number of other evidences and reasons we have detailed elsewhere—points to Christian theism as the best explanation for all the data.[1] And according to this perspective, a person's experience of the afterlife depends on the relationship that person has with the Christian God on this side of the grave.

In this chapter, we will discuss the historic Christian view of what happens immediately after death to the person who has entered a personal relationship with God by accepting the gospel of Jesus Christ, that is through accepting the death and resurrection of Christ as a payment for one's own sins. In Chapter 11, we will look at the historic Christian view of what happens to those who reject the gospel of Christ. For now, let us concentrate our attention on the Christian believer.

If a person is a Christian—has a right relationship with God—she enters into a certain sort of intermediate state of life following her physical death. This state will not be her final state, which will begin at the resurrection of her body from the grave, but it is nonetheless, a state of real life, genuine post-mortem existence.

But what is this intermediate state like? Is the person conscious, or does the soul sleep while awaiting the resurrection of the body? If the person is conscious, does he have a body or is he a disembodied soul? If the latter, how can he talk to others and be aware of his surroundings without physical sense organs? These questions are the focus of this chapter, and they are not just theoretical issues. Most Christians have loved ones or friends in Christ who have died. And we would find comfort in knowing what life is like for them now. We also wonder what we can look forward to if we die before the second coming of the Lord Jesus.

Christian Views of the Intermediate State

The Traditional Outlook

Traditionally, the intermediate state refers to the state of individuals between the time they die until they are reunited with their own resurrected bodies. The majority of theologians have held that at death, a person's soul becomes disembodied and it is translated into an entirely different, nonspatial mode of existence where time is still real. In this state the person enjoys conscious fellowship with God while waiting for a reunion with a new, resurrected body. This picture of the intermediate state is based on a number of considerations.

First, several verses in the New Testament imply that, at death, one immediately enters into the presence of God to enjoy conscious fellowship with him. Philippians 1:23 states Paul's desire "to depart and be with Christ," as does 2 Corinthians 5:8 where Paul prefers "to be absent from the body and to be at home with the Lord" (NIV). In the verses immediately preceding verse 8, Paul expresses his conviction that if our earthly body, or tent, is torn down by death, we have a new body, or house, awaiting us. Apparently, Paul's ideal choice was to be alive at the resurrection of the dead so his new body could be immediately put in place of his old one and he would not go through a period of disembodiment, which he calls being "found naked."[2] Paul's attitude does not imply that the intermediate state is bad. Far from it. But he knew that a full human state involves the soul in union with the new resurrection body, so that a state of disembodiment, while good in itself, is not our final or natural mode of afterlife existence.

In addition to Paul's statements, Jesus promised the thief crucified beside him that they would be together in paradise that very day (Luke 23:43). In the parable recorded in Luke 16:19–31—the one that pictures the poor man Lazarus and the unnamed wealthy man in different places and conditions after death—Jesus clearly implies that persons continue to be conscious in an intermediate state. It would be wrong to push the details of this parable too far, especially the spatial language, but, imagery aside, the parable expresses Jesus' conviction about the reality of the intermediate state.

Revelation 6:9–11 refers to the souls of disembodied martyrs (perhaps slain during the early days of the Tribulation period) who cry out to God for justice on the earth. As with the parable in Luke 16, the spatial imagery should not be pressed. On the other hand, disembodied existence is hard to grasp, and the Bible often depicts it in spatial language that should be taken figuratively, much as physical descriptions of God's having eyes and arms should be understood. God does not literally dwell in a spatial location named heaven, nor does he sit on a physical throne somewhere in outer space. God is not a physical being, and he is not confined to a spatial location. God is omnipresent. He is outside of space altogether. Spatial language applied to God in the Bible is figurative. The same can be said for language describing the disembodied existence of an immaterial soul.

The New Testament also gives examples of individuals who temporarily make appearances on earth—for example, the deceased Moses and Elijah appear in a transfigured state (Matt. 17:3). These appearances can most naturally be understood as individuals who are temporarily given an ability to be seen with the sense organs or to be embodied, even though, strictly speaking, they still await their resurrected bodies. In the Old Testament, the angel of the Lord made similar appearances, even though no biblical scholar would hold that this being existed in an embodied form prior to and after his appearances (Gen. 16:7–12, 21:17–18, 22:11–18).

For Christians, these passages (especially Matt. 17:3) bring tremendous comfort. They reveal that when a believer dies, she is immediately brought into conscious, intimate fellowship with Christ himself. So when Scripture uses words like *depart, be absent from the body, be with Christ,* or *be at home with Christ,* we should understand these as figures of speech, and not interpret them as spatial terms, literally conveying movement from one location to another. New Testament scholar Murray Harris confirms this, pointing out that the primary thrust of these words is to emphasize a heightened form of active, interpersonal communication between the person and the Lord himself.[3] As mysterious as this may be, what a joy it is to have a hope like this! Part of the fear of death is a dread of what it is like to die. These verses can help alleviate some of that fear, though other fears such as losing control, suffering pain, or being embarrassed may still remain.

With the traditional view in mind, let's turn to two further questions: What are the alternatives to the traditional view that claim to be more accurate representations of the biblical model? Can we gain more insight as to what exactly life will be like in an intermediate state?

The Alternatives

There are five nontraditional alternative views (and one traditional) that are equally divided between two primary categories: conscious states and unconscious ones. We can lay them out this way:

Nontraditional Outlooks

UNCONSCIOUS STATE VIEWS	CONSCIOUS STATE VIEWS
Recreation	Platonic
Perspectival	Embodied
Soul Sleep	Temporary Disembodied

We will take a look at all these options, beginning with the *unconscious-state views*. These positions agree that there is no intermediate state in which persons continue to exist in a state of consciousness between death and the future resurrection. However, they disagree about why this is so.

Before we look at some specific problems, two general refutations apply to each of the three unconscious state views. First, in 2 Corinthians 5:1–9, Paul longs for his future resurrection body, while still proclaiming his preference for the intermediate state (cf. Phil. 1:21–23). But how do we explain this desire for the final state if, at least from his vantage point, he knows he will achieve it immediately after death? Second, NDEs provide empirical evidence that there is a continuation of conscious personality after death, without any period of delay whatsoever. Now let's consider each view and its specific difficulties.

According to the *recreation* position, substance dualism is false—humans do not have substantial souls. Thus, at death a person becomes extinct, and at the general resurrection God recreates the person, not from preexisting materials but out of nothing.

We find this view inadequate. The main motivation behind it is a denial of substance dualism. But we have already seen that substance dualism is the classic Christian view of being human and a very strong case can be given on its behalf.[4] Moreover, this position has no way to account for the identity of a person throughout changes in his body (see Chap. 2). Since the recreated person has no entity in common with the person who died, the individual who exists in heaven is not literally the same person as the one who lived on earth, but a double. The recreated person may look like the person who died, but the new person is created out of nothing and has no soulish or bodily materials in common with the person who died. This is inconsistent with biblical teaching. *I* am promised eternal life, not a look-alike.[5]

Finally, the recreation position is obviously incompatible with a normal understanding of biblical passages that teach a conscious intermediate state. For those who accept the Bible's reliability and authority, this is a formidable objection.

The second nontraditional view is the *perspectival* position. It claims the following:[6] Sometimes scientific advances legitimately change our understanding of biblical passages. No one today believes the sun literally rises or sets, nor do we think that when the angels come from the four corners of the world, they cross a flat earth. Time is part of the created order and belongs entirely to this world. In the same way, we now know that time is part of the space-time physical universe, and time is relative to a frame of reference. Suppose there are twins A and B. If A remains on earth while B travels in a spaceship near the speed of light, B will be younger than A when he arrives back on earth. Time shrinks with increased velocity. Further, two events can appear simultaneous to one observer, and they can appear to happen at different times to a second observer in a rapidly moving spaceship flying overhead.

Whatever happens to persons after death, we have no reason to believe they remain in our space-time system. According to the perspectival view, when a believer dies, he goes to be with Christ and receives a resurrection body. From *his* perspective, there is no time gap between death and bodily entrance into Christ's presence. But from *our* perspective here on earth, there is a time interval between death and resurrection. The whole problem of the intermediate state's being a literal state of disembodiment arises because we erroneously view the state of the dead from our time-bound perspective.

This position, though intriguing, suffers from two main difficulties. For one thing, there is no good reason to think that time is limited to the physical universe. In fact, the very notion of timeless existence for finite conscious beings is unintelligible. (God is an infinite conscious being. He *is* outside of time because he is timeless.) Something is temporal if two questions can be asked of it: When was it? How long was it? The former is a question of temporal location, the latter of temporal duration. A timeless entity involves neither. Now in the afterlife, people will still be able to talk, ponder things, change what they are thinking about, and so forth. All of these activities require time. It is one thing to admit that people in the intermediate state are in a *different* time frame (whatever that would mean), but it is quite another to say they are in no time frame at all.

Here's the other problem. It is true that advances in science can help change the way biblical passages are interpreted. We no longer think the sun literally rises. But we cannot appeal to this phenomenon willy-nilly. There must be sufficient reason for such a change, and the new interpretation must not affect what the Bible is clearly trying to teach.

We admit this is not always an easy matter to settle. But clearly the most natural way to understand passages speaking about the intermediate state is the viewpoint captured by the traditional view. And there is no good reason for abandoning that position. Even if the scientific model of space-time relativity is granted, it does not follow that disembodied souls are timeless. It only follows that they enter a different mode of time.

Further, the relativity of real space and time is not a settled issue.[7] Empirical or measurable time may be relative, but real time, time in itself, may very well be absolute. Perhaps God himself provides an absolute reference frame for time. In any case, the perspectival position provides no good reason to abandon the natural way to interpret the Bible.

The third unconscious-state position is the *soul sleep* view. Embraced by groups such as Seventh-Day Adventists and Jehovah's Witnesses, this position claims that in the time interval between death and resurrection, persons exist in a state of sleep or unconsciousness. Several Bible passages that refer to death as a "sleep" *(koimasthai* in Greek) are used to support this view, including Daniel 12:2, Matthew 9:24, John 11:11, and 1 Thessalonians 4:13–16 and 5:10.

But several objections make this view untenable. First, numerous biblical texts (e.g., Luke 23:43, Phil. 1:23, 2 Cor. 5:1–10) clearly teach that death is a transition into conscious enjoyment of the presence of Christ. How could Christ's presence be enjoyed if one was asleep?

Second, some of these same Bible passages describe death as a gain because the deceased is with Christ. But if that person fell asleep at death, what would be the gain? In fact, why would the apostle Paul wish to go to be with Christ instead of continuing in his bodily state (Phil. 1:21–23)?

Third, 1 Thessalonians 5:10 reads, "[Christ] died for us, that whether we are awake or asleep, we may live together with Him" (NASB). This verse makes sense if it means we can enjoy Christ whether we live on earth or die, but if being asleep means being unconscious, how could this verse make sense?

Fourth, sleep is an activity of the body. The soul needs sleep because it is embodied. It is not clear, however, that a disembodied soul *could* sleep, much less need this kind of rest.

Fifth, the existence of angels shows that spirits can and do live conscious disembodied lives, so there is no problem with the idea of a conscious, disembodied intermediate state for humans.

And sixth, the word *sleep* commonly describes the appearance and posture of the body, not that of the soul. This term was used metaphorically by ancient Greek and Egyptian cultures to describe the state of the dead. Those cultures believed in conscious existence in the afterlife. This word also sometimes simply means that the person is not alive to earthly surroundings (but could still be alive to other surroundings). It is also used as a softened euphemism for death when applied to believers, and in the verb form it probably represents punctiliar action (to fall asleep or die at a point of time), not continuous action (to remain in a state of sleep). So even the history and common usage of the word *sleep* makes it very difficult for the soul-sleep advocates to justify their position by appealing to linguistics and biblical usage.

Since the unconscious-state views of the intermediate state are therefore unsound, we need to consider the other three nontraditional views that accept the perspective that the deceased in the afterlife are conscious. The first one we will look at is the *Platonic* view. According to this theory, there is no resurrection of the body. The body is composed of matter, which is evil; the immaterial soul, which is good, remains forever in a state of disembodiment after the death of the body. The real you and me is our soul; the body is completely irrelevant. This is not the classic Christian view. Christianity teaches that the soul exists, but matter is not evil. The body is important and crucial for complete, normal human existence, and the eventual resurrection of the body underscores that fact. Also, 2 Corinthians 5:1–10 teaches that the state of temporary disembodiment is not a natural, full, final way for humans to exist, which once again shows the body's importance. (We will provide further reasons for the resurrection of the believer's body in Chap. 9.) Hence, the Platonic perspective cannot be embraced in a Christian worldview.

A second position of the intermediate state is the *embodied* view.[8] John Cooper explains:

> It includes a variety of specific formulations which differ according to how each defines the term "resurrection"—whether receipt of a renewed body, transformation into a spiritual mode of existence, or simple union with God. But whatever the final resurrection amounts to, it is said to occur for the individual at the instant of death. That might involve passing into another dimension of time beyond earthly time. Or it might mean transcending time altogether. In any case, this view holds that there is no temporary mode of existence or period of nonexistence between individuals' deaths and their final resurrections. The transition is instantaneous. The New Testament depiction of a general resurrection of all people at a future time—at the second coming of Christ—cannot be taken literally. The final resurrection occurs for each person at the instant of his or her death. Thus there is no time at which persons exist without their bodies.[9]

We cannot attempt a thorough evaluation of this view in comparison to the traditional position of temporary disembodiment. The details of that debate are somewhat technical and beyond our present scope. However, we would like to respond with four brief comments. In the first place, most advocates of this view, like Murray Harris, are not dogmatic about it and admit that the traditional view is quite plausible.[10]

Second, even if this position is true, it is similar to the disembodied view at several points: Both views accept that a substantial soul or ego is part of the person; both believe that the intermediate state is a different realm of being than the earthly one; both maintain that conscious fellowship with Christ immediately after death occurs; and both accept that embodiment is the ultimate, natural destiny of believers.

Furthermore, the most natural way to understand 2 Corinthians 5:1–10 is to view Paul as teaching that those who die before the return of Christ undergo a period of nakedness, or disembodiment, in an intermediate state. The other interpretation sees Paul contrasting life in an earthly body with an immediate reception of the resurrection body at death so that the intermediate state is one in which we possess our resurrected bodies. While this is plausible, the interpretation seems strained. For example, as pointed out earlier, Paul has fewer grounds for desiring the resurrected body as soon as possible. Also, it requires us to see Paul changing his view of the resurrection from that in 1 Corinthians 15 (where it is conceived as a general resurrection at the second coming of Christ, not as an individual resurrection at one's death) to the one in 2 Corinthians 5 (we each receive our resurrected body at the time we die). Why should we adopt this change of mind on Paul's part when it is more natural to understand the two passages as complementary rather than contradictory? Sometimes, at least, this perception of a conflict in Paul's viewpoint is motivated by a denial of mind/body dualism, a denial that we showed was untenable.

Finally, in New Testament times, the standard Jewish understanding of resurrection was that all people are raised at the same time at the end of the age. The notion that each person received his or her resurrected body at the time of death was foreign to the Jews of that time.[11] So they, including the Jewish New Testament writers, most likely would not have understood the teachings of Jesus or the New Testament writings as conveying the embodied view.

Further, Paul himself always spoke of the resurrection of dead believers in the plural, referring to the corporate aspect. This means that the burden of proof is on those who do not take the natural, most literal understanding of resurrection in the New Testament. That understanding entails a future, general resurrection of the body at the second coming of Christ, preceded by a disembodied intermediate state. Advocates of the embodiment view have not been able to prove otherwise. In short, the best account of the intermediate state is the *temporary disembodiment* position, which is the traditional view.[12]

The Nature of the Intermediate State

With the traditional view established as the best expression of the Christian understanding of the intermediate state for the believer in Christ, we can take a look at the nature of this temporary disembodiment. What is it like? Unfortunately, when we look to the Bible for an answer, we find very little information. But from what little we find, we learn some things about this state.

Immediately after death, a person will continue to be truly alive and conscious, even though transformed into a different mode of being. This mode of existence is restful and happy. It is not a period of idleness and inactivity. Far from it. Theologian Loraine Boettner has pointed out that the biblical notion of rest involves the idea of satisfaction in labor and accomplishment.[13] We will continue to grow, learn, serve, and progress in the intermediate state, but these activities will not be tiring or trying. Instead, they will be joyous and directed primarily to God. Boredom will not be an issue.

Conscious, intensified fellowship with Christ will also be part of our enjoyment. We will know, feel, and partake of his presence and life richly and gratefully. To be sure, life in the intermediate state is not as good as life in a fully resurrected form, and we will look forward to receiving our resurrected bodies at the second coming. But the intermediate state is still preferable to life here on earth, as Paul tells us in Philippians 1:23.

This is all we really know from the Bible on this subject. Can we say anything more beyond this? Anything else would be speculative, but we think a few further insights can be plausibly defended.

The intermediate state will involve certain limitations. For one thing, time (understood as a succession of moments and the reality of events) will characterize such a state, but it will be a nonspatial mode of reality. Further, activities that require bodies will be impossible. Without eyes, ears, throats, tongues, and other sensory organs, we will be unable to interact with our surroundings in bodily ways.

We will, however, still have souls, so we will still be able to engage in soulish activities: believing, thinking, wishing, hoping, desiring, remembering, and (at least) feeling emotions. Time doesn't need matter. For instance, humming a tune in my mind is a series of events and takes time, and is possible even in a disembodied state.

Further, we may be able to directly communicate with God and others and be aware of their presence through a nonsensory, spiritual form of intuition. Perhaps this will be somewhat like telepathy. When one of the five senses is lost, the others are heightened. It could be that the soul's telepathic abilities are focused and strengthened with the loss of bodily sensory abilities.[14]

In this life, we are sometimes directly aware of God's presence as a being who is holy, good, loving, and so on. We are even aware of someone watching us occasionally. Perhaps these abilities will be strengthened.

Additionally, we may be able to produce thoughts and experiences in others by some form of telepathic or soulish influence. This would allow us to be aware of others and communicate without sense organs.

It is hard to speculate on how rich this sort of life will be, but on the face of it, it would seem less desirable than life that includes full-blown sensory experiences normally produced by the body interacting with physical surroundings. We all know the experience of humming a tune in our mind. That will surely be possible in the intermediate state, and it may be that others can cause us to hear such tunes through telepathy. It may even be that such tunes will be experienced in a richer and more heightened form than is possible in this life. But still, the intermediate state would be richer if this type of inner life were accompanied by the ability to experience the same kinds of sensory experiences normally produced in this life by the body. Or so it would seem.

Will we be able to feel bodily sensations in the intermediate state? That depends. Since we will not have bodies, we will not literally have, say, feelings in our toes or tastes of food on our tongues. But several people in this life have reported what is called the phantom limb phenomenon.[15] These are cases where people without a leg, for instance, still report sensations (pain, tingles, etc.) that feel as though they are still in that leg. Qualitatively speaking, these sensations are indistinguishable from those that really occur in physical limbs by means of physical events (such as being stuck with a pin). So having a limb is not a necessary condition for having such sensations.

This seems to show that sensations are really events that occur in the soul, not in the body, strictly speaking. So while these sensations usually require certain events in the body (to feel a pain, I must be stuck in the foot and, therefore, I must have a foot), it seems possible to have them without a body.

In an intermediate state, no such sensations would be painful, and they could not be caused by physical things (such as apples) interacting with bodily organs (say, the tongue). But they may still be possible, and we may be able to cause them at will, as may God. In short, the phantom limb phenomenon suggests that we may be able to have sensations of the taste of food or the sound of a song where these are caused by God, another soul, or our own wills, and not by a material object interacting with our bodies.

The phrase "I am having a tingling in my toe" is ambiguous. If it means that a tingling is being produced in my soul by virtue of the fact that my soul is present throughout my body, my toe included, and the cause of the tingling is a physical object touching my toe, then clearly this would be impossible in a disembodied state. But one could still be appeared to in a tingling way. In other words, one could still experience a tingle in the soul—if, as the phantom limb phenomenon suggests, it is really the soul that experiences sensations in the first place—if that tingle were produced by one's own will or in some other way. These experiences would be like hallucinations in this life, except they would not include the notion of being mistaken or being misled by them. For as disembodied persons, we would not take such a sensation to be an experience of a toe event but of a qualitatively identical experience produced in some other way.

Besides the phantom limb phenomenon, another consideration suggests that a disembodied soul could still enjoy a full, rich experience of sensations identical in nature to those produced in this life by the body. Philosopher H.H. Price suggested that in dreams, we have sensations of colors, sounds, tastes, and so forth.[16] Perhaps in a disembodied afterlife we could have dreamlike sensations produced in us by God, others, or an immaterial realm. This would allow us to experience a full range of sensations, even though they would not be produced by the normal means. It may even be the case that the material, spatial world could produce sensations in the soul directly without using the five senses as intermediaries. This may explain how NDEs are possible in a disembodied state.

We can add one final consideration as a supplement to Price's theory. It draws upon certain aspects of the thought of the Christian empiricist philosopher Bishop George Berkeley (1685–1753). We will have to begin with a sketchy picture of Berkeley's thought.

According to Berkeley, matter does not exist. Strictly speaking, there is no such thing as an external material world. Only two main types of things exist: souls—finite souls and the infinite soul, which is God—and mental ideas, which exist only in minds. An idea is a mental entity that has the quality of some specific sensation. A specific shade of red, taste of sweetness, feeling of warmth or hardness, hearing a sound are all ideas. For example, an apple is not composed of matter, but a bundle of precise qualities—taste, shape, texture, color, etc. Each of these qualities is a mental entity that can be in the mind of a finite person when he tastes the apple or looks at it. The "external" world is still fully real for Berkeley and, experientially speaking, it is no different from the world of matter. We still bump into things, see colors, and taste objects. But the external world is a many-faceted grouping of ideas held in existence by the mind of God as he continues to watch them.

We are not suggesting that Berkeley's picture of the physical universe is accurate. Our point is that Berkeley gave a picture of reality in which a life of mental experience (sound, taste, sight, etc.) exists that is experientially indistinguishable from the one we actually have in this life, though it does not depend on the existence of matter. No material objects, no physical bodies, no sense organs are necessary to have a full range of sensory experiences. Now while this view may not fit the physical universe this side of death, it could be that in the intermediate state God causes an objective world of ideas to exist so all disembodied persons could continue to experience that world by way of sensations identical in quality to those they experienced this side of the grave.

Of course, this is speculative.

What we can be certain about is that, in a disembodied state, souls could experience at least certain forms of mental events (thoughts, desires, etc.) and be aware of others and God through nonsensory means like telepathy. Also, the phantom limb phenomenon, Price's dream theory, and Berkeley's philosophy show that it could still be possible in a disembodied state to experience all the normal, pleasant bodily sensations of sound, sight, smell, taste, and touch.

Beyond the Intermediate

In this chapter, we have looked at different ways Christian thinkers have understood the intermediate state, and we have tried to see through a glass darkly and gain some insight about what life will be like in that state. What we found is that it is not the way God intended us to live in a final way, but it is a wonderful type of reality nonetheless. And the truth of its reality provided deep comfort for Paul, the early church, and those who have loved Christ throughout the ages. It can do so for us as well.

However, as you probably know, not everyone views the intermediate state through the lens of the Bible. Today many people have embraced various forms of reincarnation—a perspective of the afterlife that opposes the Christian viewpoint. What is reincarnation all about? What is the evidence for it? Is it true? If not, why not? These are the questions we will answer in the next chapter.

Chapter 8

Reincarnation—Is It True?

A Gallup Poll survey showed that almost one in four Americans believed in reincarnation. This is an unexpectedly high figure, especially since these data were gathered, not among followers of Eastern religions, but among Western Protestants and Catholics.[1] While we cannot, of course, decide the truthfulness of belief by head count, the influence of reincarnation and related ideas in our "Westernized" society is certainly surprising. Undoubtedly these ideas reflect the impact of such popular media as television, movies, music, novels, and even comic books, all of which have been used to present and even promote Eastern religious and philosophical concepts.

What is reincarnation anyway?

It is very difficult to provide a single definition of *reincarnation*. Meanings and nuances differ. For example, Norman Geisler and J. Yutaka Amano illustrate ten models of reincarnation, each of which emphasizes varying features, some similar and others not.[2] For our purposes, we will define reincarnation as the belief that, sometime after death, the soul or life force passes into another body before its birth. The desired goal of this process is spiritual evolution.

The more popular presentations of belief in reincarnation appeal for their justification to phenomena such as the common experience of deja vu (where we think that we have had certain experiences before) and occasional reports of hypnotized persons who "regress" to what they claim are past lives. However, beyond these more celebrated aspects, there are some serious scholars who have produced data that they think constitute evidence for reincarnation. We want to walk you through the major evidences cited on behalf of this belief, then show you why these evidences fail to establish the truth of reincarnation.

Reasons for Reincarnation

The following case reported by Ian Stevenson, a medical doctor considered by many to be the world's leading expert on reincarnation, is typical in reincarnation literature.[3]

A four-year-old boy named Prakesh began declaring that his actual name was Nirmal and that he really lived in another village. He provided details about his "real" family, such as the names of relatives and friends, as well as particulars about the family's business. He kept trying to run away to his "prior" home and talked incessantly about it, provoking the anger of his parents, who beat him for his behavior.

Five years later, Nirmal's father visited Prakesh's village and Prakesh recognized him. It was discovered that Nirmal was actually the name of the man's son, who had died prior to Prakesh's birth. Prakesh wanted to return "home" and, subsequently, was reunited more than once with those whom he claimed to have known in his previous existence. He recognized those he said were his former relatives and friends, greeted them with appropriate emotions, and provided precise details concerning the furnishings of his earlier home. Yet, he was puzzled by changes that had occurred in the intervening ten years.

Stevenson, who discovered this case three weeks after the initial reunion, listed thirty-four items Prakesh remembered, then verified their accuracy through the relevant persons. Prakesh's memory checked out, even though members of both families testified they had no prior knowledge of each other.[4]

In certain cases, reincarnation reports exhibit other evidential features. Sometimes the family reunions are arranged by persons who maintained careful watch over the situation. In one such case, Stevenson counted 47 claimed memories of a Lebanese boy named Imad before anyone attempted to authenticate the details. Although his parents tried and failed to uncover Imad's former identity, 44 of the 47 claims made by Imad himself were proved accurate.[5]

These examples provide one type of evidence for reincarnation—that which is derived from the memories of those who claim to have lived another life at some earlier time. These memories, which often fade with age, can be either produced spontaneously, as in the cases just cited, or derived regressively from hypnosis or by dreams. Many reincarnation researchers consider the former type of case more impressive, but they do not ignore the latter.

A second kind of evidence comes from cases of xenoglossy, individuals who speak in a language they seemingly do not know. There are two types of xenoglossy. One, recitative xenoglossy, refers to individuals who speak certain words or phrases in another vernacular, even though they cannot carry on a conversation in that language. The other, responsive xenoglossy, is the ability to converse and answer questions in the other language. Since the first type is more easily explained on a nonreincarnation model, Stevenson was most interested in the responsive variety.[6] Theologian Hans Schwarz thinks this latter material comprises the most impressive evidence for reincarnation.[7]

The third category of evidence comes from the presence of birthmarks and deformities in the reincarnated person that match the deceased person he claims to have been in an earlier life. The assumption here is that these blemishes provide continuity between the two persons from one life to the next.

The fourth evidential category, argues Stevenson, is even more important than the evidence from memories. It comes from the agreement between a living child's character and that of the deceased individual. These children thoroughly identify with the other person (termed *personation*)— a phenomenon that Stevenson believes constitutes one of the strongest evidences for reincarnation.[8]

The fifth category of evidence concerns Christianity and the Bible. Some people who believe in reincarnation argue that it is a doctrine that is either taught in the Bible or is at least compatible with Christian tenets. Some reincarnationists cite various biblical passages as supporting their doctrine. But these references to the Bible usually ignore careful exegesis.[9] And those reincarnationists more sophisticated in their approach to the Bible do not state their conclusions with the same finality and dogmatism as their less studious counterparts.[10]

After studying the evidence for ourselves, we believe it seems to validate something. Exactly *what* it validates is the issue. We do not think it establishes reincarnation. Let's see why.

A Major Response to Reincarnation

The heart of the issue is simple: Are there hypotheses other than reincarnation that can account for much the same data? Interestingly enough, reincarnationist advocate Ian Stevenson thinks that at least one rival option should be taken very seriously—possession of the living person by a foreign spirit. Having said this, we want to quickly point out that Stevenson does not consider demonic intrusion to be as likely as possession by the discarnate spirit of the actual person who had previously died.[11] So we need to look at these two options—reincarnation and possession—to see if either explains the data.

In both types of possession, either the demonic or the deceased human spirit could potentially explain the memories such as those in the case of Prakesh. Both types of spirit could presumably know even the sorts of intimate details concerning Prakesh's relatives, friends, and previous dwelling place. Perhaps a demonic spirit could learn the needed information from any of several sources, while the departed human spirit (of Nirmal) would, of course, be intrinsically familiar with the details of his own past human existence. Other details of the case for reincarnation could also be accounted for in this manner.

For these reasons, Stevenson admits, "For some of these cases, all the facts are better accounted for by supposing a continuing influence of the previous personality after death."[12] What views could account for such "a continuing influence" of the person? Stevenson concludes that the known data appear to support either reincarnation or possession by the enduring presence of the deceased person's spirit.

In fact, Stevenson thinks that the similarities are so close at several points that the data fall "along a continuum in which the distinction between reincarnation and possession becomes blurred."[13] Later, he writes that much of the data "do not permit a firm decision between the hypothesis of possession and reincarnation."[14] Presumably, then, Stevenson thinks that much of the evidence is difficult to dogmatically account for either one way or the other.

In fact, to illustrate his point, Stevenson follows these comments by presenting two cases of possession where this hypothesis accounts for the relevant data and reincarnation does not. In both examples, the person who died did so during the possessed individual's life, thereby ruling out reincarnation as a cause. In part, Stevenson builds his case for this conclusion because of a critical distinction he makes between reincarnation and possession. Reincarnation, he contends, is where another personality enters a body between conception and birth. Possession, on the other hand, is where entry by a discarnate personality occurs some time after embryonic development.[15]

Earlier, Stevenson presented another instance, this time from India, which fulfilled criteria very similar to his evidence for reincarnation. But here again, the deceased individual died when the second person was three and a half years old, again supporting the possession scenario.[16] Even so, Stevenson does not believe that this discarnate spirit thesis best accounts for many of the cases he cites.

But other pro-reincarnation researchers evaluate the demonic possession scenario more positively than Stevenson does. William de Arteaga concludes, concerning past-life visions: "In reference to the demonic counterfeit hypothesis, we can safely say that for many PLVs it is the most solidly verified hypothesis of all."[17] Regression hypnotist Helen Wambach, an often-cited authority, explains that she had always been aware of the reports of others in the field who testified that demonic possession was a danger in dealing with hypnotism. Then, as she had her own experiences with hypnotism, she discovered the truth involved in these initial reports.[18] Rabindranath R. Maharaj, a former Hindu guru, makes an interesting and somewhat similar observation. He explains how his religion was almost indistinguishable from occultic and demonic practices. In one place he described it like this: "My world was filled with spirits and gods and occult powers, and my obligation from childhood was to give each its due."[19] It is at least possible that Eastern religions, such as Hinduism, by their very nature and practice invite demonic possession.

Still other reincarnation critics also agree with the likelihood of possession as a viable explanation for apparent reincarnation cases.[20] One researcher tells about a well-known novelist who claimed to have been reincarnated more than a dozen times. However, the historical details of earlier ages cited in the author's novels were provided, not by her past existences, but by her personal link to a spirit "Presence."[21] This suggests another possible alternative to the reincarnation thesis and even the possession views, for it shows that the so-called evidences for reincarnation could be coming from deceptive, nonhuman spirit beings.

But if so much evidence can be explained by either discarnate or demonic possession, or even by other viewpoints, how does Stevenson choose between one of these options and reincarnation? Actually, he seems to think that while possession generally changes one's personality, the child's emotions and behavior favor the reincarnation hypothesis. Thus, true emotional responses, familiar behavior, mannerisms, habits, and skills appropriate to the situation favor natural, intimate, and personal knowledge. Stevenson believes that this is one of the strongest types of evidence in favor of reincarnation.[22]

But if this is the chief way to distinguish varieties of possession from reincarnation, it raises some serious problems. For example, how can we really be dogmatic about the differences between "possession behavior" and "reincarnation behavior"? Do we know enough about either? And doesn't the rather classic distinction between possession and obsession (the latter involves a milder power being exerted by the invading spirit, which strongly influences, but does not possess the person) blur the distinction enough to make differentiations such as Stevenson's even more questionable?

Also, if another personality or spirit has enough control to speak through a child and successfully impart large quantities of information through her, would controlling her behavior, emotions, and mannerisms be so much more difficult?[23] Wouldn't this be even more likely if, over a period of time, she had already come to (rather impressionably) accept the spirit of the other deceased person as herself?

Perhaps the most difficult issue concerns this: If one prefers the possibility of discarnate possession by the spirit of another deceased human being as the best explanation, why wouldn't the other person be genuinely excited to see his old loved ones and friends? In other words, it would seem quite proper that the appropriate emotions, behavior, mannerisms, habits, and skills would all seem to follow quite naturally from such a situation.

Lastly, since some of Stevenson's children even knew the exact location of "their" former bodies after death, this scenario provides at least equal support for possession.[24] It would appear more difficult (but admittedly still possible) to argue that such locations would be known *before* their burial by reincarnated spirits of those who had died.

In short, researchers and theorists have not proved that these cases demand reincarnation. Other alternatives remain at least equally possible. In fact, there are several cases where either discarnate or demonic possession serves as the best explanation and seems to be accepted as such by most researchers, including Stevenson himself. So the possession scenario—a spirit entering another body after birth—rules out reincarnation in those instances. And we know this has occurred in a number of cases where the deceased person died after the birth of the individual who was later influenced. Additionally, there is yet no fail-safe way to determine that another spirit must have entered before birth, as required on the reincarnation hypothesis. Hence reincarnationists have not established their claims.

In fact, to tighten this critique further, why would even prebirth spirit entry necessitate the conclusion that reincarnation had occurred? It would appear that at least demonic possession is still possible in such cases. Indeed, as far as we can tell, discarnate possession would also be feasible in such circumstances.

Perhaps one could argue that a prebirth occupancy would, by definition, be reincarnation or, conversely, that reincarnation can also occur after birth. But we would respond that, with either answer, the concept of reincarnation loses all meaning. For if all prebirth spirit entries are termed *reincarnation,* we still wonder why possession cannot also occur before birth. It certainly seems possible, and, if it is, either variety of possession in prebirth instances does nothing to further the idea that individuals are reborn many times—which is all-important in a reincarnationist model.

On the other hand, if reincarnation is possible *after* birth, it would involve the invasion of a body that already had a spirit. In this instance, the mechanism of reincarnation becomes almost identical to discarnate possession. And then what could constitute evidence specifically for reincarnation?

So the problem is this: If reincarnation is prebirth entry into a body, it is almost impossible to distinguish it from prebirth varieties of possession. On the other hand, post-birth reincarnation is not an option because spirit entry into the body at that point would be at the expense of the person's already-resident spirit. In this case, therefore, reincarnation would collapse into another form of possession. However, there are cases of post-birth possession, as we already detailed, but cases of reincarnation are extremely difficult to demonstrate, since the data could also indicate possession. No matter how you look at it, reincarnation gets the short end of the evidential stick.

More Problems for Reincarnation

But we can go farther. Consider, for instance the problem of verification, which Douglas Lackey thinks is the major problem with reincarnation data. The dilemma is this: Either the phenomena in question are evidenced, or they are not. If there is no evidence, then the claims need not be believed. But if there are corroborative findings, the person claiming to have lived the past life could have discovered the data in the same manner that the researcher did: by hearing it from someone else. In other words, if an investigation yields some evidence, could these facts not have been known or uncovered the same way by the original persons involved? Thus, it would be difficult to ever finally determine that the data *prove* reincarnation.[25]

Another problem that questions the testimony for reincarnation is causal in nature. Why is it generally assumed, both by the experiencer and the researcher, that if someone correctly remembers details of a past life, it must therefore, be *that* person's past life?

In other words, how do we jump the gap between an individual's detailed knowledge pertaining to a person who lived in the past and the assumption that the two people are one and the same? The experiencer may feel strongly that he was that other person, but the point here is how we would know this is so. All his "recollection" shows is that he possesses some knowledge of another person who once lived. The identity question requires further evidence, which reincarnationists have yet to supply.[26]

Yet another problem concerns reincarnation's supposed compatibility with Christianity. In the Judeo-Christian tradition, where resurrection is the afterlife model, God is personal and active, and history is one of the arenas of his domain. But in the reincarnation model, whatever view of deity is espoused, God is usually thought of as impersonal and passive,[27] and there is little room for miraculous intervention in history.

Further, dualism, a key tenet of Christianity, is the best model for the nature of persons. But most Eastern views accept monism, and virtually all Eastern perspectives denigrate the self and human personality, contrary to Christian teachings.

Additionally, by far most reincarnationists accept the concept of karma, which holds that all the actions in one's earlier lives affect one's future lives. Aside from the fact that Christianity maintains we live once, die, then live again in another state, never to be reborn and repeat the process, the karma doctrine opposes the biblical concepts of grace and mercy. Our past acts can be forgiven and their effects altered, minimized, and even eliminated.[28]

We are not saying that Christianity and Eastern thought are totally opposed to each other. In fact, Eastern thought is so diverse that we could find some significant traditions that would embrace some of the points just raised, such as dualism. However, in spite of a few exceptions, there exist some critical, fundamental worldview differences that cannot be reconciled, as we have just shown.

Now you may be wondering what the big deal is. So what if some Christian tenets disagree with Eastern ones? Does that automatically make the Christian tradition superior? No, but remember where we have taken you.

We have walked you through enough argumentation on the subjects of dualism (Chaps. 2–3), the resurrection of Jesus (Chap. 4), and the truthfulness of Jesus' theistic message (Chap. 9) to demonstrate some of the weighty evidence in favor of Christian theism. In fact, we think this data alone is sufficient to provide an adequate critique of the portion of the general Eastern message that opposes it. So when we show irreconcilable differences between Christianity and Eastern thought, particularly the Eastern view of reincarnation, Christianity has the upper hand because of the evidence that supports its validity.

Now let's press on to another problem with reincarnation. Many researchers think that the data used to support reincarnation can be accounted for by telepathy or other forms of extra sensory perception (ESP). While Stevenson argues, and quite well we should add, that these explanations do not explain all of the details of his research,[29] many others think that limited uses of this objection still do fit a fair amount of the data.[30] Consider an example.

Snyder introduces the case of the psychic, Peter Hurkos. He displayed the psychic ability of providing information that helped in solving crimes. In carefully documented situations, Hurkos demonstrated very precise knowledge of cases as famous as the stolen Stone of Scone (the British royal coronation stone kept at Westminster Abbey) and the Boston Strangler murders. In the case of the stolen stone, Hurkos was correct in his information about the setting of the theft, the course taken by the thieves (including street names!), their final destination, motives, time of return, and even some private items concerning the thieves. Indeed, Hurkos was "one of the most celebrated and astounding examples of retrocognition in modern history." Time and again he provided details concerning people, events, and things of the past, with an accuracy rate of 87–99 percent! Snyder concludes that the degree of precision demonstrated in his knowledge of the past is "found only occasionally in the evidence for reincarnation."

However, Hurkos's information was known completely apart from any claim to have been another individual at some time past. In these and other similarly well-documented cases, reincarnation is not a part of the scenario.[31] So if such information about the past can be gathered apart from reincarnation, could this phenomenon also account for at least some of the data used to support reincarnation? A number of researchers would answer yes.[32]

What about xenoglossy? Can it escape all these criticisms? No. Here is another place where our earlier comments on possession—either discarnate or demonic—also apply. Even Stevenson states that once the normal learning of language is dismissed, "The explanatory hypotheses become helpfully reduced and almost restricted to possession and reincarnation."[33] So while our earlier comments on possession would also explain xenoglossy (both recitative and responsive), other lesser explanations may also be helpful. One much-discussed phenomenon is cryptomnesia (also spelled cryptoamnesia), which occurs when individuals forget information they had previously learned yet still recall the data at a later time without knowledge of its source. Though we will discuss this in detail shortly, we want to note here that the later repetition of foreign terms learned (or even heard) at an earlier date is a well-known experience. This probably would account for cases of recitative xenoglossy better than the responsive variety.[34]

Researchers Badham and Badham add that, when recitative xenoglossy is the only form present, this alone constitutes a problem. Why, they ask, should such a fundamental feature of one's own claimed former life not be present? In other words, since both speaking and thinking are generally formulated in terms of one's language, to "forget" such a mainstay of one's existence while lesser points are remembered would be highly unlikely.[35]

What about birthmarks and deformities that appear to conform to similar blemishes on the deceased individual? Do these constitute solid evidence for reincarnation? No. As Stevenson, Badham and Badham all point out, just because mystics sometimes develop physical manifestations, such as the stigmata corresponding to the wounds that Jesus suffered on the cross, this does not make them reincarnations of Jesus![36]

How would wounds of any kind, however similar, prove that two people were one and the same? Similarity does not prove sameness.

On the other hand, how can we account for blemishes like these? Some researchers appeal to psychosomatic or demonic origins.[37] But by what means could a spirit (either reincarnated, discarnate, or demonic) mark a human body?[38] Even if the answer would presumably be that by some means, though perhaps unknown, they have that ability, we are no closer to discovering which of the three types of spirit involvement is the case. Possession could still very well be the answer.[39] In short, the major problems here are at least two: how any kind of marks could prove that two persons are the same, and the ambiguity involved in the type of spiritual activity causing the blemishes, if spiritual activity it is.

Finally, it is not a plausible thesis to maintain that the Bible teaches reincarnation. But because a full-scale exegesis of the relevant texts would take us well beyond the scope of this single chapter and because the more scholarly reincarnation researchers usually are unconcerned with a biblical justification for reincarnation,[40] we will keep our response brief and general.

Apart from the fact that numerous Bible passages directly contradict reincarnation, numerous theological, philosophical, and moral teachings in Scripture also oppose reincarnation. In fact, the whole tenor of the Bible is against the reincarnation hypothesis. As Snyder concludes, " 'Biblical evidence' for reincarnation amounts to little more than a short catalogue of difficult Bible references, references that are sufficiently difficult to court misunderstanding or incomprehension."[41] The Bible teaches resurrection, not reincarnation; an active, personal God, not a passive, impersonal force; grace and mercy, not the inexorable law of karma.

Some Lesser but Significant Objections

Besides the major difficulties just mentioned, there are some lesser problems that, while they are still important, do not apply as broadly to reincarnation and its alleged evidences. Nevertheless, they can still explain some of the claimed data for reincarnation.

First, we already briefly introduced the subject of cryptomnesia. Human beings consciously forget much of what they observe and learn, then selectively recall a number of those facts on later occasions as they are reminded of similar circumstances. While this certainly does not explain all (or even most) of the data for reincarnation, it can account for some hypnosis phenomena, recitative xenoglossy, and certain (sometimes specific) memories of the past, perhaps of the deja vu variety.

Badham and Badham recount a very complex example of cryptomnesia, complete with incredibly precise details of an ancient time. Yet, unconsciously known to the woman experiencing the "regression," she had an excellent capacity to remember novels and other materials she had read, sometimes adapting them in a form very close to the original source. Once she understood the source of her memories, she abandoned belief in her reincarnation.[42]

Albrecht supplies another detailed case where, under hypnosis, the subject spoke a few words in an ancient, obscure tongue. However, in another hypnosis session, it was revealed that the man had recently looked over a grammar text for that particular language.[43] Several researchers agree that cryptomnesia provides some explanatory value in such cases.[44]

A second problem concerns the cultural conditioning involved in reincarnation research. The twenty cases in Stevenson's major study were taken from India (7), Alaska (7), Ceylon (3), Brazil (2), and Lebanon (1). The strong belief in reincarnation in many of these areas can potentially explain certain conditioning factors that could encourage unconscious effects on "objective" research data. As an example, suggestive adults could play a large part in prejudicing children toward certain beliefs. In fact, why would most of the subjects be children, who are among the most suggestive of persons?[45]

Stevenson acknowledges this issue. He points out that reincarnation cases vary widely from culture to culture in both frequency of occurrence and amount of evidential particulars. American cases, for example, "are much weaker in details than those in non-Western countries, such as Asia. American children who say they remember previous lives rarely recall many details that would permit verification. When they do remember some verifiable details, they are usually those in the life of another member of the family."[46]

So it seems that the strong belief in reincarnation, in the locations where the data are frequently gathered, sometimes affects the reporting of the information. The fact that research from other regions diverges so much would lead us to this conclusion.[47]

Now we are not arguing that the geographic origin of these reincarnation accounts can explain their content. If reincarnation is true, it is true whether the evidence for it comes from one part of the world or another.[48] But, we cannot ignore that certain conditioning factors *could* impact this evidence and its reporting. Psychological and cultural factors do influence our beliefs, but that does not discount their possible truthfulness.

A third response to the reincarnation thesis comes from the suggestion of some researchers that, in Hick's words, the data are not "raw" enough—too much time can allow unconscious contamination of the findings. Hick thinks that even Stevenson's research cases are at fault here, which can only "reduce their evidential value."[49] Albrecht agrees, citing the absence of written information prior to the investigation, the unreliability of memories and perception, the general lack of neutral observation, and the average gap of three to five years between the initial symptoms and the publicity.[50] Stevenson has acknowledged at least the tenor of some of these points.[51] As with our discussion of NDEs, this would not necessarily invalidate the data, but it should make us more cautious.

Fourth, several problems with hypnosis plague those reincarnation studies that use it, generally in order to "regress" patients. For example, patients frequently wish to oblige the request of the hypnotist to produce evidence of past lives, performing what they are asked to.[52] Stevenson appears to agree with this assessment, and he does not use this technique in order to derive his own data. He explains why he shuns hypnosis:

> The "personalities" usually evoked during hypnotically induced regressions to a "previous life" seem to comprise a mixture of several ingredients. These may include the subject's current personality, his expectations of what he thinks the hypnotist wants, his fantasies of what he thinks his previous life ought to have been, and also perhaps elements derived paranormally.[53]

We commend Stevenson for disregarding hypnosis in spite of the claimed evidence for reincarnation it supposedly provides.[54] John Hick lodges a related objection to hypnosis, also refusing to believe its results: "I shall not discuss here the numerous cases of 'memories' of other lives elicited under hypnosis, because there is no support from professional psychologists for the view that these are other than examples of response to suggestion."[55] Admittedly, this specific critique may not affect the best cases proposed in favor of reincarnation. But it does apply to those instances that utilize hypnosis.

Fifth, a series of moral questions is often suggested as another sort of problem with reincarnation and the general philosophical worldview most frequently associated with it. Many are bothered by the implications of karmic theory and its repercussions. Hick, for instance, asks about the sense in which persons in the present reap what they have sown in the past.[56] Is there real, honest continuity where I gain or lose based on my perceived action in past times, especially since most persons do not recall this continuity, at least not very clearly?

Lackey poses a very similar objection. A thousand years from now, our reincarnations will have a different personality and, obviously, a different body, with nothing but the vaguest memories of our present life. So he asks, "By what stretch of the imagination is that future incarnation *me?*"[57]

Moreover, what does karma say about those who suffer greatly? Are they all moral reprobates? And do these reprobates generally get "dumped" in certain parts of the world where the conditions are quite poor? Should we also accept the caste system and other forms of social injustice on the basis of this hypothesis? Does the concept of karma even promote justice? Does karma encourage moral procrastination? And why should good karma survive more than bad karma? Or for that matter, why should good karma be commended at all?[58]

Sixth and last, the possibility of fraud (in the sense of either "outright fakery" or "inadvertent or subconscious manipulation of spurious facts and details"[59]) must be allowed, at least in some cases. Most scholars highly compliment Stevenson's work, for example, and agree that this criticism is generally inappropriate for his data.[60] But other actual examples reveal that this is a realistic concern.

The most frequently cited case of fraud is the famous Bridey Murphy episode. Under hypnosis, it was claimed that Ruth Simmons regressed to early nineteenth-century Ireland, where she had lived and was named Bridey Murphy. It was reported that she spoke Gaelic, had a deep Irish accent, and provided specialized details concerning customs and geography of the times, including details about her home and church. This information was disseminated in a widely read book and movie. An intense investigation followed, but the parish records of the county where Simmons claimed to have lived revealed no such person as Bridey Murphy. Furthermore, the church she said she had attended wasn't even built until more than one hundred years after her birth.

Other details were also uncovered. Simmons had lived with her Irish grandmother, who taught her Gaelic, and spoke with a heavy Irish brogue. She also told her granddaughter tales of the "old country." Finally, one of Simmons' next-door neighbors was actually named Bridey Murphy![61]

In this case, few will charge conscious fraud. But even unintentional misrepresentation must be considered. Albrecht describes three other cases where intentional or unintentional fraud of some sort played a major role.[62]

To be sure, other criticisms have been levelled at reincarnation, but we think that some of these responses are weak or otherwise misplaced. For example, some critics have argued the possibility of Jung's collective unconscious as the avenue for knowing precise details concerning the past, or that memory is transmitted through genetic structure. Hick thinks that reincarnation is opposed by modern genetic theory. Others have questioned the beliefs and motivations of the researchers.[63] But in our opinion, these responses tend to miss the mark, rely on unproven assumptions, or explain too little of the data. But as we have shown, there are plenty of other reasons to reject reincarnation as a viable alternative to the Christian understanding of life after death.

The Verdict

Our conclusion, therefore, is that reincarnation has no real evidence in its favor that cannot be seriously challenged on its own grounds or accounted for by other explanations. Reincarnation simply does not offer any true or distinctive answer to the nature of life after death.

In fact, possession does an even *better* job explaining several cases that exhibited all the appropriate earmarks, while, on the other hand, reincarnation was not possible in those instances. But further, it is certainly debatable if any case of reincarnation could ever be proven due to the possibility that possession could also account for prebirth examples of a spirit's entering another's body.

However, there is a strange twist to our conclusion. Even if there is no evidence for reincarnation, our discussion still produced another sort of consideration in favor of an afterlife. Since there is evidence for possession of a body by another spirit, this would appear to constitute some "back door" data in favor of a spiritual world of some sort where life after death is distinctly possible, if not likely. This being so, two points follow: At a minimum, the truth of naturalism is now even less likely, if not disproven. This is important by itself. But even further, if spirits exist and can enter and direct bodies, then we have an added support for dualism. Both of these points make life after death an even more likely fact.

Chapter 9

The Afterlife's Ultimate Model

Life after death is real. It exists. We have enough evidence to say this.

As we have also seen, life after life after life . . . is not real. The evidence for reincarnation is insufficient for us to conclude otherwise.

Then there's Jesus of Nazareth. He not only lived and died, but he did what no other human being has ever done—after three days he rose alive from the dead in a transformed state. Once again, even the minimal amount of evidence we considered is adequate to establish this event.

So where does this leave us? In a very profound position. We can know that we have one opportunity to live our current lives. Once we die, we will pass on to another type of conscious, personal existence in another realm, never to return to live the same kind of earthly life we do now. In Chapter 7, we got a glimpse of what this afterlife will be like, at least in its intermediate state. We have come a long way in our search.

But many questions still remain. One of the most pressing ones is "What else can we know about the afterlife?" An answer to this question will form the core of our inquiry in this chapter and the next two. Here we will look once again to the phenomenon of the resurrected Jesus as the ultimate model of and certainty for what life in a resurrected state will be like. In the following two chapters, we will further explore the nature of our resurrected state and consider the ultimate destinations available to us, as well as several issues these options raise. Our search is far from over. There are many more intriguing areas to explore.

The Resurrected Jesus

In one of the most inspirational texts in the New Testament, the apostle Peter explains that Jesus' resurrection provides Christians with the ultimate certainty of heaven (1 Peter 1:3–4). Because Jesus was raised, Peter tells us, believers are assured that their eternal home is indestructible and without flaw or blemish. In fact, these qualities are "reserved" or "guarded" on behalf of believers. So the nature and blessings of heaven will neither become corrupted nor be taken away. And all of this is due to Jesus' resurrection from the dead.

So Jesus' resurrection is more than some dusty historical event that has little application to our lives today or tomorrow. The New Testament relates it to a number of truths of ultimate value, some of a very personal and practical nature. And none of these are more pertinent to our futures than those that deal with our lives beyond the grave.

Jesus' resurrection provides the basis for the reality of eternal life. Yes, we have other evidence, but none as solid and verifiable as his rising from the dead.

His resurrection also gives us the ultimate model of certain facets of our future existence. For Christians, it furnishes at least an initial road map of heaven.

Perhaps we're moving too fast. We're assuming something we need to establish: a link between Jesus' resurrection and the resurrection of believers. Is there such a link? The New Testament writers thought so. They coupled these two events more than a dozen times.[1] But can this link be established? Were the New Testament writers right? Let's see.

Miracles as Evidence

The resurrection is not a natural event; it is not a regular happening in the world we experience. It is not even an irregular one. It is, however, a miracle: an event performed by the direction of God or some other supernatural agent that appears to temporarily set aside the known laws of nature. Further, miracles seem to occur in order to confirm or verify a religious message.[2]

Now what we need to know is if miracles can point beyond themselves. Can they count as evidence for something else? We think so, and here are a few considerations that indicate, in general, that this is so.

(1) Genuine miracles, by the very nature of their awe-inspiring character, tend to point beyond themselves to the confirmation of some message, usually of a religious nature. As philosopher Richard Swinburne explains, this is a common ingredient in the concept of a miracle.[3] For example, Swinburne argues that miracles can, in fact, provide some evidence for God's existence and activity.[4]

(2) Jesus specifically claimed that his miracles validated his teachings.[5] Numerous critical scholars concede this point,[6] which serves as a contemporary witness that Jesus connected his performance of miracles with the truthfulness of his claims.

(3) As Pannenberg argues, Jesus put himself in God's place by many of his teachings and actions and was therefore judged by the Jews to be a blasphemer (Mark 14:61–64; John 5:16–18, 10:32–33). When he was raised from the dead, others in the first century interpreted it as God's vindication of Jesus and his teachings.[7]

Another way to look at these three points is this: Jesus' entire life was characterized by unique theological claims, such as his offer to forgive sins, which was properly recognized as a prerogative of God alone (Mark

2:1–12); his statements regarding his unique relationship to God (Matt. 11:27; Mark 14:36); his teaching that he was the only way to God (Matt. 19:28–29), which set his testimony above that of the Jewish authorities (Matt. 5:20–48); and his affirmation of his deity in the context of the Jews' charge of blasphemy (Mark 14:61–64). Critical scholarship recognizes a number of these aspects of Jesus' career (see the next section). Therefore, since Jesus was literally raised from the dead, this miracle provides some substantiation for the truthfulness of his claims. Why would God resurrect a liar?

Moreover, Jesus' personal theistic worldview is expressed by the various aspects of his unique theological claims and teachings. And although the particulars cannot be defended here, much of Jesus' preaching, especially concerning the kingdom of God, is distinctive, even in the field of comparative religion. As Stephen Neill has attested in his well-known study of world religions, taking the Gospels seriously (but as critically as one likes) still reveals the singular nature of Jesus' message: "Jesus is not in the least like anyone else who has ever lived. The things he says about God are not the same as the sayings of any other religious teacher. The claims he makes for himself are not the same as those that have been made by any other religious teacher."[8]

When you add to this Jesus' teachings concerning the confirmatory value of his miracles (as well as the nature of miracles in general) and the reason Jewish leaders hated his message, you have a unique leader and teacher further establishing the truthfulness of his message through supernatural events. But there's still more.

Lastly (and perhaps most significantly), the evidence indicates not only that Jesus was raised from the dead, but that it is the only justifiable resurrection claim in history.[9]

So the only time that a resurrection is known to have occurred, it happened to the only person who made such unique religious claims. In short, his unique claims were ultimately validated by the miraculous nature of his resurrection from the dead.[10]

Similar arrangements of the evidence have impressed many renowned scholars. For instance, Swinburne points out that numerous claims surrounding Jesus are unique among the major theistic religions of the world and that extraordinary miraculous events are potentially a means of providing evidence for such teachings.[11] Pannenberg asserts that the unity between Jesus' declarations and his resurrection provides confirmation of his mission and of his death.[12] And even the eminent atheist Antony Flew has agreed that if the resurrection actually occurred, naturalists would have to be open to Jesus' teachings concerning the Christian theistic view of the universe, including his claims to be God, even if it meant changing their naturalistic worldview.[13]

Of course, this brief discussion does not prove the whole of Jesus' teachings or their unique qualities. Such a topic extends beyond our present purposes. But we do argue that miracles point to an additional reality beyond themselves. In particular, we want to focus on how the miracle of Jesus' resurrection guarantees the eternal life of believers.

Jesus as Spokesman for God

The Gospel texts clearly indicate that Jesus' central teaching was the kingdom of God and its entrance requirements.[14] He repeatedly called individuals to act in light of its reality by responding to his message.

Interestingly, critical scholars generally agree that this is the major area that shows Jesus firmly believed he was God's chosen spokesman. It is also the topic on which Jesus' authority is most evident, for he taught that people would be held accountable by how they responded to this message.[15] Raymond Brown states it this way: "An irreducible historical minimum in the Gospel presentation of Jesus is that he claimed to be the unique agent in the process of establishing God's kingship over men. He proclaimed that in *his* preaching and through *his* deeds God's kingship over men was making itself felt."[16] Brown adds that this message of the kingdom was the outstanding, or unique, portion of Jesus' teachings, and it was so from the beginning of his ministry.[17]

Contemporary critical scholars have generally agreed with Brown's conclusion. For instance, Rudolf Bultmann notes that in the person, deeds, and message of Jesus, the kingdom was actually dawning. Individuals had to choose whether to follow Jesus or not; he called them to decision.[18]

Reginald Fuller asserts that "God is directly present in the word of Jesus, actively demanding unreserved obedience to his will from those who have accepted the eschatological message and its offer of salvation."[19] Fuller adds that this call to salvation centered around the person of Jesus himself: "An examination of Jesus' words . . . his call for decision . . . his calling men to follow him . . . forces upon us the conclusion that underlying his word and work is an implicit Christology. In Jesus as he understood himself, there is an immediate confrontation with 'God's presence and his very self,' offering judgment and salvation."[20]

Pannenberg likewise concurs that Jesus revealed God as no other man has ever done before or since. In Jesus' person and message, God disclosed himself to man in a unique way.[21]

Thus, people could enter the kingdom of God if they responded properly to Jesus' message. As Strawson observes, "Throughout our Lord's teaching there is a continual emphasis upon the urgent need to meet the conditions God requires for entry into eternal life."[22] What were those conditions? Strawson summarizes them by saying they are fulfilled only by dependence on Jesus Christ, who is himself the way to such a life. Only then can persons be properly related to both God and humanity.[23]

The Gospels readily present the requirements for entering the kingdom.

In Jesus' teachings, all people were sinners in need of forgiveness (Luke 24:47; cf. Mark 8:38). While humans cannot save themselves (Matt. 19:25–26), Jesus stated that he would die in order to pay the penalty for their sin (Matt. 26:18; Mark 10:45). The conditions for salvation were, therefore, repentance (Luke 13:1–5) and a faith-surrender to Jesus and his message, when once met provided the means for entering into the kingdom of God and eternal life (Mark 1:15; Luke 24:47; John 6:47). The result was a changed life of service (Luke 10:25–37; 14:25–35). In brief, Jesus did what humans could not,[24] and provided the basis for their faith response to him and his message.

We need to add one related matter: Jesus also taught that eternal life was not just the life of the future world alone. In fact, believers do not even have to wait until death in order to experience it. Eternal life actually begins now, during this earthly life, for those who respond in faith to Jesus' message (John 3:36; 6:47; 1 John 5:13).[25] Thus, there is continuity between the believer's present life and the life of the kingdom.

Eternal Life: Jesus' Central Message

To repeat, Jesus' central message was the reality of the kingdom of God and the call to participation in it. This is admitted by almost all critical scholars across the entire theological spectrum; seldom is it disputed.[26] Further, the gospel texts make it clear that Jesus' call to decision regarding entrance into the kingdom cannot be separated from his offer of eternal life to those who comply with the condition, for such is the life of the coming kingdom age.[27]

Once again, critical scholars generally agree. Bultmann notes that the salvation of the kingdom consists not of national prosperity, "But in the glory of paradise." He then mentions some of Jesus' teachings concerning the activities of the redeemed in the next life.[28] Bornkamm relates that Jesus' call to a decision involved future salvation and life with God for those who respond and judgment for those who do not.[29] Strawson shows that eternal life is an integral, inseparable part of the kingdom of God.[30] And Ladd points out that entering the kingdom is essentially entering eternal life.[31]

Eternal Life: The Resurrection's Central Confirmation

Now we are prepared to move to our major point. Earlier we stated that Jesus was literally raised from the dead, and this event verified his basic teachings. Here we want to point out that Jesus' instruction about eternal life, since it was his central teaching, would be especially confirmed by his resurrection. In other words, if Jesus' resurrection validated any of his beliefs, it validated eternal life, since God would most of all have corroborated his chief message through his chief spokesman.

In fact, Jesus' resurrection actually provides two solid arguments for a Christian view of eternal life. First, as just mentioned, it establishes Jesus' authority and confirms at least his major message of kingdom immortality[32] for the believer.

But second, and easily overlooked, the risen Jesus is an actual example of the life after death that he taught. So if he was actually raised from the dead in a new, transformed body, as the eyewitnesses attested, then he provided a living example of the afterlife. And here the resurrection is unique, for no other miracle of Jesus—by its very nature—requires such a notion of life after death. Even when he raised other individuals from the dead, he raised them in their natural bodies, which meant they would die again. But a resurrection body is immortal, thus, it cannot experience death—ever.

Therefore, we have both an indirect argument for the Christian notions of eternal life and immortality (Jesus' teachings on his chief subject have been confirmed) and a direct one (Jesus actually exemplified such a transformed existence). Our case here is exceptionally strong.

To be sure, Jesus' resurrection is not the only evidence for life after death. But it is a crucial element in our strong, carefully built, multifaceted case. His resurrection provides very solid evidence for *eternal* life, as well as giving us a very personal model of some of its many characteristics. Jesus taught a personal concept of eternal life and then was raised in a glorified body as a literal example for eyewitnesses. His authority in his central teaching is established by this event, just as his post-resurrection appearances provided an actual example of the future resurrection life of Christians.

The implications of this conclusion are staggering. Renowned biblical scholar Raymond Brown points out a few for us to reflect on:

> We have indicated an area where his views were not at all those of his time, namely, the area of belief and behavior called for by the coming of the kingdom. And in this area, in my personal opinion, his authority is supreme for every century, because in this area he spoke for God. No age can reject the demand that one must believe in Jesus as the unique agent for establishing God's kingship over men (a uniqueness which the Church at Nicaea finally came to formulate in terms of Jesus' being "true God of true God").[33]

The Christian case rests on the historicity of Jesus' resurrection from the dead. This is the apostle Paul's point in 1 Corinthians 15:17-18, and this foundation is firm, as Paul also notes (vv. 20-22).

Eternal Life: Jesus, the Ultimate Model

Realizing that Jesus' resurrection provides solid evidence for eternal life, we can now deal with the model of eternal life Jesus gives us both in his teaching and by his example. In what kind of body was Jesus raised? What does this tell us about our future bodies?

Let's answer the second question first. We have already mentioned that, according to the New Testament, Christians will be raised from the dead with bodies like that of Jesus himself (1 Cor. 15:44–57; Phil. 3:21; 1 John 3:2; cf. John 14:19; Acts 4:2). This understanding is also naturally implicit in Jesus' teachings on eternal life. Now we can move back to the first question.

What were the characteristics of Jesus' resurrection body? It is common in some circles to answer this question by pitting the Gospels against Paul's writings, maintaining that the former, being written later, developed an overly strong emphasis on the bodily nature of Jesus' appearances. The Gospels show that Jesus' tomb was empty (with only his grave clothes) and present the post-resurrection Jesus in a body that displays his crucifixion wounds, a body that can be touched and heard by his disciples, a body that can consume food. It is said that Paul's writings, on the other hand, are earlier, and they champion objective but less physical appearances than the Gospels do.

Since this issue alone could be the subject of a major treatise, we will set some boundaries for our discussion. While some of the concerns here are more exegetical,[34] others tend to be more topical. Since I (Habermas) briefly addressed the former in another context,[35] I will concern myself here with the latter. It is my conviction that both the Gospels and Paul teach appearances of the risen Jesus that occurred in the same body in which Jesus was crucified.[36] Here are my reasons, concisely stated, for this conclusion.

(1) The future resurrection of the body was the predominant view in Judaism, especially among first-century Jews.[37] While this certainly does not prove Paul's view, it indicates a background against which his teachings would have been most likely viewed. When Paul identifies with or reacts to certain views of his day (see point 4 below), this general framework also provides very meaningful information.

(2) Not only is the term for resurrection *(anastasis)* best translated as referring to the body, but in one passage (Phil. 3:11), Paul specifically chose another form of this term *(exanastasis)*, which literally means the "resurrection out from among the dead." The physical body is brought back to life. Similarly, when Paul states that Jesus died, was buried, and afterward rose from the dead (1 Cor. 15:3–4), it would follow most naturally (but even more so in light of his above language) that it was Jesus' body that was raised up.

(3) In spite of the assertions of some scholars, Paul's repeated term for Jesus' appearances *(horao)* in 1 Corinthians 15:5–8 is far more frequently used in the New Testament for normal, physical sight than for visionary sight. This certainly does not solve the issue of the nature of Jesus' resurrected state in and of itself, but it is one more consideration in favor of our

overall conclusion.[38] Significantly, John in his Gospel also employs the same word to report unquestionably physical appearances of the resurrected Jesus (John 20:18, 20, 25, 29).

(4) Paul's position on the nature of the resurrection body is further clarified by those with whom he agrees and those with whom he does not. Identifying himself as a Pharisee (Phil. 3:4–5), Paul thereby indicates his previous adherence to a theological agenda. Luke tells us that Paul stated his agreement with the Pharisees specifically on the question of the resurrection of the dead, in contrast to the Sadducees who rejected this belief (Acts 23:6–8).

Then, on another occasion, we are told that the Greek philosophers who dialogued with Paul over the very subject of Jesus' resurrection disagreed with him precisely because he taught that Jesus' body was raised (Acts 17:31–34). In actuality, even without Luke's testimony, we would have a good idea of Paul's position just from his own statement that he was formerly a Pharisee (and a "Hebrew of Hebrews") on matters of theology, a comment that he did not abrogate.

(5) A crucial issue involves Paul's own anthropology. For him the term *soma* ("body") denotes a physical body, not some part of the person separated from his body. This can be seen, not only from passages where Paul addresses the subject in general, but especially where he juxtaposes *soma* with the spiritual or immaterial portion of man.[39]

After an intricate and authoritative study on this entire subject, New Testament scholar Robert Gundry concluded that there is simply massive evidence that *soma* indicates the physical body. On the topic of Paul's concept of Jesus' resurrection body, Gundry concludes that "the raising of Jesus from the dead was a raising of his physical body."[40]

John A.T. Robinson reached a similar conclusion after a critical study of Paul's anthropology, again specifically directed to Jesus' resurrection body:

All the appearances, in fact, depict the same phenomenon, of a body identical yet changed, transcending the limitations of the flesh yet capable of manifesting itself within the order of the flesh. We may describe this as a "spiritual" (1 Cor. 15:44) or "glorified" (cf. 1 Cor. 15:43; Phil. 3:21) body . . . so long as we do not import into these phrases any opposition to the physical as such.[41]

(6) The empty tomb is yet another indication that Jesus' resurrection was bodily in nature. Beyond the predominant Jewish view concerning resurrection or the meaning of the Greek term (see the first two reasons above), the most obvious interpretation for the empty tomb is that the body of Jesus, which had died and been buried, is the same one that had now been raised. It would be quite difficult for the Christian church to have started in Jerusalem, centering on the proclamation of Jesus' resurrection,

if his body was still occupying a local grave. And Paul, in recording the "died . . . buried . . . raised . . . appeared" scenario in 1 Corinthians 15:3-5, clearly implies the empty tomb and, hence, the most natural explanation that Jesus was raised in the same body.[42]

(7) Lastly, any evidence for the trustworthiness and inspiration of the Gospels would help confirm the bodily nature of the resurrection and appearance accounts they contain. Many scholars have done this, so we will not repeat their efforts here. But New Testament theologian A.M. Hunter echoes the conclusions of numerous thinkers: We have "sound reasons for believing that our Gospels are substantially reliable."[43] Of course, what is really needed is for each of the pertinent texts to be individually defended, which has also already been done.[44] But for our purposes, it is enough to know that good arguments have been marshalled in support of the Gospels and the relevant passages in particular, so we have yet more evidence that Jesus rose bodily.

For reasons such as these, then, the evidence indicates that Jesus was raised bodily from the dead and that there is no discrepancy at this juncture between the Gospels and Paul. As Gundry concludes the matter, "The resurrection of Christ was and the resurrection of Christians will be physical in nature."[45] Thus, this historical event serves as the model of and substantiation for the believer's resurrection.

A Christian's Certain Future

We have seen that genuine miracles are pointers to truths beyond themselves, and Jesus said on a number of occasions that such events indicated the truth of his message. His resurrection, as the chief miracle, was best understood as a vindication of his message.

We also saw that Jesus' central message was the reality of the kingdom of God and the entrance requirements for eternal life and immortality.[46] In this he most exhibited his influence and authority. And if Jesus' resurrection verified any message, it corroborated his chief theme.

Actually, the resurrection provides two strong reasons why Jesus' central message was true. Not only did God verify Jesus' chief message by this event, but of all Jesus' miracles, this is the only one that actually exemplifies life after death by its very nature. In fact, when the early eyewitnesses saw the risen Jesus, they actually experienced walking, talking eternal life. In short, to witness the resurrected Jesus was to witness the reality of the afterlife. It is no wonder this experience changed their lives forever.

We have presented: a number of reasons for the belief that Jesus rose and appeared in a time-space, bodily manner; the predominant first-century Jewish view of resurrection; the meaning of the New Testament terms (and especially Paul's word in Phil. 3:11); the general meaning of the word *horao* ("appeared"); Paul's identification with the view of the resurrection held by the Pharisees; the opposition to him by the Greek philosophers; his own anthropology. All of these are strong reasons to accept Jesus' bodily resurrection. But further, the empty tomb and the truth of the Gospels' resurrection texts provide additional arguments for the bodily nature of Jesus' appearances.

So, when connected with the distinctive teachings on the nature of eternal life and immortality by both Jesus and the writers of the New Testament, Jesus' resurrection from the dead provides Christians with a certainty for and a model of their own resurrection, eternal life, and immortality. And the study of the nature of Jesus' resurrection body leads to some definite hints concerning our future state. As an added benefit, Jesus even taught that eternal life begins now, in this earthly life. So Christians live in anticipation of that future state, since, as Paul tells us, we are already citizens of heaven!

So what will our bodily existence in heaven be like? This is the next topic of exploration.

Chapter 10

Heaven: The Great Adventure

Have you ever found yourself dreaming about the glories of heaven, perhaps after looking out across a starry sky? Or has heaven occupied your thoughts after the death of a loved one? Have you ever tried to answer a child's (or an adult's!) questions on this subject, realizing the implications of your own answers? Or maybe you have wondered yourself about what heaven holds in store for believers? Whatever scenario applies to you, if you are a Christian or simply familiar with Christianity, you have likely given some thought to heaven. And for good reason. If heaven will be the believer's place of eternal destiny, we ought to spend a little time dreaming about this subject. And that's just what we're going to do in this chapter.

We will attempt to do three things, moving throughout from the more known to the less known. We will begin by listing several aspects of heaven as outlined in Scripture. Then we will investigate some of the Bible's imagery of heaven, not because we should always take it literally, but because it contains some incredibly beautiful truths. Finally, we will move to a philosophical and theological treatment of certain other relevant issues where we are sometimes left more to our "sanctified guessing," which we hope will still be anything but groundless.

What Will Heaven Be Like?

Let's look at some of the more explicit biblical teachings on the nature of heaven[1] to see what Christians can look forward to.

For one thing, we will not have to look far. Eternal life *has already begun* in this life (John 6:47; 1 John 5:13). In fact, Paul tells us that believers are citizens of heaven right now. We don't even have to die to get a foretaste of the hereafter! We might encounter a bit of heaven in a longing pang for the hereafter, in a prompting of the Holy Spirit, or when we truly worship God or fellowship with him. Even a flash of insight, a movie, a good book, a piece of music, or fellowship with others can also awaken insights into the reality of heaven. This is all made possible by the resurrection of Jesus (John 11:25–26; Phil. 3:20–21).

We can also know that heaven exists as a *real* place, not as some imaginary realm or as simply the subject of children's tales or good fantasy volumes. Nor is heaven an empty "pie in the sky in the sweet by and by." We know that, since Jesus' resurrection appearances were actually the initial manifestations of eternal life, heaven is actual. It already exists; it is Jesus' current residence and our future home.

Heaven is also a *substantial* place. It is not simply a state of mind or some other sort of psychological reality. Neither is it just a place for spirits. This is revealed by the fact that Jesus' resurrection appearances were bodily in nature, and our bodies will be like his (Phil. 3:21; 1 John 3:2). Therefore, heaven is an actual place for real, substantial persons.

In addition to being both real and substantial, the life of heaven is *eternal* life. Heaven is far more than some mere utopia where people are happy and joyous but continue to get sick and die. Rather, heaven's inhabitants will never experience death again (John 11:25-26). This was the teaching of the resurrected Jesus. Believers will be like Jesus himself in this sense: they will live eternally (John 14:19; 2 Cor. 5:1; 1 Thess. 4:17).

We are also told that heaven will be *devoid of all negative qualities* (Rev. 7:15-17, 21:4). Again, beyond the kind of utopia where things are ideal most of the time, we have the assurance that heaven is qualitatively different. Sadness and those old enemies—pain and suffering—will be banished forever from our heavenly home.

Heaven will be a place of great activity. And at the top of that activity list will be *fellowship with Jesus* himself. After predicting his death, Jesus stated that he wouldn't drink "the fruit of the vine" again until he did so with his disciples in the kingdom of God (Matt. 26:27-29). Believers will have the opportunity not only to see their Lord Jesus face to face (1 John 3:2) but to spend eternity in his presence, both in the intermediate state (2 Cor. 5:8; Phil. 1:23) and in heaven itself (John 14:2-3; Rev. 22:4). What could be more glorious than to see Jesus' face at long last?

Believers will also be *glorified:* raised with Jesus, seated, and exalted with him in heaven (Eph. 2:6; Rom. 8:11, 17). Several texts teach that believers will be given positions of honor and authority in God's eternal kingdom, including reigning with him (2 Tim. 2:11-12; Rev. 5:9-10).

Still another heavenly occupation will be our *service to God* as priests (Rev. 5:10). This will be the ultimate ministry.

It appears that all believers will also join together in *praise* to Jesus Christ and his Father (Rev. 5:12). This will encompass the largest choir ever assembled, spontaneously singing praise that simply flows out of hearts filled with gratitude to God.

Moreover, the *collective aspect* of heavenly activity promises to be a blessed one. Old Testament theology emphasized the resurrection of the entire nation—the righteous would rise together (Isa. 26:19; Dan. 12:1-3). In the New Testament, Paul speaks of the resurrection of the dead in the plural: Dead and living believers will be raised together, sharing in this marvelous event (1 Thess. 4:16-17). So we will be reunited with our believing loved ones who died before us. Many other passages indicate the fellowship believers will share with each other in heaven (Matt. 8:11; 1

Cor. 12:13; Rev. 21:26–27). Even our praise to God in heaven will be done together (Rev. 5:11–13).

Another of the most stimulating aspects of heavenly life will be our *continued growth* in knowledge and truth, thereby increasing our awareness of God and his works. Paul explains that, throughout the future ages, believers will be shown "the incomparable riches of his grace" (Eph. 2:7 NIV). This conclusion concerning our future growth can also be inferred from the very nature of human beings. Although we will be resurrected, we will still be glorified, finite human beings, not omniscient wonders. And part of our very nature as sentient beings is to learn as we live.

As if all of this were not enough, the redeemed, raised, and glorified bodies of believers are not the only things to be made new. Fallen creation itself will be "redeemed" by *God's new creation* (Rom. 8:19–23, especially vv. 21–23). The new earth will be characterized by righteousness without evil (2 Peter 3:13; Rev. 21:25–27). God's newly created world will be the perfect complement for redeemed people. Here we have the hope of an entirely new universe to observe, learn from, inhabit, and enjoy.

On top of everything else, Peter explains that Jesus' resurrection guarantees that our heavenly inheritance itself "can never perish, spoil or fade" (see 1 Peter 1:3–4 NIV). Peter's specific choice of Greek terms *(aphthartos, amiantos, amarantos)* to describe these qualities of heaven insures that *our blessings are incorruptible and indestructible,* without either flaw or blemish.

Peter also declares that these benefits are "kept" or "reserved," for believers (1 Peter 1:4), using a word *(tereo)* which indicates that they are being "guarded on our behalf." This last comment is perhaps reminiscent of a somewhat related Pauline idea (2 Tim. 1:12). Heaven's very nature, characteristics, and blessings will not be stolen from believers nor otherwise become corrupted. Our eternal inheritance is not in some large bank somewhere, but guarded for us by the grace and power of God himself.

Indeed, heaven is truly a multifaceted and glorious paradise. Even though many of its details have been disclosed, we should remind ourselves that there is also very much about it that we do not yet know (1 Cor. 13:12; 1 John 3:2). In fact, we would even suggest that we adopt a type of "Christmas morning" view of heaven, which allows us to anticipate its glories and blessings without attempting to delineate exactly how all of these many details work themselves out. It is enough for believers to know and look forward to this much: Heaven will be an incomparable time of eternal fellowship with Jesus Christ and with other loved ones. Knowing that makes all the difference in the world.

The Imagery of Heaven

Throughout Scripture, a number of metaphors and other figures of speech invoke deep impressions concerning the afterlife. These images may imply more concerning what awaits us than does straightforward prose. In other words, what Scripture *doesn't* say literally may sometimes be more important than what it does spell out in specific terms.

We have already spoken of a "Christmas morning" image of heaven, whereby believers take a "wait and see" attitude toward the exact nature of the afterlife. And that's okay. The parent-child motif used to describe our relationship to God tells us that, like children, we know enough about our Father to expect the best. He won't let us down.

Jesus once remarked that the kingdom of God had been prepared for believers since the very creation of the world itself (Matt. 25:34). And while Jesus gave a fair number of details concerning eternal life, as do other biblical figures, the particulars are not as much as some might expect. Further, Scripture explains that we are not told everything about life after death.[2] So in this statement about God's preparation of the kingdom for us, our minds can roam free, within the parameters of Scripture. (We will do some of that roaming later in this chapter.) I find myself wondering what an omniscient, omnipotent God could have in store for us. The possibilities are limitless![3]

So what do we learn about the afterlife from the Bible's images? How is our imagination kindled? Some of the most profound and comforting thoughts that weave their way throughout the Scripture culminate in picturesque descriptions of heaven. Sometimes the same ideas can be traced all the way through the Old Testament, the teachings of Jesus, and the book of Revelation. These deep-seated, immensely meaningful images are tied to our concepts of eternity.

For instance, peace is one of humanity's deepest longings. Thus, Psalm 23:1-3 is a famous text in Scripture, with the Lord portrayed as the Shepherd who meets the innermost needs of his people, leading them to green pastures, beside quiet waters, and providing for their peaceful rest.[4] This same theme is found in John 10:1-16, where Jesus is the Good Shepherd who calls his sheep by name and leads them out to find pasture. The sheep hear, recognize,and follow him. The Shepherd also protects his sheep and gives his life for them.

Carrying the shepherd imagery into the heavenly scene in Revelation 7:15-17, the Lamb on the throne spreads a tent over his people who have persevered through the Great Tribulation, and then he becomes their Shepherd and leads them to springs of living water. The believers are protected from all problems and will no longer experience pain and suffering, which strongly suggests that heaven is the final culmination of our search for peace.

Closely related to our longing for peace is our desire for rest. The Old Testament teaches that God removes the burdens of his people, even on a daily basis (Ps. 68:19; 81:6-7). Jesus also promised his hearers that if all of them "who are weary and burdened" would come to him, then "I will give you rest." Then he repeated, "you will find rest for your souls"

(Matt. 11:29 NIV). This theme is also mentioned in Hebrews 4:1–11, where the promised rest is probably both temporal and eternal,[5] and in Revelation 14:13, where it is definitely heavenly: "Blessed are the dead who die in the Lord from now on. . . . They will rest from their labor" (NIV). Our rest begins here on earth; it ends in heaven.

Another favorite Old Testament image laden with meaning is one of security and protection, such as the one found in Psalm 91:1–4. Here God is a shelter for his people, who rest under the shadow of his wings. God also appears in this text as a mighty fortress and refuge in whose shadow his people dwell. The ideas revolve around finding a haven of protection and serenity.[6] In Matthew 23:37, Jesus portrays himself to the Jews as a mother hen who wanted her chickens to find protection under her wings. Then in Revelation 21, the ultimate fortress created for God's people is unveiled, and there God lives among his people (vs. 1–3). Once again, heaven is portrayed as the place where the need for refuge and protection is met to the utmost.

Beauty has always intrigued people—the sparkling river, the unbounded waterfall, the deep, silent woods, or the austere, snow-capped mountains. The Bible begins with God's creation, after which man is placed in the gorgeous Garden of Eden, with trees, rivers, scenery that was "pleasing to the eye" (Gen. 2:8–15 NIV). The Septuagint translators of the Old Testament used the word *paradise (paradeisos)* to describe this garden setting (2:8), as they did in Numbers 24:6.[7]

The same image is carried into Revelation, where God's new creation is also termed *paradise* (2:7). Then in chapters 21–22, almost half of the verses that describe the New Jerusalem are concerned with some depiction of beauty—the glory of God; the colors of the walls, city, and streets; the twelve multicolored foundations.

There are, of course, differences of interpretation as to whether these last descriptions of the New Jerusalem are literal or not. But the point we are making here can handle these differences, for the fundamental emphasis on beauty remains. What a place! More than a dozen brilliant colors to dazzle the human eye. Any science-fiction or special effects movie would pale in comparison. But rather than just seeing these things, the believer has been invited to *live* in them. As C.S. Lewis reminds us: "We want something else which can hardly be put into words—to be united with the beauty we see, to pass into it, to receive it into ourselves, to bathe in it, to become part of it."[8] And God will grant our desire beyond our wildest imagination.

Another concept carried through Scripture is an emphasis on fellowship. Few ideas can be as fulfilling as sharing with other people who love the same people and things we do. Actually, more than one metaphor of this nature can be found in the Old Testament. The thought is sometimes expressed in terms of a great feast or the merrymaking of the wedding ceremony or of the marriage relationship.[9] This is also a theme in Jesus' teaching where, for instance, there will be a great feast in God's kingdom that people will attend from all over the earth, sitting down to eat with Abraham, Isaac, and Jacob (Matt. 8:11–12). Finally, the idea of the marriage supper of the Lamb (Rev. 19:7–9), which believers attend, expresses the great rejoicing and happiness that often flow from true companionship.

Another type of fellowship is also found in Jesus' teachings: the promise of intimate and personal communion with him. He told his disciples that he would not drink from the vine again until he did so with them in the kingdom of God (Matt. 26:29). He also told them that he would be going to heaven, and they would afterward be reunited with him (John 14:1–3). Later in the New Testament, this hope is extended to all believers who "will see his face" (Rev. 22:4 NIV).

All of this imagery, then, portrays ideas that are quite desirable. Peace, rest, security, protection, beauty, and intimate fellowship are all deep-seated longings and desires that humans have throughout their lives. And Scripture testifies that, while these ideas may be partially obtainable in this life, each finds its final culmination only in heaven.

But at the foundation of all these desires lies a longing that may well be the deepest one of all.[10] According to Ecclesiastes 3:11, God has placed in each one of us a desire for eternity that cannot be fathomed in this life.[11] In Hebrews 11, one of the major characteristics of those biblical heroes who lived lives of faith is that they were strangers on earth, looking forward to future blessings (vv. 13, 26, 35). In particular, "They were longing for a better country—a heavenly one" (v. 16 NIV).

We won't pursue this last subject any further because, at this point, we are getting close to topics that arise at two other places in this book.[12] All of our highest desires find their ultimate meaning in heaven. Scripture lists specific traits of heaven and utilizes various types of imagery to provide us with hints about its nature. In both cases, the knowledge we gain is not only intellectually rewarding, but stimulating to our hearts as well.

Some Speculative Dreaming

Continuing our move from the more to the less known truths about heaven, we will now entertain a number of interesting issues that could give us more insights. We will use philosophical and theological methods to address these questions, sometimes in the absence of specific biblical criteria. Nevertheless, we think this approach can still be useful in further clarifying the subject.[13] You should also realize that there is more than one possible answer to some of these questions, many of which fit into the category of our "Christmas morning" scenario. Thus, since there is much we do not know about eternity, there is some room for differences of opinion. But none of this affects the reality of heaven. So let's do some speculative dreaming.

Is heaven a place?

John Gilmore presents three reasons supporting the conclusion that heaven is a place: (1) God created heaven, so it must be locatable; (2) Jesus ascended to heaven in a real resurrected body, which means heaven must be a place; (3) biblical texts such as Isaiah 57:15 and John 14:1-2 call heaven a place. But we cannot locate heaven on any map. In fact, we cannot say much more in biblical terms about its location other than heaven is where Jesus is now. This should cause us to ask what our relationship with him is—since he is our only means for getting there.[14]

Peter Toon points out that heaven is both a place and a state. As a place, it is where Christ is. As a state, it encompasses all of the rich blessing not true of earth, including intimate knowledge of God and fellowship with him.[15]

On the other hand, the intermediate state itself may be nonspatial, although certainly still real, as we suggested in Chapter 7. In the next chapter, we will argue that the intermediate state in hell will likely be nonspatial in addition to its reality. However, after receiving their resurrected bodies, people will be spatial beings once again, whether they inhabit heaven or hell.

Will we be omniscient in heaven?

Glorified or not, and with or without our sin natures, we are still finite human beings throughout eternity and, as such, will not know everything. In other words, to know everything would be to change our very natures and make us something other than human. Furthermore, the Bible hints that we will continue to learn, and that would lead us to believe that we will retain some human limitations.

Will we be unable to sin in heaven?

Scripture specifically tells us that sin will be kept out of the final state (Rev. 21:8; 22:15). So it is certainly possible that part of the glorification process through which we will pass will itself involve the free choice to reach the state where we can no longer sin. If this is so, then it will not be a violation of our will for us to be unable to sin. In fact, supposing we could sin after being glorified, we would then be able to do something *against* our nature, which is impossible. It would be absurd for us to complain that our free will was being violated just because we could not do wrong in a glorified state. That would be like protesting that our inability to become a bird violates our free will. In short, our new nature may *require* that we not be free to sin, just like we can't become a bird.

"Okay," you might say, "but if my nature will change regarding my ability to sin, why can't it change regarding my ability to know everything? Couldn't I become omniscient if I could become holy?" That's a good question, but it does have an answer. When we lose the ability to sin, we not only remain human, but also we find our choice to be what our Creator wanted us to be in the beginning firmly sealed. So losing the ability to sin and gaining the ability to always choose the good will cause us not to lose our humanness, but to fulfill our full potential as humans. We will finally become what God created us to be. But this doesn't seem to be the case when we consider omniscience. Coming to know everything would appear to make us something we are not. Knowing everything would require us to become something other than human. Not being able to sin would make us even more human. By sealing that choice, we would be kept from falling again.

By his very nature, God cannot sin, but this does not mean he has no freedom. His freedom is limited by his nature. For example, because he is truth, he *cannot* lie. In heaven, we may be like God in this respect.

On the other hand, it may be that we will *be able not to sin*, rather than *not being able to sin*. In this case, we would still be free to sin, but we would always choose not to because the glories and virtues of heaven would be so marvelous that no one in heaven would ever choose to act against those benefits.

But in either scenario, our certainty for believing we will never sin in heaven is made secure by the fact that an omniscient God has told us in advance that this will be the case. And God cannot lie.[16]

Will we know each other in heaven?

We have addressed this before, so we will limit ourselves here to a few brief comments. Scripture plainly teaches that we will recognize others and fellowship with them in heaven (Matt. 8:11; John 14:3; 1 Cor. 13:12). This also follows from Jesus' resurrection appearances to his disciples; they knew him and he knew them. And since we are raised in our own, albeit transformed, bodies, it would seem to follow that our being recognized by others is a natural result of our "being ourselves."[17] We might just add that corroborated NDEs further confirm this conclusion.

How can we live forever and not get eternally bored?

Of course, if we live forever, then eternal life is our lot. Period. But some people see this as an objection to the desirability of immortality.[18] It is certainly not an insurmountable objection.

The biblical description of heaven is connected to the person of God himself; it is not some realm that stands on its own. As such, the nature of heaven reflects the nature of God. And since God is omnipotent, omniscient, omnibenevolent, as well as being infinite, we need never fear boredom. In Kreeft's words: "We never come to the end of exploring Him."[19]

Also, believers will be living in God's newly created universe, which will be at our fingertips to explore and learn. And we will never come to the end of examining it, either.

Believers will also be changed and glorified, and so will have an increased capacity to continue to learn. Although we do not yet know all of the ramifications of this, these facts alone make it difficult to argue that we will be easily bored during our heavenly existence. Indeed, even our fellowship with others will become a more meaningful and constantly changing prospect. We will never cease to learn more and more about each other, nor cease to enjoy the continuing fellowship that such knowledge will bring.

Our concept of the nature of time in heaven is relevant here, too, since boredom often seems to consist of "killing time." Although we will discuss time and heaven more fully in just a moment, we can say here that we doubt we will have trouble finding something to do for eternity. And, as Gilmore points out, qualities such as fatigue, pain, selfishness, and weariness, all of which contribute to boredom, are absent in heaven.[20]

In short, the nature of God, the nature of his new creation made specifically for believers, our own glorified bodies, our new capacity to learn, our fresh relationship with others, the issue of time, and the positive qualities of heaven all argue that boredom will not be a problem. From what we know of the infinite God and what he has planned for his people, we ought to be *excited* about our future prospects, not depressed by those who doubt these things.

What age will we appear after receiving our resurrected bodies?

This is one of those topics where we have very few guidelines, biblical or otherwise, so we can only make an educated guess. Whether our appearance will be determined by our age at death, by certain identification factors (how will we most be remembered?), or by some "ideal" criteria is very difficult to tell. But one thing seems clear: Whatever our age will appear to be will be strictly irrelevant. The more important factor is that none of us will be young or old in terms of our abilities to think and act. There will be no earthly handicaps, physical or mental, in heaven.

Will there be sex in heaven?

Many scholars think that gender and sexuality are an intrinsic part of our human natures. If this is so, then one would expect that we would retain our gender differences in heaven.[21] But this does not mean that sex as a physical act will continue. We have no biblical warrant to think that procreation is needed or that sex in heaven is necessary for any other reason. But its lack of necessity does not automatically determine whether it will occur.

For most Christians, Jesus' comment on marriage solves the question: "When the dead rise, they will neither marry nor be given in marriage; they will be like the angels in heaven" (Mark 12:25 NIV). Some scholars argue from this text that both the institution of marriage (and along with it, physical sex) and gender differences ("be like the angels") will be done away with in heaven.[22] The first point seems stronger, but the last one does not necessarily follow until we know how far the likeness with angels applies. After all, we do not become angels, and we do not know for sure if angels are even genderless. But until we get more information, it would appear from all we know that physical sex will not exist in heaven.

Will there be any animals in heaven?

This is another tough question. There are very few criteria by which we may judge, so a wide range of answers has been offered.[23] Perhaps all we can say with certainty is that there appear to be no telling reasons against the existence of animals in heaven, but no clear biblical statements can be found in favor of this view either.

Will there be time in heaven?

This is also a difficult issue, but for another reason: It raises a slew of issues that can become incredibly technical. So we will give you a quick overview of the options.

Gilmore presents three basic answers to this question: heaven as timeless, as endless time, or as an everlasting present. He rejects the first option because it is plagued with problems, such as the requirement that there be no motion or sound in such an environment. Further, if Revelation 22:2 is taken literally, time is not eliminated from heaven. Gilmore thinks endless time is preferable to timelessness (and "has strong appeal"), but he judges it to be only a slight improvement over present earth-time and argues that it is not the best option in terms of the new physics.

As a result, Gilmore favors time in heaven as an everlasting present, where it "is stretched and kept. . . . No past time, no future time, just present time perfected." He also thinks that, while traditional understandings of time have been contested by the latest science, "Modern physics has enhanced the concept of eternal present-time."[24]

We are not sure what Gilmore means by this last option. We think that there will still be a flow to heavenly time, including both past and future. Moments will be realized and will recede into the past, while others await us in our future.

Along with other scholars, Kreeft differentiates between two types of time: *chronos* and *kairos*. The first, *chronos,* is what we have on earth and is measured by a clock or calendar. *Kairos,* on the other hand, is "lived time or life-time," which is relative to the purposes of human beings. On earth, *kairos* is controlled by *chronos,* but this will not be the case in heaven, where *kairos* is "measured by eternity."[25] Thus, time has both quantitative and qualitative aspects, and will be pregnant with a richness of meaning and joy unlike that on earth.

To be sure, this is a somewhat theoretical subject, and its problems are not easy to solve. Some who have attempted it, while making some strong points, have confused the issues a bit.[26] We favor the view that heaven is endless time.

How can we be happy in heaven if any loved one is in hell?

If the last two questions were difficult because of the lack of biblical criteria and scientific technicality, this one is so for another reason—our emotions. How could we enjoy bliss knowing our spouse, child, friend, or other loved one is suffering incredible agony? On this side of the grave, this is a very perplexing and emotional issue.

In the next chapter, we will explore the subject of hell and argue that hell is real and necessary. If this is so, then the key to resolving the enigma posed above must be in understanding God's perspective on the matter. He loves our loved ones more than even we could and is fully righteous, and yet he requires hell. So there must be a good reason why the awfulness of hell will not detract from the glories we will experience in heaven, even though our present limitations may make it impossible for us to understand the reason now. Perhaps philosopher Peter Kreeft has the best idea when he suggests that our love for those in hell may take a more perfect direction and operate from God's vantage point: "If our spirits are similar enough to God, we too can love without sorrow or vulnerability because we love only with the active feeling of caring, not the passive feeling of being hurt."[27] But whatever the answer, we can be assured that God will be true to his Word—heaven will still be painless, in spite of the reality of hell and who resides there.

Are there levels of punishment and blessing in heaven and hell?

It is clear that there will be differences in the degree of punishment meted out by God. In speaking about the need to watch for his coming in Luke 12:35–48, Jesus used the imagery of a servant who was charged with managing his master's estate while the master was away. The individual who misuses that trust and wrongs the other servants will be judged accordingly. Then Jesus went on to explain that the servant who knows better, but still disobeys "will be beaten with many blows." However, the one who wrongs his master by doing things that still deserve punishment, but didn't know better, "will be beaten with few blows." Jesus then concluded that judgment will entail the concept of how much has been entrusted to an individual (vv. 47–48 NIV).

This idea also occurs in Matthew 10:15, where Jesus again seems to teach that greater or lesser judgment is given in accordance with the amount of opportunity one has to turn to God. This differentiation of punishments provides an equitable means of dealing with various levels of offense.

At the same time, differing provisions are also made for blessings in heaven, which are frequently described as "crowns" or rewards.[28] These rewards are distributed in accordance with individual achievement after salvation, according to what each person has done.[29] So blessings are also accorded, not in some haphazard or aimless way or even in a singular fashion, but in a personalized manner.

What are heavenly rewards or crowns?

These treasures are the "heavenly payment" for spiritual achievement on earth after salvation. What they are exactly is difficult to know for sure, but we think it is safe to say that these awards are not physical ornaments we may parade for our own glory. Some think these crowns are the believer's eternal life itself, not additional rewards for service beyond salvation. But this position does not make the best sense of the numerous references just cited above.

On the other hand, they could be rewards (in the sense of prizes) given to the faithful by a loving Father. Or they could very well be something related to further spiritual growth and service. For example, perhaps these crowns are actually *capacities* or abilities that enable the believer to continue onward to greater spiritual heights on behalf of her Lord.

Although we cannot be positive concerning the nature of these awards, it is probably best to conclude that crowns have something to do with further spiritual development, learning, and service to the Lord. But whatever the case, the Bible makes it clear that they are well worth working and sacrificing toward.[30]

We could easily go on and on answering questions on what could well be the most interesting subject in all of Scripture.[31] But we hope that the questions we have answered will spur your further study and sanctified imaginings.

Flying Beyond the Stars

What we know about God and the eternal state he has prepared for us is certainly sufficient for us to look forward to the most fantastic "surprise" in all of God's creation. We agree with John Zoller, who writes:

> Heaven will be so vast, its beautiful valleys, its foothills and lofty mountains so extensive, its crystal clear streams and rivers, its vegetation with its marvelous forests so wonderful that it will be even far beyond our wildest imagination to conceive. I believe that it will take an eternity of years to see but a small part of God's wonderful Heaven; to meet and fellowship with the multitudes of the Redeemed who will be there.[32]

Truly, "Death is not the king of terrors; it's the doorway to Glory."[33] For heaven "is the Great Adventure, beside which moon landings and space trips pale in significance."[34]

So we close this chapter by once again quoting Francis Schaeffer: "The Christian is the one whose imagination should fly beyond the stars."[35] Schaeffer is right. Our imagination should fly *far* beyond the stars—to our eternal home in heaven!

Chapter 11

Hell: The Horrible Choice

Hell is one of those back-room topics. We may think about it from time to time, or even in our weaker or more fearful moments, talk about it with someone we trust. Some people have even pulled out the topic to scare someone into making a decision of faith. Others have brought it up and thrown it into a person's face, declaring damnation on that person for his harmful, disdainful acts.

But more often than not, the subject creeps up on us, silently, almost seditiously, until it enters our conscience and plagues us with thoughts of personal torment and judgment, or it causes us to think about the agony a loved one will face if his life doesn't turn around. The topic can bring so much concern and pain into our lives that we put it into the back room of our minds and padlock the door. We do not want to talk about hell, much less dwell on it. We would rather the topic never came up.

But locking it away will not dispel its reality. In fact, throughout history the concept of hell—some kind of judgment and punishment for wrongdoing—has played a critical role in religious life individually and communally. Certainly this has been true in the history of Judaism and Christianity—two of the most dominant religious forces in Western history.

In the Hebrew Scriptures, the prophet Daniel warned, "And many of those who sleep in the dust of the earth shall awake,/Some to everlasting life,/Some to shame and everlasting contempt" (Dan. 12:2 NKJV). Turning to the New Testament, we find Jesus himself advising his disciples not to "fear those who kill the body, but are unable to kill the soul; but rather fear Him who is able to destroy both soul and body in hell" (Matt. 10:28 NASB). Then we see Paul, the great Christian missionary, proclaiming that "these will pay the penalty of eternal destruction, away from the presence of the Lord and from the glory of His power" (2 Thess. 1:9 NASB).

These leaders and teachers did not attempt to prove hell's reality. They believed it existed and warned their audiences appropriately. Even in church history, there was a time when the reality of hell was so gripping, so pervasive, that the threat of excommunication was a powerful and feared danger.

Things have certainly changed. Today, hell is not a topic for polite conversations, and it rarely surfaces anywhere else, including sermons. We are afraid of it, embarrassed by it. Some even reject it as infantile and obnoxious. Atheist George Smith is a case in point:

> The belief in eternal torment, still subscribed to by fundamentalist Christian denominations, undoubtedly ranks as the most vicious and reprehensible doctrine of classical Christianity. It has resulted in an incalculable amount of psychological torture, especially among children, where it is employed as a terror tactic to prompt obedience.[1]

Atheist B.C. Johnson frankly states that "the idea of hell is morally absurd."[2] Morton Kelsey even notes that believers are ambivalent about the doctrine: "The idea of hell is certainly not popular among most modern Christians."[3]

Aside from our individual aversions to the concept of hell, there are a number of other factors that have attributed to its demise in our society. For example, a supernaturalist understanding of reality, which the concept of hell requires, has fallen on hard times due in large part to the rise of three antisupernaturalist schools of thought. Empiricism—the idea that we can only believe in what our senses tell us is real—has heavily influenced our perception of reality. If all we can trust is what our five senses accept, then we cannot accept the reality of hell because it is beyond the grasp of our senses. Another influential philosophical perspective is scientism: Truth is discovered by science alone. This view also rules out hell, since its reality cannot be proven by the scientific method. And, of course, the pervasiveness of physicalism cannot permit hell's existence because hell is not a part of the natural realm.

We have also adopted a form of religious tolerance that has led many people to believe that sincerity of belief is the only prerequisite to heaven. Your worldview, religious convictions, moral stance—whatever—don't matter as long as you really believe they are true and you try to live in light of your beliefs. "We're all headed to the same place," it is argued. "We just perceive the way to get there differently. God will overlook that and accept us solely on the basis of our commitment to travel our path of choice."

Another major factor against belief in hell concerns our cultural shift in values. We do not appreciate or extol the "hard" virtues of holiness, justice, and righteousness. Instead, we are preoccupied with the "soft" virtues of love, mercy, and kindness.

This shift in values has led to another factor that affects our acceptance of hell: the change from a morality emphasizing duty and obligation to one that emphasizes individual rights and liberties.

Consequently, the idea of hell has become outdated. It no longer fits with our modern perception of reality, so its existence is usually ignored or even denied. And we frequently twist the ancient teachings on hell so we can justify our new understanding of hell's irrelevance.

We (the authors) think this modern attitude toward hell should not be accepted at face value. What if our society is wrong? What if hell is real? What if heaven is not the destination of all people after death? If heaven is for believers and hell for unbelievers, what will happen to unbelievers right after their death? What will their intermediate state be like? And, assuming hell is real, does it really have flames of fire? Is it a place of torture and unrelenting torment? If people go there, will they have to stay? Will they receive a second chance? In fact, when faced with the prospect of hell, will people in the afterlife be given the chance to repent before having to suffer hell? Or, will those who experience hell eventually be annihilated by God rather than suffer endlessly? After all, wouldn't everlasting punishment be unjust for a comparatively brief life of sin?

These are serious and important questions. And their answers will influence the way we live our lives here and now. So we want to deal with these questions in this chapter, and our discussion will begin by clarifying the Bible's teaching about hell.

Why should we start with the Bible? Because, if our case for life after death is correct, then the Christian view of the afterlife is true, and the Bible is Christianity's most reliable source of information about life beyond the grave. Let's consider what the Bible has to say.

The Scriptures on Hell

Two New Testament passages provide the clearest definition of hell we have. Second Thessalonians 1:9 says, "And these [who do not know God or obey the gospel] will pay the penalty of eternal destruction, away from the presence of the Lord and from the glory of His power" (NASB). The other passage, Matthew 25:41 and 46 states: "Then He will also say to those on His left, 'Depart from Me, accursed ones, into the eternal fire which has been prepared for the devil and his angels'; . . . And these will go away into eternal punishment, but the righteous into eternal life" (NASB).

From these (and other) verses we see that the essence of hell is the end of a road away from God, love, and anything of real value. It is banishment from the very presence of God and from the type of life we were made to live. Heaven, which is full of God's presence, is a place of supreme happiness, where we can cultivate our freely chosen friendship with God and others who love him, where we can grow in our knowledge of and intimacy with God and others who love him, where we can serve God and others who love him. Hell is the opposite of all this.

The Bible describes hell primarily in relational terms—it is "away from" God. Therefore, it involves banishment from his presence, his purposes, and his followers. Like heaven, hell is a freely chosen destination. What we decide to believe and do in this life sets us on a road leading to a final destination in the next.

Hell is also a place of shame, sorrow, regret, and anguish. This intense pain is not actively produced by God; he is not a cosmic torturer. Undoubtedly, anguish and torment will exist in hell. And because we will have both body and soul in the resurrected state, the anguish experienced can be both mental and physical. But the pain suffered will be due to the shame and sorrow resulting from the punishment of final, ultimate, unending banishment from God, his kingdom, and the good life for which we were created in the first place. Hell's occupants will deeply and tragically regret all they lost. As Jesus said, "For what profit is it to a man if he gains the whole world, and loses his own soul?" (Matt. 16:26).

Finally, hell was not a part of the original creation. It was not part of what God made and declared "good" (Gen. 1). Hell is a later addition meant to accommodate the banishment of the Evil One and his rule over fallen angels and people who have rebelled against God.

The Bible uses several words to describe this place of pain. In the Old Testament, *sheol* is the main word used.[4] It sometimes means the grave itself, but more often it refers to the nether world, the realm of the dead. *Sheol* was seen as a shadowy, dark mode of existence (Job 10:21–22; Ps. 143:3) and a place where one could talk with others (Isa. 14:9–20) and be reunited with friends (Gen. 15:15, 37:35). It was pictured with two compartments (Gen. 37:35; Deut. 32:22): the lowest part and the highest one (also called, prior to Christ's resurrection, "Abraham's bosom" in Luke 16:22 and "paradise" in Luke 23:43). Thus, *sheol* contained both unbelievers and believers, and therefore, cannot be identified as the place of the wicked's final punishment.

In the New Testament, *hades* takes the place of *sheol,* and it appears that Christ's resurrection changed the nature of *hades* (Eph. 4:8–9; 1 Peter 3:18–22). Before Christ's resurrection, *hades* is used as a synonym for *sheol* as a whole, including the lowest and highest components. However, after Christ's resurrection, *hades* becomes identified with the lowest part of *sheol* only (Luke 16:23). *Hades,* then, becomes viewed as a temporary place of banishment during the unbeliever's intermediate state (2 Peter 2:9), which will be done away with at the final judgment (Rev. 20:13–15). During the intermediate state, people remain conscious and disembodied, as they await the final resurrection of their bodies and the final judgment.

The New Testament also uses *tartarus* (only in 2 Peter 2:4), *gehenna,* and *the lake of fire* to stand interchangeably for the final state of the banished brought about at the final judgment at the end of the world (Matt. 23:33; Rev. 20:1–15). In *gehenna,* people will have bodies as well as souls (Matt. 5:22, 10:28), and they will experience conscious, everlasting banishment from heaven.

Finally, the Bible describes hell's occupants as experiencing different degrees of punishment. Just as there are different degrees of rewards for believers in heaven (2 Cor. 5:10), so there are different degrees of judgment and shame for unbelievers "according to the works" that have been done in this life (Matt. 11:21–24; Luke 12:47–48; Matt. 23:23; and, perhaps, James 3:1; Rev. 20:12–13).

Two further questions about the biblical picture need to be answered. First, is hell a place somewhere in space? Most likely not.[5] When the Bible uses spatial language of God, heaven, and hell, the language is metaphorical. God doesn't literally have a right hand, nor does he literally sit on some throne spatially located somewhere. God is omnipresent and spaceless, not localized or spatial. Similarly, the intermediate state known as hades is surely real, but it is an entirely different nonspatial mode of reality suited for disembodied existence. It is a mistake to think that if something is real, it must be located somewhere and have certain spatial dimensions.

At the final judgment there will be resurrected bodies; the saved and unsaved will be embodied. So human life will again be spatial, but we should be cautious in trying to picture in detail what life will be like then, because of the unusual nature of Christ's resurrection body and the fact of a new heaven and new earth.

Second, are the flames in hell literal, physical things, or are they symbolic? For several reasons we believe they are symbolic. Metaphors are often used in Scripture to depict God and the future life. We saw this in our chapter on heaven. If heaven is handled this way, hell probably is also.

Moreover, if the metaphors for hell are taken physically and literally, contradictions result. Hell is called a place of fire and darkness, but how could there be darkness if the fire is literal? Hell is also described as a bottomless pit and a dump. How can it be both? In addition, Scripture calls God himself a consuming fire (Heb. 12:29) and states that Christ and his angels will return surrounded "in flaming fire" (2 Thess. 1:8). But God is not a physical object as is fire, and the flames surrounding the returning Christ are no more literal than is the sword coming out of his mouth (Rev. 1:16). Flames are used as symbols for divine judgment. In reference to hell, flames depict human shame, punishment, sorrow, and anguish.

The Bible's picture of hell, therefore, indicates that upon death, some people will be translated into a different, nonspatial mode of existence. They will be conscious, and they will await the resurrection of their bodies, at which time they will be banished from heaven and secured in hell where they will experience unending, conscious exclusion from God, his people, and anything of value. This banishment will include conscious sorrow, shame, and anguish to differing degrees, depending on the person's life on earth.

This is a good place to say something about the Catholic doctrine of purgatory. Catholics and Protestants agree on a great deal regarding God, Jesus Christ, and the afterlife. However, we and our fellow Protestants cannot bring ourselves to accept the full-blown notion of purgatory.[6] Very roughly, the notion of purgatory includes the following: Purgatory is closely associated with the idea of temporal punishment. According to tradition, it is a place where certain people go immediately after death to prepare themselves for heaven. It is a temporary state of misery, suffering, and punishment. In purgatory, people are punished for certain sins committed in this life, they make reparation and amends for those sins through repentance and penance (acts of self-abasement and devotion that earn God's forgiveness and establish restoration with God and others), and they are purified and made righteous again in God's sight. Theologian Loraine Boettner gives a helpful summary of the doctrine of purgatory:

> The Roman Catholic Church has built up a doctrine in which it is held that all who die at peace with the Church, but who are not perfect, must undergo penal and purifying suffering in an intermediate realm known as purgatory. Only those believers who have attained a state of Christian perfection go immediately to heaven. All unbaptized adults and those who after baptism have committed mortal sin go immediately to hell. The great mass of partially sanctified Christians dying in fellowship with the Church, but who nevertheless are encumbered with some degree of sin, go to purgatory where, for a longer or shorter time, they suffer until all sin is purged away, after which they are translated to heaven.[7]

Some theologians, such as Morton Kelsey, claim that the doctrine of purgatory includes the notion of getting a second chance to go to heaven after death.[8] In purgatory, one gets a fresh start on life altogether.

What should we make of this belief? For one thing, the notion of a second chance or a fresh start will be discussed later in this chapter, so let's set it aside for now. What about the rest of the doctrine? We do not think that the traditional understanding of purgatory is rationally acceptable. We can only say briefly why we think this way.[9]

To begin with, a major support for the doctrine is a passage of 2 Maccabees 12:39–45. However 2 Maccabees is a disputed book in Christian circles. It was written after the completion of the Old Testament and prior to the New Testament, and Protestants consider it to be an apocryphal book that is not part of the true canon of Holy Scripture. It may have some historical validity and scholarly interest, but it is not divinely inspired or authoritative for belief and practice.

Furthermore, the idea of purgatory goes against biblical teaching. The Bible says nothing about purgatory or the need to be purged after death. Rather, the Bible claims that Christ himself did all that was necessary to earn our joyous entrance into God's presence at death. Paul states in Philippians 3:9 that his right standing with God was not something he earned or secured through acts of penance or reparation.

Furthermore, Paul claims that at death, we who are believers in Christ immediately go to be in Christ's presence (Phil. 1:21–24; 2 Cor. 5:8); there is no stopping-off place. This experience is to be joyously anticipated. But purgatory involves no such joyous anticipation, nor does it include the intimate fellowship depicted by Paul. The Bible consistently affirms that Christ himself has purged our sins and washed them away, and on this basis believers confidently and joyfully anticipate being directly in his presence in the intermediate state at the moment of death.

Does our rejection of the full-blown doctrine of purgatory mean that we do not find anything true in the idea? No, it doesn't. What we find false and misleading are those aspects of the theology of purgatory that picture the intermediate state as a place of punishment, misery, penance, and reparation for sin. True, the intermediate state is incomplete. It is also a form of life that involves joy in fellowship with God and others. But it is not the believer's final destination. It is a place of growth and incompleteness in joy and fellowship. Only when we receive our new resurrected bodies will we enter heaven the way it was meant to be. So, if purgatory is understood as a temporary, incomplete, joyful existence that involves growth and anticipation of reembodiment in heaven, then we can accept it, as long as we remain clear about what the concept really means and includes.

Returning to our points about the biblical teaching on hell, we are reminded of how serious the business of living really is. We are not evolutionary "accidents" or modified monkeys who have no purpose in life. We are creatures with intrinsic dignity. Our choices really matter. They affect us and others in this life and beyond. With great dignity comes great responsibility and the real possibility of gain or loss, partnership with God or alienation from him. Freedom is a serious and awesome gift.

The Justification of Belief in Hell

The severity and finality of the Bible's view of hell has been thought by some to be too horrendous, too absolute, too tragic to accept. It is no surprise, then, that the biblical picture has had many detractors. So now we want to examine the justification of hell by focusing on some of the issues, objections, and alternatives that have been proposed.

Some Reasons to Believe in Hell

Oxford University philosopher Richard Swinburne has offered an important defense of the orthodox view of hell.[10] Swinburne asks, "Why is it that you have to have right beliefs and a good will (one that desires God, salvation, and heaven) to go to heaven? Why are people with wrong beliefs and a bad will left out?"

His basic answer is twofold: Heaven is the type of place where people with wrong beliefs and a bad will would not fit, and heaven must be freely and noncoercively chosen.

According to Swinburne, heaven is a place where people eternally enjoy a supremely worthwhile happiness. This happiness has three important aspects. First, it is not the mere possession of pleasant sensations. You could have pleasant sensations, say, by taking drugs all day or by having people constantly lie to you about how wonderful and intelligent you are. But for that you should be pitied. You would not have a supremely worthwhile happiness.

Second, such a happiness can only be possessed if you do what you truly want to without any conflicting desires. You could be happy doing something, even if you experienced conflicting desires about that activity, but it would be better to do something you freely wanted to do and it be free from conflict.

Third, a supremely worthwhile happiness must come from true beliefs and things that are truly and supremely valuable. We all know that happiness can be obtained from false beliefs. You can be happy in the belief that someone loves you even if that belief is false. So happiness can come from either true or false beliefs, but happiness is more worthwhile if it comes from true beliefs. If given a choice between a lot of happiness from false beliefs or a little happiness from true beliefs, we would choose the latter. Furthermore, happiness can come from doing silly or even immoral actions. Some people gain happiness from killing or stealing. But a supremely worthwhile happiness comes from true beliefs and activities that are really valuable.

To sum up then, a supremely worthwhile happiness is a deep happiness, not a shallow one. It does not involve the mere possession of pleasant sensations, but it is obtained by freely choosing to do activities when that choice is based on true beliefs and those activities are truly worthwhile. Deepest happiness is found in successfully pursuing a task of supreme value and being in a situation of supreme value, when I have true beliefs about these and I only want to be doing these tasks in this situation without any conflict of my desires.

What are these supreme tasks and situations? Swinburne claims they include developing a friendship with God, learning to care for others who have that same friendship, caring for and beautifying God's creation, and the like. Heaven is not a reward for good action; it is a home for good people. Heaven intensifies and fulfills a certain type of life that can be chosen, in undeveloped form, in this life. Only people of a certain sort are suited for life in heaven: those who have a true belief about what it is like and really want to be there for the right reasons.

People with different beliefs about the good life or heaven will value and practice different activities, so even if they are seeking the good in some sense, their character will develop in a different way than will the character of the Christian. For example, a Buddhist who spends his whole life trying to remove his desires would not find heaven a place that fulfills the things he really wants. People with a bad will or people with a good will, but with false beliefs about what God, heaven, and the good really are, will not be suited for life in heaven.

Can God force the bad to become good? No, says Swinburne, not if he respects our freedom. God can't make people's character for them, and people who do evil or cultivate false beliefs start a slide away from God that ultimately ends in hell. God respects human freedom. We could add here that it would be unloving, a sort of divine rape, to force people to accept heaven and God if they did not really want them. When God allows people to say no to him, he actually respects and dignifies them. We may rush in to force our children to do something in their best interests, but our paternalism drops out when they grow up, because we wish to respect them as adults. Similarly, God dignifies people and treats their choices as significant by allowing them to choose against him, not just for him.

So, Swinburne's argument is that heaven is suitable for people of a certain sort (those who really want to be there and who base their choice on true beliefs), and their decision to go there must be made freely. Hell is a place for people of a different character who freely choose to be there.

As it is, Swinburne's case seems to be a good one, but we can add to it too. For example, more can be said about how hell is the result of God's respect for persons. It is reasonable to argue that it is wrong to destroy the type of intrinsic value humans have. If God is the source and preserver of values, and if persons have the high degree of intrinsic value Christianity claims they have, then God is the preserver of persons. He would be wrong to destroy something of such value just because it has chosen a life it was not intended to live. Thus, one way God can respect persons is to sustain them in existence and not annihilate them. Annihilation destroys creatures of intrinsic value.

Another way to respect persons is to honor their free, autonomous choices, even if those choices are wrong. God respects persons in this second way by honoring their choices. As philosopher Eugene Fontinell has noted:

> The question that must be raised here is whether the doctrine of universal salvation, highly motivated though it may be, does not diminish the 'seriousness' of human experience. . . . At stake here, of course, is the nature and scope of human freedom. . . . There is a profound difference between a human freedom whose exercise *must* lead to union with God and one that allows for the possibility of eternal separation from God. . . . A world in which there can only be winners is a less serious world than one in which the possibility of the deepest loss is real.[11]

Since God cannot force his love on people and coerce them to choose him, and since he cannot annihilate creatures with such high intrinsic value, then the only option available is quarantine. And that is what hell is.

There are three other considerations to ponder concerning hell. First, some of God's attributes—particularly his justice and holiness—seem to demand the existence of hell. Justice demands retribution, the distribution of rewards and punishments in a fair way. It would be unjust to allow evil to go unpunished and to reward evil with good, even if the good was not sought in a genuine, informed way. Thus hell is in keeping with God's justice. As Paul put it, "For after all it is only just for God to repay with affliction those who afflict you, . . . dealing out retribution to those who do not know God and to those who do not obey the gospel of our Lord Jesus" (2 Thess. 1:6, 8 NASB).

Similarly, God's holiness requires him to separate himself entirely from evil, and hell is essentially a place away from God. Thus, hell is in keeping with God's holiness. It may very well be that our current hostilities toward the notion of hell result, not from an enlightened conscience, but quite the reverse. Our culture embraces a contentless formalism where individual liberties prevail, come what may.[12] But as a society we have little concern or appreciation for holiness, and this dulling of our moral sensibilities may have inevitably led to our failure to appreciate the morality of hell as seen in the light of the demands of holiness and justice.

This matter leads to a second point. In ethics, there is a theory known as *virtue ethics*. The details of this theory are beyond our present concern, but one thing about virtue ethics is very important. This theory maintains that people who have a well-developed, virtuous character are in a better position to have moral sensibilities and genuine insight into what is right and wrong than those who do not have such a character. In other words, true moral experts are possible, and they are those people who have cared deeply about virtue and goodness and who have labored to develop in-grained virtues and moral sensibilities. Jesus Christ and his apostles were moral experts. They were remarkable people who exhibited lives of staggering dedication to goodness, virtue, and the moral way of life. Now if they, being as virtuous as they were and having well-developed moral sensibilities, did not balk at the notion of hell but even embraced it as just, loving, and fair, then our current distaste for the doctrine says more about us than about the doctrine itself. To deny this conclusion is tantamount to claiming that our modern moral sensibilities are more developed than those of Jesus and his apostles, not to say those of the overwhelming number of godly people who have followed Jesus since. But this claim is clearly arrogant and unreasonable.

Third and finally, the doctrine of hell gains support from a notion called the defeat of evil.[13] Let us begin with some examples. It is possible to have pleasure or displeasure in something bad. For instance, we could take pleasure in the fact that someone else is hurt or that could displease us. Or take fear. The feeling of fear is bad, but it is a necessary part of exercising courage, and courage is good. Now in these examples, we have the following: Some part P is bad, considered in and by itself, but it is part of a larger whole, W, that is good, and W is better off for having P as a part than it would be if P were not a part.

Does this sound complicated? It really isn't. Let P stand for the mental state of displeasure. Now displeasure, considered in and by itself, is bad. Just ask yourself if, all things being equal, you would prefer to be in a state of pleasure or displeasure, without taking anything else into consideration. Now suppose P (displeasure) becomes part of a whole, W. Say the displeasure is in the fact that someone else is hurt. In this case, W has two parts: a state of displeasure (P) and the state of affairs this displeasure is directed toward (the fact that someone else is hurt).

Now, even though displeasure is bad in comparison with pleasure, considered in and of themselves, a whole state of displeasure in the fact that someone else is hurt is good and, in fact, better than an alternative whole where one has pleasure in the fact that someone else is hurt. In this case, the evil found in displeasure is defeated; while bad in and of itself, it is offset and overbalanced by being an important part of a larger perspective. It is better to have displeasure in another's misfortune than to take pleasure in it, even though displeasure is worse than pleasure.

We can see the same thing when we look at fear. Being fearful is worse than not being in a state of fear. But fear can be a part of a larger whole exhibiting courage, which defeats the evil of fear. When we apply these observations to the notion of hell, we discover this: Even though the suffering, shame, and banishment of people in hell is bad, considered in and of itself (it would be better it these people were in heaven, all things being equal), nevertheless, such a bad state is defeated if it is part of a larger purpose that is good and that has hell as an essential part. That larger whole is (1) the creation of free individuals who can freely desire and choose heaven based on true beliefs, or reject heaven, and who have enough intrinsic value to make annihilation wrong; and (2) the justice and holiness of God. The evil of hell, therefore, is defeated because hell is part of a larger whole that is good (and better than it would be without hell).

This, then, constitutes some of the reasons the biblical doctrine of hell is morally and intellectually justifiable. But there are still some objections to consider.

Some Objections Answered

The Problem of Universalism

According to universalists, God will eventually reconcile all things to himself, including all individuals, even if this means that God will continue to draw them to himself in the afterlife. Morton Kelsey has said, "To say that men and women after death will be able to resist the love of God forever seems to suggest that the human soul is stronger than God."[14] John Hick claims that because of God's goodness, mercy, grace, and love, "God will eventually succeed in his purpose of winning all men to himself in faith and love."[15]

Universalists appeal to various arguments in support of their views but three are central. One argument is that the doctrine of eternal banishment is immoral and unjust and, for that reason, unacceptable. Second, they argue that the doctrine of eternal banishment is incompatible with some of God's attributes, such as omnipotence, love, and mercy. God's mercy must surely triumph over human resistance. Finally, certain Bible texts (Acts 3:21; Rom. 5:18, 11:32; 1 Cor. 15:22–28; Eph. 1:10; 1 Tim. 2:4) are cited in favor of universalism. However, these arguments do not succeed. Let's look at each one more closely to see why.

We have already considered some reasons for rejecting the first argument—the injustice of eternal banishment. The state of hell is fair and, in fact, an indication of human dignity. Heaven is unsuited for certain types of people and life-styles. People can freely resist God. God's love respects human freedom, making human choices and human history truly significant. And God will not extinguish people of intrinsic value. Eternal punishment is sad, even to God, but we must not confuse sadness with injustice. There are possibilities of real, eternal gains in this life, and this brings with it the possibility of real, eternal loss.

Regarding God's attributes, we can make a similar case. Omnipotence has nothing to do with the issue of hell. Consider the task of creating a square circle. This is a logical contradiction. The task of creating such an entity is a pseudotask. It is not something you could do by, say, working out with weights. Power is irrelevant to such pseudotasks. The same can be said with regard to free choices. All the power in the world cannot *guarantee* that a free choice will be a good one. Determining a good result of a free choice is a logical contradiction.

Furthermore, while hell is in some sense a defeat to God (his *desire* is that all men be saved), in another sense it is not a defeat. Because it is a quarantine that respects the freedom and dignity of his image-bearers while separating hell from his special presence and the community of those who love him (heaven).

Finally, regarding divine love, we all know that resistance to love does not always break down. Love, even divine love, cannot coercively guarantee a proper response to it.

What about the Bible, then? Does it teach universalism? No. In fact, it contains very clear passages that contradict universalism (cf. Matt. 8:12, 25:31–46; John 5:29; Rom. 2:8–10; Rev. 20:10, 15). And the passages that appear to support universalism should be understood as doing one of two things. Either they are teaching what God's desire is without affirming what will happen, or they are describing not the ultimate reconciliation of all of fallen humanity, but a restoration of divine order and rule over creation taken as a whole.

So universalism is not an adequate stumbling block to belief in hell. As C.S. Lewis wisely observed:

> If a game is played, it must be possible to lose it. If the happiness of a creature lies in self-surrender, no one can make that surrender but himself (though many can help him to make it) and he may refuse. I would pay any

price to be able to say truthfully, "All will be saved." But my reason retorts, "Without their will, or with it?" If I say, "Without their will," I at once perceive a contradiction: How can the supreme voluntary act of self-surrender be involuntary? If I say, "With their will," my reason replies, "How if they *will not* give in?"[16]

A Second Chance After Death?[17]

The Bible is clear that people do not get a second chance to go to heaven after death. Hebrews 9:27 says, "It is appointed for men to die once, and after this comes judgment" (NASB). But is this teaching really fair and just? Yes. At least three factors tell us why.

For one thing, certain passages indicate that God gives people all the time they need to make a choice about eternity. Second Peter 3:9 teaches that God is postponing the return of Christ because he is "not wishing for any to perish but for all to come to repentance" (NASB). From this, we can infer that if all a person needed was more time to make a decision, God would see to it that she got the extra time instead of dying prematurely. No one will go to hell who would have gone to heaven if he had needed one more chance. Those who would have responded to a second chance after death will have their deaths postponed and given that chance this side of the grave. God "desires all men to be saved and to come to the knowledge of the truth" (1 Tim. 2:4 NASB).

Another factor to consider is this: It is arguable that people do not have the ability to will or choose heaven after death. Character is shaped moment by moment, day by day, in the thousands of little choices we make. Each day our character is increasingly formed, and in each choice we make we either move toward or away from God. As our character grows, some choices become possible and others impossible. The longer one lives in opposition to God, his truth, and his ways, the harder it is to choose to turn that around.

This is one of the reasons most religious conversions occur early in life. If God permits a person to die and go to hell, it seems reasonable to think that God no longer believes that this person is saveable. Only God could make that type of judgment, but that judgment could clearly be true. Those who claim God has created purgatory as a place in which he continues to work on people to draw them to himself forget two things. First, purgatory seems to imply God was somehow lax and did not do all he could to save the person this side of death, but this view is morally and theologically repugnant. Second, the doctrine of purgatory fails to acknowledge that the longer a person is away from God the harder it is for him to turn around. A choice of heaven would be more difficult after death, not easier. One's choice to live apart from God would be more settled in hell than it would have been on earth.

Third, one may think that the shock of judgment after death may be what people need to push them over the edge and cause them to respond to a second chance. But again, this seems to imply that God has not dealt fairly and earnestly with people in this life. Furthermore, people who would "choose" heaven in a second chance after death would most likely not really be choosing heaven, but choosing to avoid hell. The two are not the same. Heaven is for people who really desire to be there and where this desire is unmixed, as we saw in Swinburne's defense. People who would "choose" in a second chance would not really be choosing God, his kingdom, and his ways, nor would they be suited for life in such a kingdom. They may actually be making a prudential choice to avoid judgment only. Such a choice would be like a child who tells his sister he is sorry because he now knows that discipline is on the way. His repentance is not genuine. The same could be said of second chances after death.

Maybe God Annihilates Those Who Do Not Go to Heaven?

A growing number of advocates, evangelical and nonevangelical, embrace a position called *conditional immortality* or *annihilationism*. Sometimes these terms are synonymous. Sometimes they refer to slightly different positions. When used differently, conditional immortality is the notion that humans are by nature mortal, God gives the gift of everlasting life to believers, and at death God simply allows unbelievers to become extinct. Annihilationism often refers to the view that everyone survives death and participates in the final resurrection, but the judgment passed on unbelievers is extinction. Non-Christians undergo everlasting punishment, not everlasting punishing, in that the result of their judgment—annihilation—lasts forever.

While there have been various non-Christian religious groups associated with annihilationism, we must point out that a number of solid evangelical Christians—such as John Stott, Clark Pinnock, John Wenham, P.E. Hughes, and Stephen Travis—have defended the view.[18] While we are not convinced their view is true, we must say two things. First, these people are committed Christians, and they have appropriately reminded us of the importance of not being glib, much less gleeful, about the doctrine of hell. However justifiable the traditional justification of hell is, hell's presence in God's universe saddens him and us as well. Second, we who call ourselves evangelical Christians must base our views on the authoritative Word of God, supplemented by right reason. This means that we should listen and always be open to objective biblical, theological, and philosophical defenses of an idea.

Thus, while we (the authors) are not persuaded by the case for annihilationism, we do not disparage our evangelical brothers who wish to be given a chance to make a biblical case for their views. The issue itself is what should be in focus, not our personalities. So we will push on to do just that, to look at the main issues involved.

Before proceeding, though, one more preliminary is in order. We do not accept the idea that hell is a place where God actively tortures people forever and ever. There will indeed be everlasting, conscious, mental and physical torment in various degrees according to the lives people have lived here on earth. But the essence of that torment is relational in nature: the banishment from heaven and all it stands for. Mental and physical anguish result from the sorrow and shame of the judgment of being forever relationally excluded from God, heaven, and so forth. It is not due to God himself inflicting torture.

The traditional doctrine of hell has been embraced by the vast majority of theologians throughout church history and not without reason. A fairly straightforward reading of Scripture lies behind the traditional view. For example, a number of passages use images that imply everlasting, unending, conscious existence in hell: the figures of everlasting fire that will not be quenched and of the worm that never dies, as well as figures that imply the final judgment is constant, conscious, and everlasting (Isa. 33:14, 66:24; Matt. 3:12; Mark 9:42–48). Isaiah 33:14 says, "Who among us can live with continual [everlasting] burning?" (NASB). Mark 9:47–48 warns that offenders will be cast into hell where their worm does not die and the fire is not quenched. It would seem clear that the worm and fire stand for a type of judgment that involves everlasting, conscious awareness.

Similarly, the Hebrew word *olam* and the Greek word *aionios* are translated as "eternal," "everlasting," "forever." And while these terms can, on rare occasions, be used to refer to an age or long period of time (or when the end of the age is in view, cf. Jer. 17:4, 18:16), the context must clearly show this because their normal meaning is an unending period of time. The term *aionios* occurs 71 times in the New Testament. Sixty-four of these refer to God himself and divine plans or realities. In these cases an unending period of time is clearly in view. The term is used seven times in regard to perdition and should be understood in an everlasting sense there as well (cf. Matt. 18:8, 25:41, 46; Jude 6–7, 13; Rev. 14:11, 20:10).

Daniel 12:2 and Matthew 25:41, 46 are particularly important and clear. Daniel 12:2 says, "And many of those who sleep in the dust of the ground will awake, these to everlasting life, but the others to disgrace and everlasting contempt" (NASB). In Matthew 25:41 and 46, Jesus announces, "Then He will also say to those on His left, 'Depart from Me, accursed ones, into the eternal fire which has been prepared for the devil and his angels'; . . . And these will go away into eternal punishment, but the righteous into eternal life" (NASB). Some annihilationists would agree that divine punishment is not for a brief time, but is endless. However, they would claim that the punishment is endless, not the punishing. That is, the punishment is extinction, and the results of this judgment will last endlessly, with smoke and fire as symbols of the everlasting result of being consumed. However, the passages in Daniel and Matthew make it clear that the final states of the just and unjust are exactly analogous—both are conscious, continuous modes of living—except for their respective destinations.[19] If heavenly bliss is endless, so is hellish agony.

With these overall considerations in mind, let's delve into some of the main arguments for annihilationism and consider their flaws. This discussion will also answer many of the questions we raised at the beginning of the chapter.

Argument #1: Our immortality is not a natural attribute of being human; it is God's gift. Eternal life is given only to believers at the resurrection.

Response: It is true that only God has immortality in himself (1 Tim. 6:15–16). But it does not follow from this that extinction at death, though a logical possibility, actually becomes a reality. After all, God has conferred unending existence on angels and (arguably), in a different sense, on abstract objects (numbers, triangularity, and other Platonic forms). Further, annihilationists seem to believe that death (extinction) is a punishment for sin, and immortality (continued existence) is a reward for faith. But in Scripture, while death *is* a punishment for sin (Gen. 2:17; Rom. 5:12), it is viewed as separation from God, not extinction. Further, the Bible does not teach that immortality (continued existence) is a reward for faith. The eternal life received by believers is not mere endless existence as opposed to extinction, but rather a certain quality of life together with God and others in his kingdom, in contrast to life separated from God and others in his kingdom.

Argument #2: Everlasting punishing implies an unending cosmological dualism that cannot be allowed if God will eventually become "all in all" (1 Cor. 15:28) and is "making all things new" (Rev. 21:5). In other words, the Bible cannot accept an everlasting evil coexisting with an everlasting good.

Response: This argument is one of the weakest offered by annihilationists. For one thing, there will always be some sort of cosmological dualism, at least in the sense that God will always be separate from his creation. And if an ultimate dualism of this type can be accepted, there is no problem in embracing other types of dualism, including the one of heaven and hell.

Moreover, it is question-begging to claim that everlasting punishing is more evil and a greater defeat for God than annihilation and everlasting punishment. Preserving in existence creatures of intrinsic value may be more in keeping with the demands of a moral universe and a just God than annihilating those creatures. Hell may be a part of what it means for God to be all in all and not count as a counterexample to it.

Finally, phrases like "all in all" and "making all things new" are left vague and general in the Scriptures. They are not precise enough in meaning to sustain the weight of an argument. According to the Bible, God is already the sovereign Lord of the world, but this does not rule out libertarian freedom, evil, and things not in keeping with God's desires. Phrases like "all in all" may announce God's desire, or they may refer to creation as a whole, not to each and every part. For example, God will bring a new world discontinuous with the old one, but the existence of hell, traditionally conceived, is not contradictory to a new world taken as a whole.

Argument #3: Biblical words and imagery like *fire, death,* and *destruction* imply extinction and annihilation.

Response: First, these words and images should be seen in light of clear passages, such as Daniel 12:2 and Matthew 25:41 and 46, which show that unending consciousness is in view.

Second, eternal life in the Bible is the only life worth having, because of its qualitative nature of being in a right relationship with God. But if one is cut off from a relationship with God, one can be said to be destroyed or to die. In the Bible, death usually means separation, not annihilation. *Death* and its cognates signify the ruin and loss of deep happiness, not nonbeing. So the main contrast between eternal life and its opposite is two very different types of life, not existence verses nonexistence.

Lastly, the biblical words cited above have a wide range of meanings. As David Wells states:

> Sinners are "cut off" (Ps. 37:9, 22, 28, 34, 38), but so is the Messiah (Dan. 9:26); sinners are "destroyed" (Ps. 143:12), but so was Israel (Hos. 13:9; cf. Isa. 9:14) and so were the sheep and coins (Luke 15:4, 8) that were then found; unbelievers are said to "die," but then all of us have always been "dead" (Rom. 6:13; 7:4; Eph. 2:1, 5; cf. Rom. 7:10, 13; 8:2, 6; 1 Tim. 5:6; Col. 2:13; Rev. 3:1), and that surely does not mean we have been without existence and consciousness.[20]

Argument #4: The doctrine of unending consciousness in hell is unjust and immoral. It serves no purpose, it amounts to an infinite punishment for a finite life of sin and, thus, it is a disproportionate punishment, which contradicts divine justice.

Response: In our view, this argument is the strongest one, and in light of this argument, we attempt to go back to scriptural exegesis and see if annihilationism can be made consistent with this problem of injustice and immorality.[21]

In response, we should first point out that we would agree that an unending hell of moment by moment, active torture by God would be unjust and hard to square with his love and the intrinsic dignity of man. But we have already shown that our understanding of hell is different from the torture-chamber model.

Second, the future is only a potential infinite, not an actual infinite. Our life in the future will increase without limit, but it will always be finite in duration. We will never have lived an actual, infinite number of days; we will only live a day at a time forever. So technically speaking, the comparison should be between a finite life before death and a finite, though always increasing, life after death.

In addition, if people reject an ultimate God who is the greatest being that could possibly exist, then an ultimate judgment where one pays with one's life in a final, irrevocable sense is just.[22] Since the term *ultimate* is used differently when applied to God (he is ultimate in the sense of being the most perfect being possible) and to the final state of the unbeliever (which is ultimate in the sense of being final and complete), then it must be admitted that annihilationism cannot be ruled out by simply focusing on the notion of ultimacy. An annihilationist could argue that extinction is, in fact, ultimate. But our point is that the same claim can be made for the traditional doctrine of hell. An ultimate judgment (in an everlasting, conscious sense) could be the proper and proportionate response for the rejection of a maximally perfect being and his offer of love. At the very least, such a scheme is not clearly immoral and unjust, as some of the annihilationists would seem to have us believe. In this regard, Alan Gomes has made the following point about the idea that sins committed in finite time are not worthy of eternal hell:

> [This objection] assumes that the heinousness of a crime is directly related to the time it takes to commit it. But such a connection is nonexistent. Some crimes, such as murder, may take only a moment to commit, whereas it may take a thief hours to load up a moving van with someone's possessions. Yet, murder is a far more serious crime than theft. Second, the nature of the *object* against which the sin is committed, as well as the nature of the sin itself, must be taken into account when determining the degree of heinousness.[23]

The length of punishment for a wrong act, therefore, is not a direct function of the length of time the act took to accomplish, but a function of the seriousness of the act itself. And that, in turn, is partly a function of the nature of the act and the object toward which that act is committed.

But there is a more important, fundamental consideration than the ones just listed: For the sake of argument, if we compare extinction with life in hell, *it is clearly more immoral to extinguish humans with intrinsic value than to allow them to continue living in a state with a low quality of life.* In fact, we do not believe the second alternative is immoral at all, but the first alternative *is* immoral.

Consider the parallel situation in certain end-of-life ethical issues like infanticide (intentionally taking the life of a defective newborn) and euthanasia (intentionally taking the life of a person, which is often justified by appeals to mercy and benevolence).[24] Sometimes people argue that it is morally permissible to intentionally take the life of a person with a low quality of life.

Sanctity of life advocates have argued against this position on several grounds: (1) It calls for the intentional taking of human life, which is wrong (except in war, self-defense, or capital punishment). (2) It fails to respect the incredible intrinsic value and dignity of persons by extinguishing them. (3) It treats persons as means to an end (people and death are used as a means to the end of removing a low-quality-of-life state by killing the patient) rather than as ends in themselves. (4) In light of reasons 1–3, the burden of proof lies on the quality-of-life advocate, not the sanctity-of-life advocate. The former must not only answer points 1–3, but also show that a life of low quality is morally preferable to extinction and death. But showing this is very difficult because such quality-of-life judgments are subjective. Who's to say who has a low quality of life and who doesn't? And on what objective grounds? Moreover, there are no moral things in common between extinction and an existence in a low quality of life to serve as a moral basis for such a judgment.

In our view, annihilationism versus the traditionalists regarding hell form a precise parallel to quality-of-life versus sanctity-of-life positions regarding infanticide and euthanasia. Remember, hell is not a torture chamber, and people in hell are not howling like dogs in mind-numbing pain. There are degrees of anguish in hell. But the endlessness of existence in hell at least dignifies the people there by continuing to respect their autonomy and their intrinsic value as persons. Extinction does not. As Germain Grisez has argued, "The hypothesis of annihilation also is incompatible with . . . God's love of all that is good; for although the damned abuse their freedom, their reality and their freedom remain great goods."[25] So, far from being morally preferable, annihilationism, as its quality-of-life counterparts in infanticide and euthanasia, is morally inferior to the sanctity-of-life view embodied in the traditional doctrine of hell.

We take no glee in nor are we trying to be glib about hell. Hell saddens all of us, God included, but we believe that the traditional notion of hell is both biblically and morally sound.

Argument #5: What about people who, through no fault of their own, never have a chance to hear the gospel of Christ? Do they receive or deserve unending punishing? Furthermore, why did God create people whom he knew would go to hell in the first place?

Response: We must first affirm with Scripture that Jesus Christ is the only way to God. Christ is unique in his claims to be God (John 8:58, 10:30), to forgive sins (Mark 2:10), and in his miracles and resurrection from the dead. Buddha, Confucius, Mohammad, and other religious leaders are still in their graves; Jesus is not. Furthermore, Jesus himself claimed to be the only way to God (John 3:18, 8:24, 11:25–26, 14:6) and this claim is reasserted by Peter in Acts 4:12.

The main issue in religion is truth, not belief. Believing something doesn't make it true. If four people have different beliefs about the color of my mother's hair, they can't all be right, and believing that her hair is red does not make it so. While all religions have certain truths in common, nevertheless, they significantly differ over what God is like, what God believes, what the afterlife is to be, and how we have a relationship with God. The real issue is truth, not belief. If Jesus was who he claimed to be, then he is unique and the only way to God.

We also need to observe that, according to the Bible, God desires all men to be saved (1 Tim. 2:4; 2 Peter 3:9; Ezek. 18:23, 32), and he judges fairly (Job 34:12; Gen. 18:25) and impartially (Rom. 2:11). The biblical God is not a cold, arbitrary being, but a God who deeply loves his creatures and desires their fellowship and worship.

Also, all humans have some light from creation and conscience that God exists, he is personal and moral, and they are guilty before him (Rom. 1:18–20, 2:11–16).

Moreover, the Bible is very clear about the state of those who hear the gospel and reject it (John 3:18, 5:21–24). They will be banished from heaven and sent to judgment in hell. Remember, the most kind, virtuous person who ever lived said these words.

With all this in mind, we can begin to address the first question raised: What about those who don't have a chance to hear the gospel? The Bible doesn't address this question explicitly and for obvious reasons. The Word of God doesn't usually offer a plan B if the church chooses to reject God's plan A. Scripture commands us to go to the world and be sure no one fails to hear the gospel. It doesn't explicitly say, "Here is what will happen if you decide not to act on God's command." So whatever view we reach here must be formulated theologically from God's attributes and general considerations in Scripture.

Here is another point: We must distinguish between the *means* of salvation and the *basis* of salvation. Christ's death and resurrection have always been the basis for our justification before God. However, the means of appropriating that basis has not always been a conscious knowledge of the content of the gospel. Saved individuals before Christ (and surely justice includes people who lived and died within a few years after Christ's execution when the gospel couldn't reach them) were saved on the basis of Christ's work, but they did not know the content of the gospel. They were saved by responding in faith and mercy to the revelation they had received at that point (Gen. 15:6).

Furthermore, most theologians believe that those who cannot believe (infants and those without rational faculties capable of grasping the gospel) have the benefits of Christ applied to them. Many argue this on the basis of 2 Samuel 12:23, where David expresses his conviction that he will be reunited with his deceased infant in heaven. They also appeal to the fact that there is no mention of perdition for children in all the Bible, and they cite God's clear desire to save all humanity, his justice, and his love.[26]

So we believe it is certainly possible that those who are responding to the light from nature that they have received will either have the message of the gospel sent to them (cf. Acts 10) or else it may be that God will judge them based on his knowledge of what they would have done had they had a chance to hear the gospel. The simple fact is that God rewards those who seek him (Heb. 11:6). It does not seem just for another to be judged because of my disobedience in taking the gospel to others, and it is surely possible, and actually the case, that the gospel has not been taken to others in the way God commanded. We (the authors) are not sure this line of reasoning is true, but it does seem plausible in light of the information we have.

If our case is correct, then why reach out to others with the gospel? For three reasons. As we admitted, our answer is somewhat speculative (remember, the Bible does not address the question explicitly). While we think we are right, we should evangelize just in case we are wrong. Also, God commands us to tell others about his Son, and we should obey him out of our love for him. We are also told to spread God's teachings and broaden his family, not merely for what happens in the future state, but to spread his rule now. Why delay and give evil more victory now? Why not bring people mercy and forgiveness and release from sin as soon as possible? Good news should not be delayed.

New Testament scholar Leon Morris puts this whole discussion in perspective:

> Peter told [Cornelius] that God is no respecter of persons, "But in every nation he who fears him and works righteousness is acceptable to him" (Acts 10:35). This surely means that people are judged by the light they have, not by the light they do not have. We remember, too, that Paul says, "It is accepted of a man according to what he has and not according to what he does not have" (2 Cor. 8:12). Long ago Abraham asked, "Shall not the Judge of all the earth do right?" (Gen. 18:25), and we must leave it there. We do not know what the fate of those who have not heard the gospel will be. But we do know God, and we know that he will do what is right.[27]

But a final question remains: Why did God create people whom he knew would not choose him? In our view, Christian philosopher William Lane Craig has provided a very helpful answer to this question.[28]

Craig points out that there are three different moments or forms of knowledge God possesses. First, God has *natural* knowledge. This is God's knowledge of all possible worlds that God could have created. A possible world is one whose description does not contain a contradiction. For example, a possible world could be one where unicorns lived in Montana and goats did not exist. A possible world could not contain square circles, however, because such entities are contradictory.

Second, God has *free* knowledge. This is his knowledge of the actual world from beginning to end concerning what actually happens. God knows everything about the actual world—past, present, and future.

Third, God has *middle* knowledge. This is God's knowledge of what every possible free creature would do under any possible set of circumstances. This is knowledge of those possible worlds God can make actual. For example, I do not have a sister, but God knows a possible person who would have been my sister if my parents had married earlier and given birth to a daughter. Again, I was raised in Missouri and never challenged to become a lawyer, but God knows what would have happened if I had moved to Illinois as a teenager and what I would have freely done had I been challenged as a boy to become a lawyer.

We can further clarify middle knowledge with a biblical example. In 1 Samuel 23:6–13, David was staying at Keilah, having just delivered it from the Philistines. King Saul, who was pursuing David, gathered an army to go to Keilah and besiege David and his men. David, knowing about the plot, inquired of the Lord by asking whether or not Saul was going to come to Keilah, and if so, whether or not the people of Keilah would deliver David over to Saul. The Lord responded by telling David that Saul would come down and the people would turn David over to him if David stayed in Keilah. Hearing this, David left Keilah and Saul gave up the pursuit.

In this example, *God knew what would have happened if David had stayed in Keilah, even though David did not, in fact, stay.* Craig describes this as middle knowledge—knowledge of what a free creature would do in certain circumstances, even if those circumstances do not happen. God knows all the possible creatures he could have created but didn't, and he knows all the free choices all his creatures—those he actually created and those he did not create—would make in all the circumstances they could be placed in (some actually happening, some not happening).

What does this have to do with the doctrine of hell? God knows every possible creature and every possible response they would make to the gospel in every possible circumstance. Given this knowledge, why did God create a world in which people are not saved (he knew before they were born that they would not trust Christ)? Furthermore, because God knows what circumstances need to happen for each person to trust Christ, why didn't God bring those circumstances about instead of other circumstances such that persons placed in them freely reject Christ?

Craig breaks down this problem into four statements:

(1) God has middle knowledge.
(2) God is omnipotent (all-powerful).
(3) God is all-loving.
(4) Some persons freely reject Christ and are lost.

According to Craig, the problem is this: If we accept the first three statements, an objector would claim that we cannot also accept statement 4. For if we accept statements 1–3, the objector holds that we also ought to accept these statements:

(1 ') God knows under what circumstances any possible person would freely receive Christ.

(2 ') God is able to create a world in which all persons freely receive Christ.

(3 ') God holds that a world in which nobody rejects Christ is preferable to a world in which somebody does and consequently is lost.

The objector claims, then, that since God has middle knowledge, he would know for every possible creature just what circumstances need to happen to bring him to Christ, and since God prefers a world in which nobody rejects Christ over a world in which some reject Christ, then God would have the knowledge and power to create a world in which everyone is saved.

Craig's solution to this problem is to reject 1 '–3 ' and replace them with these statements that are more likely to be true:[29]

(1 '') There are some possible persons who would not freely receive Christ under any circumstances.

(2 '') There is no possible world in which all persons would freely receive Christ.

(3 '') God holds that a world in which some persons freely reject Christ but the number of those who freely receive him is maximized is preferable to a world in which a few people receive Christ and none are lost.

Let us look at these in more detail. We have already discussed 1 '' in conjunction with universalism. There we saw that God cannot guarantee that a free creature would accept Christ. That is just what it means to be free. Therefore, of all the possible persons God could have created or did create, some would freely reject Christ no matter what the circumstances. How could God *guarantee* a set of circumstances for each person in which that person *freely* receives Christ? Statement 1 '' seems clearly true then.

For all we know, of all the possible persons God could have created, the vast majority of those who would have rejected Christ never get created in the first place. The number of people who reject Christ may be an act of mercy on God's part. But still, Craig reminds us, the objector may respond by asking why God created *anyone* whom he knew would not trust Christ.

Craig's answer is 2 ''. Perhaps there is no world God could have created in which all persons freely receive Christ. Now on the surface of it, 2 '' does not seem plausible. Suppose of all the possible persons God could have created (including some he did create and some he did not create), there is a set *n* composed of all and only those people who would trust Christ. Then why couldn't God just create a world composed only of people in set *n*? What is the problem here?

Craig's solution is this:[30] It may not be possible to create just those persons and just the right circumstances for all to be saved. Why? It may well be that if God changes the circumstances that allow Smith to freely trust Christ, this alteration may bring it about that Jones will freely reject Christ even though Jones would have accepted Christ in a world without the circumstances needed to bring Smith to saving faith.

An example may help to illustrate this point. Suppose God can bring about two circumstances, one in which my father is offered a job in Illinois while I am a young boy and one in which no offer is forthcoming. In the former case, suppose my father freely accepts the offer and we move to Illinois. In the latter case, we stay in Missouri. Let us call these events C and D, respectively. Suppose further that in circumstance D, three years after the offer could have been given (but wasn't), I will meet just the right person in just the right circumstances and come to Christ. It is entirely possible that I would have had no such opportunity in circumstance C. So my salvation is dependent upon D obtaining as opposed to C. In addition, suppose that if D obtained, I would lead five others to Christ in Missouri in my lifetime, but if C had obtained, then a neighbor of mine in Illinois would have come to Christ by watching my non-Christian life fall apart, but without my bad example he would freely reject Christ. Now suppose this neighbor would have led ten people to Christ. In circumstance D, six people come to Christ (I and five others), and in C, eleven come to Christ. C and D cannot both obtain and, thus, free human choices responding to different influences make it impossible for God to bring about the conversion of all seventeen people.

This example shows that adjusting the circumstances in a possible world has a ripple effect. Not even God can change things piecemeal and respect freedom. If one thing is changed, this has an impact on other things. Additionally, the more people God creates, the greater the chance that some of the people he makes will not trust Christ. So 2″ seems reasonable and quite plausible.

There is another point that can strengthen 2″. In the ancient church there were two major views about the origin of the soul: creationism and traducianism. According to creationism, our bodies are passed on to us through normal reproduction by our parents, but God creates each individual soul out of nothing, most likely at fertilization. According to traducianism, both the body and soul are passed on to us by our parents. Now the soul is the thing that makes us the unique individuals we are. I could have had a different body, but I could not have had a different soul. My soul makes me, *me.*

For the creationist, I could have had different parents from the ones I had. Why? Because God could have created my soul out of nothing and placed it into a different body formed by different parents. In this case, I would have been united to a different body and born to different parents. For the traducian, I could not have had different parents from the ones I had. Why? Because essential to my identity is the fact that I have this very soul, and essential to a particular soul's being the very soul it is, is that it come from just these two people. The soul is passed on from the parents—different parents, different soul.

If we accept traducianism, then God could not have created me without creating my specific parents, and he could not have created my specific parents without creating their specific parents, and so on. In other words, God could only get to me, as it were, by reaching me through my entire ancestral chain. If my great grandparents had married different people, I could not have existed. So when God is comparing alternative possible worlds, he is not just comparing alternative individuals, but alternative ancestral chains in their entirety. It may be that God allows some chains to come about, with some individuals in them who reject Christ (say my great, great grandfather), but which allow for others to be born who do trust Christ. In this case, God would be balancing alternative chains and not just alternative people. Of course, if one accepts creationism regarding the soul (not to be confused with creationism as opposed to evolution), then this solution would be unavailable.

These considerations show that creating a world with a large number of people may have the result that a number of them may be permitted to be lost for some justifiable reason in order to respect human freedom and accomplish some task known by God. What might that task be? Statement 3″ gives us an answer: God prefers a world in which some persons freely reject Christ but the number of saved is maximized over a world in which a few trust Christ and none are lost.

Consider two worlds, W1 and W2. In W1, suppose 50 million are saved and 5 million are lost, while in W2, 5 million are saved and none lost. It is not clear that W2 is morally preferable to W1.[31] If W2 *is* morally preferable, then hell has veto power over heaven. God's purpose becomes the negative one of keeping people from hell, not the positive one of getting people to heaven. In contrast, it may be worth having more people go to heaven to allow more to go to hell. At least this is not clearly immoral. If something like this is correct, then, with Craig, we can affirm the following and add it to his opening four statements:

> (5) The actual world contains an optimal balance between saved and unsaved, and those who are unsaved would never have received Christ under any circumstances.

This would seem to explain why God would create individuals whom he knew would not trust Christ in any circumstances.

A Plea

In this chapter, we have looked at the traditional Christian understanding of hell, and we have responded to alternatives and objections. Our discussion was basically intellectual in nature. We felt this was necessary in order to have the space to lay out the issues.

But no one should treat the doctrine of hell in a cold, uncaring way. Hell may be justifiable, but it saddens God and all who love people. Hell will forever remind us of the significance of human life, its history, and its choices. It will also forever be a memorial to the tragedy of bad choices. Those of us who love Jesus Christ and other people must get about the task of taking the gospel to the world. Action, not just intellectual assent, is the appropriate response to the Bible's teaching about hell.

PART 3

The Implications of Immortality

Chapter 12

Becoming Heavenly Minded

"Christians are so heavenly minded that they are of no earthly good." Have you ever heard this complaint? Maybe it's true that believers are not involved enough in worthwhile "earthly" pursuits. But ironically, why is it often assumed that we *are* heavenly minded? Although we often imagine we really are, perhaps we aren't as much as we think. How can Christians become heavenly minded in such a way that our lives on earth are *truly* changed and for the better? Can our knowledge of heaven and its glories have lasting, intensely practical effects in this life?

We have spent several chapters building a case for the reality of eternal life and catching a glimpse of what it will be like. For the rest of this book, we want to focus on what difference all of this evidence and information really makes where the "rubber meets the road"—in life's day-to-day ups and downs. We will begin in this chapter by viewing the larger picture. We think the truths we have presented can be applied in such a way that it changes one's entire outlook. When we are truly heavenly minded, we will be of great earthly good.

We believe that the New Testament outlook on heaven and its relation to the believer's life is the most revolutionary idea (next to salvation) ever penned. The key here is perspective. The God of the universe invites us to view life and death from his eternal vantage point. And if we do, we will see how readily it can revolutionize our lives: daily anxieties, emotional hurts, tragedies, our responses and responsibilities to others, possessions, wealth, and even physical pain and death. All of this and much more can be informed and influenced by the truths of heaven. The repeated witness of the New Testament is that believers should view all problems, indeed, their entire existence, from what we call the "top-down" perspective: God and his kingdom first, followed by various aspects of our earthly existence. From such an outlook, the upper level remains the same, while the lower tier changes and can even experience transformation for the better. Our assurance of heaven allows us to function from its vantage point, making us free to enjoy our life more while still being committed first and foremost to God.

Let's turn to the New Testament and consider several passages that develop this idea. Then we will look ahead to see how these truths can be applied.

The Divine Outlook

Key Bible Passages

Matthew 6:19–34

This text is perhaps the chief "top-down" teaching of Jesus. Located in the middle of the three-chapter Sermon on the Mount, it is well-known for its prohibition of worry. We are told not to fret over life's needs, since God's care of the birds, lilies, and grass indicates that he will care for us too (vv. 25–32). Besides, why should we worry when anxiety will not change anything, including increasing the length of our life or an inch of our height (v. 27)? Therefore, we should trust God instead of being distressed.

As worthwhile as these thoughts are, they are subpoints of Jesus' overall message here. What he says about worry begins with the word *therefore,* which tells us that his counsel on this subject is not self-contained. It is part of a wider context and depends on it. So let's do some backtracking.

In Matthew 6:19–24, Jesus commands us to store our treasures, not on earth where they can be destroyed or stolen, but in heaven where they are incorruptible (vv. 19–20). Our heart will coincide with the placement of our treasures, wherever they are "invested" (v. 21). And since it is impossible to be equally committed to two different masters simultaneously, we cannot pursue heavenly and earthly treasures at the same time (v. 24).[1]

So Jesus' central teaching is that if God and his kingdom are *genuinely* preeminent in our lives, as they ought to be, *we will have no real reason to be anxious over our earthly affairs.* Problems will certainly arise in our everyday lives, but they should not become our *ultimate* concern. God and his kingdom come first. There should be no competitors.

Looking at this text from another angle, we can see that Jesus is also teaching how incredibly secure our real treasure in heaven is. We have no need to worry, since our heavenly wealth cannot be disturbed.

But here is the rub: If we are usually anxious over temporal problems, our hearts are not centered on what is properly our first love. We are more occupied with transient realities than Jesus intended. So here we have a ready-made test by which we can assess our true motives and the depth of our beliefs.[2]

Interestingly, Jesus also says that, if our priorities are properly attuned, our earthly needs will be met as well (6:33b). What a deal! God *is* concerned about our needs and will supply them (vv. 30–32). But he has also told us in this passage that our daily essentials are his concern, not ours. Our job is to concentrate on his "top-down," heavenly perspective.[3]

So when our lives are beset by worry over our daily needs, we betray our first love, which ought to be God and his kingdom. This is *not* to say that we can arrive at a state where nothing bothers us; believers are not called to detach from living in the world.[4] But we are repeatedly challenged to shift our priorities to God's perspective in order to live above these problems so they will not characterize our lives. By God's power, we *can* conquer at least the more debilitating aspects of these fears. The Christian hope is not a "pie-in-the-sky" perspective unrelated to life's concerns and problems.

Matthew 10:28 and 16:26

In Matthew 10:28, Jesus tells his listeners not to be afraid of those who kill the body but cannot harm the soul, but rather "fear Him who is able to destroy both soul and body in hell." Jesus is saying that the eternal judgment of God should be of more concern than any physical death to which human beings can subject us. The verses that follow (vv. 29–31) speak of God's personal care (reminding us of Jesus' teaching in 6:19–34) and warn of denying Jesus (vv. 32–33). However, the major point is that one's perspective of eternal destiny is even more important than temporal issues of life and death. We should not pay primary attention to our own earthly life or even our death, but to our eternal future.[5]

In Matthew 16:26, Jesus makes an even more striking assertion. He goes beyond the thought that our life should not be considered more dear than our soul, and claims that *everything* the world has to offer is not a fair trade for our soul. So not only is eternity of great value, it is *much more* precious than the *sum total* of earth's enjoyable experiences. That's incredible.

Luke 10:25–37

Here Jesus answers a lawyer's question about how to obtain eternal life. He directs the lawyer to the Mosaic Law and focuses on two important commands. In two parallel passages (Matt. 22:34–40; Mark 12:28–34), Jesus refers to these commands as the two most significant directives in the entire Law. Then he tells a parable to illustrate his point. Also in these texts, he teaches that our relationship to God takes precedence even over service to our neighbors.

The "top" perspective is a radical love of God that places him first and foremost in our lives. We are to love God with all of our heart, soul, strength, and mind.

The "down" perspective is, in this case, not a negative one (such as worry) but an incredibly positive one—love for our neighbors. And Jesus' second command is also radical—it is to be done in the same way we love ourselves.

Only Luke relates the lawyer's follow-up question about the identity of his neighbor, which is followed by Jesus' story of the good Samaritan (Luke 10:29–37). Jesus tells of a traveler, presumably a Jew, who was assaulted by robbers. Although the thieves left him close to death, both a priest and a Levite passed by him without offering to help. However, a

Samaritan pitied him, stopped, and bandaged his wounds. Then he took him to an inn to be cared for and paid all of his expenses.

This story startled Jesus' audience. Jews and Samaritans generally avoided each other out of racial and religious prejudice. Jesus calls us to move beyond these factors in love. But even more than this, Jesus' approval of the Samaritan's sacrifice of time and money to help even a stranger tells us how radical our love commitment to others should be. The Samaritan sacrificed valuable time out of a perhaps already busy schedule, financing a stranger's medical bills from his own pocket, including any future expenses of recovery. Jesus presented a radical view of both financial and time commitment. Then he drove his point home by challenging us to "go and do likewise" (v. 37 NIV).

Jesus' central teaching here is that the order of our love commitment should be God first, others second. We should be *radically*[6] committed to both, since the correct way to love God is with our entire being and the proper way to love others is by our self-sacrificial involvement in their lives, even to the degree we love ourselves.[7]

2 Corinthians 4:7–5:10

Death may be the underlying reality that causes the most potent fear known to mankind. Here Paul handles the subjects of persecution, pain, and death head-on, challenging believers to think about these subjects in light of the top-down perspective.

Paul begins by mentioning the persecution he and others are undergoing, realizing that it will all ultimately lead to his own resurrection (4:14). His present circumstances are not nearly as important as eternal life with the resurrected Lord. Turning to afflictions that affect believers, Paul teaches that, because pain is only temporal, believers ought to shift their thoughts to the reality of eternal life (4:17–18). In some of the most inspirational words in all of Scripture, Paul writes:

> For our light and momentary troubles are achieving for us an eternal glory that far outweighs them all. So we fix our eyes not on what is seen, but on what is unseen. For what is seen is temporary, but what is unseen is eternal.[8] (4:17–18 NIV)

What were some of the "light and momentary troubles" Paul experienced? Elsewhere he tells us what some of them were:

> Five times I received from the Jews the forty lashes minus one. Three times I was beaten with rods, once I was stoned, three times I was shipwrecked, I spent a night and a day in the open sea, I have been constantly on the move. I have been in danger from rivers, in danger from bandits, in danger from my own countrymen, in danger from Gentiles; in danger in the city, in danger in the country, in danger at sea; and in danger from false brothers. I have

labored and toiled and have often gone without sleep; I have known hunger and thirst and have often gone without food; I have been cold and naked. (2 Cor. 11:24–27 NIV)

How can anyone in his right mind call these "light and momentary troubles"? Only a person who is deeply convinced by and committed to a top-down perspective. Here is a life that is truly well lived. There is a longing in our hearts to be like this and, we trust, in your heart as well. However, this quality of life is not primarily a goal to be sought. Instead, it is a by-product of the top-down perspective to be enjoyed.

Paul draws upon the time-space truthfulness and power of eternal life to focus one's thinking. His point is that suffering Christians have no more worthwhile theme to pursue than this. And as we will see, in a real sense this truth can actually alleviate some of their pain.

Next Paul addresses the subject of death itself (5:1–10). Even after bodily death, he says, believers never face the prospect of extinction; they will live forever. God will provide the new bodies for which believers long (5:2, 4). Death is even preferable to earthly life since, while we are in our physical bodies, we do not see Christ, and we are in a real sense separated from him (5:6–7). So death is preferable because we will be with Christ (5:8; Phil. 1:21–23).

Once again, the top-down perspective concerns eternal life. In the light of heaven, earthly life takes on new meaning. Comfort and hope are plentiful even in the face of persecution, pain, and death.

1 Timothy 6:17–19

What about the issues of personal finances and wealth? The scriptural perspective captures these as well. Speaking to the rich, Paul warns them to not be proud of or trust in their possessions. Instead they ought to trust in God, realizing that he is responsible for their wealth and the enjoyment of it. They should also be involved in good works, being generous with their finances, willing to use them to help those with needs (6:17–18). Reminiscent of Jesus' words in Matthew 6, we are told that this use of personal funds, whether we are wealthy or not, builds one's heavenly treasures and even affects the quality of one's eternal life (6:19).

1 Peter 1:3–9

This passage's counsel is couched between two contrasts—heaven and persecution. And the peg anchoring Peter's advice is Jesus' resurrection. This actual historical event is the foundation for the believer's eternal life and the reason for the believer's hope (v. 3). And the term "hope" *(elpis)* in this context indicates that our future prospects rest on a firm, proven cornerstone, not on a mere wish or desire.

Peter tells us that our heavenly inheritance "can never perish, spoil or fade" (v. 4 NIV). The choice of words indicates that the believer's blessings are incorruptible and indestructible, without any blemish whatsoever.[9] He adds with assurance that these qualities are "kept" or reserved for Christians, using a military term *(tereo)* that signifies they are being guarded (or "garrisoned") for us.

The outcome of all this is that the nature, characteristics, and blessings of heaven will never be snatched away from us or become contaminated. Our eternal inheritance is kept eternally secure by the grace and power of God himself. In fact, Peter praises God because these blessings are entirely due to him. God's mercy saved us (v. 3), and his power makes the victory over evil possible (v. 5).

That all of this is God's work and not ours is crucially important. Believers do not deal with earthly problems in their own power. While we *are* called upon to be willing to change our thinking and to act accordingly, we are *not* told to do these things in our own might. We cannot overemphasize this point. Spiritual attainment in thought and behavior does not come from our own human striving and our own abilities to "hang in there." It comes through our obedience to God and his work in us.

Against such an eternal backdrop, Peter implores Christians to consider their present persecution as a temporary obstacle through which God will help them persevere, so they will emerge with a proven and much stronger faith (vv. 6–9). With this heavenly perspective, Peter directs these embattled believers to *rejoice* in the reality of their salvation *even during* their suffering (v. 6)! Similar to Paul's injunction to suffering Christians that they meditate on eternal life even while they are suffering, Peter explains that having a correct perspective on God and immortality ought to cause believers to rejoice even in the heat of persecution. In one sense, the worst scenario would be the believer's death, yet that would usher him or her into Christ's heavenly presence. So although suffering is painful, especially when it also involves our loved ones, and while eternity is not presently visible, our salvation is assured (vv. 8–9) and we will be with Jesus forever.

A similar message is briefly repeated in 1 Peter 5:10–11, where we are told that God himself, through the suffering, would make these believers "strong, firm and steadfast" (NIV). Thus, even beyond the "eternal glory" that is ours in Christ, temporal blessings also proceed from such persecution. And once again, it is God's power that accomplishes all of this, not our own.

Imagine, the knowledge of Jesus' resurrection could be applied in such a way that Christians could actually rejoice in the face of deadly persecution! What a forceful reminder that, even in life-and-death situations, we can find victory over our fears and other evils, experience enduring strength and a proven, strengthened faith, and even add to our heavenly bank account, all by refocusing our priorities heavenward.

These Bible passages are remarkable. With a unified voice, they declare that the upper level of the top-down perspective remains the same: God, his kingdom, and eternal life. Our highest goal is to seek the kingdom of God, where our imperishable treasures and God's righteousness are found. We should be more concerned with our eternal souls than with our own earthly lives and everything the world has to offer. We should keep always before us the hope and magnificent reality of eternal life with Christ and build our lives on this heavenly foundation so that, regardless of what we face, we can handle it in God's strength and from his vantage point.

On the lower level, where the subject changes, life can take on new meaning in the light cast upon it by the upper tier. We can control worry and anxiety if we are investing our treasures in heaven. Our earthly treasures, including money, do not need to control us either; by using them for good on earth we add to our account in heaven. Even fear has no hold on us if we are living with a heavenly mindset. This perspective will also help us reach beyond ourselves with a radical love that can extend to even our enemies. And if people turn on us, hurting us, persecuting us, even threatening our lives, we can find the resources to handle that through God and his power.

In light of these incredible truths, how could any message be more cherished in the hearts of believers? What is intuitively more precious than life itself and true fellowship with other persons? What could be more desirable than a personal eternity spent with loved ones, fellow Christians, and with Jesus Christ, the Creator and Sustainer of the universe? And what message could liberate and enable us more to live as fully as possible here and now—freeing us from the time and energy it takes to worry about paying the bills, how we treat others, death, and even worrying about fear itself? How much we miss on earth when our eyes are not turned toward heaven.

More from Scripture

So far we have only scratched the surface of what the New Testament teaches about the top-down, heavenly perspective. It is probably the most frequent theme instructing Christians on how to cope with the daily grind of earthly existence. So let's dip below the surface to explore what else awaits us.

Hebrews 11

Here we discover an enticing element in the top-down perspective. Believers are pilgrims on a lifelong journey, and our true home is not on earth, but in heaven.

The Old Testament saint Abraham obeyed God's call and traveled great distances, but he was ultimately looking for a city that was not on earth—and this city was built by God (vv. 8–10). Likewise, Moses preferred to be identified with his own people rather than enjoy all of the riches the Egyptians had to offer, because he was seeking his eternal reward (vv. 24–27). Hebrews 11 tells about numerous saints who were like Abraham and Moses, "aliens and strangers on earth" (v. 13b NIV). Their aim was to reach another land; they were seeking a heavenly country (vv. 13–16). None of them, however, received these promises in their own lifetimes. Their rewards were yet future (vv. 13, 39–40).

What were they looking for? What all believers seek—heaven (v. 16). This is a revolutionary aspect of the top-down perspective. The believer's time on earth is a pilgrimage toward heaven. And in a certain sense, believers are finally fulfilled only after they arrive home. Until then, we experience a "longing" for that country (v. 16). Yet, like those who have gone before us, we do not spend our time on earth sitting in easy chairs, doing nothing for the kingdom. We travel onward, committed to the Lord and, in the lower perspective, lovingly involved in the lives of others.

Philippians 3:18–21

In this passage, Paul again uses a top-down motif. He begins by contrasting those who pursue earthly desires with those who prefer spiritual goals. The former crave physical items such as food or their own glory. He sorrowfully regards these persons as enemies of Christ (vv. 18–19). Believers, on the other hand, even while they are still on earth, are already citizens of heaven. And they will eventually receive bodies like the glorious resurrection body of Jesus himself (vv. 20–21). Perhaps one reason we long for God's heavenly city is precisely because we are presently citizens of that country.

Paul's words exude encouragement and comfort, and they remind us of Jesus' repeated teachings that believers *currently* have eternal life.[10] Because we *now* possess both eternal life and citizenship in heaven, we should be even more motivated to lay up treasures there and think and act in a "top-down" manner.

2 Corinthians 8:1–5

This passage deals with possessions. But is is not written to rich Christians—it describes the activities of poor believers. The Macedonian Christians willingly donated to the needs of other believers, even though they lived in poverty themselves. Yet their interests were not only in the material needs of others, for they presented themselves to the Lord *first* and then *afterward* to those in need (v. 5). So regardless of the financial conditions of the persons involved, whether they are wealthy, poor, or in between, the order of perspective and priority is the same: God first, others second.

We could continue to explore other New Testament texts (for example, Phil. 1:21–26, 4:14–17; Heb. 10:34–35), but the heart of their message would remain the same: "Set your minds on things above, not on earthly things" (Col. 3:2 NIV). Our earthly actions ought to be performed from the top-down perspective of God and his kingdom. This primary emphasis on Christians' loving God and spending eternity in relationship with him and other believers should be a tremendous catalyst to help us obey Jesus' second command of radically loving our fellow human beings. But how can this be carried out? How can we really apply heaven's perspective to earth's concerns?

Bringing Heaven to Earth

Even a perusal of certain trends in contemporary Christian thought would lead one to wonder what has become of the message of the centrality of God and his kingdom. It does not often take center stage. But even when it does, that does not guarantee it will be applied. Knowing something is true does not necessarily translate into knowing what to do with that truth.

So when and how can this central Christian message become a signal to guide our entire lives? Scripture indicates that we *should* be transformed. Numerous Christian thinkers have also highlighted this theme. One such person was the nineteenth-century American philosopher Jonathan Edwards. In an essay entitled "The Christian Pilgrim," he admonished believers to pursue eternal life in a single-minded manner:

> Therefore, it becomes us to spend this life only as a journey toward heaven, as it becomes us to make the seeking of our highest end and proper good the whole work of our lives; to which we should subordinate all other concerns of life. Why should we labor for or set our hearts on any thing else, but that which is our proper end, and true happiness?[11]

So how should our lives change? How can we bring heaven to earth? Let's consider some real-life needs and concerns, beginning with evangelism.

Since God and his kingdom should be first in our lives (Matt. 6:33), we should strive to obey Jesus' command to tell others about God's offer of eternal life (Matt. 28:18–20; Luke 24:47; Acts 1:8). How could we share his love more clearly than by seeking to meet the eternal needs of others? In fact, what could be closer to fulfilling Christ's command to love our neighbors as we do ourselves? The method of evangelism we choose will vary with the circumstances, but the fact that we share the gospel should remain a constant.

What about helping other believers discover this top-down perspective for themselves? After all, teaching is also of vital interest in the body of Christ (cf. Matt. 28:20).

Consider also our finances. This is not the place for a long diatribe, but it often seems that even Christians who already give a tithe (or something like it) to the Lord's work find it very difficult to sacrifice much more for such priorities as spreading the gospel or assisting individuals in need.

Admittedly, we, too, are pressed by bills, repaying loans, and just "trying to make it" in these burdensome times. And granted, many of our resources are spent on true needs. Nevertheless, to be fair, many of our other expenditures do not easily fall into these categories. Each of us needs to answer to the Lord concerning what portion of our income would truly be available for his work if we were properly motivated. After all, hasn't it been clear from the biblical witness that to place our treasures in heaven, sending them ahead of us, so to speak, is actually the *greatest* use of our possessions (Matt. 6:19–24)? Doesn't it just make more sense to "save" where the greatest return is achieved? And isn't it far better to store up our treasures where they can *never* be stolen or fail to yield their proper return? Jesus told his followers: "Sell your possessions and give to the poor. Provide purses for yourselves that will not wear out, a treasure in heaven that will not be exhausted, where no thief comes near and no moth destroys. For where your treasure is, there your heart will be also" (Luke 12:33–34 NIV).

What difference will our earthly possessions make one thousand years from now, anyway? When we think about it, where would our finances have been better spent?

However, you may recall that selfish goals, such as accumulating treasures for the sake of the rewards themselves or for our own glory, are certainly not the aim of these biblical passages.[12] We have said that the biblical goal for believers, among other heavenly pursuits, is to fellowship with Jesus and our loved ones forever. Beyond Scripture, the loftiest declaration of any human ecclesiastical creed may be what is contained in the Westminster Shorter Catechism, where we are told that the "chief end of man is to worship God and enjoy Him forever" (Article 1).

How, then, may we actually begin to apply the New Testament teachings on the top-down use of our finances? We could begin by internalizing the biblical instruction on the use of our finances in light of eternity. This would help convince us that cheerful giving to biblical causes is crucial.[13] After all, we are most committed to projects we are convinced are worthy[14] and especially to those in which we are personally involved. We may recall Jesus' words that an individual's treasure is stored wherever his heart is (Matt. 6:21).

Then, we may wish to begin simply by extending ourselves little by little, progressively giving more than we do now. A more radical procedure would be to do a very careful and prayerful assessment of our current spending practices, endeavoring to determine which expenditures can be biblically justified as actual needs. Eliminating unjustifiable expenses can free us to better use our funds in a biblical manner.[15] The sacrificial spirit many of us apply to purchasing a nice "extra" for our home, a new car, a vacation, or other desire could well be applied to our giving to the Lord. While Christians do not like being called materialists, Jesus' words about not worrying are relevant here in a different sense: If we continue to ignore or violate biblical instruction, we are simply demonstrating where our true treasures lie.

Someone could object: "All this talk about 'saving' and laying up treasures for ourselves sounds like it could be pretty selfish in its own way. Shouldn't we share and otherwise act properly just because it is *intrinsically* the right thing to do?" This is a powerful challenge and even has a sort of "ring of truth" about it.

But we have already noted our agreement that the biblical texts we discussed do not teach that the *selfish* accumulation of heavenly treasures for their own sake is a *Christian* motive. It is also clear that the New Testament actually tells Christians to expand their heavenly bank account.[16] Moreover, why is it wrong to desire heaven when we are told that God himself has placed this longing in us and approves of such motives (Eccl. 3:11; Heb. 11:16)?

We should be careful not to throw the baby out with the dirty bath water. Simply because our motives *can* be impure does not indicate that they, in fact, *are*. And since Scripture *does* teach these truths, we know that the core desire for eternal life in heaven with God and our loved ones is proper and ought to be our goal throughout our earthly existence.

Yet, we have also clearly said that biblical teachings such as these are not an excuse for Christians to seek heavenly rewards for their own benefits. So, the flip side is that believers should constantly examine and reassess their own motives and determine to keep the top-down perspective in check so that their heavenly desires are biblical. Our purpose is not to selfishly accumulate heavenly treasures for ourselves. And we can check this by carefully and frequently balancing our priorities.

Admittedly, assessing our perspective in these matters is not always easy, but it is not impossible either. Perhaps a thought experiment may help.[17] If Jesus promised you, "Create your own heaven—you may have whatever you desire," for what would you privately wish? Would you desire power, pleasure, wealth, peace, or great glory and honor from all persons everywhere? What about all of these? Then what if while you are contemplating each of these possibilities and any other wonderful options, you hear Jesus add, "However, there is only one condition to my promise—you will never see my face." What was the very first thought that passed through your mind? Did you perceive a sudden chill? Were you crestfallen? Or were you secretly (of course!) satisfied in spite of Jesus' only condition?

If you realized that the presence of God makes heaven what it is, this may indicate that your desires may at least be pointed in the proper direction. In fact, as we saw in Chapter 9, heaven isn't even heaven without the presence of God.

On the other hand, if the earthly goals still appeared inwardly desirable to you, you need to do some honest reflection. Maybe repentance and the healing work of the Holy Spirit is in order. Perhaps you need to meditate on the teachings and promises of Jesus regarding heaven. That might burn the delight of his presence and fellowship deeper into your consciousness.

If you still wonder whether living with a view toward heaven exhibits a misplaced desire, perhaps a couple of illustrations would be helpful. Do you think the large number of adults who regularly go jogging or participate in other forms of exercise are inherently wrong for desiring not only to improve the quality of their lives but also the length? Or, perhaps as a closer comparison, if you went to the doctor's office to have an ailment treated and were told that you must do certain things in order to live longer, wouldn't you attempt to obey the doctor's instructions? Wouldn't the prospect of lengthening your life provide plenty of incentive?

Would you call persons who participated in either of these activities sinful or intrinsically mistaken because their actions were performed with another, very personal motive in mind concerning their own welfare? To desire life, and eternal life in particular, is a natural, God-given longing. It can be misappropriated, to be sure. But it is not intrinsically evil or misplaced. Yet, because it can be abused, we need to regularly examine our own motives for desiring heaven and living in its light.

Before we press on, there is one more matter about this objection that is bothersome. We think a crude notion of rewards often sneaks into discussions such as these. If rewards are seen as literal ornaments that adorn individuals for their own sakes and have the purpose of enhancing their own glory or centering attention on themselves, this would be a proper concern. But we have already said that humans are endowed with intrinsic value by their Creator. So rewards may be the recognition of a loving Father affirming individuals as made in his image, with the praise ultimately reverting to God himself. Or, as another exciting possibility, what if, instead of extrinsic manifestations, rewards are *capacities* granted by God for greater service and personal growth? At any rate, the natural and appropriate seeking of rewards defined in manners such as these, especially when they are actually prompted by God-given longing, can be very appropriate.

Another way we can bring heaven to earth is by providing assistance to those in need and becoming involved in the lives of others. Jesus certainly did this during his earthly tenure, and, through the story of the good Samaritan, he exhorted his listeners to "go and do likewise" (Luke 10:37 NIV).

However, some might object that this confuses salvation with good works. We wish to be very clear that salvation is not in view here. Our commitment to others comes *after* our surrender to the Jesus of the gospel message. It is a response to what he has already done for us through his death and resurrection. It is not a way to earn the salvation gift.

Other people may think that the top-down scenario actually creates the sort of persons who were described at the opening of this chapter: those who are "so heavenly minded that they are of no earthly good." But it should certainly be clear by now that not to be committed to others sets one against the commands of the Lord Jesus and the New Testament authors. We should aid, serve, and support others precisely because we do value eternity.

How can we begin to reach out? Perhaps the place to start would be to assess our current time priorities. We make time for what we value. What are you spending your time on?

Another step we can take is to pray about being led to persons in need, then to start helping out as we are able. We may need to enlist the help of others, as well. By offering such help, we often open the door to presenting the gospel or meeting other spiritual needs. In fact, helping others can often earn us the right to be heard.

Another way we can apply a heavenly perspective concerns suffering and pain. How do we respond when a loved one, or we ourselves, suffers? If we become depressed, irritable, or resentful, we are encouraged to refocus our thought patterns *during* the pain from earthly concerns to heavenly, eternal ones (2 Cor. 4:16–18; cf. 1 Peter 1:3–9).

Some people have balked at this suggestion, arguing that it alters nothing of consequence because it fails to reduce the actual level of pain, which is the immediate problem. This reply fails on at least two counts.

Since eternal life is a reality and the Bible makes the nature of heaven a high priority in our thinking and acting, the biblical advice is correct *even if* our pain is not thereby lessened. Eternal life is still ultimate reality, even long after the pain actually subsides.

Even aside from this, we maintain that this heavenly perspective *can,* in fact, actually lessen the pain. Perhaps an analogy will help make this clear. A promising word from a medical doctor regarding the absence of any serious sickness often lessens pain, since the patient's emotional fear has been reduced. Similarly, a correct perspective on eternal life can adjust our thinking from the immediate situation and give us the assurance that, at least ultimately, everything will turn out fine (even eternally so!). This heavenly conviction can cause us to react more calmly by refocusing our attention away from the pain, thereby reducing the pain's emotional component. This is a valuable result, since the emotional element of pain is frequently the most painful one.

Two last areas where we need very much to apply these principles are anxiety (especially the fear of death) and religious doubt. However, since the subject of the fear of death is integral to our overall thesis in this book, it will be the sole topic for the next chapter. The remedy (changing our thinking) is also relevant and applicable to the general issue of worry.[18] The question of doubt, on the other hand, takes us to a very broad field far beyond this book.

The Top Line

In business, people talk about the bottom line. They want to know how expenses and revenues will hurt or enhance a venture's success. The bottom line is all-important.

From a Christian perspective, the bottom line gains its value from the top line. Earthly gains equal zero if heaven's perspective is ignored. The top line, then, is all-important. And if it is properly in place, the bottom line will flourish. In essence, that's what this chapter has been about.

God and his eternal kingdom are to be sought above all other pursuits. Said another way, we are to view everything from his heavenly perspective. And when we do, we will begin to experience freedom from at least the more painful effects of life's worries and fears, and we will discover innumerable opportunities to bring heaven into the lives of others. Then we will be both heavenly minded and of significant earthly good. And the people we touch will get to taste heaven in the personal way God intended them to.

Chapter 13

Overcoming the Fear of Death

Have you ever been shocked by a sudden confrontation with the reality of your own mortality? Perhaps the catalyst was the funeral of a loved one or friend, or your own close brush with an accident or disease. Maybe the prompting came in the form of a reminder of your age (however young), or from something as simple as a picture of a casket. At moments such as these, the whispered truth is that we, too, will die someday.

The dread that sometimes fills our hearts at the mere mention of the subject of death is a common experience for humans. Often this anxiety lasts only for a moment; other times it initiates a downward emotional spiral. But whether the experience is spontaneous and short-lived or lingering for long periods of time, it is usually discomforting and even traumatic.

We have said that, for believers, ordering our lives from a "top-down," heavenly perspective can affect our entire outlook and actions. Now we want to know what it can do for our fear of death. How does the reality of eternal life and even a partial knowledge of its nature help us deal with our own mortality?

It is probably true that the ultimate fear known to humankind is caused by the reality of death. Believers are not exempt from such fears. The biblical writers frequently reflect on the anxiety associated with this topic.[1] In one penetrating passage, we are told that many persons are in bondage to the terror of death throughout their lives. However, Jesus came to release them from that fear (Heb. 2:14–15).

One text that graphically presents a life-and-death struggle is 2 Kings 20:1–11. Here we are told that King Hezekiah is quite sick, and he is informed by the prophet Isaiah that he will die. Hezekiah is grief-stricken by the news, praying to God and weeping bitterly (vv. 1–3). The king, righteous though he was, had no desire to die; he was even fearful that his earthly life would soon end. On this occasion God responded to Hezekiah's prayer by granting him a fifteen-year extension on his life (vv. 4–11).

Perhaps you can identify with Hezekiah. We, too, frequently experience dread at the prospect of death, either our own or that of a loved one. Maybe we even fight these emotions every time we undergo a painful or nagging illness, or even suspect the threat of such situations. Why do we have such a fear of dying? Is it possible to get to the place where we can successfully deal with at least the anxiety-producing portions of this fear? These are the areas of focus for this chapter, and they are practical ones indeed.

Why We Fear Death

There are several reasons we may experience anxiety at the thought of dying. For many of us death is associated with pain, and this is even thought to be the chief evil. So we want to go quickly and painlessly. If we could just "go in our sleep," that would be the best.

This last thought points to another aspect of our consternation: We often suffer trepidation at the prospect of looking forward to an imminent demise predicted by our doctor. We sometimes fear that every illness may be our last. In such cases, it is almost as if we would rather deal with death itself than with its anticipation. We would rather have death come silently and swiftly so we will not have time to think about its arrival.

Another factor that causes a great degree of dread is the thought of terminating our relationships with our loved ones on earth. Ironically, this may even be the case with those who, because their priorities are properly placed, value relations with persons over their enjoyment of things. So they worry about the possibility of being separated from those they have loved so much. This emotion usually intensifies when the anxious individual is a parent with small children.

Visions of funerals, caskets, and bodily decomposition also plague many believers. With such concerns, we probably have specific examples of anxiety causing our imaginings of our death.

Perhaps the chief fear we have of death involves apprehension over the unknown. In spite of the Bible's teaching on the nature of the afterlife, believers bemuse in "what if" terms. What if Christianity is *not* true? What if our interpretation of the Bible's teaching is incorrect? Admittedly, it is so easy to constantly wonder if one is right, after all.

Closely related to our apprehension is the horror of nonexistence. Doubts arise concerning the reality of an afterlife—*any* kind—even though the Bible clearly affirms one. What if nothing exists after death? Few things are as violently opposed to the nature and desires of humans as utter extinction.

Still another worry comes from the fear of being alone. Nothing changes the basic fact that dying is something we do by ourselves.

Some believers even tend to be afraid of judgment or at least of standing before God. This fear can persist in spite of our knowing the biblical attestation that Christians will not be judged to determine their final destination, but to determine their rewards.

It is doubtful if many human beings ever escape from experiencing one or more of these fears about death, and this includes Christians. Fancy or smooth talking will not remove these fears entirely either, at least not in most cases. As long as individuals insist on allowing emotions to judge the facts, including entertaining visions of their most horrible anxieties and "what if" scenarios, such fears will plague them.

So where does this leave us? Doesn't Hebrews 2:14–15 say that Jesus came to deliver us from our fear of death? Aren't we told that even those who were tormented all their lives by this paralyzing anxiety may be freed from it? Didn't Paul add that the death of loved ones need not cause believers to grieve as do persons who have no future hope (1 Thess. 4:13)? Absolutely, but none of these passages (nor any others in Scripture) claim that we will be totally free of the emotional struggles that arise from time to time. We are told, however, that victory over at least the more crippling elements of this fear is possible. Let's see how.

Finding Victory Over Our Fears

The basic New Testament response is that the death and resurrection of Jesus, viewed along with the heavenly perspective these events provide, ultimately supplies the chief answer to our dilemma. This is the uniquely Christian response to death, and it provides the basis for how we can handle our fears of death.

For instance, it is undeniable that pain frequently accompanies death. And yet, we have already seen that Paul counsels believers to focus their attention on eternal life instead (2 Cor. 4:7–18).[2] He carefully explains that this perspective follows from the fact that the Christian's troubles are only momentary and terminal—they will not last long. On the other hand, the afterlife is eternal, blissful, and of inestimable value, so it warrants our concentration (vv. 17–18). The reality of Jesus' resurrection provides the firm ground for Paul's concept of eternal life in this passage. Believers will be resurrected by the same God who raised Jesus from the dead (v. 14). And as we saw in the last chapter, this "top-down" perspective can actually lessen our pain (and especially the emotions) associated with death. But even so, eternal life is true and is still a reality long after the pain actually does wane.

While granting that looking forward to the prospect of our death is unpleasant, it is also true that this says more about the state of our thinking processes than it does about our actual demise. An extremely important part of maintaining a "top-down" perspective involves the ordering of our thoughts so we can replace unedifying ideas with truthful, encouraging ones. We must learn to not allow concentration on temporary conditions, however real, to supplant eternal truths. Certainly suffering is real and death will come, but these realities are not ultimate. And when we treat them as such, we blind ourselves to eternity's vantage point—in fact, we replace eternal reality with temporal vision. We must keep Paul's words before us, allowing them to clear our vision: "I consider that our present sufferings are not worth comparing with the glory that will be revealed in us" (Rom. 8:18 NIV).

In Philippians 4:6–9, Paul also addressed the topic of worry and challenged his readers' anxious thinking (v. 6), commanding them to pray, give thanks and, perhaps most importantly, exchange their anxious thoughts for edifying, truthful ones (v. 8). Then he exhorted his readers to practice this process until it became a way of life (v. 9). How can we do this?

It is best to apply these steps *precisely during* the time of anxiety. We must learn to cultivate the disciplines of prayer and thanksgiving. Then we need to identify the things we tell ourselves that are not only misplaced but merely contribute to our worry. Lastly, we must substitute godly thoughts for anxious ones. Practicing these truths during our roughest moments, whether we feel like it or not, is the key. As Paul says, constantly rehearsing this process until it becomes a habit will lead to peace.

We should also remind ourselves that this process of perspective transformation is not a mind game meant to manipulate our thinking or con us into believing reality is something other than it is. This process is based firmly on the truths of Jesus' resurrection and eternal life. So it is when we *fail* to participate in mind renewal based on truth that we actually fall prey to falsehood and illusion.

This subject of redirecting our thinking patterns is much more than a nice-sounding, quickly stated suggestion to stem the tide of fear. It is thoroughly biblical, and for those interested in scientific verification, it is also based on well-proven psychological methods. It has been tested in a variety of circumstances and demonstrated that it really, truly works.[3] Now let's turn to how we can handle the fear of death or of losing a loved one.

While we cannot escape the fact that earthly relationships temporarily cease at death, we are clearly told in Scripture that true knowledge of and fellowship with others will occur only in the future state (1 Cor. 13:12). We will be reunited with believing family and friends, either by death or by the coming of the Lord (1 Thess. 4:17–18). Our relationships will broaden and deepen in the afterlife too (Matt. 8:11; 2 Cor. 5:8). So, while the sting of death still separates us temporarily from loved ones, ironically it is also the only way to achieve true and lasting fellowship with them.

Consider also the fear of extinction fostered by visions of funerals, caskets, and bodily decay. This fear is directly due to improper thinking patterns we can correct. It is also misplaced factually, because eternal life, not eternal extinction, is a reality. So, however unpleasant and scary these imaginings may be, they will not hinder us from experiencing immediate consciousness after death. We do, in fact, survive our own funerals and bodily decomposition. A blissful existence awaits believers (2 Cor. 5:8).

In 1 Corinthians 15:53–57, Paul also states that after our bodies are raised, death will finally be conquered. The grave will have lost its bite (vv. 53–56); it will maintain no more control over the destinies of human beings. And once again, the certainty of these events is an empirical, factual one: Because of Jesus' resurrection from the dead (v. 57; 2 Cor. 4:14), our bodily resurrection and the defeat of death are definite.

Although we will not deny that death embodies the chief unknown ever encountered by man, Jesus did experience it, and he conquered it by rising from the dead. And while Jesus' resurrection does not tell us everything we may wish to know about the nature of eternal life, it does reveal enough that there is no need to be so fearful of death. Because of Jesus' experience, death and its aftermath are no longer a frightening mystery. We really can know their most important aspects and calm our sometimes raging fears. In fact, in this book we have even developed a "Christmas morning" picture of heaven. We do, indeed, have some good ideas of what heaven will be like, and we will also be pleasantly surprised by what we don't know about it or can only speculate about. Therefore, while we perhaps know very little about what follows death, what we do know is abundantly able to soothe our fears if we will only allow it.

From this we can also find reasons for calming our worries about the threat of nonexistence. We know certain details about heaven, including our immediate existence after death, because of Jesus. And Scripture confirms that we will still be alive after our bodies die (Phil. 1:21–23; 2 Cor. 5:1–8). So this is yet another place where practicing proper thinking is imperative. Nonexistence is simply an unbiblical and untrue prospect, so why concentrate on it?

For similar reasons, we can rest assured that we will not be alone after death. We experience fellowship, and that even more fully, after our passing to the next world (Matt. 8:11; 2 Cor. 5:8). Jesus exemplified this fellowship during his post-resurrection appearances to his disciples. So there is no factual basis for the belief that the afterlife is a separate, lonely existence. The facts argue otherwise. The sooner we align our thinking with these facts, the sooner we will experience our own personal victory over the fear of death.

Standing before Christ's judgment seat (see 2 Cor. 5:10) is another worry for some Christians, but it doesn't need to be. Believers will be present with the Lord after death (v. 8; cf. Phil. 1:21–23), not rejected by him. Christians will not be condemned (John 3:16–18, 36; 5:24–29), because of Christ's actions on our behalf, accomplished through his death and resurrection (Eph. 2:4–7). Anxieties to the contrary dominate us because we do not think biblically about them. Only unbelievers need to fear condemnation. So the answer to any worries we have about death is to trust the Lord in light of the known facts of the gospel (2 Cor. 6:2). The certainty of our future should not give us an excuse to be proud or calloused (1 Cor. 10:12), but it should help us realize deep within our being that our eternal destiny is not at stake.

Now none of this means that death is our friend. Death is an enemy, a consequence of our wrongdoing, a bitter pill that goes down hard, choking joy out of life. Thinking about it often hurts. And suffering through it as it claims loved ones (or even just contemplating this event) tears at our hearts and minds.

As painful as all this is, though, we can find hope and solace in the fact that death is not the end. It does not have the final say. For Christians, ultimate victory lies on the other side of death. And there we will find the best in (eternal) life. God through Christ has turned death into the door that opens to the fullest possible joy—heavenly bliss (Ps. 16:11). As believers, we can stare death in the face and see it as an evil from which God brings good. For us it can even be a blessing to die so we can be at home with Christ (Phil. 1:21–23; 2 Cor. 5:8).[4] The more we can bring our thoughts in line with these truths, the greater will be our opportunity to conquer even the most painful side effects of the fear of death.

Of course, we are not suggesting that we can (or should even try to) progress to the place where even the thought of our own death or that of a loved one does not bother us. But this is not a defeat. The temporal separation and pain we experience even affected Jesus after the death of his friend Lazarus. Jesus stood in front of Lazarus' tomb and wept (John 11:35). And Jesus even knew that he would raise Lazarus from the dead! Feelings of loss and sadness are appropriate. But we don't have to fear death and what lies beyond it. Like all human beings, Christians struggle with their emotions, but they do not have to be overcome by them. Believers can still achieve victory over the most painful results of mankind's greatest fears. That's the testimony of Scripture. And it's the witness and example of Jesus, who even though he wept over death, came to free us from the bondage-creating elements of this king of anxiety.

A Strategy for Facing Death

Here we will outline three steps to handling our fears of death: (1) internalizing the truth that eternal life is an actual reality; (2) shifting our pattern of thinking to God's heavenly, "top-down" perspective; and (3) replacing our anxious thoughts of death with these biblical truths. In other words, we need to be sure of the reality of eternal life, apply this truth to everyday life, and then allow these new attitudes to transform our fearful thoughts about death. Now we want to walk back through these steps, showing you even more specifically how you can rely on them to help you overcome your fears.

Internalizing the Truth That Eternal Life Is Real

Throughout this book we have provided numerous evidences and arguments that eternal life is real. Just one of these evidences, Jesus' resurrection from the dead, provides a strong, twofold argument for the believer's eternal life. First, the very nature of his resurrection indicates victory over death. When the disciples saw the risen Jesus, they beheld walking, talking, eternal life. Second, Jesus' central message was the kingdom of God and the necessary requirements for entrance into eternal life. So if any of Jesus' messages were vindicated by the resurrection, his teachings about the afterlife were, since they were his chief focus.

Since eternal life is a fact, to reject it involves accepting a falsehood, and to believe it as true lays the foundation we need to shoulder sickness, disappointment, and fear. Since Christians will live after the death (or even the final corruption) of our earthly body, we have no ultimate reason to fear its power. The glories of heaven can even make the prospect of our future abode an enjoyable longing (Phil. 1:20–24; 2 Cor. 5:8). At the very least, while still viewing death as an enemy and a necessary evil, we do not have to be overcome with worry over its reality.

Shifting Our Thought Pattern to God's Heavenly Perspective

Once we embrace the truth that eternal life is real, we must learn to view death and immortality from God's eternal perspective. This is yet another facet of what it means to seek God and his kingdom above everything else (Matt. 6:33). We need to turn our thinking from suffering, pain, and death, however real and painful they may be, and redirect our thoughts toward eternal life (2 Cor. 4:14–5:10; Phil. 1:21–23).

The heavenly perspective is the theme of Hebrews 11. The heroes of the faith are extolled for having spent their entire lives in pursuit of their eternal home. This lifelong quest is far more meaningful than any earthly, mundane aspiration (Heb. 11:8–10, 13–16, 24–27). Elsewhere, believers are told not to pursue or be satisfied with physical gratification because their citizenship is already in heaven (Phil. 3:18–21).

This perspective is a life-changing principle—perhaps even the chief general guideline for Christian ethics in all of the New Testament. Living by the "top-down," heavenly perspective is radically liberating because it calms and frees us from life's usual worries to live for God and his kingdom, which ought to be our first love.

So how does all of this relate to the fear of death? Once believers know eternal life is a reality, they need to think and act in light of that reality. By changing our vantage point to a "top-down" one, we have actually prepared ourselves to practice the third step to defeating our fears.

Replacing Our Anxious Thoughts with Biblical Truths

Every time we experience anxiety over death, we need to replace that thought with a biblical, edifying one. Maybe the truth that will help you will be the fact of Jesus' resurrection. Or maybe it will be some other aspect of the reality or nature of eternal life, such as what we know about heaven. Or perhaps God's promises about immortality will be the most comforting. Regardless what biblical truth or truths you're drawn to, you need to recall and rely on them when potentially debilitating fears raise their ugly heads. In fact, cultivating this practice even when the fears are not present will help you build a strong, edifying, biblical mindset (Rom. 12:2).

For example, topics such as the resurrection of Jesus or scriptural promises concerning heaven would be excellent themes for personal, daily meditation. This practice would provide "preventive therapy" before the specter of doubt ever rose in your mind or heart.

Specific occasions for death anxiety such as funerals, close brushes with death, or startling portrayals of the reality of the grave (such as cemeteries and pictures of caskets) are more of a challenge. In these cases we need to immediately review such truths as those listed above. It would also help to constantly remind ourselves of the evidence for eternal life and that the contrary images before us do not represent ultimate reality. Even concentrating on the nature of the afterlife would offer us positive reinforcement for countering fearful thoughts *that are contrary to the evidence anyway.*

Aside from the idea of death, everyday sorts of struggles such as finances, the best use of time, sickness, worry, and doubt are constant reminders of the need to apply the "top-down" perspective to our thinking. With financial and time concerns, we can assess our current priorities, eliminate poor choices, and begin acting by extending ourselves into those projects that are more in keeping with our heavenly priorities. And before sickness, worry, and doubt get us down, we need to weed out truth from error, identify misbeliefs, confront them with what's really true, and replace them with truthful conceptions.[5] The truth will set us free (John 8:32). Lies always enslave.

We readily admit that weeding out unbiblical thoughts can be hard and demanding. But its rewards are incalculable. It cannot only correct our bad habits (Phil. 4:8–9) and allay our fears, but also revolutionize our entire lives.[6] The key here is to *practice* substituting biblical truths for nonbiblical ones until our emotions are corrected.

Are you convinced of the reality of eternal life? Will you commit, with God's help, to reorienting your thinking toward a heavenly perspective? Do you really want to face your fears and directly and repeatedly confront them with God's truth? You can enjoy a taste of heaven on earth. This strategy[7] for dealing with the fear of death can bring some of the nectar of heaven's fruit to even the most bitter fact of life.

Some Thoughts on Handling Grief

Before moving on, we would like to deal briefly with the subject of grief, because it is a close companion of death and our fears of the grave. Losing a loved one can be traumatic, no matter how the loss occurs. We can feel disoriented, abandoned, alone, resentful, angry, and despondent. We may even wish to end our own lives so we can join our deceased loved ones. How can the truths of eternal life help us through such a loss? Let's see how Jesus himself dealt with this so we can gain some ideas on how to deal with it in our own lives. More than once, Jesus counseled those who were grieving after the death of a family member or friend. And he taught that something could be done about their emotions (and ours).

When Jesus first spoke to his beleaguered disciples after his own death, his resurrected presence and comforting words changed them from doubt and fear to joy and faith (John 20:19-20, 27-29). Just seeing and hearing their resurrected Lord was enough to calm their fears and comfort their sorrowful hearts.

Sometime before Jesus' crucifixion, he comforted Martha and Mary after the death of their brother Lazarus (John 11:17-44). In response to Martha's expression of grief, Jesus reminded her that Lazarus would be raised from the dead (v. 23). Martha misunderstood him at first. She thought he was just reminding her of the commonly accepted Jewish doctrine of the day: Her brother would rise again at the final resurrection along with all of the other righteous dead (v. 24). Jesus gently corrected her and explained that he was the resurrection and the life and that those who exercise faith in him will live even immediately after death (vv. 25-26a). Martha embraced these truths, hoping in their reality (vv. 26b-27).

Jesus was not disputing the doctrine of the future resurrection of the righteous dead. He was informing Martha that the resurrected state involves immortality—deathlessness. As a result, believers remain conscious after death and before their resurrection. Jesus taught her what he would later say to the believing thief on the cross next to him (Luke 23:43) and what his disciples would perceive much more clearly after witnessing Jesus' resurrection appearances: One's consciousness does not cease at death. Then, to show both Martha and Mary that he was indeed the Lord of life, Jesus raised their brother Lazarus from the dead (vv. 34-44).

So, with Martha and later with his own disciples, Jesus counseled grieving persons with the facts and their implications.[8] His own resurrection appearances were the chief answer for his disciples, while, for Martha, the answer was found in the theological instruction about the true meaning of immortality: Believers do not cease to exist after death and before the final resurrection of the body. The reality of personal life after death was the foundational truth on which Jesus' comments were based, and his counsel shows that comforting the bereaved is important and it can be successful, even during stressful times.

Perhaps you have recently lost someone close to you. Or maybe that person died some time ago, but you still grieve the loss. Maybe you know someone who is struggling over the death of a loved one, and you're not sure how to help that person. Whatever the case, know that the risen Jesus intimately understands the grief, the loss, the sense of abandonment. And he has promised that all those who follow him will join him in blissful fellowship in heaven, reunited with their believing loved ones, feasting on the sweet, incorruptible fruit of eternal life. This will not make the pain go away, but drawing from this well of truth will bring healing balm to the aching wounds. "Come to Me," says Jesus, "and drink" (John 7:37).

Chapter 14

Dealing with Abortion, Infanticide, and Euthanasia

In the fall of 1987, a retired couple—we'll call them Betty and Fred—entered a nursing home. Fred appeared to be in good health as did Betty, except for the fact that her kidneys had failed and she was on kidney dialysis. Betty's life revolved around two things—her husband and her activities as a concert pianist. Within a month of entering the nursing facility, Fred suffered a massive heart attack and died unexpectedly. Betty was shattered, but kept herself together by focusing on an upcoming Christmas performance of Handel's *Messiah* at her church. A week after the performance, Betty experienced a mild stroke that left her unaffected except for one thing. The slight paralysis in her hands left her unable to play the piano. Faced with the loss of her husband and musical ability, Betty felt life was no longer worth living. She petitioned the nursing home administrator to permit her to forego her dialysis treatments. He agreed. A few days later, Betty passed away.

Technology had kept Betty alive, and its removal led to her death. Should her request have been granted? Should technological assistance have been removed? The rise of advanced medical technologies has brought to center stage a number of ethical dilemmas at the end of life. Is it permissible to take a patient's life if that person is suffering intractable pain or no longer wishes to live? Recently, a physician thought so, and he invented a suicide machine for a woman patient who used it to take her own life. We can keep people alive indefinitely in a comatose state. Is that morally obligatory? And how does the afterlife figure into such questions? Should it have made a difference to the nursing home administrator, morally speaking, if Betty had been an unbeliever or a believer?

These are difficult and complicated questions and a whole book would be required to do them justice. Obviously, even if we had all the answers to them, which we do not, we could not detail them here. But we would like to wrap up our treatment of immortality by seeing how it impinges on end-of-life ethical issues. We want to survey some important distinctions involved in end-of-life ethical decisions, especially focusing on medical issues. Then we want to look at how the doctrines of heaven and hell can inform our moral views about these issues, particularly about abortion, infanticide, and euthanasia—three of the most controversial and practical ethical/medical issues in our day.

Ethics for the End of Life

Critical Concepts

Natural moral law

Before we step into the sometimes murky and treacherous waters of end-of-life ethical issues, we need to understand some key concepts so we won't lose our way or crash into hidden reefs. We will begin with a lesson on natural moral law.

For the Christian, the Bible is an authoritative source of moral rules, principles, and insights. However, throughout church history, Christian thinkers have acknowledged something called natural moral law found in general revelation—that revelation of God and his truth found in creation.[1] According to natural moral law theory, there are moral laws or norms that are true and knowable to all people without the special revelation found in the Bible. Passages like Genesis 18:22–25, Amos 1 and 2, and Romans 1 and 2 teach that believers and unbelievers alike have a basic insight into the nature of justice, stealing, murder, and truth-telling. Humankind may not always acknowledge or live in keeping with natural moral law, but the norms are still there. They come from God, and they are rooted in creation.

Natural moral law is important for believers because it provides, at least in principle, common moral ground to argue moral issues in a pluralistic culture and a secular state. Natural moral law also provides believers with a basis for what we believe to be the appropriate Christian view of civil government: Believers should not try to Christianize the civil government or put it under the church or Scripture; instead, we should work for a just government.[2]

The natural moral law contains moral absolutes. What is a moral absolute?[3] Basically, it is a moral rule (like "Do not murder" or "Keep your promises") that guides actions, tells us what ought to be the case, is objectively true whether anyone believes it or not (we discover morality, we do not invent it), and is universal—it applies at all times, in all places, and to all cases that are similar in a morally relevant way.

To sum up, then, natural moral law comes from God, it provides absolutes, it is knowable through nature by all people, and it provides moral grounding for debate in a pluralistic culture and a secular state. Granting the existence of natural moral law, why doesn't everyone interpret it the same? Why do people differ over what they believe is right or wrong? This leads us to lesson two.

Moral theories

One of the tasks of a moral theory is to organize, clarify, justify, and apply moral rules and principles.[4] Such rules and principles are prescriptions like "respect persons," "tell the truth," and so on.[5] Regarding moral rules and moral theories, two main competitors fight for our allegiance: utilitarianism and deontological ethics.[6]

Although there are several types of utilitarianism, they boil down to basically this: An act (such as, "Am I going to lie now or tell the truth?") or moral rule ("keep promises" or "break promises to save people embarrassment") is right if and only if it produces as much overall good consequences (called "utility") as any other act or rule open to the person acting. No act or rule is intrinsically right or wrong. The rightness or wrongness of an act or rule is *solely* a matter of the consequences it produces.[7] What kind of consequences? According to utilitarianism, the important consequences are the nonmoral goods produced by the act or rule: pleasure vs. pain, friendship, health, love, the satisfaction of individual liberties and preferences, and so on.

The other main competitor is deontological ethics. *Deontological* comes from the Greek word *deon,* which means "binding duty." Deontological ethics are usually associated with theological ethics and with the moral thought of philosopher Immanuel Kant (1724–1804). A deontological approach to ethics has three important features.

First, duty should be done for duty's sake. The rightness or wrongness of an act is, at least in part, a matter of the intrinsic moral features of that kind of act. For example, acts of lying, promise-breaking, or murder are intrinsically wrong regardless of the consequences produced by them. Consequences may help me discover how to do my moral duty, but they do not make something my moral duty. If I have a duty to benefit a patient and not harm him, then the consequences of various medical treatments may help me discover which treatment best helps me do my duty. But the intrinsic rightness of the rule itself, not its consequences, is what makes this duty binding on me.

Second, humans and persons ought to be treated as objects of intrinsic worth—as ends in themselves and never as mere means to some other end. If a person is treated as a mere means to an end (say, by letting the police department punish an innocent man to deter other criminals who mistakenly think the police are efficient and swift enough to capture criminals), then this is immoral, even if the consequences are good (crime goes down because of social impressions of police efficiency).

Third, some duties are more binding than others. Jesus taught that there are greater and lesser matters of the law (Matt. 23:23), and most deontologists believe in what are called *prima facie* duties.[8] A prima facie duty is a duty that can be overridden by a more stringent duty, but when such a situation occurs, the prima facie duty does not disappear but still makes its

presence felt. A prima facie duty is always to be acted upon unless it con-
flicts on a particular occasion with an equal or stronger duty. Consider the
following example.

Suppose an elderly man in a nursing home is engaging in certain forms
of self-destructive behavior. He pulls out his feeding tube and tears off the
bandages protecting his bed sores. A nurse has two duties to the man: she
has the duty to benefit the patient and not harm him; she has the duty to
preserve the autonomy of the patient and his individual liberty of action
and movement.

In this case, the presence of self-destructive behavior makes the first
duty more important than the second. So the first duty overrides the second, making it morally justifiable to restrain the elderly man's liberty of
action. But the duty to preserve autonomy, even though prima facie and
overridden, still makes its presence felt. How? The nurse is not justified in
constraining him in any way she wishes (e.g., taping his mouth shut so he
cannot talk). She is only justified in constraining him as little as necessary
to protect him. Thus, the prima facie duty, though taking a back seat, is
still present informing the situation.

In short, deontological ethical theory holds that duties, principles, and
commands have intrinsic moral value, duty should be done for duty's sake,
persons have intrinsic moral value and should be treated as ends in themselves and never merely as means to an end. Neither are all moral duties
equally binding and weighty. The following chart compares and contrasts
the deontological view with utilitarianism.

Two Competing Moral Theories

Deontological	Utilitarian
Command focused	Consequences focused
Duty is intrinsic	Duty is instrumental
Moral value performed	Nonmoral value produced
Regulations are primary	Results are primary

We cannot evaluate these two theories here.[9] But you should know that
we, along with the vast majority of Christian philosophers and theolo-

gians, believe that deontological ethics is philosophically and theologically superior to utilitarian theories. Throughout the rest of this chapter, we will draw on a deontological viewpoint to guide our navigation through moral waters. Which brings us to consider a number of critical principles.

Many key moral principles are relevant to assessing ethical issues at the end of life. Some of these moral rules, as understood in a deontological sense, are:

(1) *The principle of autonomy.* A competent person has the right to determine her own course of medical action in accordance with a plan she chooses. We have a duty to respect the wishes and desires expressed by a competent person.

(2) *The principle of nonmaleficence.* One should refrain from inflicting harm (or unduly risking the infliction of harm) on another. Nonmaleficence requires me to refrain from doing something harmful to someone.

(3) *The principle of beneficence.* One should act in order to further the welfare and benefits of another and to prevent evil or harm to that person. Beneficence requires me to do something helpful for someone.

(4) *The principle of justice.* Everyone should be treated fairly and receive the benefits and burdens due him. I have a duty not to discriminate unfairly against a person and not to distribute benefits and burdens in a disproportionate way.

(5) *The preservation of life principle.* People have a moral duty to preserve and protect innocent human life whenever possible.

Most of these principles are self-explanatory, but two comments may help to shed further light on them. Let's begin by considering the principle of autonomy. Why should we accept it and how is it justified? Ethicist James Childress has argued that the principle is derived from and justified in terms of a more basic principle—the respect for persons.[10] We have a fundamental duty to respect persons as ends in themselves because they have intrinsic value. Respecting a person as a self-legislator or respecting a person's individual liberty of thought and choice are captured in the principle of autonomy and, thus, acting in accord with it is one way to respect persons.[11]

On the other hand, it should be obvious that the duties listed above can come into conflict. Recall the case of Betty and Fred. There was a conflict between the principle of autonomy, which would imply that Betty's request to forego dialysis treatments should be honored, and the principles of beneficence and nonmaleficence, which would imply that no action should be taken to harm and not benefit Betty, and causing her death is clearly a great harm.

The distinctions we have just made shed considerable light on moral questions of death and eternal life. For example, if utilitarianism is true, then some argue that abortion could be justified as a means of ensuring the heavenly salvation of aborted fetuses. Others argue that annihilationism is wrong because it violates the deontological principle that one should not treat people as a means to an end. Snuffing out someone's life as a means to removing suffering in hell goes against this principle. Still others claim that it is permissible to allow a terminally ill patient to die if she is a believer, but not if she is an unbeliever. Why? Because allowing an unbeliever to die violates the principles of beneficence and nonmaleficence, since it sends people to hell and harms them.

We want to deal with these issues in more depth, but before we do, we need to explore one more important concept.

The law of double effect

When we evaluate the morality of someone's action, we take into account the intention of the person who acted. For example, if a person drives recklessly through a residential area and kills someone, he is morally culpable. We charge such a person with manslaughter. But if that person drove through the same residential area and *intentionally* ran over someone, we should consider him even more culpable. He would be guilty of murder. Morally speaking, our intentions, or lack thereof, make a difference.

When we evaluate the morality of someone's action, we also take into account whether or not that person uses an immoral means to accomplish some end that may be either morally good or neutral. For example, suppose your next-door neighbor was a self-centered egotist who constantly bothered the rest of the neighborhood with excessively loud noise, lewd behavior, and physical intimidation. Now suppose that you knew that your neighbor hated children and would move if you put a swingset in your backyard. Two situations could arise. You could put the swingset up with the sole intention of harassing and harming your neighbor. If you followed through with the swingset, you would accomplish a good result—the neighbor would move and peace would be restored to the community. But you would accomplish this result by means of an evil, namely, a malicious intent.

You could follow through with a second possibility, however. You could put up the swingset solely for the purpose of providing a place for your children to play, even though you could foresee that such an action would cause your neighbor to move. Morally speaking, the second situation would be better because the good result was obtained not by means of an evil action, but by means of a good action (providing a place for your children to play).

These two moral insights—the importance of intentions and the avoidance of using bad means to accomplish good or neutral ends—have long been a part of Catholic and Protestant moral thought. Christian ethicists captured these and other insights in what is called the principle of double effect. This principle states that when an action has good and bad consequences, it may be performed under these circumstances: (1) The act is good, or at least indifferent, regarding the end that one directly intends; (2) the good and evil effects follow immediately from the act—that is, the good effects are not obtained by means of evil effects; (3) one only intends the good effect and merely tolerates the bad effect, even if that bad effect was foreseen prior to the act; (4) there is a proportion between the good and bad effects—the good must be at least equal to the bad. An illustration may help clarify these four conditions.

Suppose someone was terminally ill with only a few weeks to live. He was in terrible pain, wanted to die, and had no hope for recovery. An injection of morphine would alleviate his suffering, but also shorten his life from a few weeks to a few days.

Now think about this illustration in light of the four conditions just mentioned. According to the first condition, one should not inject the morphine into the patient with the express intent of killing him. This act would have death as its intended end, so it would amount to the intentional taking of innocent human life. But suppose a person really intended to alleviate suffering by bringing about the death of the patient through the morphine injection. Here the intent is different, but condition two still forbids it. Why? Because it accomplishes a good effect (the alleviation of suffering) by means of an evil effect (directly causing the death of the patient). But a third option could be chosen. One could honestly intend only to treat the patient's suffering by the injection, even though death could be a foreseen but unintended and tolerated result. In this case, suffering is not alleviated by means of an evil (death), but by means of a good (the intentional use of a pain medication). The principle of double effect says that such an action is permissible because death is not intended nor is suffering alleviated by means of an evil.

This example may make you think that the principle of double effect is unduly nitpicky with its emphasis on intentions and means to ends. "After all," you may reason, "the results are the same in each case, so who cares about intentions?" Because our society is so pragmatic and results oriented, we often feel impatient with finely tuned discussions, including those over moral issues. We want to press on to the bottom line and not "waste" time with minute distinctions. Nevertheless, the principle of double effect is extremely important because it captures the centrality of intentions and means to ends that figure crucially in moral actions. To grasp this point, let's look at another scenario.

Suppose Patty, Sally, and Beth each has a grandmother who will leave behind a large inheritance. Each woman visits her grandmother on a Saturday afternoon and brings her a cherry pie. Patty, motivated by respect for her relative, intends to love her grandmother by staying with her for the afternoon and giving her a cherry pie. Sally, who is motivated by greed, intends to secure a place in her grandmother's will by staying with her grandmother for the afternoon and giving her a cherry pie. Beth, motivated by hate for her grandmother, intends to secure a place in the will by giving her grandmother a cherry pie with poison in it.

Each woman has a motive, an intent, and a means to accomplish that intent. A motive is why one acts, an intent is what one is deciding or purposing to do, and a means is a step one takes to accomplish that intent. Patty had a good motive (respect for a relative), a good intent (to love her grandmother), and a good means to accomplish that intent (spending time with her grandmother and giving her a pie). Sally had a bad motive (greed), a bad intent (selfishly to secure a place in the will), and a good means to that end (the same as Patty used). Beth had a bad motive (hate), a bad intent (the same as Sally's), and a bad means to that end (poisoning her grandmother). This illustration shows that motives, intents, and means to ends, far from being irrelevant and nitpicky, are all crucial to assessing a moral action. The law of double effect tries to capture these important notions.

Withdrawing vs. withholding treatment

This distinction is fairly straightforward. If a person withholds medical treatment, he does not start that course of action. If someone withdraws treatment, he stops what has already begun. Emotionally, some people feel it is morally preferable to withhold treatment rather than withdraw it, perhaps because it seems more dramatic to stop something than not to start it in the first place. But ethically speaking, it is hard to see any relevant difference between the two. If it is morally permissible to withdraw a treatment, then it would have been morally permissible, all things being equal, to withhold the treatment, and vice versa. The issue is not starting or stopping a treatment per se, but whether the treatment, considered in itself, is appropriate or inappropriate for this patient in this condition. Thus, there is no important moral distinction between withholding and withdrawing treatment.

The ordinary/extraordinary distinction

Ethicists frequently distinguish ordinary means of treating an illness from extraordinary means. Ordinary means are all medicines, treatments, and operations that offer a reasonable hope of benefit for the patient without placing undue burdens (such as pain or risk of serious harm) on him or her. They are morally mandatory. Extraordinary means are those that are not ordinary—they involve excessive burdens on the patient and do not offer reasonable hope or benefit. They are morally optional.

The six basic concepts are extremely valuable for our ability to navigate accurately through the ethical issues that arise at the end of life. Now that we know what they are, we need to push out into the water and use these navigational tools to work through two critical, practical ethical issues: euthanasia and infanticide.

End-of-Life Ethical Issues

Euthanasia

The term *euthanasia* comes from the Greek language and literally means "good death" or "easy death." More broadly, euthanasia refers to the ending of a person's life regardless of whether such an act is active or passive, or voluntary or involuntary. Since these latter distinctions— active/passive and voluntary/involuntary—are important, we need to spell them out in some detail.

The active/passive distinction amounts to this: Passive euthanasia refers to the withholding or withdrawing of life-sustaining treatment in certain justifiable circumstances and allowing a patient to die. The distinction between voluntary/involuntary is also important. Voluntary euthanasia proceeds with the informed, autonomous consent of the person involved. Involuntary euthanasia proceeds without this consent because the person involved is incapable of granting informed consent.

Currently, there are two schools of thought regarding the morality of euthanasia: The traditional approach has been embraced by the vast majority of Christian ethicists and theologians. According to this view, there is an important distinction between active and passive euthanasia. The former is morally forbidden, but the latter is morally permissible in certain circumstances—medical treatment may be foregone when the patient is terminal, death is imminent, treatment is extraordinary, and death is not directly intended. We (the authors) accept this position.

Recently, however, a more radical view has been growing in popularity through the influence of groups such as the Hemlock Society and the Society for the Right to Die.[12] The radical view sees no distinction between active/passive euthanasia and it implies that the intentional and direct killing of an innocent human being is morally permissible in certain circumstances (for instance, the patient requests death, or the patient is in terrible agony and death is allegedly the only merciful option). Physician-assisted suicide, where a doctor helps a patient commit active euthanasia against himself (say, by prescribing sleeping pills to a hopelessly ill patient with knowledge of their intended use), is an example of active euthanasia.

The radical view is morally inadequate for several reasons. First, a mistaken diagnosis can be reversed in passive euthanasia. If treatment is withdrawn or withheld and the patient was not as severely sick as thought, he or she will get well. Obviously, no such possibility exists if active euthanasia is allowed.

Second, advocates of the radical view justify active euthanasia on the grounds that it is often the only merciful way to alleviate suffering and pain. But this is not the case. For one thing, if proper medical care is administered, then cases will be very rare where medication cannot manage pain and suffering and stay within acceptable limits. This would not degrade or inappropriately distress the sufferer. Furthermore, even in cases where pain cannot be so easily managed, a doctor can offer medication that is not intended to bring about death, even if death is a foreseen consequence of the medication. In such cases, medication is given to contain pain and not to kill, even if the dosage required will shorten life as a foreseeable result. Finally, though this can be abused, suffering and pain are not without meaning and purpose and should not be avoided at all costs. If the goal of life was to avoid suffering and pain no matter what, even at the expense of what is morally right, then human life itself would be radically devalued.

Third, active euthanasia violates the special duties health care professionals have to patients, namely to preserve their lives and "be present to them" in a caring way when a cure is impossible. If we allowed active euthanasia as a medical practice, it would seriously alter our trust and respect for the health care profession, and it would cause an overall weakening in our value of and respect for human life.

Fourth, and most importantly, active euthanasia is wrong because it involves the direct, intentional killing of an innocent human being. Such an act removes a creature of intrinsic value. It is an act of murder. It treats the person as a means to some end, even if that end is an appropriate one (the removal of pain). And it accomplishes that end via an evil act.[13]

Infanticide

Infanticide refers to the practice of intentionally taking the life of a defective newborn or allowing the newborn to die. The former would be a case of active euthanasia, so it must be judged morally inappropriate for the reasons listed above. The latter would be an example of passive euthanasia, so the question arises: "Under what circumstances, if any, is it morally permissible to allow a defective newborn to die?" There are five major views about infanticide, and three of them are especially relevant to our present concerns.[14]

One perspective is the *third-party-harms* view. Advocates of this view claim that decisions to treat or not treat defective newborns should include a benefits/harms consideration to those other than the infant. If an infant's continued existence would seriously harm a marriage, adversely affect a family, or require an undue amount of society's resources, then it is morally permissible to allow the infant to die.

Several objections have been leveled against this position, but one is especially important. The third-party-harms view dehumanizes defective newborns by treating them as a mere means to the end of benefiting others. Humans are ends in themselves and should never be treated as mere means to ends. Further, humans have incredible intrinsic value simply as humans. How can a monetary price be put on an individual infant?[15] This view fails to respect the infant, so it must be judged a failure.

Another view is called the *quality-of-life* position. According to this view, it is morally permissible, and some would argue obligatory, to forgo treatment for a defective newborn and let the newborn die if its quality of life drops below a certain threshold. Different phrases are used by different advocates to state this idea. The infant's life is "a life not worth living." Or it is not "meaningful life," nor does it have the potential to be one. Or it is not an "acceptable life." Or it is a "poor quality of life."

Different criteria have been offered for what counts as a poor quality of life: The infant has low potential for social utility; his life would not be subjectively satisfying to most people; he fails to exemplify an ability to have a self-concept, use language, have meaningful relationships with God and others, autonomously pursue chosen goals and ambitions, etc.

Critics have raised numerous objections to the quality-of-life view, but three are central. In the first place, quality of life judgments are highly subjective and, thus, inadequate as objective claims about the morality of a practice. As we noted, advocates of this view hold to different criteria, and no general agreement exists as to the number, importance, and identity of those criteria. Moreover, evaluations of quality of life change throughout a person's life. What is often acceptable at one period of life is not judged acceptable at another. Also, quality-of-life judgments generally reflect cultural and socioeconomic bias and prejudice.

Another major problem with the quality-of-life position is that its advocates must show that some infants are better off dead than alive. But merely showing that they are in bad shape does not prove that they are better off dead than alive. The fact is that there is no way of comparing a life with defects to a state of death and showing that the former is morally inferior to the latter, because there is no clear, common basis of comparison between them.

One final problem is this: The quality-of-life view has a defective view of what it means to be human. It fails to treat infants as entities with intrinsic dignity and value, and it tends to reduce the value of human beings to their social utility or to a view of persons as bundles of pleasant mental and physical states or capacities. The value of our continued existence does not reside in the pleasantness of our life or in our usefulness, but in the simple fact that we are made in the image of God.[16]

A third view regarding infanticide is the *sanctity-of-life* view. It holds that all infants have equal intrinsic worth and dignity simply because they are human beings. So if it is wrong to withhold treatment from a normal infant, it is wrong to withhold it from a defective infant. Additionally, the only cases where foregoing treatment is justifiable are those where passive euthanasia in general would be justifiable. In short, we should treat all nondying infants as equally valuable in themselves.

This position has at least five strengths. It preserves our basic, considered intuition that all human beings have equal and intrinsic worth and dignity by basing that dignity in the only thing we all have in common—being human. If value accrues to us in virtue of possessing something else, say rationality or a self-concept, then since we do not all share these equally, we should not be treated equally. But this is morally repugnant.

This position also places the proper focus of infanticide on the infant alone, and it preserves the principle of justice, which requires that we do not discriminate against the weak and helpless.

Third, it locates the real issue about nontreatment within the broader discussion of euthanasia rather than focusing on issues specifically involved with infants.

The sanctity-of-life view also preserves the basic moral insight that humans have special, intrinsic value compared to animals (humans, not animals, are made in the image of God), though we ought to respect the (lesser) rights of animals as well. If we are valuable because of our quality of life, then some higher, healthy primates are more valuable than defective newborns, because the former can have a higher quality of life.

Fifth, this view lines up with the basic conviction that it is simply wrong to kill babies.

In summary, we have seen that infanticide should be viewed as a special case of the broader issues surrounding euthanasia.[17] We have also seen that active euthanasia is morally forbidden, but passive euthanasia can be morally permissible. Ethical dilemmas at the end of life are not easy, and they often involve heartbreaking options, but we show love, respect, and care to each other if we try to face these dilemmas in a morally sensible and correct way. This brings us to the crux of our exploration.

The Afterlife and Moral Decisions

How do the realities of heaven and hell figure into ethical decision-making at the end of life? Do they make a difference? These are hard and complex questions, but we want to offer some very brief, but we hope helpful, comments on certain aspects of two important end-of-life issues—abortion and euthanasia. Since we have seen that infanticide is really just an application to infants of the broader questions about euthanasia, we will not look specifically at infanticide. But what we say about euthanasia below also applies to infanticide. We'll begin with abortion.

Abortion

A consistent deontological, sanctity-of-life position holds that abortion is morally forbidden (except in rare cases where the life of the mother is clearly in jeopardy) because, among other things, such an act treats a human as a means to an end, it violates the most basic right of all (the right to life), it involves the intentional taking of innocent human life, and it is not in keeping with what a virtuous person would do to another, regardless of one's legal rights.

However, one might think that the doctrine of hell changes this situation. Infants who die go to heaven. If a child is allowed to grow up, that child may reject Christ and go to hell. Therefore, it is merciful to have abortions to insure heaven as a future state.

This line of argument is morally inadequate. As we saw in our treatment of the law of double effect, it is wrong to accomplish a good end (heaven for aborted fetuses) by means of an evil (the intentional killing of innocent human life). God does not honor evil acts, and he does not need us to kill people to insure that his universe is just and merciful.

Furthermore, this argument proves too much, for, if it's true, it shows we ought to kill all children before they leave the womb or reach a certain age, say four years old. But this alleged moral and merciful act cannot be consistently universalized; everyone cannot nor dare not practice it. Because this act of will (killing all babies before they can reject the gospel) would result in removing all future acts of will, since the human race would become extinct. It turns out to be a self-refuting moral legislation that eliminates future moral legislations. This line of thought, then, is irrational and immoral.[18]

Euthanasia

The traditional view of euthanasia provides an argument against annihilationism. Remember, according to the traditional view, it is wrong to intentionally take a person's life, even if there is a low quality of life present. We need to take seriously the biblical notion that people are made in God's image, they are ends in themselves, and they are objects with incredible intrinsic value even if they have low social usefulness or quality of life.

We do not wish to caricature the annihilationist view, but two things appear to be implicitly contained in this position. First, annihilationists seem to believe that extinction is morally superior to a state of low quality of life and that God can treat people as means to an end—that is, as a means to a state of no shame or anguish due to annihilation. In other words, it is morally permissible (and perhaps, morally obligatory) to annihilate people as a means to the end of obtaining an anguish-free state (a state of nonexistence). But this is very hard to prove, as we saw in the case of infanticide. On what basis or according to what criteria could one show that a state of misery was *morally* inferior to nonexistence? In fact, how can you compare any state of being with nonbeing? What's to compare between something and nothing? In any case, annihilationism disrespects persons by treating them as means to an end.

Second, when annihilationists claim that everlasting hell serves no purpose, their argument comes perilously close to treating hell and persons in hell in utilitarian terms. The argument seems to be that the utility of humans in hell is absent, therefore, such persons and such a state are of no value. But this is wrong. Hell may serve as a perpetual reminder of human dignity and freedom, of justice, and of God's style of noncoercive rule. More importantly, the mere existence of individuals is good, since they have value in themselves, regardless of what further purpose they fulfill.[19]

Besides questions about annihilationism, there are other important aspects of euthanasia and the afterlife. We have already seen that active euthanasia is wrong. But what about heaven and hell and the permissibility of passive euthanasia?

Let's begin by looking at the case of a believer. No one denies that passive euthanasia is morally permissible, given certain circumstances (the person is terminal, death is imminent, the treatment foregone is ordinary, and death is not directly intended or caused but merely foreseen and tolerated). Passive euthanasia is an attempt to recognize that death is inevitable, and there comes a time when a person should be allowed to pass away. However, for the believer, such a decision should not be made by simply focusing on that person's desires, individual liberties, and rights. Believers are members of God's kingdom. Everything in our lives, including the way we face death, is not just done for ourselves, but for God and others. Also, we will be rewarded in heaven for what we have done here on earth. So while living wills are certainly appropriate vehicles for expressing our desires in case we reach a point when we are no longer able to do so, our expressed desires should not be formed by merely reflecting on our individual rights, liberties, and desires.

Happiness is not the point of life, but rather serving God and others. Suffering gives me an opportunity to teach others in the community how to live well. I should try to face my death in a way that increases my influence on others, allows me to teach them by my example how to face life's various hardships, and give them hope and courage. When I am trying to decide what to do in a painful situation, my consideration should not be simply to try to avoid pain. I should also try to consider the opportunity pain gives to grow, teach others, trust God, and model a concern for virtue to others. And I should also remember that the way I die will leave behind a good or bad model, and I will be rewarded in heaven for this final act of service.

We are not trying to glorify pain, nor are we saying that a person should continue to live no matter what. But believers should face death with a broader picture in mind than simply that of avoiding hardship and preserving their individual liberties and rights. That broader picture will include the rewards of heaven for a death well faced and the impact we have on others. Sometimes, the only thing a person still has to give to others is a virtuous, courageous, instructive approach to death.[20]

What about passive euthanasia and the unbeliever? Remember our earlier discussion of the principles of beneficence (we should act to benefit others) and nonmaleficence (we should refrain from harming others). It could be argued that allowing an unbeliever to die, in cases where passive euthanasia would otherwise be justifiable, is morally inappropriate because the fact that he would go to hell introduces serious harm and violates the principle of nonmaleficence.

This argument makes an important point. We should consider life after death as a harm in deciding when it is morally appropriate to allow passive euthanasia. And we should use every appropriate means to share Christ with those facing such decisions whom we suspect to be unbelievers. We should be sure people have had a clear chance to trust Christ in these situations.

But it does not follow that we should never allow an unbeliever to die. Passive euthanasia can still be morally appropriate. Why? For one thing, we should respect a person's autonomous choices. God respects such choices so much that hell is a part of his universe. Following God's model, it is morally correct to respect a person's choice to be allowed to die (in cases where passive euthanasia is justifiable).

Furthermore, we must trust providence. If God has allowed the person to reach a terminal state where death is inevitable, and if we recall that God desires all to be saved and, in fact, will postpone a person's death if all that person needs to be saved is more time, then we can rest confident that he would not have allowed this state to be realized if more time was all that was needed. True, only God knows when that state is reached for a person, and we should continue to try to give people opportunities to trust Christ. But we should also be wise in recognizing providence as well. If it appears that passive euthanasia is morally justifiable, we should trust that God has allowed this to come about, knowing full well that he would not have done so if more time for repentance was all that the person needed.

Valuing Life

Issues at the end of life are among the most important things that should matter to us. Living and dying in morally sensitive ways signal the value and purpose of life and give honor to God. As Paul reminded us, whether we live or die, we are the Lord's. And we should treat one another, regardless of age, health, usefulness, and the like, as valuable in God's sight and in ourselves as creatures made in God's image. In this light, what we become and what we do on earth have a staggering impact on what our lives will be like beyond the grave. And they certainly influence what others around us think and do about the afterlife. Ethical decision-making is no exception.

Eternity in the Balance

The topic of immortality is here to stay. And it is imminently relevant to each of us and those who will come after us. In this book we have tried to demonstrate this relevance by first establishing that eternal life is a reality. We examined many arguments that claimed to provide *evidence* for an afterlife, and we considered counterarguments against each one. We rejected some arguments as poor ones (like the simplicity of the soul and a human's kinship with God). We judged others to provide some value, though they did not solve the issue of immortality by themselves (such as the connection with theism,[1] the nature of the self, and the argument from desire).

We also presented three independent arguments that we think are the strongest ones for eternal life—the case for substance dualism, the resurrection of Jesus, and near-death experiences. Each of these topics was explained and defended in depth. Immortality is a fact.

We then moved to what we can know about eternal life. Our purpose in discussing several integral topics regarding the *nature* of eternal life was to emphasize the most important subjects and those that had solid grounds upon which to draw conclusions. We did not present or assume any certain eschatological outlook, but rather developed a more generalized overview of immortality.

We supported what we termed a "Christmas morning" view of the nature of the afterlife. We can be persuaded of the general outline of the future, and even of some of its details, but we don't have to be overly particular about how and when everything will fall into place. Basically, what we know about God, combined with some of the key notions about the future, lead us to also expect very pleasant surprises about eternity.

Then we shifted to the "so what" section: What *implications* should the afterlife have *for* our "here-life"? We applied our arguments and conclusions to concerns of daily living and ethical decision-making. Because immortality is a fact, it should entail a radical commitment at least on the part of Christians.

We hope we have convinced you, if you didn't already believe this, that there are few subjects more important than eternal life. We have tried to take you from theory to application in one volume. Immortality is a theoretical issue concerned with truth and a practical matter that begs for our response. Life after death screams at us that this world is not all there is to our existence. And because the afterlife is eternal, it should have some priority in our earthly lives. In short, eternal life has both qualitative and quantitative precedence over our lives here and now.

For believers in Jesus Christ, the truths of immortality lead to issues of application. What does the truth of eternal life say about this present life? What decisions should we make? How should we bring our thoughts and actions in line with its precepts? Granted, the concerns of this earthly existence ring loudly in our ears. Jobs, bills, traffic jams, fears, and relationships clamor for our attention. Yet we must recognize above all else that our priorities should be viewed from the top down. Since heaven lasts for all eternity, and as a far superior place, we should give more thought to it than we do to preparing for anything else. We must become heavenly minded in order to become of any great earthly good.

For unbelievers, the reality of the afterlife is no less important. And the first decision they need to make involves their destination. If Jesus is indeed the only way to eternal bliss in heaven, then unbelievers must come to grips with his gospel message. Surrender to him is the prescribed means of obtaining this afterlife. Failure to surrender to him puts one on the road away from heaven toward everlasting anguish. No one needs to or must choose hell over heaven. Eternal happiness is open to all, but only those who choose it will receive it. Eternity hangs in the balance of our free choices. We, the authors, have made our choice. What will yours be?

Notes

Beyond Life's "Certainties"

1. For the truth of Christianity, see J.P. Moreland, *Scaling the Secular City* (Grand Rapids, MI: Baker, 1987); J.P. Moreland and Kai Nielsen, *Does God Exist?: The Great Debate* (Nashville: Thomas Nelson, 1990). For the historicity of Jesus and his resurrection, and the New Testament, see Gary Habermas, *The Verdict of History* (Nashville: Thomas Nelson, 1988); Terry L. Miethe, ed., *Did Jesus Rise from the Dead? The Resurrection Debate* (San Francisco: Harper & Row, 1987).

Chapter 1   Reasons to Believe

1. See Alvin Plantinga, "Reason and Belief in God", in *Faith and Rationality,* ed. by Alvin Plantinga and Nicholas Wolterstorff (Notre Dame, IN: University of Notre Dame, 1983), pp. 16–93; Roderick Chisholm, *Theory of Knowledge* (Englewood Cliffs, NJ: Prentice-Hall, 3rd ed., 1989).

2. See Chisholm, *Theory of Knowledge,* pp. 8–17.

3. It is possible to be an atheist and believe in life after death, and to be a theist and deny life after death. For examples of the former, see C.J. Ducasse, *Nature, Mind, and Death* (La Salle, IL: Open Court, 1951), pp. 423–502; G.M.E. McTaggart, *Some Dogmas of Religion* (London: Edward Arnold, 1906), pp. 77–111. But this does not imply that life after death is equally plausible and at home in a non-theistic vs. a theistic universe.

4. Elton Trueblood went so far as to claim that "apart from theism or some similar belief, . . . evidences for immortality have little persuasiveness. The reality of God is the only assurance we have of ultimate rationality." See *Philosophy of Religion* (Grand Rapids, MI: Baker, 1973), p. 302. Cf. Richard Purtill, *C.S. Lewis's Case for the Christian Faith* (San Francisco: Harper & Row, 1985), pp. 120–131. In our opinion, this claim is an overstatement.

5. Cf. William J. Wainwright, *Philosophy of Religion* (Belmont, CA: Wadsworth, 1988), pp. 108–109.

6. Geddes MacGregor, *Introduction to Religious Philosophy* (Washington, DC: University Press of America, 1981), p. 206. MacGregor does not focus simply on the value of persons, but on the value of ideal goals realized only in persons. Either way, extinction appears to be morally unacceptable.

7. See H.P. Owen, *Christian Theism* (Edinburgh: T & T Clark, 1984), p. 132. Cf. John H. Hick, *Death and Eternal Life* (San Francisco: Harper & Row, 1980), pp. 152–156. The argument from justice can be given a non-theistic formulation. An argument of this sort takes its starting point from some abstract principle of justice as a principle of being and goes on to assert that reality unfolds according to the moral requiredness of the uni-

verse and such an unfolding includes life after death. For a picture of what an argument of this sort would look like, even though life after death is not specifically mentioned, see John Leslie, *Universes* (London: Routledge, 1989), pp. 165–183.

8. Patrick Sherry offers another argument relating God's existence to life after death. The argument is too detailed to be considered here. See Patrick Sherry, *Spirit, Saints, and Immortality* (Albany, NY: State University of New York, 1984).

9. For examples of this, see Eugene Fontinell, *Self, God, and Immortality* (Philadelphia: Temple University, 1986), pp. 165–199. Cf. J.P. Moreland, review of *Self, God, and Immortality* in the *International Philosophical Quarterly* 29 (Dec. 1989), pp. 480–483.

10. Plato's dialogue *Phaedo* contains different examples of this type of argument, especially *Phaedo* 100b–107a.

11. Cf. Plato, *Phaedo* 60c ff.; McTaggart, *Some Dogmas of Religion*, pp. 107–109; Augustus H. Strong, *Systematic Theology* (Old Tappan, NJ: Revell, 1907), pp. 984–986.

12. Some philosophers believe that so-called abstract objects (properties, sets, propositions, numbers) are self-existent like God, and therefore, God did not create them. See Nicholas Wolterstorff, *On Universals* (Chicago: University of Chicago, 1970), pp. 290–300. For an alternative view that embraces the existence of abstract objects while allowing that God "created" them, see Alvin Plantinga, *Does God Have a Nature?* (Milwaukee: Marquette University, 1980).

13. It is fairly standard to define simplicity in terms of the absence of parts, but that is not really correct. Something can fail to be simple if it has an internal differentiation of properties or parts. A property (e.g., redness) is a universal that can be in more than one thing (e.g., my flag and your apple) at the same time. A part is a particular that cannot be in more than one thing at the same time. Thus, if an apple is annihilated, its parts are destroyed but its properties are not. Furthermore, there are separable and inseparable parts. Separable parts are those that can be separated and still exist, e.g., the skin and the core of an apple. Inseparable parts cannot be separated and continue to exist: in a tiny spread of surface area of an apple, the two states of affairs—the shape-of-the-spread and the redness-of-the-spread—are inseparable parts. Something can lack simplicity by possessing more than one property or more than one separable or inseparable part.

14. It is sometimes suggested that when an electron jumps from one orbital to another, it ceases to exist at the moment it leaves the first orbital and comes to be at the moment it arrives at the second orbital. If true, this would be a case of annihilation. See Michael Peterson, William Hasker, Bruce Reichenbach, and David Basinger, *Reason and Religious Belief* (New York: Oxford, 1991), p. 75. However, several problems arise if we take cases like these as real examples of ceasing to be and coming to be. First, there would be no reason why an electron, as opposed to something else, say a water molecule or grain of sand, comes to be at the location occupied by the second orbital. Since nothing exists at the moment before something comes to be, literally nothing exists at the moment of coming to be that could control the process and determine what it was that popped into existence. Second, even if an electron came to be at the second orbital, why would it be the same electron as the one that ceased to be instead of a brand-new electron? Third, this would appear to violate the first law of thermodynamics, namely, that energy can be neither created nor destroyed. It is better to take cases like electrons' jumping orbitals as either cases of transformation (the electron changes form during the interval "between" the two orbitals) or, even better, as cases where our current theories simply do not define the state of affairs between the two orbitals. By the way, if someone believes there are time atoms (ultimate, smallest intervals of time possible such that divisions of time reach ultimate intervals of time beyond which no further divisions are possible), then an electron could jump in such a way that there simply was no interval between the two orbitals. But in this case, neither would there be a ceasing to be nor a coming to be, but simply a discontinuous jump.

15. See Ducasse, *Nature, Mind, and Death,* pp. 161–173; W.E. Johnson, *Logic Part III: The Logical Foundations of Science* (New York: Dover, 1924), pp. 78–101; C.D. Broad, "The 'Nature' of a Continuant," in *Examination of McTaggart's Philosophy,* vol. I (Cambridge: Cambridge University, 1933), pp. 264–78.

16. See McTaggart, *Some Dogmas of Religion,* pp. 108–9; Richard Purtill, Michael Macdonald, and Peter J. Kreeft, *Philosophical Questions* (Englewood Cliffs, NJ: Prentice-Hall, 1985), pp. 378–9. Wainwright lists McTaggart's argument as one regarding the simplicity of the soul. See William J. Wainwright, *Philosophy of Religion* (Belmont, CA: Wadsworth, 1988), pp. 104–6. But McTaggart's argument involves the unity of the soul, not its simplicity. It should also be pointed out that the body of a living organism, e.g., the human body, is not simply a physical object, because the soul diffuses throughout the body and makes it a distinctively and irreducibly *human* body while it is ensouled. Sometimes philosophers speak of the lived body and the body as object. The former refers to the body-as-*mine,* that is, the body as that in which and by which I relate to the world. The latter refers to the body-as-*object* or the empirical body, that is, the body as a mere object of knowledge or study. The lived body includes the notion of the body as ensouled, whereas the body as object need not utilize the notion of a soul at all.

17. Robert C. Solomon, *The Big Questions* (San Diego: Harcourt Brace Jovanovich, 1982), pp. 157–158.

18. See Roderick Chisholm, *The First Person* (Minneapolis: University of Minnesota, 1981), p. 89.

19. See Richard Swinburne, *The Evolution of the Soul* (Oxford: Clarendon, 1986), pp. 147–153. Cf. Geoffrey Madell, *The Identity of the Self* (Edinburgh: Edinburgh University, 1981).

20. Actually, a better way of putting this is that the table, taken as a whole, ceases to be, and part of the table survives in each new table. For more on issues regarding sameness through change, see David Wiggins, *Sameness and Substance* (Cambridge, MA: Harvard University, 1980).

21. Cf. Thomas Nagel, "Brain Bisection and the Unity of Consciousness," in *Mortal Questions* (Cambridge: Cambridge University, 1979), pp. 147–64, especially pp. 154–155.

22. Bernard Williams, *Problems of the Self* (Cambridge: Cambridge University, 1973), pp. 46–63.

23. Immanuel Kant, *Critique of Pure Reason,* trans. by Norman Kemp Smith (New York: St. Martin's, 1929), p. 373.

24. Roderick Chisholm, *On Metaphysics* (Minneapolis: University of Minnesota, 1989), p. 56.

25. Thomas Aquinas, *Summa Theologica* (Westminster, MD: Christian Classics, 1981), Pt. I, Q. 75, Art. 6.

26. See C.S. Lewis, *The Weight of Glory* (Grand Rapids, MI: Eerdmans, 1949), pp. 1–15; *The Problem of Pain* (New York: Macmillan, 1962), pp. 144–154.

27. For more criticisms of this view, see Bruce Reichenbach, *Is Man the Phoenix?* (Grand Rapids, MI: Eerdmans, 1978), pp. 124–126; John Beversluis, *C.S. Lewis and the Search for Rational Religion* (Grand Rapids, MI: Eerdmans, 1985), pp. 8–31. Cf. Richard Purtill, *C.S. Lewis's Case for the Christian Faith* (San Francisco: Harper & Row, 1985), pp. 120–131.

28. For a discussion of further arguments for life after death, see Reichenbach, *Is Man the Phoenix?* pp. 113–134; Wainwright, *Philosophy of Religion,* pp. 99–112.

Chapter 2   Body and Soul

1. We will argue that dualism and the soul are important for eternal life and that dualism is the only option to physicalism. But this is not quite right. There is a third live

option today called personalism. Personalists hold that a person is a basic metaphysical category, different from matter and mind, and that the latter two are different aspects of persons. See Raziel Abelson, *Lawless Mind* (Philadelphia: Temple University, 1988). Nothing will be lost, however, if we fail to consider personalism because personalists (1) still hold to a metaphysical reality beyond the body (the person), (2) acknowledge mental entities, and (3) treat persons as substances in much the same way as substance dualists treat the soul.

2. Some have claimed that physicalism is consistent with life after death (both can be held without affirming a contradiction). This may be true, but nevertheless, physicalism and life after death do make odd bedfellows and have rarely been advocated jointly. Furthermore, physicalism has not been the traditional Christian view regarding eternal life. See John W. Cooper, *Body, Soul, and Life Everlasting: Biblical Anthropology and the Monism-Dualism Debate* (Grand Rapids, MI: Eerdmans, 1989).

3. John H. Hick, *Death & Eternal Life* (San Francisco: Harper & Row, 1980), p. 92. Hick's comments are made regarding belief in life after death, but they apply with equal force to belief in the soul. Materialism has long been a reason for skepticism regarding God, the soul, and immortality. See J.C.A. Gaskin, ed. *Varieties of Unbelief* (New York: Macmillan, 1989), pp. 11–12, 17–26.

4. Our preference for sensory experience is not merely due to certain trends in philosophy and science. Sociological factors (e.g., television) have also had a significant influence on us. See Neil Postman, *Amusing Ourselves to Death* (New York: Penguin, 1985).

5. Abelson states that "With the birth of modern science in the seventeenth century, purposive explanation in terms either of innate strivings or of divine will was dispensed with in favor of mechanistic explanations of defining things in terms of measurable ('primary') properties linked by mathematical laws." See *Lawless Mind,* p. xiv. Lynne Baker says that "Physicalism is the product of a claim about science together with a particular conception of science. The claim is that science is the exclusive arbiter of reality. . . . On this view, scientific knowledge is exhaustive." Lynne Rudder Baker, *Saving Belief: A Critique of Physicalism* (Princeton, NJ: Princeton University, 1987), p. 4.

6. It is interesting to note that empiricism and scientific realism (roughly, the idea that science gives us an increasingly true picture of a theory-independent world, especially of unobservable, theoretical entities like electrons that are causally responsible for observational phenomena, and science does so in a rationally justifiable way) have always been at odds with each other. Thus, the more one is an empiricist, the less one is able to accept the truth claims of science, construed along realist lines (because one cannot observe many theoretical entities like electrons and must infer their existence from observations and such inferences go beyond what is empirically observable). See Stanley Jaki, *The Road of Science and the Ways to God* (Chicago: University of Chicago, 1978); J.P. Moreland, *Christianity and the Nature of Science* (Grand Rapids, MI: Baker, 1989), chaps. 4 and 5. The same has been true of empiricism and materialism, because more extreme empiricists have claimed that one cannot see matter (it is a mere "I know not what" as John Locke put it), but one can directly see one's own private, mental sense data. For more on this, see A.J. Ayer, *The Central Questions of Philosophy* (New York: Holt, Rinehart and Winston, 1973), pp. 112–136.

7. Cf. D.W. Hamlyn, *Metaphysics* (Cambridge: Cambridge University, 1984), pp. 161–218; Cooper, *Body, Soul, & Life Everlasting.*

8. As mentioned in note 1 above, we are not considering the views of thinkers like Raziel Abelson or P.F. Strawson. Their views are called personalism. In our opinion and for our purposes here, personalism is close enough to substance dualism to be considered a version of the latter because most personalists and substance dualists unite in rejecting physicalism, and holding that there is an immaterial substance (a crucial ingredient of the person for a personalist, the substantial soul for a substance dualist). Furthermore, there

are six different views of a human being that have been offered as adequate representations of Christianity: (1) physicalism; (2) property or event dualism; (3) substance dualism, where the soul's existence is dependent upon the existence of the body; (4) substance dualism, where the soul's existence is not dependent upon the body (it has a foothold in being independent of its embodiment, even though embodiment may be the soul's natural mode of existence); (5) substance dualism, where the soul has a natural immortality within itself; (6) the view that the person is identical to his or her soul, and the body is not part of the person. In our view, position 4 is the most accurate representation of historic, biblical Christianity.

9. For excellent treatments of the notion of substance in the Aristotelian/Thomist tradition, see David Wiggins, *Sameness and Substance* (Cambridge, MA: Harvard University, 1980); Michael Loux, *Substance and Attribute* (Dordrecht, Holland: D. Reidel, 1978); C.J. Ducasse, *Nature, Mind, and Death* (La Salle, IL: Open Court, 1951), pp. 161–173; W. E. Johnson, *Logic Part III: The Logical Foundations of Science* (New York: Dover, 1924), pp. 78–101; C.D. Broad, "The 'Nature' of a Continuant," in *Examination of McTaggart's Philosophy,* vol. I (Cambridge: Cambridge University, 1933), pp. 264–278; Richard J. Connell, *Substance and Modern Science* (Notre Dame, IN: University of Notre Dame, 1988); Michael Ayers, "Substance: Prolegomena To A Realist Theory of Identity," *The Journal of Philosophy* (Feb. 1991), pp. 69–90. For a critique of Loux, see J.P. Moreland, "How to Be a Nominalist in Realist Clothing," *Grazer Philosophische Studien* 39 (Summer 1991), pp. 75–101.

10. The way substances change gives rise to another issue regarding the nature of substance—the issue of law. Substances change in lawlike ways. For example, the growth of an acorn into a mature oak tree will follow a series of stages that unfold in lawlike stages. This is best explained by postulating a ground in organisms treated as wholes (and not mere heaps of parts or property things wherein all activities are to be explained in terms of mechanical, material relations among the atomic parts of those property things). This ground will treat a substance as a unity of capacities or dispositions to behave in certain ways, given certain circumstances (e.g., given water and soil, an acorn will do such and such).

11. See J.P. Moreland, *Universals, Qualities, and Quality-Instances: A Defense of Realism* (Lanham, MD: University of America, 1985). For a critique of Moreland, see Keith Campbell, *Abstract Particulars* (Cambridge, MA: Basil Blackwell, 1990), pp. 45, 54, 65–74.

12. There is a time-honored debate between Platonic and Aristotelian advocates of the existence of properties as universals, the former claiming that properties can exist even if they are not actualized by any particulars (redness can exist even if there are no red particulars), the latter denying this claim. Thus, Platonists would hold that redness could, as it were, exist "all alone by itself" without being instanced. But Platonists could still agree that there is an ontological asymmetry in the predication relation: that is, substances have properties and properties are had by substances.

13. Actually, this characterization of an event is a bit too narrow, because events can involve the coming, going, or having of relations among substances. For example, an event takes place when one ball is moved closer to another. This does not necessarily involve a change in the internal constitution of either ball, but rather, a change in the relations between them. However, this aspect of events is not relevant for our present purposes. The account of events we are advocating is called the property exemplification account of events: $[x,P,t] = [y,Q,t']$ if and only if $x=y$, $P=Q$, $t=t'$, where x and y are substances, P and Q are properties, t and t' are moments of time. For an alternative account of events designed to save physicalism, see Cynthia Macdonald, *Mind-Body Identity Theories* (New York: Routledge, Chapman, and Hall, 1989), chap. 4.

14. Cynthia Macdonald, a physicalist who holds to what is called a token-token identity

theory (individual mental events are identical to individual physical events), admits that "It is clear that a workable conception of the physical is at least as, if not more, difficult to come by as is an adequate conception of the mental." See *Mind-Body Identity Theories,* p. 11. Cf. Howard Robinson, *Matter and Sense* (Cambridge: Cambridge University, 1982), pp. 108–123; John Foster, *The Case For Idealism* (London: Routledge & Kegan Paul, 1982), pp. 51–88. For example, one cannot define matter as something impenetrable, because this invites the question "impenetrable by what?", and the answer will turn out to be other chunks of matter. In this case, matter is defined in a circle, viz. Matter is something that cannot be penetrated by *other matter.* In the history of philosophy, there has been a very large, respectable tradition that asserts that mind is much clearer and less problematic than matter. The present preference for physicalism seems out of touch with the problems surfaced by that tradition.

15. The possible exception is those physicists who claim that the material world owes its existence to its being observed by a mind. See Nick Herbert, *Quantum Reality* (Garden City, NY: Anchor, 1985), pp. 15–29, especially pp. 17–18, 24–29. Obviously, this understanding of quantum physics would have disastrous implications for physicalism if we grant that an act of observation is what it appears to be, namely, a mental act.

16. Richard Swinburne defines mental properties as "ones to which one subject has privileged access, which he is necessarily in a better position to know about than anyone else." See *The Evolution of the Soul* (Oxford: Clarendon, 1986), p. 6.

17. Cf. David G. Myers, *The Human Puzzle* (New York: Harper & Row, 1978), pp. 77–88.

18. For brief or beginning treatments of the nature of identity, see Swinburne, *The Evolution of the Soul,* pp. 46–53; Jenny Teichman, *Philosophy and the Mind* (New York: Basil Blackwell, 1988), pp. 17–21. For a more detailed treatment, see Tom V. Morris, *Understanding Identity Statements* (Great Britain: Aberdeen University, 1984); Saul Kripke, *Naming and Necessity* (Cambridge, MA: Harvard University, 1972).

19. Some philosophers claim that this understanding of identity, more specifically, identity statements, makes them trivial because they merely assert that something is identical to itself and this is hardly informative. See Panayot Butchvarov, *Being Qua Being* (Bloomington, IN: Indiana University, 1979), pp. 9–63, for an example of this charge. A response to claims of this sort can be found in Baruch Brody, *Identity and Essence* (Princeton, NJ: Princeton University, 1980), pp. 3–17.

20. In other words, the identity relation is necessary. That is (x) (y) (x=y $\rightarrow$ $\Box$) (x=y). For all x and y, if x is identical to y, then, necessarily, x is identical to y. There is no possible world where x obtains without y or vice versa.

21. Actually, a weaker argument is all that is required to establish dualism: (1) No physical properties are self-presenting. (2) Some mental properties are self-presenting. Therefore, (3) some mental properties are not physical properties. For more on the definition of self-presenting properties, see Roderick Chisholm, *Theory of Knowledge* (Englewood Cliffs, NJ: Prentice-Hall, 3rd ed., 1989), pp. 18–25; *The First Person* (Minneapolis: University of Minnesota, 1981), pp. 79–83; *On Metaphysics* (Minneapolis: University of Minnesota, 1989), pp. 99–106.

22. Even if a neurophysiologist could know about my mental state by reading a scientific instrument that measured my brain state, this would not refute the argument. Why? In order for a neurophysiologist to do such a thing, he would first have to come up with an elaborate set of correlations of mental and brain states, and these would allow him to infer a certain mental state when he read the presence of a certain brain state. Unfortunately, such correlations would rely on first person psychological reports because the scientist would only have access to one side of the correlations, namely, the brain states. Far from replacing such first person awarenesses and the reports of them, such correlations presuppose them.

23. Of course, one can have a vague awareness of one's own consciousness through inattention, or one can have an awareness of a vague object (e.g., one that feels halfway between an itch and a pain) and label or report it wrongly. For more on arguments about incorrigibility, see Chisholm, *Theory of Knowledge,* p. 25.

24. Paul Churchland in *Matter and Consciousness* (Cambridge, MA: MIT, 1984), pp. 31–33 criticizes the argument we are advancing. According to Churchland, the argument is an example of the intensional fallacy in logic. In normal, truth-functional logic, the connectives ("if, then," "if and only if," "or," "and," "not") are extensional—equals can be substituted for equals and truth is preserved. Thus, if one has P if and only if Q, then one can substitute Q for P in the following syllogism: If P, then R; P; therefore, R.

But in intentional contexts where words like *believe* or *know* are used, equals cannot be substituted for equals and preserve truth. I may know that Muhammad Ali was the world champion, but I may not know that Cassius Clay was the world champion if I fail to know that Clay is identical to Ali. It is the intensional fallacy to assume that such substitutions can be made in intentional contexts.

Similarly, I may know my mental states and not know my brain states, but the two may still be identical, says Churchland, if I fail to appreciate that such an identity holds. There are at least two problems with Churchland's remarks.

First, our arguments using private access and incorrigibility do not turn on a supposed ignorance of an identity between mental and brain states, but on the fact that the former are and the latter are not self-presenting as evidenced by private access and incorrigibility. If two entities have different properties (one is self-presenting and the other is not), then they cannot be identical.

Second, the very existence of irreducibly intentional contexts that defy extensional treatment is evidence for dualism. See George Bealer, "The Logical Status of Mind," in *Midwest Studies in Philosophy: Studies in the Philosophy of Mind,* vol. 10, ed. Peter A. French, Theodore E. Uehling, Jr., and Howard K. Wettstein, (Minneapolis: University of Minnesota, 1986), vol. 10, pp. 231–274.

25. See Thomas Nagel, "What Is It Like to Be a Bat?" *Mortal Questions* (Cambridge: Cambridge University, 1979), pp. 165–180; Frank Jackson, "Epiphenomenal Qualia," *Philosophical Quarterly* 32 (Apr. 1982), pp. 127–136; Saul Kripke, *Naming and Necessity,* pp. 134–155.

26. Robinson, *Matter and Sense,* p. 7.

27. Nagel, *Mortal Questions,* p. 167. Nagel seems to present two arguments instead of one: the argument from the subjective, phenomenal quality of an experience, and the argument about the irreducibility of a first person point of view to a third person perspective. For a critique, see Macdonald, *Mind-Body Identity Theories,* pp. 20–23. For a dualist defense of physicalist rejoinders to the argument from the subjective nature of experience, see Richard Warner, "A Challenge to Physicalism," *Australasian Journal of Philosophy* 64 (Sept. 1986), pp. 249–265.

28. Frank Jackson, *Perception* (Cambridge: Cambridge University, 1977), p. 121. Jackson assumes a representative theory of perception in the tradition of John Locke (e.g., I directly see sense data of chairs, not chairs themselves). But the argument does not require that assumption. For more on different theories of perception, see Jonathan Dancy, *Introduction to Contemporary Epistemology* (Oxford: Basil Blackwell, 1985), pp. 143–159.

29. At least six differences have been listed between intentionality and physical relations: (1) When we represent a mental act to ourselves (e.g., an act of thinking about something), there are no sense data associated with it; this is not so with physical states and their relations. (2) Intentionality is completely unrestricted with regard to the kind of object it can hold as a term—anything whatever can have a mental act directed upon it, but physical relations only obtain for a narrow range of objects (e.g., magnetic fields only

attract certain things). (3) To grasp a mental act I must engage in a reflexive act of self-awareness (e.g., to grasp my awareness of a tree, I must be aware of an awareness), but no such reflexivity is required to grasp a physical relation. See Dallas Willard, *Logic and the Objectivity of Knowledge* (Athens, OH: Ohio University, 1984), pp. 55–57. (4) For ordinary relations (x is to the left of y), x and y are identifiable objects irrespective of whether or not they have entered into that relation; this is not so for intentional contents (e.g., one and the same belief cannot be about a frog and later about a house). (5) For ordinary relations, each of the participants must exist before the relation obtains (x and y must exist before one can be on top of the other); but intentionality can be of or about nonexistent things (e.g., I can think about Zeus). (6) Intentional states are intensional, but physical relations are extensional. See this article entitled "Intentionality" in Richard L. Gregory, *The Oxford Companion to the Mind* (Oxford: Oxford University, 1987). For physicalist treatments of intentionality, see William Bechtel, *Philosophy of Mind* (Hillsdale, NJ: Lawrence Erlbaum, 1988), pp. 40–78.

30. Insofar as I am an embodied soul, then I am a unity of soul and body. Thus, I *have* a soul in that it is an entity that is part of a whole that includes my body. But I have my soul in a different way from it has mental experiences.

31. See J.P. Moreland, "An Enduring Self: The Achilles' Heel of Process Philosophy," *Process Studies* 17 (Fall 1988), pp. 193–199; Richard M. Zaner, *The Way of Phenomenology* (Indianapolis: Bobbs-Merrill, 1970), pp. 125–174.

32. Cf. Geoffrey Madell, *The Identity of the Self* (Edinburgh: Edinburgh University, 1981), pp. 1–48.

33. Cf. David Wiggins, *Sameness and Substance* (Cambridge, MA: Harvard University, 1980); Richard Swinburne, *The Evolution of the Soul,* pp. 145–73; "The Structure of the Soul," in *Persons and Personality,* ed. by Arthur Peacocke and Grant Gillett (Oxford: Basil Blackwell, 1987), pp. 33–55.

34. So far as we can tell, no one denies the fact that physicalism is inconsistent with libertarian freedom except Clifford Williams, "The Irrelevance of Immaterial Minds," *Christian Scholar's Review* 12:4 (1983), pp. 310–323. But Williams does not make his case. He merely asks why matter cannot be free (couldn't God create matter with free will?), and claims that arguments for dualism based on free will assume that matter is passive. In response to Williams, it can be pointed out that (1) most examples of matter are passive, but even if some cases of matter are such that they exercise their casual powers, they do not do so as human agents do—as substances that act freely and intentionally in order to (final cause) realize an aim; (2) he must supply us with an example (apart from citing conscious beings) for the thesis that matter acts freely in a libertarian sense; (3) his thesis, even if correct, will differ only semantically from dualism, because he will have established two kinds of "matter"—passive and active in a libertarian sense; but almost all "matter" is the former, and dualists call active "matter," in Williams's sense, a soul. How does his active "matter" differ substantially from a soul? It seems to be soul by a different name. What is at stake here is essentialism. If matter has a certain nature or essence, or at least if material substances have certain natures or essences, then God himself could not have created matter (or material substances) without those properties. Based on our knowledge of material things, it would seem that the capacity for libertarian freedom is not part of the essence of matter (or material substances); thus, for God to "create matter with free will" would be for him to create a different kind of matter than the kind he did, in fact, create. But then, how would this new "matter" differ from soul stuff? No difference is no difference at all.

35. See Bruce Reichenbach, *Is Man the Phoenix?* (Grand Rapids, MI: Eerdmans, 1978), pp. 105–111. W.S. Anglin has argued that if libertarian freedom is denied, then no account can be given for the following: true rationality, real artistic creativity, full moral responsibility, the ability to choose our values, genuine cooperation among humans, true

love, the ability to love unconditionally, the real ability to make promises. See *Free Will and the Christian Faith* (Oxford: Clarendon, 1990), pp. 10–24. Anglin also claims that libertarian freedom is hard to square with physicalism. See p. 155.

36. Richard Taylor, *Metaphysics* (Englewood Cliffs, NJ: Prentice-Hall, 1963), p. 28.

37. For more on the differences between state-state and agent causes, see William L. Rowe, "Two Concepts of Freedom, in *Proceedings and Addresses of the American Philosophical Association Supplement to Vol. 61* (Sept. 1987), pp. 43–64; Steward C. Goetz, "A Noncausal Theory of Agency," *Philosophy and Phenomenological Research* 49 (Dec. 1988), pp. 303–316; Swinburne, *The Evolution of the Soul*, pp. 85–102; *The Existence of God,* (Oxford: Oxford University, 1979), pp. 22–50; Roderick Chisholm, *On Metaphysics,* pp. 3–15; Ernest Le Pore, Barry Loewer, "Mind Matters," *The Journal of Philosophy* 84 (Nov. 1987), pp. 630–642. The importance of agent causation for freedom is missed by Dennis M. Senchuk, "Consciousness Naturalized: Supervenience Without Physical Determinism," *American Philosophical Quarterly* 28 (Jan. 1991), pp. 37–47. Senchuk admits that strict physicalism is deterministic for ordinary macro-objects like chairs and dogs, but he claims that emergent event dualism is not. He argues that consciousness is a genuine emergent property of wholes, that it can cause things to happen in the world, among which are behaviors (e.g., my conscious experience of pain can cause me to say, "Ouch!"), and that a specific state of consciousness does not uniquely determine a specific behavior. This allows for a certain indeterminate flexibility between a given conscious state (e.g., a feeling of pain) and a behavioral outcome as the "goal" of that conscious state (e.g., shouting, "Ouch!" or shouting, "That hurt!").

However, Senchuk's proposal will not do the job. For one thing, it will not appeal to those who wish to see physics as exhaustively capable of predicting the physical behaviors of macrosystems (e.g., human action). But more importantly, Senchuk does not tell us what it is that is ultimately responsible for behaviors or, for that matter, for some of our mental states themselves, such as what is responsible for my having a certain belief. For Senchuk, behaviors are either states caused by prior states or else they are inherently indeterminate. Either way, it is not I myself who acts toward goals and ends I chose (or who freely adopts certain conscious states themselves) and that is what is needed for real freedom and responsibility.

38. J.R. Lucas, *Freedom of the Will* (Oxford: Clarendon, 1970), pp. 114–115.

39. H.P. Owen, *Christian Theism* (Edinburgh: T & T Clark, 1984), p. 118.

40. A.C. Ewing, *Value and Reality* (London: George Allen & Unwin, 1973), p. 77. Cf. Hans Jonas, *On Faith, Reason, and Responsibility* (Claremont, CA: The Institute for Antiquity and Christianity, 1981), p. 43; Lynne Rudder Baker, *Saving Belief: A Critique of Physicalism* (Princeton, NJ: Princeton University, 1987), pp. 134–148; Keith Lehrer, *Knowledge* (Oxford: Clarendon, 1974), pp. 241–249.

41. H.D. Lewis, *The Self and Immortality* (New York: Seabury, 1973), p. 34. For more detailed defenses of dualism, see Robinson, *Matter and Sense;* Swinburne, *The Evolution of the Soul;* John R. Smythies and John Beloff, *The Case for Dualism* (Charlottesville, VA: University of Virginia, 1989).

Chapter 3   Dualism and Eternal Life

1. Cf. Peter Smith and O.R. Jones, *The Philosophy of Mind* (Cambridge: Cambridge University, 1986), pp. 45–67; Paul Churchland, *Matter and Consciousness* (Cambridge, MA: MIT, 1984), pp. 13–21; Jenny Teichman, *Philosophy and the Mind* (Oxford: Basil Blackwell, 1988), pp. 87–126; Douglas Lackey, *God, Immortality, and Ethics* (Belmont, CA: Wadsworth, 1990), pp. 53–68; James W. Cornman and Keith Lehrer, *Philosophical Problems and Arguments: An Introduction* (New York: Macmillan, 1974), pp. 237–264.

2. C.D. Broad, *The Mind and Its Place in Nature* (London: Routledge & Kegan Paul,

1925), p. 98. Cf. C.J. Ducasse, *Nature, Mind, and Death* (La Salle, IL: Open Court, 1961), pp. 424–443.

3. See Mark Bedau, "Cartesian Interactionism," in *Midwest Studies in Philosophy: Studies in the Philosophy of Mind*, vol. 10, ed. by Peter A. French, Theodore E. Uehling, Jr., and Howard K. Wettstein (Minneapolis: University of Minnesota, 1986), pp. 483–502; see also John Foster, "In Defense of Dualism," in *The Case for Dualism*, ed. by John R. Smythies and John Beloff (Charlottesville, VA: University Press of Virginia, 1989), pp. 1–25.

4. If there is any place that a request for a mechanistic explanation of how a causal process takes place should be fruitful, it would be in science. But as these examples show, even in science it is often the case that a picture of how causation takes place is lacking and yet belief that causation is present is still justified. In metaphysics, the request for a mechanism of causation is even more dubious if that request is taken as a necessary condition for justifying belief that causation is real. For example, we know that if we burn a green leaf, we "cause" the color green to no longer be instanced by the leaf. But how a physical event of burning can cause a universal—a nonspatial, nontemporal entity—to no longer enter into an instancing relation with a particular (the leaf) is unclear.

5. As an example of this, Peter Smith and O.R. Jones "argue" against dualist interactionism by claiming that such an interaction "goes clean against a fundamental principle of the physical sciences, namely that the causes of physical changes are other entirely physical events." See *The Philosophy of Mind*, p. 58.

But they seem to reverse the order between philosophy and science, and this reversal results in the question begging claim just mentioned. If dualism is true, then the physical sciences are not the only thing needed to account for human nature and action. Thus, the philosophical case for and against dualism is epistemologically prior to scientific considerations, not vice versa.

Further, their view entails determinism, which we demonstrated in Chap. 2 to be far from reasonable.

Finally, if one tries to offer a physicalist account of how human action and cognitive abilities are possible, then this strategy backfires in the face of something called the frame problem. See Daniel Dennett, "Cognitive Wheels: The Frame Problem of AI," in *Minds, Machines, and Evolution*, ed. by Christopher Hookway (Cambridge: Cambridge University, 1984), pp. 129–151. An intelligent creature is able to learn from past experience, anticipate future scenarios to alternative actions available to the creature, and think things out before it acts. Dennett acknowledges (pejoratively) that dualism can explain this ability to "look before one leaps" by the simple notion that the soul can learn from experience. But the physicalist is hard pressed to explain this ability, and the frame problem may be fairly presented as a counterargument to those who demand an explanation of how a causal process takes place before we are justified in believing that it takes place, especially when the explanation must operate within physicalist constraints.

6. For a caricature of the substance dualist understanding of interaction, see Paul Churchland, *Matter and Consciousness*, pp. 18–20.

7. For more on scientism, see J.P. Moreland, *Christianity and the Nature of Science* (Grand Rapids, MI: Baker, 1989), chap. 3.

8. Teichman, *Philosophy and the Mind*, p. 105.

9. Some have claimed that dualist interaction is inconsistent with the First Law of Thermodynamics—the principle of the conservation of energy. If an immaterial mind can act upon the body, then there will be a gap between the state of the brain before a mental event has had its effect and the state of the brain after the mental event has had its effect. In other words, a brain event at time t_1 will not be sufficient to produce a brain event at time t2, the latter event being produced by the brain event at t_1 and the mental event (or simply the self) at t_1. In this case, energy is created and introduced into the system.

But this objection is inconclusive. Robert Larmer argues that we must distinguish two forms of the First Law. A strong form states that energy can neither be created nor destroyed. A weak form states that in a causally closed system, the total amount of energy remains constant. Dualism is inconsistent with the strong form but not the weak form, because for the dualist interactionist, the human body is not a causally closed physical system. The dualist will maintain that the evidence for dualism is stronger than the evidence that supports the strong form of the First Law. For more on this, see Robert Larmer, "Mind-Body Interaction and the Conservation of Energy," *International Philosophical Quarterly* 26 (Sept. 1986), pp. 277–285.

10. Howard E. Gruber, *Darwin on Man: A Psychological Study of Scientific Creativity* (Chicago: University of Chicago, 1974), p. 211.

11. Richard Swinburne argues that the existence and nature of the soul and its states are issues that lie outside the bounds of science. See *The Evolution of the Soul* (Oxford: Clarendon, 1986), pp. 183–196. Among his arguments, one is particularly interesting. Swinburne points out that if science is going to offer a law correlating two or more phenomena, then all those phenomena must be well defined for science. For example, a law correlating the pressure, volume, and temperature of a gas would be within the bounds of science because all three notions are clearly scientific. But a scientific law correlating brain states with mental states or trying to explain how and why souls emerged at a certain point in evolutionary history would be impossible, because one of the terms in the law (the soul and its states) is not accessible to or definable for science.

12. Churchland, *Matter and Consciousness,* p. 21. Two things should be noted in regard to Churchland's comment. First, dualist statements are not always theoretical explanations but reports. For example, the statement "I am in pain" is not a theory of folk psychology to the effect that if something grimaces, it is in pain; I am grimacing; therefore, I am in pain. Rather, the statement is a simple first person, descriptive report of a self-presenting property: having a pain. Second, Churchland's physicalism entails determinism, so he needs to clarify what sort of responsibility he includes in his admonishment that "we should learn" to live with physicalism. If physicalism is true, how can there be any shoulds at all?

13. D.M. Armstrong, *A Materialist Theory of Mind* (London: Routledge & Kegan Paul, 1968), p. 30.

14. Arthur Peacocke and Grant Gillett, eds., *Persons and Personality* (Oxford: Basil Blackwell, 1987), p. 55.

15. David Hull makes the following observation: "The implications of moving species from the metaphysical category that can appropriately be characterized in terms of 'natures' to a category for which such characterizations are inappropriate are extensive and fundamental. If species evolve in anything like the way that Darwin thought they did, then they cannot possibly have the sort of natures that traditional philosophers claimed they did. If species in general lack natures, then so does *Homo sapiens* as a biological species. If *Homo sapiens* lacks a nature, then no reference to biology can be made to support one's claims about 'human nature.' Perhaps all people are 'persons,' share the same 'personhood,' etc., but such claims must be explicated and defended *with no reference to biology.* Because so many moral, ethical, and political theories depend on some notion or other of human nature, Darwin's theory brought into question all these theories. The implications are not entailments. One can always dissociate *'Homo sapiens'* from 'human being,' but the result is a much less plausible position." See David Hull, *The Metaphysics of Evolution* (Albany, NY: State University of New York, 1989), pp. 74–75.

In other words, Darwin's theory makes less plausible the existence of a human nature possessed by all humans (which has been taken by many to be the human soul), as well as ethical and other theories built on the existence of human nature. Our point is that if one has good ethical, theological, and philosophical grounds for believing in human nature, then these count against Darwinian evolution as being the whole story of our origin. See Moreland, *Christianity and the Nature of Science*, pp. 46–56.

16. See Roderick Chisholm, *On Metaphysics* (Minneapolis: University of Minnesota, 1989), p. 12; Swinburne, *The Evolution of the Soul*, pp. 183–196.

17. Actually, we are being too generous in allowing the notion of a symbol and a rule to be used of computers. These two notions are also intentional. Even if they are simply syntactical, they are not a part of physics or chemistry. See John Searle, "Is the Brain a Digital Computer?" *Proceedings and Addresses of The American Philosophical Society* 64 (Nov. 1990), pp. 21–37.

18. John Searle, *Minds, Brains, and Science* (Cambridge, MA: Harvard University, 1984), pp. 32–33. Cf. John Searle, "Minds, Brains, and Programs," *The Behavioral and Brain Sciences* 3 (1980), pp. 417–424. For a detailed critique of strong artificial intelligence models of being human, see Jeffrey Koperski, "Frames, Brains, and Chinese Rooms: Problems in Artificial Intelligence," unpublished M.A. thesis, Liberty University (Spring 1991).

19. See Hilary Putnam, *Reason, Truth, and History* (Cambridge: Cambridge University, 1981), pp. 8–12. Putnam asks us to imagine a case where two computers are connected in such a way that the output of one feeds into the input of the other and vice versa. In such cases, the two computers could "talk" to each other forever and "refer" to things in the world (both are mental, intentional notions), even if the world disappeared. This example illustrates that intentionality cannot be identified with a functionalist analysis of it in terms of artificial intelligence.

20. It should be pointed out that Ockham's Razor is controversial, to say the least, especially when it is applied to the area of metaphysics (unless, of course, it is interpreted merely as the benign principle that one should not postulate an explanatory entity unless it is needed). There is no general agreement about how the principle should be interpreted or how it is to be applied in metaphysical debate.

21. A further argument against dualism is the problem of our knowledge of other minds along with a related problem known as the private language argument. For a dualist response to these, see Swinburne, *The Evolution of the Soul*, pp. 11–16.

It is also objected that the notion of a soul is not particularly useful or fruitful compared to the tremendous fruitfulness of models of the brain, evidenced by the progress in the brain sciences. But this is a question-begging claim, because "useful" and "fruitful" mean "empirically, scientifically fruitful in guiding us in a search for new physical (even mechanistic) discoveries." However, a nonphysical entity may not be useful in guiding one in a search for new, physical/scientific information. And in any case, a notion can be true even if it is not helpful in the search for material causes. For more on this last point, see Etienne Gilson, *From Aristotle to Darwin and Back Again* (Notre Dame, IN: University of Notre Dame, 1984).

22. Three main physicalist alternatives to dualism are currently being debated: the identity thesis (which, in turn, comes in three versions: type-type, causal role, and token-token identity theories), functionalism (which comes in different versions), and eliminative materialism. For an overview of these, see Churchland, *Matter and Consciousness;* Teichman, *Philosophy and the Mind;* William Bechtel, *Philosophy of Mind* (Hillsdale, NJ; Lawrence Erlbaum, 1988); David M. Rosenthal, ed., *Materialism and the Mind-Body Problem* (Englewood Cliffs, NJ: Prentice-Hall, 1971); Joseph Margolis, *Philosophy of Psychology* (Englewood Cliffs, NJ: Prentice-Hall, 1984); Cynthia Macdonald, *Mind-Body Identity Theories* (New York: Routledge, Chapman, and Hall, 1989). Most of the works just listed are sympathetic to physicalism (except for Teichman), but they do contain critiques of the different physicalist theories.

For brief criticisms of different versions of physicalism, see A.J. Ayer, *The Central Questions of Philosophy* (New York: Holt, Rinehart and Winston, 1973), pp. 126–132.

More detailed critiques of physicalism can be found in Swinburne, *The Evolution of the Soul;* Lynne Rudder Baker, *Saving Belief: A Critique of Physicalism* (Princeton, NJ: Princeton University, 1989); Howard Robinson, *Matter and Sense* (Cambridge: Cambridge University, 1982); Jaegwon Kin, "The Myth of Nonreductive Materialism," in *Proceedings and Addresses of the American Philosophical Association* 63 (Nov. 1989), pp. 31–47.

23. Eugene Fontinell argues for a form of life after death without a literal, substantive, enduring I. See *Self, God, and Immortality* (Philadelphia: Temple University, 1986). For a critical review of Fontinell, see J.P. Moreland, review of *Self, God, and Immortality* in *International Philosophical Quarterly* 29 (Dec. 1989), pp. 480–483.

24. Cf. John Gilmore, *Probing Heaven: Key Questions on the Hereafter* (Grand Rapids, MI: Baker, 1989), pp. 130–133; Peter J. Kreeft, *Everything You Ever Wanted to Know About Heaven . . . But Never Dreamed of Asking* (San Francisco: Harper & Row, 1982), pp. 45–46.

25. Cf. *Summa Theologica,* Ia., Q. 75, Articles 2, 3, and 6. For introductory expositions of Aquinas' argument, see Ralph McInerny, *St. Thomas Aquinas* (Notre Dame, IN: University of Notre Dame, 1982), pp. 46–49; Herbert McCabe, "The Immortality of the Soul," in *Aquinas: A Collection of Critical Essays*, ed. by Anthony Kenny (Notre Dame, IN: University of Notre Dame, 1969), pp. 297–306; Jacques Maritain, "A Proof of the Immortality of the Soul," reprinted in *Religious Belief and Philosophical Thought*, ed. by William P. Alston (New York: Harcourt, Brace & World, 1963), pp. 345–352.

26. See J.P. Moreland, *Scaling the Secular City* (Grand Rapids, MI: Baker, 1987), chap. 3.

27. Recently, Patrick Sherry has offered an argument for eternal life based on the nature of religious experience. Roughly, Sherry argues that religious experience provides evidence for the existence of God and, further, that the nature of religious experience is that of a taste of the first fruits of life after death. See *Spirit, Saints, and Immortality* (Albany, NY: State University of New York, 1984).

Chapter 4   The Resurrection of Jesus

1. If you wish to pursue these alternative theories (including other options not discussed here) in more detail, see Gary R. Habermas, *The Resurrection of Jesus: A Rational Inquiry* (Ann Arbor, MI: University Microfilms, 1976), pp. 114–171, 198–224, 286–299, 323–326.

2. For a similar treatment, see Gary R. Habermas, *The Verdict of History: Conclusive Evidence for the Life of Jesus* (Nashville: Thomas Nelson, 1988), pp. 127–130.

3. In his classic work on the nineteenth-century liberal search for the Jesus of history, Albert Schweitzer lists no adherents to these fraud theories after 1778 (Hermann Reimarus). See his volume *The Quest of the Historical Jesus,* trans. by W. Montgomery (New York: Macmillan, 1968).

4. For an engaging discussion and an excellent bibliography, see William D. Edwards, Wesley J. Gabel, and Floyd E. Hosmer, "On the Physical Death of Jesus Christ," *Journal of the American Medical Association,* vol. 255, no. 11, 21 Mar. 1986.

5. Parallels to John's account are found in Quintillian, *Declamationes Maiores* 6, 9, and in the anecdotal accounts of early Christian persecution related by sixteenth-century Oxford fellow John Foxe in *Foxe's Christian Martyrs of the World* (Westwood, NJ: Barbour & Co., 1990)), p. 96.

6. An incredible aspect of this subject is the large number of medical doctors who have investigated this and other details of the crucifixion of Jesus. For just a few examples, see Edwards, Gabel and Hosmer, "On the Physical Death of Jesus Christ," pp. 1462–1463, including the bibliography; Robert Bucklin, "The Legal and Medical Aspects of the Trial and Death of Christ," *Medicine, Science and the Law* (Jan. 1970); C. Truman Davis, "The Crucifixion of Jesus: The Passion of Christ from a Medical Point of View," *Arizona*

Medicine, Mar. 1965; Pierre Barbet, *A Doctor at Calvary* (Garden City, NJ: Doubleday, 1953).

7. Edwards, Gabel, and Hosmer, "On the Physical Death of Jesus Christ," p. 1463.

8. For details, see Nicu Haas, "Anthropological Observations on the Skeletal Remains from Giv'at ha-Mivtar," *Israel Exploration Journal* 20 (1970), pp. 38–59.

9. For particulars, see Martin Hengel, *Crucifixion in the Ancient World and the Folly of the Message of the Cross,* trans. by John Bowden (Philadelphia: Fortress, 1977).

10. David Strauss, *A New Life of Jesus,* 2 vols. (Edinburgh: Williams and Norgate, 1879), vol. I, p. 412.

11. For two older works that noted the absence of advocates for the swoon theory in their day, see Eduard Riggenbach, *The Resurrection of Jesus* (New York: Eaton and Mains, 1907), pp. 48–49 and James Orr, *The Resurrection of Jesus* (Grand Rapids, MI: Zondervan, 1908, 1965), p. 92.

12. However, this is not the only, or perhaps even the most natural, way of interpreting the disciples' doubts. We already mentioned the idea that, rather than an hallucination, the disciples may have thought that Jesus was a spirit of some sort, albeit one who was objectively present among them. Certain contemporary ideas are similar, so it may be helpful to distinguish such a view (sometimes called the *objective* vision theory) from the hallucination hypothesis (also called the *subjective* vision theory) and to make a brief response.

If someone claims that the appearances of Jesus' spirit were objective, thereby meaning that he was literally raised from the dead and present to witnesses but without a physical body, she is not proposing a naturalistic theory. The spiritual realm, including life after death, would still be a viable possibility for reasons we will point out in Chap. 8. Our chief dispute with this theory might then be over the *nature* of Jesus' resurrection body, not over the fact that Jesus was actually raised. The testimony of the Gospels in particular would need to be discussed. (Again, see Chap. 8 for a brief response.)

On the other hand, the "appearing" of Jesus' "spirit" might be taken in some nonliteral sense in which Jesus did not *actually* rise or appear at all (which would include some views that the resurrection was only the ongoing spiritual or psychological influence of Jesus). This stance would still fall prey to an entire host of problems, including many of the same criticisms leveled at the hallucination theory and to some of those aimed at the legend theory discussed later. It would also run up against the various reasons for holding that Jesus rose bodily, as pointed out in Chap. 8.

13. One of the rare attempts to argue that collective hallucinations are possible (without any application to the resurrection) is made by Leonard Zusne and Warren H. Jones, *Anomalistic Psychology: A Study of Extraordinary Phenomena of Behavior and Experience* (Hillsdale, NJ: Lawrence Erlbaum, 1982), pp. 135–136. But this type of approach falls prey to literally myriads of critiques such as the ones listed here.

The chief examples of these "collective hallucinations" are supplied by references to Fatima-like group religious experiences. But since the known instances of such phenomena are said to be basically religious in nature (Zusne and Jones, p. 135), this is problematic because it begs the question of whether such experiences could possibly be objective ones. In other words, if the instances of such collective phenomena tend to be religious, why must they all be assumed to be subjective, untrue experiences? Further, this view is unfalsifiable—it could be applied to many purely natural one-of-a-kind group sightings without much fear of refutation. So how could anyone know when it was explaining an experience accurately or when it was explaining away what had truly happened?

If this view were applied to the New Testament accounts of Jesus' resurrection, its explanatory power would be annulled. The truth is that much of the New Testament data not only differs from, but contradicts, the necessary conditions for "collective hallucinations."

For instance, Zusne and Jones attest that "expectation" and "emotional excitement" are "prerequisites" for such group sightings. In fact, the former "plays the coordinating role"

(p. 135). But such a scenario did not apply to the witnesses of Jesus' resurrection appearances, especially since they were confronted with the utter realism of the recent and unexpected death of their dear friend, the One they were hoping would rescue Israel. This is *totally unlike* those in the other experiences above, who exuberantly gathered with the explicit desire to see something.

Other crucial differences also exist, which indicates that Jesus' resurrection appearances are not to be considered in the same category. For example, the resurrection accounts present a much greater variety of times, settings, and circumstances, including the element of surprise. Further, James and Paul are two enemies whose lives were entirely transformed after meeting the risen Jesus, even in terms of being willing to give their lives for this belief. Also, the empty tomb would require another, unrelated explanation.

There's still more this theory could not explain. For instance, the disciples were especially exacting in their teachings about the resurrection, since it was the *central* claim in the New Testament. Moreover, no early text reports that any disciple ever recanted; they were even willing to die for their belief in the resurrection. Additionally, the report of Jesus' resurrection contradicted early Jewish beliefs about the general resurrection, which was believed to happen only corporately and at the end of time. So the question here would concern how hallucinations would ever give rise to the belief that an individual (Jesus) had been raised in their time.

Finally, even if it could be established that groups have hallucinated at the same time, it does not at all follow that these experiences are collective. If hallucinations are private events peculiar to individuals (see sources below), how could *exactly the same* subjective visual perception be shared? It is much more likely that the phenomena in question are either perceptual misinterpretations of actual, physical manifestations (as Zusne and Jones suggest on p. 136) or individual hallucinations experienced along with others who may or may not be hallucinating individually. But if individual hallucinations are required, the odds that each person would be in such a frame of mind decrease exponentially.

But we have already said that Zusne and Jones do *not* attempt to apply this data to Jesus' resurrection at all. Rather, the authors even end their discussion with the admission that these group hallucinations have a "dubious status" because it is not possible to ascertain whether these individuals are actually hallucinating (p. 136; cf. pp. 134–135)! For a different assessment, see J.P. Brady, "The Veridicality of Hypnotic, Visual Hallucinations," in Wolfram Keup, ed., *Origins and Mechanisms of Hallucinations* (New York: Plenum, 1970), p. 181; Weston La Barre, "Anthropological Perspectives on Hallucinations and Hallucinogens," in R.K. Siegel and L.J. West, eds., *Hallucinations: Behavior, Experience and Theory* (New York: John Wiley and Sons, 1975), pp. 9–10.

14. Clinical psychologist Gary R. Collins, personal correspondence, 21 Feb. 1977.

15. See especially 1 Cor. 15:5–7; Matt. 28:9–10, 16–20; Luke 24:13–32, 36–53; John 20:19–21, 26–29; 21:1–23; Acts 1:1–9; 10:39–43; 13:25–33; cf. Mark 16:7. Contemporary critical scholars often favor Paul's account of Jesus' appearances as recorded in 1 Cor. 15:5–8, so we should note that Paul's list alone is enough to reach our conclusion here.

16. For references for each of these appearances, see endnote 15 above.

17. Just for the record, here are some other problems hallucination theories face. (1) There are several evidences that Jesus' appearances were *physical* in nature, as we will point out in Chap. 8. (2) Hallucinations are comparatively rare under normal circumstances. Could we expect the large number needed in order to explain all of the data here? (3) If it is held that all such religious phenomena are self-generated and basically everyone is a candidate, then why does the New Testament differentiate between the resurrection appearances of Jesus and religious visions? While we are told that the former basically ended after forty days, being marked by the specific event of Jesus' ascension (Acts 1:3), the latter was an earmark of the early church. For some instances, see Acts 10:9–17; 27:21–25; 2 Cor. 12:1. (4) For that matter, why did the resurrection appearances stop at

all? If they were self-created hallucinations, why should they not have continued, perhaps as an initiation rite into Christianity? (5) Since the basically unanimous Jewish hope was for a future and corporate resurrection of the dead, and hallucinations come from within an individual's own mind, why would the earliest followers of Jesus have invented such a contrary picture—of a single resurrection, in the present, and in a glorified body?

18. For examples, see Paul Tillich, *Systematic Theology* (Chicago: University of Chicago, 1971), vol. II, especially p. 156; Hans Grass, *Ostergeschehen und Osterberichte,* 2nd ed. (Gottingen, Germany: Vandenhoeck u. Rupert, 1962), p. 96; Gunther Bornkamm, *Jesus of Nazareth,* trans. by Irene and Fraser McLuskey with James M. Robinson (New York: Harper & Row, 1960), p. 185; Joachim Jeremias, "Easter: The Earliest Tradition and the Earliest Interpretation," *New Testament Theology: The Proclamation of Jesus,* trans. by John Bowden (New York: Charles Scribner's Sons, 1971), p. 302; John A.T. Robinson, *Can We Trust the New Testament?* (Grand Rapids, MI: Eerdmans, 1977), pp. 123–125; Reginald H. Fuller, *The Formation of the Resurrection Narratives* (New York: Macmillan, 1971), pp. 46–49; Pinchas Lapide, *The Resurrection of Jesus: A Jewish Perspective* (Minneapolis: Augsburg, 1983), pp. 125–126; A. M. Ramsey, *The Resurrection of Christ* (London: Collins Clear-Type, 1961), pp. 41, 49–50; Neville Clark, *Interpreting the Resurrection* (Philadelphia: Westminster, 1967), pp. 100–101.

19. Wolfhart Pannenberg, *Jesus: God and Man,* trans. by Lewis L. Wilkins and Duane A. Priebe (Philadelphia: Westminster, 1982), p. 96. For other critical scholars who also reject this particular thesis, see the discussion in the main text.

20. To begin with, (1) Jesus was an historical individual while most of these mythical or semi-mythical personages were not. Also, (2) the mystery religions, for example, were not very influential in Palestine at all. (3) Certain parallels between Christian and pagan messages do not explain the far greater and more important differences. Lastly and perhaps most crucially, (4) there is no clear and early case where one of these pagan myths teaches a resurrection in a text that dates before the late second century A.D. This is actually devastating to the critic's position since none of these resurrection stories can be shown to pre-date the Christian teaching concerning Jesus' resurrection. So while we are not asserting this here, one could even presumably hold that these mystery religions, in their typically syncretistic manner, borrowed the idea of resurrection from the Christian message! For these and other details, see Habermas, *The Resurrection of Jesus: A Rational Inquiry,* pp. 146–171; Habermas, *The Verdict of History,* pp. 35–36. For the last point on the dating of these mystery myths, see the important research by Bruce Metzger, *Historical and Literary Studies: Pagan, Jewish and Christian* (Grand Rapids, MI: Eerdmans, 1968), especially pp. 18–19; Ronald Nash, *Christianity and the Hellenistic World* (Grand Rapids, MI: Zondervan, 1984).

21. See endnote 35 for sources that provide some excellent arguments for the empty tomb.

22. Pannenberg, *Jesus: God and Man,* p. 91.

23. For more detailed critiques and evidence, see Habermas, *The Resurrection of Jesus: A Rational Inquiry,* pp. 114–171.

24. Hume's major thesis is located in his volume, *An Enquiry Concerning Human Understanding* (Peru, IL: Open Court, 1988), sec. X, "Of Miracles," part 1. Hume's four subpoints, which pertain mainly to the nature and strength of the evidence for miracle claims, are delineated in Part 2.

25. For this argument in more detail, see Chap. 8, including the sources provided there.

26. See Richard Swinburne, *The Concept of Miracle* (New York: Macmillan and St. Martin's, 1970); Francis J. Beckwith, *David Hume's Argument Against Miracles: A Critical Analysis* (Lanham: University Press of America, 1989); Gary R. Habermas, "Skepticism: Hume," *Biblical Errancy: An Analysis of Its Philosophical Roots,* ed. by Norman L.

Geisler (Grand Rapids, MI: Zondervan, 1981), pp. 23–49. For a more popular critique, see C.S. Lewis, *Miracles: A Preliminary Study* (New York: Macmillan, 1963). For a summary of the views of both Hume and several others who generally follow him, see Norman L. Geisler, *Miracles and Modern Thought* (Grand Rapids, MI: Zondervan, 1982). It should be carefully noted that we are only addressing the issue of the historicity of Jesus' resurrection in this chapter, not its miraculous nature as an act of God. These are two distinct issues in the current dialogue. The interested reader should see Chap. 8 for an initial treatment of the question of God's miraculous actions in this event. The endnotes in that chapter provide more detailed references.

27. Stephen T. Davis, "Is it Possible to Know that Jesus was Raised from the Dead?" *Faith and Philosophy,* vol. 1 (Apr. 1984), pp. 148, 150.

28. See Friedrich Schleiermacher, *The Christian Faith,* ed. by H.R. Mackintosh and J.S. Stewart (New York: Harper & Row, 1963), vol. II, p. 420; Schweitzer, *The Quest of the Historical Jesus,* pp. 211–214. For example, Paulus was impressed that the physical reality of Jesus' appearances, chiefly as depicted in the Gospel accounts, ruled out phantom apparitions.

29. For a description of Keim's three-volume life of Jesus, published from 1867–1872, see Schweitzer, *The Quest of the Historical Jesus,* pp. 211–214. On the impact of Keim's critique, see James Orr's 1908 assessment in *The Resurrection of Jesus,* p. 219. After actually stating the subjective vision theory in its strongest form (Sparrow-Simpson thinks that it was expressed "more learnedly and forcibly than Strauss"), Keim judged that the hypothesis still fails. The lack of emotion in the apostolic age, careful distinction in the New Testament between the resurrection appearances and early religious visions, the apostles' reserved reaction to the appearances, as well as their sudden cessation all argue against subjective, self-generated phenomena. For a detailed discussion of these and other related points, see the 1911 study by W.J. Sparrow-Simpson, *The Resurrection and the Christian Faith* (Grand Rapids, MI: Zondervan, 1965), pp. 110–120.

30. Schweitzer lists no proponents of the fraud theses since the work of Reimarus in 1778 (pp. 21–22).

31. One nineteenth-century liberal theologian who exhibits a remarkable degree of self-criticism, especially as to how legends cannot explain the original disciples' experiences, is Otto Pfleiderer, *Early Christian Conception of Christ* (London: Williams and Norgate, 1905), pp. 153–159. Subsequent critical thought agrees with his criticisms. Examples are provided by Fuller, *The Formation of the Resurrection Narratives,* pp. 46–49; Bornkamm, *Jesus of Nazareth,* p. 185; Lapide, *The Resurrection of Jesus: A Jewish Perspective,* pp. 120–122; Pannenberg, *Jesus: God and Man,* p. 91.

32. Karl Barth, *The Doctrine of Reconciliation,* vol. IV, part I of *Church Dogmatics,* ed. by G.W. Bromiley and T.F. Torrance (Edinburgh: T & T Clark, 1956), p. 340.

33. Raymond Brown, "The Resurrection and Biblical Criticism," *Commonweal,* Nov. 24, 1967, especially p. 233.

34. See Tillich, *Systematic Theology,* vol. II, especially p. 156; Bornkamm, *Jesus of Nazareth,* pp. 181–185; Jeremias, "Easter: The Earliest Tradition and the Earliest Interpretation," p. 302; Robinson, *Can We Trust the New Testament?,* pp. 123–125; Pannenberg, *Jesus: God and Man,* pp. 88–97; Ulrich Wilckens, *Resurrection,* trans. by A.M. Stewart (Edinburgh: Saint Andrew, 1977), pp. 117–119; Lapide, *The Resurrection of Jesus,* pp. 120–126; cf. A.M. Hunter, *Bible and Gospel* (Philadelphia: Westminster, 1969), p. 111.

35. For some strong arguments for the empty tomb, see Edward Lynn Bode, *The First Easter Morning,* Analecta Biblica 45 (Rome: Biblical Institute, 1970), pp. 155–175; William Lane Craig, "The Empty Tomb of Jesus," *Gospel Perspectives: Studies of History and Tradition in the Four Gospels,* vol. 2, ed. by R.T. France and David Wenham (Sheffield, England: JSOT, 1981), pp. 173–200; Robert H. Stein, "Was the Tomb Really Empty?"

Journal of the Evangelical Theological Society, vol. 20, no. 1 (Mar. 1977), pp. 23–29.

36. Fuller, *The Formation of the Resurrection Narratives,* pp. 37, 42–47.

37. This is without even considering other strong evidences such as the empty tomb or the five hundred persons who reportedly saw Jesus at one time (1 Cor. 15:6).

38. William Wand, *Christianity: A Historical Religion?* (Valley Forge, PA: Judson, 1972), pp. 93–94. Wand also makes similar comments concerning the evidence for the resurrection as a whole (see pp. 51–52, 70–71, 116).

39. The ensuing discussion follows more-or-less closely from part 2 of a recent journal article by the author. For details, see Gary R. Habermas, "Jesus' Resurrection and Contemporary Criticism: An Apologetic," *Criswell Theological Review,* vol. 4, no. 2 (Spring 1990).

40. For some examples, see Lapide, *The Resurrection of Jesus,* pp. 97–99; Fuller, *The Formation of the Resurrection Narratives,* pp. 10–11; Raymond E. Brown, *The Virginal Conception and Bodily Resurrection of Jesus* (New York: Paulist, 1973), pp. 81, 92; Robinson, *Can We Trust the New Testament?,* p. 125; Rudolf Bultmann, *Theology of the New Testament,* trans. by Kendrick Grobel (New York: Charles Scribner's Sons, 1951, 1955), vol. I, p. 296; Paul van Buren, *The Secular Meaning of the Gospel* (New York: Macmillan, 1963), pp. 126–127; Cf. Willi Marxsen, *The Resurrection of Jesus of Nazareth,* trans. by Margaret Kohl (Philadelphia: Fortress, 1970), p. 80; Bornkamm, *Jesus of Nazareth,* p. 182; Joachim Jeremias, "Easter: The Earliest Tradition and the Earliest Interpretation," p. 306.

41. Jeremias, "Easter: The Earliest Tradition and the Earliest Interpretation," p. 306.

42. Wilckens, *Resurrection,* p. 2.

43. See Grass, *Ostergeschehen und Osterberichte,* p. 96; Reginald Fuller, *The Foundations of New Testament Christology* (New York: Charles Scribner's Sons, 1965), pp. 142, 161; Fuller, *The Formation of the Resurrection Narratives,* pp. 10, 14, 28, 48; Oscar Cullmann, *The Early Church: Studies in Early Christian History and Theology,* ed. by A.J.B. Higgins (Philadelphia: Westminster, 1966), pp. 65–66; Leonard Goppelt, "The Easter Kerygma in the New Testament," *The Easter Message Today,* trans. by Salvator Attanasio and Darrell L. Guder (New York: Thomas Nelson, 1964), p. 36; Pannenberg, *Jesus: God and Man,* p. 90; C.H. Dodd, *The Apostolic Preaching and Its Developments* (Grand Rapids, MI: Baker, 1980), p. 16; Hunter, *Bible and Gospel,* p. 109; Raymond Brown, *The Virginal Conception and Bodily Resurrection of Jesus,* p. 81; Thomas Sheehan, *First Coming: How the Kingdom of God Became Christianity* (New York: Random House, 1988), pp. 110, 118; George Eldon Ladd, *I Believe in the Resurrection of Jesus* (Grand Rapids, MI: Eerdmans, 1975), p. 105. Gerald O'Collins attests that he is unaware of any scholars who date Paul's reception of this material after the A.D. 40s. Our major conclusions in this chapter would still follow even with a later date such as this. See O'Collins, *What Are They Saying About the Resurrection?* (New York: Paulist, 1978), p. 112.

44. Goppelt claims that most scholars hold that this creed is Palestinian in its form ("The Easter Kerygma in the New Testament," p. 36). Most of the scholars in the previous endnote favor the Jerusalem scenario. However, Grass prefers the city of Damascus as the locale, indicating an even earlier date *(Ostergeschehen und Osterberichte,* p. 96). Sheehan does not answer the question in his immediate context.

45. Dodd, *The Apostolic Preaching and Its Developments,* p. 16.

46. For the possible meaning of *historeo* in Gal. 1:18 and its relevance in determining the nature of Paul's inquiring of Peter during his visit to Jerusalem, see the study by William R. Farmer, "Peter and Paul, and the Tradition Concerning 'The Lord's Supper' in 1 Cor. 11:23–25," *Criswell Theological Review,* vol. 2 (1987), especially pp. 122–130. On the Petrine and, hence, apostolic nature of this creed, see pp. 135–138.

47. While it may be objected that Paul's explicit point in Gal. 1:11–17 is that he did not

receive his message of the gospel from any man, including any other apostles, this is surely to miss his overall intent. He is speaking in these verses *specifically* about his initial and direct call by the Lord, in which he *was* given the gospel message, presumably before he ever met another apostle. But he is also equally clear that his consultation with the other apostles concerning his message came *later*. Therefore, to say that he *never* consulted any other apostle on this subject is to miss his second point.

48. Hans von Campenhausen, "The Events of Easter and the Empty Tomb," *Tradition and Life in the Church* (Philadelphia: Fortress, 1968), p. 44.

49. Lapide, *The Resurrection of Jesus*, p. 99.

50. Dodd, *The Apostolic Preaching and Its Developments*, p. 16.

51. Michael Grant, *Jesus: An Historian's Review of the Gospels* (New York: Charles Scribner's Sons, 1977), especially p. 176.

52. Carl Braaten, *History and Hermeneutics*, vol. II of *New Directions in Theology Today*, ed. by William Hordern (Philadelphia: Westminster, 1966), p. 78.

53. Fuller, *The Foundations of New Testament Christology*, p. 142.

54. Wolfhart Pannenberg, "The Historicity of the Resurrection: The Identity of Christ," *The Intellectuals Speak Out About God*, ed. by Roy Abraham Verghese (Chicago: Regnery Gateway, 1984), p. 260.

55. James D.G. Dunn, *The Evidence for Jesus* (Louisville: Westminster, 1985), pp. 73–75.

56. In the *Gospels*, see Matt. 27:26–56; Mark 15:21–47; Luke 23:26–56; John 19:16–42. Other early *New Testament creeds* that report the death of Jesus include Rom. 4:25; 1 Cor. 11:23–26; Phil. 2:8; 1 Tim. 2:6; 1 Peter 3:18.

Critical research has shown that some of the early passages in Acts (and Peter's speeches, in particular) reflect early tradition from the Jerusalem community. The death and resurrection of Jesus are frequently reported in these early teachings (Acts 2:22–23, 31; 3:15, 4:10, 5:30, 10:39, 13:28–29).

Early *non-New Testament Christian* sources incorporate Clement of Rome (cf. *Corinthians* 7, 12, 21, 49), Ignatius *(Trallians* 9; *Smyrneans* 1), *Barnabas* (5), and Justin Martyr *(First Apology* XXXII; XXXV; L; *Dialogue with Trypho* XCVII; CVIII). *Non-Christian* texts of mixed value that record the death of Jesus number at least 10 and include Tacitus *(Annals* 15:44), a disputed portion by Josephus *(Antiquities* 18:3), the *Talmud (Sanhedrin* 43a; cf. 106b), Lucian of Samosata *(The Death of Peregrine* 11–13), Mara Bar-Serapion (letter, British Museum, Syriac manuscript, additional 14,658), the lost *Acts of Pilate* (Justin Martyr, *First Apology* XXXV), the lost history of Thallus (from a fragment of Julius Africanus), *The Gospel of Truth* (20:11–14, 25–29). *The Gospel of Thomas* (parable, 45:1–16), *The Treatise of Resurrection* (46:14–21). The *Toledoth Jesu* reports Jesus' death, but is much later. For details, see Habermas, *The Verdict of History,* chap. 4.

57. Reports from the *Gospels* are found in Matt. 28, Mark 16:1–8 (Jesus' appearances predicted), Luke 24:13–51, John 20:14–21:23. Appearance accounts are also found in the early tradition of *Acts* (1:1–11, 2:32, 3:15, 5:30–32, 10:39–43, 13:30–31). Besides 1 Cor. 15:3ff, *New Testament creeds* that report the resurrection include Luke 24:34 and 2 Tim. 2:8. Early *non-New Testament Christian* accounts are found in Clement of Rome *(Corinthians* 42), Ignatius *(Smyrneans* 3), and Justin Martyr *(First Apology* L). A disputed *non-Christian* reference to Jesus' resurrection is found in Josephus *(Antiquities* 18:3), while highly theological mentions occur in Gnostic works such as *The Gospel of Truth* (25:25–34) and *The Treatise on Resurrection* (44:27–29; 45:14–23; 46:14–21; 48:10–19). Allusions to Jesus' post-death exaltation are found in *The Gospel of Thomas* (45:15–17) and *The Apocryphon of John* (1:5–12).

58. See Matt. 26:56, 69–74; Mark 14:50, 66–72; Luke 22:55–72; John 18:25–27.

59. For some examples of their changed attitude, in contrast to those in the previous endnote, see Acts 2:41–47; 4:1–4, 8–21, 29–31; 5:17–32, 40–42. Paul's post-creedal re-

port concerning the work of the apostles as a whole is seen in 1 Cor. 15:9–11, while 1 Tim. 3:16 records another early creed that notes this apostolic ministry. Regarding the apostles' willingness to die, see Acts 7:57–60, 12:1–3, 21:13, 25:11; Rom. 14:8; 1 Cor. 15:30–32; Phil. 1:20–24; cf. 2 Peter 1:13–15. For some other accounts of the deaths of the apostles, see Eusebius, *Ecclesiastical History,* Book II:IX, XXIII, XXV.

60. This message is contained in both early extra-New Testament Christian writers such as Clement of Rome *(Corinthians* 42), Ignatius *(Smyrneans* 3), *Barnabas* (5), as well as secular sources like Tacitus *(Annals* 15:44), the much-discussed portion in Josephus *(Antiquities* 18:3) and is implied in the letter by Mara Bar-Serapion (British Museum).

61. An impressive feature of the early apostolic preaching in the book of Acts is that there is not one sermon or testimony in the first five chapters where the resurrection of Jesus is not central. (See Acts 1:21–22; 2:22–24, 29–33; 3:13–15, 26; 4:2, 10; 5:30–32; cf. Acts 10:39–43; 13:30–37; 17:1–4, 18, 31.) A good summary text is Acts 4:33, where Luke specifically states that the resurrection was at the core of the apostles' message.

62. Well over three hundred verses are concerned with the subject of Jesus' resurrection in the New Testament. We are told that this event is a sign for unbelievers (Matt. 12:38–40; cf. John 20:24–29) as well as the answer for the believer's doubt (Luke 24:38–43). It serves as the guarantee that Jesus' teachings are true (Acts 2:22–24; 1 Cor. 15:12–20) and is the center of the gospel itself (Rom. 4:24–25, 10:9; 1 Cor. 15:1–4). Further, the resurrection is the impetus for evangelism (Matt. 28:18–20; Acts 10:39–43), the key indication of the believer's daily power to live the Christian life (Rom. 6:4–14, 8:9–11; Phil. 3:10) and the reason for the total commitment of our lives (Rom. 7:4; 1 Cor. 15:57–58). The resurrection even addresses the fear of death (John 11:25; 1 Cor. 15:54–58; cf. Heb. 2:14–15) and is related to the second coming of Jesus (Acts 1:11; Rev. 1:7). Lastly, this event is a model of the Christian's resurrection from the dead (Acts 4:2; 1 Cor. 6:14; 1 Thess. 4:13–18) and provides a foretaste of heaven for the believer (Phil. 3:20–21; 1 Peter 1:3–5). For a popular treatment that addresses these and other aspects, see Gary R. Habermas, *The Centrality of the Resurrection,* forthcoming.

63. See Clement of Rome *(Corinthians* 42), Ignatius *(Smyrneans* 3), and *Barnabas* (5).

64. Fuller, *The Formation of the Resurrection Narratives,* p. 48.

65. See Acts 9:1–9, 22:5–11, 26:12–18. We discuss Paul's conception of Jesus' resurrection body in Chap. 8.

66. See Acts 21:13; 1 Cor. 15:30–32; 2 Cor. 4:7–14, 5:8–9, 11:23–33; Eusebius, *Ecclesiastical History,* II:XXV.

67. It has been suggested that Stephen's death and other matters affected Paul to the extent that he was ready for a conversion. But not only is there no evidence of such remorse, Paul even states that he carried on his persecution of Christians with zeal, being faultless *(amemptos)* with regard to the Law (Phil. 3:6; cf. Acts 22:3). Besides, such guilt would appear to be a very weak basis for his unbending Christian conviction, even to the death. That there is no sign of Paul's doubting his conversion in light of his exceptionally strong background in Judaism should also indicate much more than a reaction to any remorse in his life.

An hallucination has also been suggested, with critics citing the facts that Paul's companions in the Acts accounts neither saw Jesus (9:7) nor understood the words of the voice (22:9 NIV). But to cite only these subjective elements is not to do justice to the corresponding objective ones. Paul's companions did hear the voice, although without comprehension (9:7), they saw the light (22:9; cf. 26:13), and they fell to the ground along with Paul (26:14). Further, Paul was blinded by the light for three days (9:8–9, 22:11).

There is no sufficient reason to prefer some of these elements while disregarding other ones from the same texts. On the other hand, to dismiss the Acts accounts altogether appears to be to lose the very basis for the claim of the subjective components in the appearance to Paul. The objective data therein do militate strongly against hallucinations, as does also the same lack of remorseful preconditioning just mentioned. Lastly, it is crucially important that Paul apparently had no objections to thinking that what he saw could also be seen by 500 people at once (1 Cor. 15:6, 8), so he plainly does not think of his appearances as being *characterized* by subjective elements.

In short, there is *no known reason* why Paul should have either desired to forsake his deep and pious roots in Judaism or yearned to be struck down by an appearance of the glorified Jesus in whom he did not believe. Conversely, we *do know* that his conversion, like that of James, had all of the earmarks of a sudden act of God: an undeniably powerful commitment to the Christian faith, probably ending in his own martyrdom, the decided lack of any reconsidering or recanting, and the total assurance that Jesus had appeared to him (complete with certain objective elements), enough so that he was willing to risk his life on this alone (1 Cor. 15:18-20, 30-32).

68. See Fuller, *The Formation of the Resurrection Narratives,* pp. 42-49; Pannenberg, *Jesus: God and Man,* pp. 92-96; Brown, *The Virginal Conception and Bodily Resurrection of Jesus,* pp. 85-92; Murray J. Harris, *Raised Immortal* (Grand Rapids, MI: Eerdmans, 1983), pp. 46-49; Grant R. Osborne, *The Resurrection Narratives: A Redactional Study* (Grand Rapids, MI: Baker, 1984), pp. 231-233. Daniel Fuller defends Luke's three accounts of Paul's conversion, as well as the historicity of the appearance to Paul, at great length. See Daniel Fuller, *Easter Faith and History* (Grand Rapids, MI: Eerdmans, 1965), pp. 188-261.

69. These five facts are so widely recognized that even a sampling would be massive. We will list here more than thirty New Testament scholars, theologians, historians, and philosophers who hold each of them: Bultmann, *Theology of the New Testament,* vol. I, pp. 44-46, 60, 77, 80-83, 293-295; Tillich, *Systematic Theology,* vol. II, pp. 153-158; John Hick, *Death and Eternal Life* (San Francisco: Harper & Row, 1980), pp. 171-177; Bornkamm, *Jesus of Nazareth,* pp. 179-186; Helmut Koester, *Introduction to the New Testament,* two vols. (Philadelphia: Fortress, 1982), vol. II, pp. 84-86, 100; Barth, *Church Dogmatics,* vol. IV, part one, pp. 334-336, 351-353; Emil Brunner, *Dogmatics,* three vols., trans. by Olive Wyon (Philadelphia: Westminster, 1952), vol. II, pp. 363-378; Jurgen Moltmann, *Theology of Hope,* trans. by James W. Leitch (New York: Harper and Row, Publishers, 1967), pp. 165-166, 172, 197-202; C. H. Dodd, "The Appearances of the Risen Christ: An Essay in the Form Criticism of the Gospels," *More New Testament Essays* (Grand Rapids, MI: Eerdmans, 1968), pp. 104-105, 123-125, 131-133; Norman Perrin, *The Resurrection According to Matthew, Mark, and Luke* (Philadelphia: Fortress, 1977), pp. 11, 78-84; Robinson, *Can We Trust the New Testament?,* pp. 113-129; Reginald Fuller, *The Formation of the Resurrection Narratives,* pp. 27-49; Grant, *Jesus,* pp. 174-179; Pannenberg, *Jesus: God and Man,* pp. 66-73, 88-106; Wilckens, *Resurrection,* pp. 6-16, 112-114; Jeremias, "Easter," pp. 300-311; Werner Georg Kummel, *The Theology of the New Testament: According to its Major Witnesses: Jesus—Paul—John* (Nashville: Abingdon, 1973), pp. 102-105; Brown, *The Virginal Conception and Bodily Resurrection of Jesus,* pp. 80-82, 128; Goppelt, "The Easter Kerygma in the New Testament," pp. 36-37, 43-53; Elaine Pagels, *The Gnostic Gospels* (New York: Random House, 1979), pp. 6-12; Lapide, *The Resurrection of Jesus,* pp. 32-36, 91-99, 125-131; Sheehan, *First Coming,* pp. 101-114; Marcus Barth and Verne H. Fletcher, *Acquittal by Resurrection* (New York: Holt, Rinehart and Winston, 1964), Part 1 (Barth), pp. 3-6, 11-14, 38-39; Van Buren, *The Secular Meaning of the Gospel,* pp. 126-134; Wand, *Christianity,* pp. 51, 59, 84, 93, 108; A. M. Hunter, *Jesus: Lord and Saviour,* pp. 98-107; Ramsey, *The Resurrection of Christ,* pp. 35-45; W. T. Jones, *A History of Western Philosophy,* 5 vols., 2nd ed. (New York: Harcourt Brace Jovanovich, 1969), vol. II, pp. 34-35, 39; Ladd, *I Believe in the Resurrection of Jesus,* pp. 36-43, 93, 109-111; Daniel Fuller, *Easter Faith and History,* pp. 208-229; Thielicke, "The Resurrection Kerygma," *The Easter Message Today,* pp. 59-62, 86-91; Osborne, *The Resurrection Narratives,* pp. 231-233,

276–277, 281–288; Harris, *Raised Immortal,* pp. 5–11, 60; Clark, *Interpreting the Resurrection,* pp. 89–101.

Chapter 5   Near-Death Experiences

1. Raymond A. Moody, Jr., *Life After Life* (Atlanta: Mockingbird, 1975).

2. There appears to be some imprecision as to *how many* of these signs should be present, especially if it was impossible to check thoroughly at the time of the crisis.

3. For an enlightening discussion, see the treatment by cardiologist Michael B. Sabom, *Recollections of Death: A Medical Investigation* (New York: Harper & Row, 1982), pp. 5–9, including the helpful definitions provided by the Russian scientist, Professor Negovskii. Cf. the brief, but similar, definitions given by cardiologist and CPR expert Maurice Rawlings, *Before Death Comes* (Nashville: Thomas Nelson, 1980), p. 18.

4. Moody, *Life After Life,* pp. 101–104. Sabom also discusses the relevance of "brain death," but doesn't seem to be quite sure where to place it on the definitional scale (pp. 8–9).

5. We will follow the lead of many others and view pre-death visions and near-death experiences as types of basically the same phenomena. One example of this contention is found in Michael Grosso, "Toward an Explanation of Near-Death Phenomena," *Anabiosis,* vol. 1, no. 1, July 1981, pp. 4–5. For an earlier statement of some of the points in this section of the chapter, see Gary R. Habermas, "Paradigm Shift: A Challenge to Naturalism," *Bibliotheca Sacra,* vol. 146, no. 584, Oct.–Dec. 1989, pp. 444–449, in particular.

6. Habermas has interviewed or collected from the published literature more than seventy corroborative reports in these four categories. These cases include a tremendous amount of variety and the reader should realize that such evidenced accounts are not rare.

7. Katie's own physician, the pediatrician who revived her and investigated the details, reports this account along with many others. See Melvin Morse with Paul Perry, *Closer to the Light: Learning from the Near-Death Experiences of Children* (New York: Random House/Villard, 1990), pp. 3–9.

8. Ibid., pp. 152–154.

9. Raymond A. Moody, Jr., "Almost Dying," a lecture given at Louisiana State University, 26 Apr. 1987. Moody also relates a similar experience in which a dying girl thought she had left her body and went to her older sister in another hospital room and heard her crying and pleading with her not to die. She, too, surprised her older sister when she later told her exactly where she was and what she had been saying *(Life After Life,* p. 71).

10. Kenneth L. Woodard, "There is Life After Death," *McCall's,* Aug. 1976, p. 136; J. Kerby Anderson, *Life, Death and Beyond* (Grand Rapids, MI: Zondervan, 1980), p. 91; Elisabeth Kubler-Ross, *On Children and Death* (New York: Macmillan/Collier Books, 1983), p. 208.

11. For this discussion, quotation, and source, see Sabom, *Recollections of Death: A Medical Investigation,* p. 8. This is why longer periods of heart stoppage with corroboration are still evidential.

12. Morse, *Closer to the Light,* pp. 24–26, 165.

13. Ibid., pp. 32–33.

14. Sabom, *Recollections of Death,* pp. 87–91, 94–99, 105–111.

15. Maurice Rawlings, *Beyond Death's Door . . .* (Nashville: Thomas Nelson, 1978), pp. 73–75, 93–95. In the second case here, that of a Christian, the patient also reported a glimpse of a heaven-like place: "There was a river below me, and it was becoming dawn. Everything was getting brighter. I noticed that I was crossing over a beautiful city below, as I followed the river like a soaring bird. The streets seemed to be made of shining gold and were wonderfully beautiful. I can't describe it. I descended onto one of the streets and

people were all around me—happy people who were glad to see me! They seemed to be in shining clothes with a sort of glow" (pp. 94–95).

Although it is not our purpose here to reproduce many of these descriptions of heavenly environments (for reasons we will discuss in the next chapter), this is one example of many similar portraits.

16. John Audette, "Denver Cardiologist Discloses Findings After 18 Years of Near-Death Research," *Anabiosis*, 1, 1979, pp. 1–2; Dina Ingber, "Visions of An Afterlife," *Science Digest*, vol. 89, no. 1, Jan.–Feb. 1981, pp. 94–97, 142; personal conversation with Fred Schoonmaker, 1 June 1982.

17. Exceptions are cases of "drug overdose or extreme hypothermia," where brain function may be repressed. See "Definitions of Death," *Science Digest*, vol. 89, no. 1, Jan.–Feb. 1981, p. 96; "A Definition of Irreversible Coma: Report of the Ad Hoc Committee of the Harvard Medical School to Examine the Definition of Brain Death," *Journal of the American Medical Association*, vol. 205, 1968, pp. 337–340.

18. This particular case is reported by Elisabeth Kubler-Ross. For example, Elizabeth Kubler-Ross, "The Experience of Death," in *The Vestibule*, ed. by Jess Weiss (New York: Pocket Books, 1972), pp. 57–64; "When Face to Face With Death," *Reader's Digest*, Aug. 1976, p. 84; cf. "Life After Death?" *Newsweek*, July 12, 1976, p. 41.

19. Natalie Kalmus' article appeared in *Guideposts* magazine in 1947. It was reproduced in John Myers, ed., *Voices From the Edge of Eternity* (Old Tappan, NJ: Revell/Spire, 1968), pp. 17–20.

20. John Myers, ed., *Voices from the Edge of Eternity,* pp. 55–56. One of Myers's older cases is an account that was reproduced from a book written by Judson Palmer, a minister who included the account as it had been given to him by an eyewitness and friend, A.D. Sandborn, also a minister. Sandborn regularly visited a seriously ill young woman in Iowa on his way to work. One day while Sandborn was present, she testified that she was seeing the gates of heaven, along with two old friends (who now lived at opposite ends of the country), and that they had died. The three friends were waiting to be taken into heaven. A few days after the death of the woman, Sandborn researched the matter and discovered that the other two friends had both died on exactly the same day (pp. 97–99).

21. Morse, *Closer to the Light,* pp. 51–55.

22. Rawlings, *Beyond Death's Door . . . ,* pp. 17–22.

23. Kubler-Ross, *On Children and Death,* p. 208.

24. Ibid., p. 210.

25. For example, in the Kalmus case above, the cousin had died the previous week. But in our modern world of instant communication, time lapses are not what they used to be. Still, the instances where the other person in question died at the same time would appear to be more evidential in nature since there is little way that the death could have been previously known by the near-death experiencer.

26. Kubler-Ross, *On Children and Death,* p. 210.

27. Karlis Osis and Erlendur Haraldsson, *At the Hour of Death* (New York: Avon, 1977).

28. Kenneth Ring, *Life at Death: A Scientific Investigation of the Near-Death Experience* (New York: Coward, McCann, and Geoghegan, 1980). In the Introduction, Moody describes this volume as a more systematic, sophisticated study than his own (p. 13).

29. Ibid., pp. 265–270, 275–279, respectively.

30. Sabom, *Recollections of Death,* chap. 7 in particular. Also, Michael B. Sabom, "The Near-Death Experience: Myth or Reality? A Methodological Approach," *Anabiosis,* vol. 1, no. 1, July 1981, pp. 44–56.

31. Morse, *Closer to the Light,* pp. 17–24, 40–42.

32. Moody, *Life After Life,* pp. 107–120; Osis and Haraldsson, *At the Hour of Death,* pp. 187–204; Ring, *Life at Death,* pp. 206–217; Sabom, *Recollections of Death,* pp. 151–

178; Morse, *Closer to the Light*, pp. 183–193. In *Anabiosis* vol. 1, no. 1 (July 1981), three philosophers also responded to such alternative theories: Michael Grosso, "Toward an Explanation of Near-Death Phenomena," pp. 12–23; Mark Woodhouse, "Near-Death Experiences and the Mind-Body Problem," pp. 57–58; Stephen Vicchio, "Near-Death Experiences: Some Logical Problems and Questions for Further Study," pp. 69–73.

33. Wilder Penfield, *The Mystery of the Mind: A Critical Study of Consciousness and the Human Brain* (Princeton, NJ: Princeton University, 1975), pp. 76–77.

34. Ibid., pp. 77–78.

35. A more technical treatment is found in Roger W. Sperry, "Mind-Brain Interaction: Mentalism, Yes; Dualism, No," *Neuroscience,* vol. 5, 1980, pp. 195–201. Cf. Roger Sperry, "Changed Concepts of Brain and Consciousness: Some Value Implications," *Zygon,* vol. 20, no. 1, Mar. 1985.

36. See in particular Sir John C. Eccles and Sir Karl Popper, *The Self and Its Brain* (New York: Springer-Verlag, 1981). Popper, an influential philosopher, is a dualist even though he is a religious agnostic.

37. Sir John C. Eccles, "Modern Biology and the Turn to Belief in God," *The Intellectuals Speak Out About God,* ed. by Roy Abraham Varghese (Chicago: Regnery Gateway, 1984), pp. 47–50.

38. For details, sources, and an excellent summary of recent research such as this, see Laurence W. Wood, "Recent Brain Research and the Mind-Body Dilemma," *The Asbury Theological Journal,* vol. 41, no. 1, 1986, p. 60.

39. Ibid., p. 60.

40. Ibid., pp. 60–61.

41. Ibid., p. 72. Wood also concludes: "The dogmatists now appear to be the reductionists. . . . Thanks to the recent research in neurophysiology and computer-based psychology, a greater appreciation for the inexhaustible depth of life can be obtained. . . . Philosophical materialism seems both scientifically and philosophically indefensible" (pp. 72–73).

42. Penfield, *The Mystery of the Mind,* p. 80.

43. Ibid., p. 89.

44. Wilder Penfield and T.B. Rasmussen, *The Cerebral Cortex of Man* (New York: Macmillan, 1950). For details, see Morse, *Closer to the Light,* pp. 99–104, 169–172.

45. Morse, *Closer to the Light,* p. 170.

46. John Beloff, in 1965, as cited in David Winter, *Hereafter: What Happens After Death?* (Wheaton, IL: Harold Shaw, 1972), pp. 33–34.

47. "Near-Death Experiences Defy Single Explanation," *Brain-Mind Bulletin,* 14 Sept. 1981, pp. 1, 3.

48. A.J. Ayer, " 'What I Saw When I Was Dead': Intimations of Immortality," *National Review,* 14 Oct. 1988, pp. 38–40.

49. Ibid., pp. 39–40.

50. Articles on the subject in some of the most prestigious scholarly journals are another sign of the growing respect for near-death research. See Ian Stevenson and Bruce Greyson, "Near-Death Experiences: Relevance to the Question of Survival After Death," *Journal of the American Medical Association,* vol. 242, no. 3, 20 July 1979, pp. 265–267; Bruce Greyson and Ian Stevenson, "The Phenomenology of Near-Death Experiences," *American Journal of Psychiatry,* vol. 137, no. 10, Oct. 1980, pp. 1193–1196.

Chapter 6   NDEs: Questions and Objections

1. This Associated Press report of an interview with George Gallup, Jr., was issued from Virginia Beach on 24 June 1982. Also see George Gallup, Jr., with William Proctor, *Adventures in Immortality* (New York: McGraw-Hill, 1982).

2. Maurice Rawlings, *Before Death Comes* (Nashville: Thomas Nelson, 1980), pp. 18–19.

3. Michael B. Sabom, *Recollections of Death: A Medical Investigation* (New York: Harper & Row, 1982), pp. 56–57. For his method, cf. p. 6.

4. Kenneth Ring, *Life at Death: A Scientific Investigation of the Near-Death Experience* (New York: Coward, McCann, and Geoghegan, 1980), p. 32.

5. Dina Ingber, "Visions of An Afterlife," *Science Digest,* vol. 89, no. 1, Jan.–Feb. 1981, p. 96.

6. For one example, see Raymond A. Moody, Jr., *Reflections on Life After Life* (New York: Bantam, 1985), p. 87.

7. Melvin Morse, *Closer to the Light, Learning from the Near-Death Experiences of Children* (New York: Random House/Villard, 1990), pp. 27–28, 35–36, respectively. But concerning the first NDE, Morse concludes: "Chris just didn't forget the staircase. He had been treated with many narcotics and Valium™, all of which cause amnesia. His case and those similar to it make me think that everyone who has almost died may possibly have had a near-death experience. Perhaps they frequently don't remember because the drugs given to them erase memory" (p. 28).

We would contend that this conclusion is not necessarily warranted at all. Because drugs may affect some memories does not give us strong grounds to think that they could very well affect all such recollections. Aside from that, however, Morse has made a good observation: Drugs do sometimes affect our memories.

8. Moody argues that "a certain percentage" might be explained this way *(Reflections on Life After Life,* p. 87).

9. But on the other hand, two other patients had three to five and eight to ten crises, respectively, and had a NDE each time. Sabom, *Recollections of Death,* Table VII, p. 203; cf. Raymond A. Moody, Jr., *Life After Life* (Atlanta: Mockingbird Books, 1975), p. 25.

10. Moody, *Reflections on Life After Life,* p. 87.

11. Ring, *Life at Death,* fig. 1, p. 40.

12. Sabom, *Recollections of Death,* Table IX, p. 206.

13. For example, both Ring and Sabom list peace and separation from one's body as the two most commonly observed elements, but Ring's occurrence is much lower (60 percent and 37 percent, respectively) than Sabom's (100 percent each, along with the return to the body). Further, both list darkness at the same rate of incidence (23 percent). Ring's light phenomena (16 percent) appears less than the same feature in Sabom (28 percent).

14. Moody, *Life After Life,* p. 39.

15. Moody, *Reflections on Life After Life,* p. 97.

16. Moody, "Foreword," in Morse, *Closer to the Light,* p. xi.

17. Morse, *Closer to the Light,* pp. 17–24, 40–42.

18. In Ring's study, 16 percent reported the light and 10 percent said that they entered it *(Life at Death,* p. 40, Figure 1, pp. 56–66). In Sabom's research, 28 percent witnessed the light *(Recollections of Death,* p. 206, Table IX). Although Morse does not provide details, he states that about 20 percent of adults see the light. Incredibly (even for its possible relevance to theology), Morse recounts that almost every child included some element of light in his or her experience *(Closer to the Light,* p. 115).

19. Osis and Haraldsson report almost exactly three times as many human beings (418 examples) being seen as religious persons (140 persons). See *At the Hour of Death* (New York: Avon, 1977), Table 2, p. 218. Sabom also lists far more humans than religious personages *(Recollections of Death,* Table XIII, pp. 210–211).

20. For details, see Osis and Haraldsson, ibid.

21. Ibid., Table 2, p. 218.

22. Ibid., pp. 59, 91–95, 98. These data also militate against those who argue that all of the religious figures are really manifestations of the same God.

23. William L. Rowe and William J. Wainwright, eds., *Philosophy of Religion* (Belmont, CA: Wadsworth, 1988), pp. 113–130.

24. Osis and Haraldsson, *At the Hour of Death*, p. 92.

25. Morse presents two such cases in *Closer to the Light,* pp. 156, 167.

26. Ring states that a feeling of peace was perceived by 60 percent of his sample (*Life at Death*, fig. 1, p. 40). Sabom reports that 100 percent of his nonsurgical cases experienced "calm and peace" (*Recollections of Death*, Table IX, p. 206).

27. Maurice Rawlings, *Beyond Death's Door . . .* (Nashville: Thomas Nelson, 1978), chaps. 1, 7 for example. Cf. Maurice Rawlings, "Hell is for Real," *Christian Life,* Jan. 1979, pp. 32–33, 55–56, 78. For another popular account of a case like those reported by Rawlings, see Irwin Fisher, "I Died for 20 Minutes and Went to Hell," *Weekly World News,* 4 Oct. 1988, p. 33. Habermas has also been told of two hell experiences of this type. Incidentally, Rawlings also presents examples where people became Christians during a hellish near-death experience, including Rawlings himself after witnessing these cases! See Maurice Rawlings, *Before Death Comes,* pp. 19–25.

28. Rawlings, *Beyond Death's Door . . . ,* pp. 20–21, 111–112, 120.

29. Ring describes Rawlings's thesis as *"not proven,"* objecting to several factors and favoring the view that such cases are more probably hallucinations. Yet Ring still thinks that all of Rawlings's examples cannot be dismissed and that hellish near-death experiences "sometimes do occur," but much less frequently than Rawlings thinks. Ring lists some other researchers who have also found some examples of a hell-like state (Ring, *Life at Death,* pp. 192–198, 248–250, 259).

30. Not all reports of hell are like the traditional "hellfire" cases. A fictional account that has had an immense influence on contemporary views of hell (in spite of the warnings of the author not to apply these ideas to reality—pp. 7–8) is C.S. Lewis's *The Great Divorce* (New York: Macmillan, 1946). In this fantasy, nothing is truly real in hell, but deception, crime, and unfulfilled, meaningless desires are some of the major characteristics of life. See Chap. 11 below.

Interestingly, a number of near-death experiences seem to fall into this type of hell genre. For examples, see George G. Ritchie with Elizabeth Sherrill, *Return from Tomorrow* (Waco, TX: Word, 1978); Burris Jenkins, "I Was an Atheist—Until I Died," *The Vestibule,* ed. Jess E. Weiss (New York: Pocket Books, 1972), pp. 35–36; Moody, *Reflections on Life After Life,* pp. 18–22; John Myers, ed., *Voices From the Edge of Eternity* (Old Tappan, NJ: Revell/Spire, 1968), pp. 239–241; cf. Osis and Haraldsson, *At the Hour of Death,* p. 167. Further, Osis and Haraldsson found that a large number of Indian patients in both terminal and nonterminal cases reacted negatively to the pre-death visions, in that they often "cried out for help or tried to hide" (p. 87; Table 1, p. 217; Table 5, p. 221). Also, only Indian patients identified the messenger as the god of death or a spokesman for that god (Table 2, p. 218).

31. J. Kerby Anderson agrees with this assessment (see *Life, Death and Beyond* [Grand Rapids, MI: Zondervan, 1980], p. 110). Although he thinks that the hell cases are real but not plentiful, Ring still concludes the matter this way: "What may happen *after* the initial stages of death—something this research cannot speak to—remains an open question" (italics his; *Life at Death,* p. 250).

32. This barrier might be almost any form of separation such as a river, fence, or wall. Two of those Habermas interviewed spoke about crossing a lake and walking up a stairway. If they had finished the task, they believed it would have indicated final death.

33. Rawlings, *Beyond Death's Door . . . ,* pp. 53, 88, 92, 100, 102. Anderson appears to agree (*Life, Death and Beyond,* pp. 140–141).

34. For instance, Zaleski found that medieval accounts of near-death experiences, in much contrast to contemporary examples, give an especially prominent place to the torments of hell, since that was probably the central feature of the Church's teaching at that

time. Today, in keeping with the common belief that God is not judgmental and will accept everyone, the typical near-death interpretation is that the experience is blissful. So Zaleski concludes that the interpretation given to these incidents is largely conditioned by current beliefs. However, these explanations are still to be separated from the issue of whether the phenomena are objective. See Carol Zaleski, *Other-World Journeys: Accounts of Near-Death Experiences in Medieval and Modern Times* (New York: Oxford University, 1987).

35. Even apart from the aspects of heaven and hell, most researchers have noted that there is little (or no) corroboration for any of what Sabom calls the "transcendental" aspects of the near-death experience (Ring, *Life at Death*, pp. 238–239; Sabom, *Recollections of Death*, p. 185; cf. Moody, *Reflections on Life After Life*, pp. 138–139). The fact is that some veridicality does exist, but not for the religious persons who are met, or for heaven and hell itself. See Ring, *Life at Death*, pp. 238–239; Osis and Haraldsson, *At the Hour of Death*, p. 180. Habermas has also found (and interviewed) a detailed case where two persons had "transcendental" experiences at the same time in different parts of the country, later verifying aspects of each other's accounts.

36. In *Life After Life* (pp. 107–108), Moody considers this view as an alternative explanation and rejects it. In *Reflections on Life After Life* (p. 84), he entertains the question of occult involvement on the part of those he interviewed.

37. Anderson, *Life, Death and Beyond*, pp. 120–126; Mark Albrecht and Brooks Alexander, "Thanatology: Death and Dying," *SCP Journal*, vol. 1, no. 1, Apr. 1977, pp. 4–11. Robert A. Monroe explains an experience while he was traveling out of his body (but not in a near-death setting) where he met a boy who was "humanoid," but Monroe thought he seemed "more animal, or somewhere in between." (Incidentally, he entitles the chapter "Intelligent Animals.") Joined by a second one in a later meeting, "Each turned into a good facsimile of one of my two daughters" before turning back again. Monroe wasn't sure if it was an hallucination or something else. Robert A. Monroe, *Journeys Out of the Body* (Garden City, NJ: Doubleday, 1971), pp. 136–140. In light of Monroe's report here and our own discussion of near-death experiencers who met previously deceased loved ones, see the various comments below (such as those in endnote 41, for instance).

38. Anderson thinks not only that spirit intervention is possible in near-death experiences (*Life, Death and Beyond*, p. 116), but that some are due to the immaterial natures of persons (pp. 94–116). Still, a number of near-death experiences appear to be genuine and biblical (pp. 126, 135–144).

39. For two popular sources, see Charles Ryrie's notes in *The Ryrie Study Bible* (Chicago: Moody, 1978), p. 1766; Merrill F. Unger, *Unger's Bible Handbook* (Chicago: Moody, 1966), p. 657.

40. See Phil. 1:23. See also Chap. 7 on the intermediate state.

41. Incidentally, for those who wonder if NDEs are satanic counterfeits where (like the episode just mentioned above with Monroe) some sort of spirits mimic deceased loved ones, it should be mentioned that at least one of the incidents included in these two chapters was reported by a Christian, while two others were described by children. Habermas has also interviewed some of those involved in another such example, all of whom were Christians.

42. Therefore, Morey is surely right to warn about any involvement in the occult, but should be more cautious in the implication that near-death experiences are automatically in this category (Robert Morey, *Death and the Afterlife* (Minneapolis: Bethany, 1984), pp. 258–266). For some of the biblical warnings, see Lev. 20:6, 27; Deut. 18:9–14; Rev. 21:8.

43. Snyder asserts that near-death experiences are "open to a variety of interpretations" and, just by their nature, they do not solve the issue of which religious phenomena are true. See John Snyder, *Reincarnation vs. Resurrection* (Chicago: Moody, 1984), pp. 44–45.

44. As possibilities, Morse lists anesthetic agents such as ketamine, as well as morphine, marijuana, LSD, and heroin (*Closer to the Light*, pp. 183–187).

45. Osis and Haraldsson, *At the Hour of Death*, p. 71; cf. pp. 82–83, Table 3, p. 219.

46. Morse, *Closer to the Light*, p. 21.

47. Moody, *Life After Life*, p. 110; Ring, *Life at Death*, pp. 211–212.

48. In one case, Habermas was told about an elderly woman who, prior to her death, thought she saw a choir of people singing in the doorway to her bedroom and on the front porch. At the time of these experiences, she had also been taking the drug phenobarbital.

49. Osis and Haraldsson, *At the Hour of Death*, pp. 73, 82–83, 104–105, 156, 188.

50. Morse, *Closer to the Light*, pp. 21–22.

51. Ring, *Life at Death*, p. 210, referring to Sabom's work, as well.

52. Another case personally related to Habermas included beautiful heaven-like scenery and a visit from Jesus. However, the experience occurred while the individual in question had an unresponsive fever of 105 degrees. This is not to say that the incident did not happen, but the physical condition should not be ignored either.

53. Osis and Haraldsson, *At the Hour of Death*, p. 71, Table 3, p. 219.

54. Ingber, "Visions of An Afterlife," p. 142.

55. Morse, *Closer to the Light*, pp. 191–192. See Moody, *Life After Life*, p. 111; Moody, *Reflections on Life After Life*, p. 109; Ring, *Life at Death*, p. 213; Sabom, *Recollections of Death*, p. 178. Physicist Timothy Ferris has recently charged that NDEs are trauma- and stress-related. The human body dumps chemicals into the bloodstream, including polypeptides that attach to the brain's endorphin receptors, and reduces pain and creates euphoria. He calls this the "most telling objection" to NDEs, claiming that it has "dispelled the myth that NDEs shed light on the question of whether there is an afterlife." But such attempts to use subjective criteria are woefully inadequate to explain the objective, corroborative aspects of NDEs such as those we outlined in the last chapter. See Timothy Ferris, "Death Trip," *Detroit Free Press Magazine*, 12 Jan. 1992; Timothy Ferris, *The Mind's Sky* (New York: Bantam, 1992). For penetrating medical critiques of such a model, see Morse, *Closer to the Light*, pp. 190–191; Sabom, *Recollections of Death*, pp. 171–173.

56. Sabom, *Recollections of Death*, p. 173.

57. Osis and Haraldsson concluded the following on the topic of hallucinations: "No evidence was found in our sample to suggest that psychological factors known to facilitate hallucinations also cause afterlife-related deathbed visions" (*At the Hour of Death*, p. 188).

58. For a number of relevant details and responses, see Grosso, "Toward an Explanation of Near-Death Phenomena," pp. 15–16; Moody, *Life After Life*, pp. 113–120; Ring, *Life at Death*, pp. 207–210; Sabom, *Recollections of Death*, pp. 160–168, 174–178; Morse, *Closer to the Light*, pp. 187–190.

59. Another natural objection that does *not* address the veridical material is that near-death incidents are derived from memories of the human birth experience. Again, similarities do not prove the cause of something. Moreover, this response does not account for the evidential examples we cited in the last chapter. For other responses, see Morse, *Closer to the Light*, p. 188, and Grosso, "Toward an Explanation of Near-Death Phenomena," pp. 18–19.

60. Another person interviewed by Habermas seemed to recall words spoken in the emergency room after medical personnel thought they were "losing" her. The perceived comment was brief, not very detailed, and appeared to indicate something she naturally sensed. Cf. Sabom, *Recollections of Death*, pp. 153–156.

61. Anderson, *Life, Death and Beyond*, pp. 70–72.

62. Douglas P. Lackey, *God, Immortality, and Ethics* (Belmont, CA: Wadsworth, 1990), pp. 46–47.

63. Morse was the doctor who resuscitated Katie and interviewed her very soon after her recovery. The cases reported by Schoonmaker were also largely his own patients, so much of interviewing occurred soon after NDEs. Rawlings personally resuscitated two of the three patients whose hearts stopped, and interviewed the first one just two days after she recovered from her coma. Natalie Kalmus was present at the death of her sister and heard her testimony as it was given. Kubler-Ross was also present with the little boy as he came out of the coma and announced that he was going with his mother and Peter, his brother, presumably to heaven.

64. Sabom, *Recollections of Death,* Table IV, pp. 196–200.

65. Ibid., Table XI, p. 208; Osis and Haraldsson, *At the Hour of Death,* p. 193.

66. Osis and Haraldsson, *At the Hour of Death,* pp. 140–145, 192–194.

67. Interestingly, even after raising the above issues (*Life, Death and Beyond,* pp. 70–73), Anderson himself concludes that natural causes cannot explain all near-death experiences. Rather, some of them are due to "the immaterial part of man" (p. 94). For this view in more detail, see pp. 99, 101, 116, 126, 135–144.

68. Cf. Sabom, *Recollections of Death,* pp. 156–160.

69. Moody, *Reflections on Life After Life,* pp. 111–112; Ring, *Life at Death,* chaps. 8 and 9; Sabom, *Recollections of Death,* p. 186; Morse, *Closer to the Light,* chap. 7.

70. Fully 35 percent of Sabom's interviewed patients reported multiple crisis events where they were close to dying. Of these, by far the majority had no other near-death experiences (Sabom, *Recollections of Death,* pp. 56–57, Table VII, p. 203).

71. If it is supposed that the telepathic message was "received" at some other time, either before or after the actual crisis, this only removes the aspect of receiving such material at that crucial moment. It still doesn't answer the truthfulness of the super-ESP hypothesis itself, or the question of why such mundane and everyday material such as home activities, clothing, or jewelry, was ever communicated or received. Further, the content of the ESP would have to include the correct activities being done at home or the clothing and jewelry worn at the time of the crisis, since it was properly identified. Additionally, the problems with the *vantage point* of the perception itself and the visits with deceased relatives also need to be explained.

72. We may recall the case of Kalmus's sister, who suddenly stretched out her arms and happily said, "I'm going up." We learn similarly from the case of the little boy who smiled and told Kubler-Ross, "Everything is all right now. Mommy and Peter are already waiting for me." Kubler-Ross relates another such case, as well *(On Children and Death* [New York: Macmillan/Collier Books, 1983], pp. 208–209).

73. There is the possibility that the near-death patient communicated with the loved one just prior to the loved one's biological death, thereby leaving a chance that the loved one's consciousness was derived from his own brain. However, this could not have been so in cases like the Kalmus example, where the cousin had died the week before (Myers, *Voices from the Edge of Eternity,* pp. 17–20) or Rawlings's report of his patient who met (and later correctly identified a picture of) his mother (who had been dead for about 47 years!), whose picture he had never seen before *(Beyond Death's Door . . . ,* pp. 17–22), or Kubler-Ross's instance of the girl who met the brother she never knew she had, who had died several years before *(On Children and Death,* p. 208).

If it is thought that, in these "older" cases, the information could have been telepathically received from another relative who knew the information, this would suffer from all the other problems we have raised regarding this proposal, including the joyful desire to be with the deceased person.

Further, it would be an incredible—better, incredulous—coincidence if every case of this nature happened at the precise moment of the loved one's own near-death experience but always just before their final death and the sudden deterioration and cessation of the other's "image" or "transmission"! In Kubler-Ross's case of the little boy who wanted to be with "Mommy and Peter" *(On Children and Death,* p. 210), we would need *three* simultaneous NDEs, each before death!

Finally, very strange evidence of another (rare) sort would then exist if this scenario were true—we would have corroborated examples of simultaneous near-death experiences, which would be useful themselves in establishing their veracity.

Therefore, it would surely appear that those who opt for such a theory do so against the evidence.

74. Osis and Haraldsson even argue that ESP is the means by which near-death patients "become aware of post-mortem existence" *(At the Hour of Death,* pp. 139–140).

75. Similar ideas are expressed in Lackey, *God, Immortality, and Ethics,* p. 47, and Vicchio, "Near-Death Experiences: Some Logical Problems and Questions for Further Study," *Anabiosis,* vol. 1, no. 1, July 1981, p. 67.

76. See "Definitions of Death," *Science Digest,* vol. 89, no. 1, Jan.–Feb. 1981, p. 96. Sabom includes all three concepts, but does not list them in a progressive order. Because of confusion over the definitions, he simply gives his own concept and proceeds from there. He defines "near-death" as: "Any bodily state resulting from an extreme physiological catastrophe, accidental or otherwise, that would reasonably be expected to result in irreversible biological death in the majority of instances and would demand urgent medical attention, if available" *(Recollections of Death,* pp. 8–9).

Moody lists the three concepts in 1–2–3 order (clinical, brain wave loss, biological), favoring the last definition, but stating that it is "pointless" to spend time debating which definition to use. As he notes, the issue is really whether any biological function left in the body could account for the experience. See *Life After Life,* pp. 101–104.

For further discussion, see "A Definition of Irreversible Coma: Report of the Ad Hoc Committee of the Harvard Medical School to Examine the Definition of Brain Death," *Journal of the American Medical Association,* vol. 205, 1968, pp. 337–340.

77. At the end of his study, Ring concludes that there is "abundant empirical evidence" that supports the existence of NDEs and "that there is highly suggestive evidence that death involves the separation of a second body—a double—from the physical body." Here we even have "an empirical referent for the possible origin of the concept of the soul. . . . I do endorse the proposition that consciousness (with or without a second body) may function independently of the physical body" *(Life at Death,* pp. 232–233).

Sabom speaks in a more reserved manner, but still does so in terms of dualism. Using Penfield's work as a conceptual model, he states: "Since I suspect that the NDE is a reflection of a mind-brain split, I cannot help but wonder why such an event should occur at the point of near-death" *(Recollections of Death,* p. 185).

Chapter 7 Life in Between:
The State Between Death and Eternity

1. See J.P. Moreland, *Scaling the Secular City* (Grand Rapids, MI: Baker, 1987); J.P. Moreland and Kai Nielsen, *Does God Exist? The Great Debate* (Nashville: Thomas Nelson, 1990); Gary R. Habermas, *The Verdict of History: Conclusive Evidence for the Life of Jesus* (Nashville: Thomas Nelson, 1988); Terry L. Miethe, ed., *Did Jesus Rise from the Dead? The Resurrection Debate* (San Francisco: Harper & Row, 1987).

2. See John W. Cooper, *Body, Soul, and Life Everlasting* (Grand Rapids, MI: Eerdmans, 1989), pp. 155–63.

3. Murray J. Harris, *Raised Immortal* (Grand Rapids, MI: Eerdmans, 1983), pp. 136–7.

4. For treatments of substance dualism and Christianity, see Cooper, *Body, Soul, and Life Everlasting;* Robert Gundry, *Soma in Biblical Theology: With Emphasis on Pauline Anthropology* (Cambridge: Cambridge University, 1976; Grand Rapids, MI: Zondervan 1987); W.S. Anglin, *Free Will and the Christian Faith* (Oxford: Clarendon, 1990).

5. The ontological aspects of personal identity must be kept separate from the epistemological ones. The former focuses on what *constitutes* personal identity—what *is* personal identity and what makes it *real*. In our view, sameness of soul is what constitutes personal identity. The epistemological aspects of personal identity focus on how it is possible to *know* if a person at time t_2 is the same person as a person at time t_1, which was earlier than t_2.

The epistemological problem must be broken down further into a first and third person issue. I may simply be aware of being the very same person from moment to moment; I may simply find identity given to me in consciousness. This immediate awareness could be supplemented by other considerations, say, sameness of memory and, less important, sameness of body. The third-person perspective is the issue of how others can recognize me as the same person as the one existing earlier. How could someone recognize a disembodied soul as the same individual as I am before death? Perhaps in the following ways: (1) through reporting sameness of memories; (2) through the similarity of character traits; (3) through the lack of a double who is present with memories and traits similar to mine (this would not be a conclusive but only a supporting reason); (4) through trust in my word as I report that I am the same (and this may be known by me through direct introspection); (5) through trust in God as he tells them who I am.

For more on these issues, see John Perry, *A Dialogue on Personal Identity and Immortality* (Indianapolis: Hackett, 1978); Stephen T. Davis, "The Resurrection of the Dead" in *Death and Afterlife*, ed. by Stephen T. Davis (New York: St. Martin's, 1989), pp. 119–144; Richard L. Purtill, "The Intelligibility of Disembodied Survival," *Christian Scholar's Review* 5 (1) (1978), pp. 3–22; George I. Mavrodes, "The Life Everlasting and the Bodily Criterion of Identity," *Nous* 11 (1977), pp. 27–39; Paul Helm, "A Theory of Disembodied Survival and Re-embodied Existence," *Religious Studies* 14 (Mar. 1978), pp. 15–26; Peter van Inwagen, "The Possibility of Resurrection," *International Journal for Philosophy of Religion* 9 (1978), pp. 114–121; Philip Quinn, "Personal Identity, Bodily Continuity and Resurrection," *International Journal for Philosophy of Religion* 9 (1978), pp. 101–113.

6. See Stephen H. Travis, *Christian Hope and the Future* (Downers Grove, IL: InterVarsity, 1980), pp. 110–112.

7. Cf. J.L. Mackie, "Three Steps Towards Absolutism," in *Space, Time, and Causalty*, ed. by Richard Swinburne (Dordrecht, Holland: D. Reidel, 1983), pp. 3–22.

8. See Harris, *Raised Immortal*.

9. Cooper, *Body, Soul, and Life Everlasting*, pp. 117–118.

10. Harris, *Raised Immortal*, pp. 138–142.

11. Cooper, *Body, Soul, and Life Everlasting*, pp. 86–89.

12. There are two other key issues surrounding a Christian understanding of the intermediate state: purgatory and the correct interpretation of 1 Peter 3:18–20. More will be said about purgatory in Chap. 11. But for now, we offer the following as a critique of the notion of purgatory: Loraine Boettner, *Immortality* (Philadelphia: Presbyterian & Reformed, 1956), pp. 124–137. Interestingly, the notion of purgatory in Catholic theology is still both a conscious state view and a temporary, intermediate abode. Some, like Kreeft, argue that it is actually a realm of positive, joyful growth rather than a place of correction, punishment, and retribution. (See Peter J. Kreeft, *Everything You Ever Wanted to Know About Heaven . . . But Never Dreamed of Asking* [San Francisco: Harper & Row, 1982], pp. 13–14, 20–22.) In Chap. 11, we will reject the full-blown Catholic doctrine of purgatory, but we will accept Kreeft's modest reformulation of it. Regarding 1 Peter 3:18–20, it is said that Christ made proclamation to spirits now in prison who were disobedient during Noah's day. At least four orthodox interpretations have been offered: 1) This is a proclamation of the gospel by Christ through his apostles to men who rejected the gospel, died, and are now in hell. 2) This refers to the preincarnate Christ who preached to men in Noah's

day through Noah, they rejected Noah's warning, and they are now in hell. 3) Between Christ's death and resurrection he visited the realm of the dead and announced his victory to human spirits there. 4) After Christ's death, he visited tartarus, the realm of imprisoned angels who, perhaps, sinned in Genesis, and proclaimed his victory to them.

13. Boettner, *Immortality*, pp. 91–97, especially pp. 92–93.

14. It is often reported that other senses are strengthened when one of the senses is lost. It could also be the case that the soul has latent telepathic abilities that emerge upon disembodiment. Furthermore, some philosophers have argued that the soul possesses a faculty of intuitive perception that enables us to have insight into the laws of logic, synthetic a priori truths (e.g., red is a color), and so forth, as well as a faculty of spiritual perception exercised in religious experience. Perhaps these faculties will be available in the intermediate state as well. The point to remember is this: our goal here is to suggest possible scenarios that make disembodied existence intelligible. We cannot be sure our speculations are correct.

15. Frank Jackson, *Perception* (Cambridge: Cambridge University, 1977), pp. 54–56, 77.

16. H.H. Price, "Personal Survival and the Idea of 'Another World,'" *Proceedings of the Society for Psychical Research* 50 (Jan. 1953), pp. 1–25. For a critique of Price, see John Hick, *Death & Eternal Life* (San Francisco: Harper & Row, 1980), pp. 265–277. For a favorable elaboration of Price's view, see H.D. Lewis, *The Self and Immortality* (New York: Seabury, 1973), pp. 141–177. It should be noted that we do not agree with Price's suggestion of a possible dream world scenario where, after death, a person's desires would be transformed into a subjective wish world almost solipsistically produced for him alone, as if he were the only existent being. Our reasons for rejecting this view should be obvious from the entire tenor of our argument in this volume.

Chapter 8   Reincarnation—Is It True?

1. This figure includes 21 percent of Protestants and 25 percent of Catholics. See George Gallup, Jr., with William Proctor, *Adventures in Immortality* (New York: McGraw-Hill, 1982). For a summarized overview, see Kenneth L. Woodward, "Life After Death: What Americans Believe," *McCall's,* June 1982, pp. 47–48.

2. See Norman L. Geisler and J. Yutaka Amano, *The Reincarnation Sensation* (Wheaton, IL: Tyndale, 1986), pp. 167–171.

3. Stevenson, along with his associates, has reportedly investigated about 1,300 cases in recent years. See the insightful evaluation of this data by Paul Badham and Linda Badham, "Claimed Memories of Former Lives," in Ralph W. Clark, *Introduction to Philosophical Thinking: Readings and Commentary* (St. Paul, MN: West, 1987), pp. 260–269.

4. Ian Stevenson, *Twenty Cases Suggestive of Reincarnation* (New York: American Society for Psychical Research, 1966), pp. 20–30. This volume was later reissued by the University of Virginia Press (1966, 1974, rev.). References here are to the 1966 edition.

5. Ibid., pp. 119, 257, 271–274, 290.

6. Ian Stevenson, *Xenoglossy* (Charlottesville, VA: University of Virginia, 1973).

7. Hans Schwarz, *Beyond the Gates of Death: A Biblical Examination of Evidence for Life After Death* (Minneapolis: Augsburg, 1981), chap. 4, "Reincarnation," p. 101.

8. Stevenson, *Twenty Cases Suggestive of Reincarnation,* p. 5.

9. Ernest Wilson argues that when Jesus called Peter "Bar-Jonah," the "use of 'son' here is figurative, implying that the present incarnation is the 'son' or offspring of the previous life." Likewise, when Jesus called himself the son of David, he meant that "He was the reincarnation of David." Without trying to be nasty here, we must confess that sloppy exegesis such as this convinces very few. Ernest C. Wilson, *Have We Lived Before?* (Kansas City, MO: Unity School of Christianity, 1946), pp. 40–41.

10. Geddes MacGregor devotes several chapters to the issue of the compatibility of

reincarnation with Christianity. Rather than making broad claims of how the Bible teaches reincarnation, he is satisfied to state, "I wish to present a vision of the afterlife such as will show how reincarnationism could not only fit into but clarify Christian hope concerning human destiny" (p. 159). In his concluding paragraph he states: "We may conclude that there is nothing in biblical thought or Christian tradition that necessarily excludes all forms of reincarnationism. . . . We have seen no reason why it must be in conflict with the historic teachings that have come to us through the Bible and the Church" (p. 173).

We will argue that MacGregor is incorrect in his assessment of the compatibility of reincarnation with the tenets of biblical Christianity. But our point here is to contrast Mac-Gregor's method of argument with that of Wilson's as presented in the previous endnote. Geddes MacGregor, *Reincarnation in Christianity* (Wheaton, IL: Theosophical Publishing House, 1978).

11. It is not immediately obvious why demonic possession should be taken any less seriously than discarnate possession. If the former is considered less "modern," so must the latter be, including reincarnation. Historically, all these views have old, deep roots.

Furthermore, why should belief in demons be rejected as ancient, anyway? The laws of gravity are old but no one discounts them because of that. Finally, if possession by discarnate persons is considered to be a serious option, as Stevenson thinks it is, then we already have, in principle, a mechanism for demonic possession as well.

The question of demons involves considerations that are certainly beyond the limits of this book and will not be addressed in detail here. Nevertheless, we would like to point out that the facticity of the resurrection of Jesus, the truth of dualism and eternal life, all previously argued, also involve worldview considerations that make belief in demonic possession even more believable.

12. Stevenson, *Twenty Cases Suggestive of Reincarnation,* pp. 339–340.

13. Ibid., p. 340. Cf. Badham and Badham in Clark, p. 269, for a similar assessment.

14. Stevenson, *Twenty Cases Suggestive of Reincarnation,* p. 351.

15. The details on the two cases just mentioned are from Stevenson, ibid., pp. 228–229, 340–347.

16. Ibid., p. 48, although Stevenson still seems to consider this case an example of reincarnation!

17. William de Arteaga, *Past Life Visions: A Christian Exploration* (New York: Seabury, 1983), p. 174, as cited by Geisler and Amano, *The Reincarnation Sensation,* p. 80.

18. Helen Wambach, *Reliving Past Lives: The Evidence Under Hypnosis* (New York: Harper & Row, 1978; New York: Bantam Books, 1978), pp. 41–42.

19. Rabindranath R. Maharaj, *Death of a Guru* (Philadelphia: H.J. Holman, 1977), later (with Dave Hunt) retitled *Escape into the Light* (Eugene, OR: Harvest House, 1984), p. 24.

20. Schwarz thinks that possession by a deceased personality is a "probable" cause in certain cases (*Beyond the Gates of Death,* pp. 98–99). Geisler and Amano seem to prefer demonic possession as one of several viable alternative explanations (*The Reincarnation Sensation,* pp. 78–80). Snyder appears to be closer to Geisler and Amano, without necessarily ruling out discarnate possession. See John Snyder, *Reincarnation vs. Resurrection* (Chicago: Moody, 1984), pp. 38–41. Albrecht thinks that either type of possession is possible. See Mark Albrecht, *Reincarnation: A Christian Appraisal* (Downers Grove, IL: InterVarsity, 1982), pp. 71–79.

21. Albrecht, *Reincarnation,* p. 72.

22. Details are provided in Stevenson's *Twenty Cases Suggestive of Reincarnation,* pp. 5, 324.

23. Concerning the "fading" of the child's memories of the past as she grows older, this also presents no problem for the possession scenario. Not only does it seem that these

childhood memories do not always fade, but possession can also occur in adults. Finally, sometimes the possession cases are characterized by the spirit leaving the person alone after a time, which could also account for the cessation of memory recall. Details are contained in Stevenson, *Twenty Cases Suggestive of Reincarnation*, pp. 340–347; Badham and Badham in Clark, *Introduction to Philosophical Thinking*, pp. 262–263; Albrecht, *Reincarnation*, pp. 74–76; Snyder, *Reincarnation vs. Resurrection*, pp. 38–39.

24. Geisler and Amano, *The Reincarnation Sensation*, p. 80.

25. In the same context, Lackey states that his point "is a systematic criticism that can be made of *all* reports that allege reincarnation" (p. 48, his emphasis). However, we think that he somewhat overstates his own case. While this is a serious criticism that should be considered carefully by reincarnation researchers, it is certainly possible that certain types of evidence are most likely revealed through serious investigation alone, which did not seem to have been present at the time of the reports themselves. Further, perhaps the "patient" reported something that was not known by anyone else and that, by its nature, had not yet been verified or falsified. We conclude that Lackey's criticism is a strong one, but that it is not necessarily determinative in all instances. See Douglas P. Lackey, *God, Immortality, Ethics* (Belmont, CA: Wadsworth, 1990), p. 48.

26. See Snyder, *Reincarnation vs. Resurrection*, pp. 29, 34.

27. Eastern philosophies include a variety of different beliefs about God, ranging from theistic to pantheistic concepts, and on to the possibility of agnosticism. For some background and details, see Sarvepalli Radhakrishnan and Charles A. Moore, ed., *A Source Book in Indian Philosophy* (Princeton, NJ: Princeton University, 1957).

28. For details on the issues in the last three paragraphs, see Schwarz, *Beyond the Gates of Death*, pp. 94–96; Geisler and Amano, *The Reincarnation Sensation*, pp. 113–121; Albrecht, *Reincarnation*, pp. 88–89, 95–97; Snyder, *Reincarnation vs. Resurrection*, chaps. 6–7; cf. John H. Hick, *Death and Eternal Life* (San Francisco: Harper & Row, 1980), pp. 339–340.

29. Stevenson, *Twenty Cases Suggestive of Reincarnation*, pp. 305ff.; *Xenoglossy*, pp. 87ff.

30. By "limited uses" here, we agree with many other scholars in holding that the so-called "super-ESP" hypothesis, which would attempt to explain almost all data in terms of some as yet unproven (and even seldom detailed), all-inclusive hypothesis, has too many problems of its own to be useful against reincarnation. However, *some* of the data might still be explained in this way.

31. For details, quotations, and documentation, see Snyder, *Reincarnation vs. Resurrection*, pp. 30–32.

32. For details besides Snyder's in the previous note, see *Death and Eternal Life*, p. 376; Schwarz, *Beyond the Gates of Death*, pp. 99, 105–106; cf. Badham and Badham in Clark, *Introduction to Philosophical Thinking*, p. 269. Albrecht prefers ESP and possession in cases that cannot be explained naturally (*Reincarnation*, p. 77). Snyder seems to be more positive about mixing ESP with personation (when one person closely identifies with another and behaves like him or her) in order to explain more of the data (*Reincarnation vs. Resurrection*, p. 38).

33. Ian Stevenson, *The Evidence for Survival from Claimed Memories of Former Incarnations* (New York: American Society for Psychical Research, 1961 reprint), p. 43, as quoted by Badham and Badham in Clark, *Introduction to Philosophical Thinking*, p. 269.

34. Some details are provided in Schwarz, *Beyond the Gates of Death*, p. 101.

35. They also note, however, that responsive xenoglossy is another matter (Badham and Badham in Clark, *Introduction to Philosophical Thinking*, p. 266).

36. Badham and Badham in Clark, *Introduction to Philosophical Thinking*, p. 265.

37. See, respectively, Schwarz, *Beyond the Gates of Death*, p. 99, and Geisler and Amano, *The Reincarnation Sensation*, p. 82.

38. Cf. Snyder, *Reincarnation vs. Resurrection,* pp. 34–35.

39. Of the three types of spirit involvement just mentioned, it might even be argued that demonic possession would be the most likely cause, due to the harm sometimes perpetrated on the persons involved.

40. For details by those who do address this subject, see Geisler and Amano, *The Reincarnation Sensation,* chap. 9; Hick, *Death and Eternal Life,* pp. 365–368; Schwarz, pp. 88–96; Snyder, *Reincarnation vs. Resurrection,* chap. 5; Pat Means, *The Mystical Maze* (USA: Campus Crusade for Christ, 1976), pp. 102–105. When we think about this issue, with the exception of those who are trying to win converts on a popular level, why would most reincarnationists want to argue from the biblical data at all? From their perspective, would the doctrine be true just because the Bible taught it? It isn't likely.

41. Snyder, *Reincarnation vs. Resurrection,* p. 55. Other scholars agree. For example, conclusions expressed by those in note 37 after their own study of the biblical data are similar to Snyder's. Geisler and Amano summarize: "None of the verses in Scripture that are used by reincarnationists support the doctrine of reincarnation" (*The Reincarnation Sensation,* p. 154). Hick affirms: "Reincarnation is not, and never has been, an orthodox Christian [sic] belief" (*Death and Eternal Life,* p. 365). Schwarz states: "Although its environment was certainly familiar with this kind of thinking, there do not seem to be any traces of reincarnational thought in the Bible" (*Beyond the Gates of Death,* p. 94). Means concludes: "The Bible teaches resurrection after death rather than reincarnation" (*The Mystical Maze,* p. 104).

42. Incidentally, the authors note that some reincarnationist literature has not sufficiently noted the subject's relinquishing belief in her own rebirth. See Badham and Badham in Clark, *Introduction to Philosophical Thinking,* p. 267.

43. Albrecht, *Reincarnation,* p. 62.

44. For example, see Geisler and Amano, *The Reincarnation Sensation,* pp. 75–76; Snyder, *Reincarnation vs. Resurrection,* p. 37. In views that are not necessarily in conflict, Snyder seems to think that the best of the claimed reincarnation cases cannot be explained in this way (p. 37), while Albrecht thinks that cryptomnesia "is probably the most common source of past-life recall experiences" (*Reincarnation,* p. 78). Badham and Badham propose combining cryptomnesia with dramatization for added value (in Clark, *Introduction to Philosophical Thinking,* pp. 265–266).

45. Hick, *Death and Eternal Life,* p. 374; Schwarz, *Beyond the Gates of Death,* p. 99.

46. This quotation is found in Albrecht (*Reincarnation,* p. 65), where it was reproduced from an article in a newspaper supplement. For other similar details see Ian Stevenson, "The Explanatory Value of the Idea of Reincarnation," *The Journal of Nervous and Mental Disease,* Sept. 1977.

47. See Schwarz, *Beyond the Gates of Death,* pp. 97, 105; Geisler and Amano, *The Reincarnation Sensation,* pp. 76–78; Albrecht, *Reincarnation,* pp. 59, 64–65. Interestingly enough, some near-death researchers have reported no accounts of reincarnation even after hundreds of cases. See Raymond A. Moody, Jr., *Life After Life* (Atlanta: Mockingbird, 1975), who remarked, "Not one of the cases I have looked into is in any way indicative to me that reincarnation occurs. However, it is important to bear in mind that not one of them rules out reincarnation, either" (p. 99). Although Moody could not, of course, rule out reincarnation by the absence of any evidence, it is still interesting that no such cases were found. In another, perhaps more relevant, study conducted by Osis and Haraldsson, more than 1,000 near-death cases were studied, more than half of which were from India. Yet, reincarnation was never mentioned. See Karlis Osis and Erlendur Haraldsson, *At·the Hour of Death* (New York: Avon, 1977), pp. 190–191.

48. This is why our argumentive form would not commit the informal logical fallacy termed the Genetic Fallacy. (It is improper to argue that an idea's origin explains its content.)

49. Hick, *Death and Eternal Life,* pp. 374–375.

50. Albrecht, *Reincarnation,* p. 59.

51. Stevenson, *Twenty Cases Suggestive of Reincarnation,* p. 4.

52. Badham and Badham in Clark, *Introduction to Philosophical Thinking,* p. 267.

53. Stevenson, *Twenty Cases Suggestive of Reincarnation,* p. 3; cf. also Albrecht's thoughtful comments about hypnosis (*Reincarnation,* pp. 63–64, 68–69).

54. On some of the difficulties associated with hypnosis, see Elizabeth Stark, "Hypnosis on Trial," *Psychology Today,* Feb. 1984, pp. 34–36.

55. Hick, *Death and Eternal Life,* p. 378.

56. Ibid., p. 392.

57. Lackey, *God, Immortality, Ethics,* p. 69, author's emphasis.

58. For these and similar questions, see Geisler and Amano, *The Reincarnation Sensation,* chap. 7, and Albrecht, *Reincarnation,* pp. 89–104.

59. This is Albrecht's definition (*Reincarnation,* p. 62).

60. Albrecht, for instance, cites Stevenson's scientific research as a "sane, cautious approach . . ." (Ibid., p. 59). Badham and Badham respond that fraud is "one option [that] seems not to be open" in regard to Stevenson's approach, but it is still at least partially apparent in the work of others (in Clark, *Introcuction to Philosophical Thinking,* p. 263). Snyder states concerning fraud that, "in Stevenson's and my view it is an inadequate explanation for the more sophisticated evidence" (*Reincarnation vs. Resurrection,* p. 37). Geisler and Amano agree that fraud certainly cannot be applied to all cases (*The Reincarnation Sensation,* p. 75). In spite of Stevenson's voluminous work and fine reputation, he is, of course, not the only pro-reincarnation researcher. Although we have cited the work of others (MacGregor, Wambach, de Arteaga, Wilson), we have relied heavily on Stevenson's research. But we wish to note that the types of arguments on behalf of reincarnation that we have detailed represent the field of research in general.

61. For details and research sources, compare Lackey, *God, Immortality, Ethics,* p. 48; Geisler and Amano, *The Reincarnation Sensation,* p. 75; Albrecht, *Reincarnation,* p. 61; Robert A. Morey, *Death and the Afterlife* (Minneapolis: Bethany, 1984), pp. 181–182.

62. Albrecht, *Reincarnation,* pp. 61–63, cf. p. 78. Badham and Badham give some examples of "twisting" information to fit the needs of the reporter (*Introduction to Philosophical Thinking,* p. 263).

63. For examples, see Schwarz, *Beyond the Gates of Death,* p. 106; Albrecht, *Reincarnation,* pp. 63, 78–80; Hick, *Death and Eternal Life,* pp. 381–388; Snyder, *Reincarnation vs. Resurrection,* p. 38.

Chapter 9   The Afterlife's Ultimate Model

1. For some examples, see Acts 4:2; 1 Cor. 6:14, 15:20; 2 Cor. 4:14; 1 John 3:2.

2. For the relationship between Jesus' resurrection and a miracle as an act of God, see Gary R. Habermas and Antony Flew, *Did Jesus Rise from the Dead?* (San Francisco: Harper & Row, 1987), pp. 15–19, 39–42.

3. Richard Swinburne, *The Concept of Miracle* (New York: Macmillan and St. Martin's, 1970), pp. 7–10.

4. Richard Swinburne, *The Existence of God* (Oxford: Oxford University, 1979), chap. 12.

5. Matt. 11:1–6; 12:38–40; 16:1–4; Mark 2:1–12; Luke 11:20; John 5:36–37; 10:25, 38; 14:11 for examples.

6. For instance, see Rudolf Bultmann, *Theology of the New Testament,* trans. by Kendrick Grobel (New York: Charles Scribner's Sons, 1951, 1955), vol. I, p. 7; Reginald Fuller, *The Foundations of New Testament Christology* (New York: Charles Scribner's Sons, 1965), p. 107; Wolfhart Pannenberg, trans. by Lewis L. Wilkins and Duane A

Priebe, *Jesus: God and Man,* (Phildelphia: Westminster, 1982), pp. 63–64; Raymond E. Brown, *Jesus: God and Man* (New York: Macmillan, 1967), p. 97.

7. Pannenberg, *Jesus: God and Man,* p. 67–68.

8. Stephen Neill, *Christian Faith and Other Faiths,* 2nd ed. (Oxford: Oxford University, 1970), p. 233. See also J.N.D. Anderson, *Christianity and World Religions: The Challenge of Pluralism* (Downers Grove, IL: InterVarsity, 1984); Stephen Neill, *The Supremacy of Jesus* (Downers Grove, IL: InterVarsity, 1984).

9. See Gary R. Habermas, "Resurrection Claims in Non-Christian Religions," *Religious Studies* 25, pp. 167–177.

10. It is not being asserted that all of Jesus' teachings are unique to him. As we mentioned, we are chiefly speaking about theological claims he made in reference to himself. We do not deny there are parallels, for instance, in certain moral teachings between Jesus and others. We would even expect this in light of the moral conscience given to each person (see, for example, Rom. 2:14–15).

We also want to note that our purpose in this chapter is not to prove that Jesus' theological teachings are unique. Indeed, even if you wondered whether there were possibly some parallels to Jesus' self-claims, this would still not necessarily affect the corroboration of Jesus' teachings provided by his resurrection. Some of these subjects are addressed in Gary R. Habermas, *The Resurrection of Jesus: An Apologetic* (Grand Rapids, MI: Baker, 1980; Lanham, MD: University Press of America, 1984), especially chaps. 2–3.

11. Swinburne, *The Existence of God,* pp. 222, 225–226, 233–234, 241–243.

12. Pannenberg, *Jesus: God and Man,* p. 73; Pannenberg in Roy Abraham Varghese, *The Intellectuals Speak Out About God* (Chicago: Regnery Gateway, 1984), pp. 263–264.

13. Habermas and Flew, *Did Jesus Rise from the Dead?* pp. 49–50; cf. p. 3.

14. For examples of the centrality of the kingdom of God in Jesus' preaching, see Matt. 6:33; 13:44–52; Mark 1:14, 15; 4:3–34. For Jesus' part as the central figure in the call to faith and obedience in light of the kingdom of God, see Matt. 10:32–39, 25:31–46; Luke 11:20, 14:25–35; John 3:15–16, 6:47.

15. See examples such as Fuller, *The Foundations of New Testament Christology,* pp. 103–106; Rudolf Bultmann, *Jesus Christ and Mythology* (New York: Charles Scribner's Sons, 1958), p. 11; Bultmann, *Theology of the New Testament,* vol. I, pp. 4–11; Gunther Bornkamm, *Jesus of Nazareth,* trans. by Irene and Fraser McLuskey with James M. Robinson (New York: Harper & Row, 1960), pp. 64–95; Wolfhart Pannenberg, *Theology and the Kingdom of God,* ed. by Richard John Neuhaus (Philadelphia: Westminster, 1969), p. 51; Brown, *Jesus: God and Man,* pp. 101–104.

16. Brown, ibid., pp. 96–97, emphasis added.

17. Ibid., pp. 59, 98.

18. Bultmann, *Theology of the New Testament,* vol. I, pp. 4–11.

19. Fuller, *The Foundations of New Testament Christology,* pp. 105–106.

20. Ibid., p. 106.

21. Wolfhart Pannenberg, "Dogmatic Theses on the Doctrine of Revelation," *Revelation as History,* ed. by Wolfhart Pannenberg, trans. by David Granskou (New York: Macmillan, 1968), pp. 139–145 for example.

22. William Strawson, *Jesus and the Future Life* (Philadelphia: Westminster, 1959), p. 226. In his second edition of this volume (1970), Strawson states, "We assume then that there are conditions to be met if we are to obtain everlasting life" (p. 227).

23. Ibid., 2nd ed. (1970), pp. 227–228.

24. See Martin Hengel, *The Atonement: The Origins of the Doctrine in the New Testament,* trans. by John Bowden (Philadelphia: Fortress, 1981) for a defense of this concept in the teachings of Jesus and in the earliest church.

25. Paul even asserts that Christians are already citizens of heaven (Phil. 3:20).

26. This is not to say that there are not differences in the interpretation of these con-

cepts. For a discussion of some major trends in contemporary theology, as well as an indication of general elements of agreement, see Habermas, *The Resurrection of Jesus: An Apologetic,* chap. 4.

27. For Jesus' teaching that the life of the kingdom is eternal life, see Matt. 25:46; Mark 9:43–46, 10:17–31; Luke 20:36; John 3:1–17. Incidentally, eternal life, however, is not synonymous with the kingdom, in that eternal life was a reality even before Jesus' preaching of the dawning of the kingdom (see Mark 12:18–27; cf. Luke 16:19–31). For a stimulating treatment, see George Eldon Ladd, *The Pattern of New Testament Truth* (Grand Rapids, MI: Eerdmans, 1968).

28. Bultmann, *Theology of the New Testament,* vol. I, pp. 5–6.

29. Bornkamm, *Jesus of Nazareth,* pp. 92–95.

30. Strawson, *Jesus and the Future Life,* 2nd ed., chap. 6.

31. George Eldon Ladd, *The Last Things* (Grand Rapids, MI: Eerdmans, 1978), pp. 104–118.

32. While none of the actual terms for immortality are found in the gospel teachings of Jesus, he addresses the subject in passages such as Luke 20:27–40 and John 11:25–26. Strawson claims that, for Jesus and his Jewish contemporaries, immortality was synonymous with resurrection (*Jesus and the Future Life,* p. 209). Murray Harris holds that, while the two terms are distinct, they are also inseparable, for the resurrection inevitably involves the acquiring of immortality. They are interdependent sides of the same truth. See his volume, *Raised Immortal: Resurrection and Immortality in the New Testament* (Grand Rapids, MI: Eerdmans, 1983), pp. 199–201, 209–214, 232–236, for a stimulating and detailed study of this subject.

We also want to be clear that the term *immortality* is not to be confused with notions such as the Greek concept of the immortality of the soul. Actually, three Greek synonyms (*athanasia, aphtharsia, aphthartos*) are used only eleven times in the New Testament (ten by Paul and one by Peter) to refer to the believer's life after death. In no case are these terms applied directly to the human soul. In fact, the Greek teaching had very little influence in Palestine anyway. For several reasons why Paul, in particular, opposed this Greek belief, see the next section in this chapter. Further, Paul specifically used immortality and eternal life in a related manner in Rom. 2:7 (cf. Gal. 6:8; 2 Tim. 1:10), while interchanging his references to immortality and the resurrection of the body in 1 Cor. 15:50–55. He thereby indicated that he was defining such terms in a Hebrew sense, as Jesus had also done. Harris asserts that the term *eternal life* in the New Testament "refers primarily to quality . . . secondarily to quantity. . . . Immortality, on the other hand, refers primarily to quantity . . . and secondarily to quality" (see p. 199; cf. pp. 273–275). But because of the close similarities of these concepts, we will speak throughout of *resurrection, eternal life,* and *immortality* as interrelated terms.

33. Brown, *Jesus: God and Man,* p. 101.

34. For examples, concerns in this category include various details in the accounts of Paul's conversion in the Book of Acts (9:1–9, 22:6–11, 26:12–18), why Paul places Jesus' appearance to him in the list with others in 1 Cor. 15:3–8, Paul's reference to Jesus as a "life-giving spirit" in 1 Cor. 15:44–45, and his statement that flesh and blood cannot enter God's kingdom in 15:50. See endnote 45 below for some brief comments.

35. See Habermas and Flew, *Did Jesus Rise From the Dead?* pp. 163–169.

36. This does not necessarily mean, however, that Jesus' resurrection body was not changed in any way. While it was his same body, he was, at a minimum, no longer mortal. Later, he was also glorified.

37. More than one view was taught in the inter-testamental and first-century Jewish literature that both influenced and reflected important ideas on this issue.

An afterlife existence such as that in sheol seems to be taught in Ecclesiasticus (14:16, 22:11; cf. 17:30). While it is difficult to ascertain, immortality of the soul may be the view favored in The Wisdom of Solomon (2:23, 3:1-5). While the same idea appears in 1 Enoch 103:4, an early portion of this book also teaches that the spirits of the departed dead would later reassemble (9:3). And the resurrection of the body, sometimes in glorified form, is additionally taught in a number of writings, such as 2 Maccabees (12:43-45, 14:46), the Apocalypse of Baruch (51:1-10), 1 Enoch (51:1-2, 62:13-16), 4 Ezra (7:97), and in the Testaments of the Twelve Patriarchs (Test. Jud. 25:1-4; Test. Benj. 10:6-9; Test. Zeb. 10:4).

In the time of Jesus and afterward, the Pharisees taught the resurrection of the body, while the Sadducees denied it (Acts 23:7-8). The Jewish Talmud clearly taught it (for example, see Israel W. Slotki, ed., *The Babylonian Talmud* [Seder Nashim, Kethuboth], trans. by S. Daiches [Rebecca Bennett Publications, 1959], vol. III, XII. 103a), while the view of the Essenes is debated.

So while different views are represented, the resurrection of the body (expressed either in very physical terms or as a transformed state) appears to be the far more frequently-taught position in the extant literature of this period.

38. For the importance of this term in the discussion, see Edward Lynn Bode, "The First Easter Morning," *Analecta Biblica* 45 (Rome: Biblical Institute, 1970), pp. 93-96.

39. For a more general study in just one of Paul's books, see 2 Cor. 1:8-10; 4:10-12, 16; 5:1-4, 6, 8-9; 10:10. For texts where Paul provides a clear contrast between *soma* as the physical body and the immaterial portion of persons, see 1 Cor. 5:3; 2 Cor. 12:2-3; Eph. 5:28-29; Phil. 1:20-24; Col. 2:5; 1 Thess. 2:17.

40. See Robert H. Gundry, *Soma in Biblical Theology: With Emphasis on Pauline Anthropology* (Cambridge: Cambridge University, 1976; Grand Rapids, MI: Zondervan, 1987), p. 182. See also chaps. 1, 5-6, 12 and, in particular, chap. 13, "The Soma in Death and Resurrection."

41. John A.T. Robinson, "Resurrection in the New Testament," *The Interpreter's Dictionary of the Bible,* ed. by George Buttrick (Nashville: Abingdon, 1962), vol. 4, p. 48.

42. See Chap. 4, including endnote sources, for a brief discussion of the empty tomb, and why some historians think that this fact may be established even apart from the New Testament evidence, which is still very strong in itself.

43. A.M. Hunter provides four arguments for this conclusion: (1) The earliest Christians were careful to preserve the essence of Jesus' words and actions. (2) The Gospel authors were able to discover the facts of Jesus' life. (3) The authors repeatedly show that they are honest reporters. (4) Together the Gospels present an authentic, unified picture of Jesus *(Bible and Gospel* [Philadelphia: Westminster, 1969], pp. 32-40).

44. For an example of such an enterprise, see Grant R. Osborne, *The Resurrection Narratives: A Redactional Study* (Grand Rapids, MI: Baker, 1984). C.H. Dodd, after an investigation of each of the gospel appearance accounts, has argued that several of them are "concise" reports, containing material that is quite valuable in understanding the nature of Jesus' appearances. Specifically, Dodd lists Matt. 28:8-10, 16-20; John 20:19-21 and, to a lesser extent, Luke 24:36-49 as appearance narratives that rely on early tradition. C.H. Dodd, "The Appearances of the Risen Christ: An Essay in the Form Criticism of the Gospels," *More New Testament Essays* (Grand Rapids, MI: Eerdmans, 1968).

45. Gundry, *Soma in Biblical Theology,* p. 182. Incidentally, Gundry also addresses himself to issues such as Paul's meaning in texts like 1 Cor. 15:44-45, 50. Concerning 15:44-45, Gundry concludes that, just as Adam was not a soul without a body (v. 45a), Jesus did not become a spirit without a body (v. 45b). Rather, Jesus was raised in "a physical body renovated by the Spirit of Christ and therefore suited to heavenly immortality" (pp. 165-166). With regard to 15:40a, "the phrase 'flesh and blood' connotes the present body's weakness and perishability . . . but does not imply immateriality of the resurrected body" (p. 166). We would add to this last point that such an interpretation does

more justice to the context in 15:50b, where Paul's thought seems to be that mortal bodies cannot inhabit immortal abodes.

46. On the interrelation of the New Testament concepts of resurrection, eternal life, and immortality, see the study in Harris, *Raised Immortal*, pp. 182–184, 199–201, 232–236, 273–275. For my disagreement with his formulation of the nature of Jesus' resurrection body, see my review article, "The Recent Evangelical Debate on the Bodily Resurrection of Jesus: A Review Article," *Journal of the Evangelical Theological Society*, vol. 33, no. 3, Sept. 1990, pp. 375–378. But my critique is not concerned with Harris's excellent work on the above terms.

Chapter 10   Heaven: The Great Adventure

1. Perhaps we should remind you of something we have said all along. We have not tried to argue for the trustworthiness or inspiration of Scripture in this book because that would require a book in itself. But both of us have addressed these subjects elsewhere [J.P. Moreland, *Scaling the Secular City* (Grand Rapids, MI: Baker, 1987), chap. 5; Gary R. Habermas, *The Resurrection of Jesus: A Rational Inquiry* (Ann Arbor, MI: University Microfilms, 1976], app. 2, also we began this volume by carefully explaining that this topic was beyond the scope of this present volume, and we referred you to other books for reference.

Another important item we need to mention is this: Even if all we knew about heaven was what follows from the verified resurrection of Jesus and its implications (see chaps. 4, 9), most of the details in the first section would still follow, or at least be implied. For details concerning how this is so, see Gary Habermas, *The Centrality of the Resurrection*, chap. 12, "A Foretaste of Heaven," forthcoming. A few hints might even come from near-death experiences. Additionally, we would still be able to do our speculation in this book's final section.

2. There may be a hint in 1 Cor. 2:9 that God has also prepared eternal things for his followers that they have never fathomed. It is true that the context does not discuss eternal life at all, plus we are told in the next verse that the Holy Spirit does reveal these things to believers. Yet, it is plain that all things have not been revealed to us; in fact, it may be argued that eternal life is one area where there is still much to learn (and experience!). So the text still seems to be saying that God has planned numerous inscrutable things for us, some that the Holy Spirit has made known to us by his revelation. Thus, even though the afterlife is not directly in view here, this could well be a subject where God has many things planned for us, some that have been revealed, and some that have not.

In fact, when Paul visited paradise (in what was possibly a near-death experience) in 2 Cor. 12:1–4, he heard certain items he would not repeat. So it is apparent that not all aspects of the afterlife have been revealed. Likewise, 1 John 3:2 states that it has not yet been made known what we will become in the future.

3. Francis Schaeffer said this about the imagination of the Christian *(Art and the Bible* [Downers Grove, IL: InterVarsity, 1973], p. 61): "Christian man has a basis for knowing the difference between subject and object. The Christian is the really free man—he is free to have imagination. This too is our heritage. The Christian is the one whose imagination should fly beyond the stars."

4. The image of God as a Shepherd leading his people is a very common Old Testament theme. For examples, see Ps. 28:9, 37:3, 74:1, 79:13, 80:1, 95:7, 100:3; Isa. 40:11, 53:6.

5. For a brief summation, see Homer A. Kent, Jr., *The Epistle to the Hebrews: A Commentary* (Grand Rapids, MI: Baker, 1972), pp. 80–83.

6. The idea that God is the believer's refuge, shield, rock, fortress, stronghold, shelter, and protector is also a very common idea in the Old Testament. See 2 Sam. 22:3; Ps.

3:3, 5:11, 9:9, 11:1, 16:1, 17:8, 18:2, 18:30, 25:20, 27:1, 28:7, 31:1–4, 31:20, 32:7, 36:7, 46:1–7, 144:2; Isa. 17:10, 25:4–5, 31:5, 57:13; Jer. 16:19, 17:17.

7. Num. 24:5–7 (NIV) reads:

> How beautiful are your tents, O Jacob,
>   your dwelling places, O Israel!
> Like valleys they spread out,
>   like gardens *[paradeisos]* beside a
>   river,
> Like aloes planted by the LORD,
>   like cedars beside the waters.
> Water will flow from their buckets;
>   their seed will have abundant water.

8. C.S. Lewis, *The Weight of Glory and Other Addresses* (Grand Rapids, MI: Eerdmans, 1949), p. 13. Then Lewis adds on the same page:

> For if we take the imagery of Scripture seriously, if we believe that God will one day *give* us the Morning Star and cause us to *put on* the splendour (sic) of the sun, then we may surmise that both the ancient myths and the modern poetry, so false as history, may be very near the truth as prophecy. At present we are on the outside of the world, the wrong side of the door. (Lewis's emphasis)

9. See examples in Ps. 45; Isa. 54:1–10; Zech. 14:16–19.

10. C.S. Lewis said: "There have been times when I think we do not desire heaven but more often I find myself wondering whether, in our heart of hearts, we have ever desired anything else." See Lewis's *The Problem of Pain* (New York: Macmillan, 1962), p. 145. For an excellent investigation of this subject, see Peter J. Kreeft, *Heaven: The Heart's Deepest Longing* (San Francisco: Harper & Row, 1980). A different but relevant discussion is found in Norman L. Geisler, *Philosophy of Religion* (Grand Rapids, MI: Zondervan, 1974), part 1. For some other brief thoughts on this subject, see Robert A. Morey, *Death and the Afterlife* (Minneapolis: Bethany, 1984), pp. 66–70; Jack MacArthur, *Exploring in the Next World* (Minneapolis: Bethany Fellowship/Dimension, 1967), pp. 21–26.

11. It has been said that this is the most difficult verse in the Book of Ecclesiastes and more than one translation has been proposed. For example, see the differences between O.S. Rankin (exegesis) and Gaius Glenn Atkins (exposition) in vol. 5 of *The Interpreter's Bible,* ed. by George Arthur Buttrick (New York: Abingdon, 1956), pp. 46–49. While Rankin prefers another option, Atkins's comments are more in keeping with our thoughts here.

12. The argument from the presence of this desire in persons to the existence of eternal life is evaluated in Chap. 1. The idea that heaven should serve as the perspective from which to view life and its decisions is the subject of Chap. 12. It should be carefully noted that our discussion on the desire for heaven at this point in the text does not depend on the truthfulness of the argument from desire we discussed in Chap. 1. Our current discussion is based on empirical realities and the actual existence of heaven.

13. It is certainly impossible in the course of a chapter section to do what others have taken books to develop. For some stimulating examples, see Kreeft's volume *Heaven,* plus his *Everything You Ever Wanted to Know About Heaven . . . But Never Dreamed of Asking* (San Francisco: Harper & Row, 1982) and John Gilmore, *Probing Heaven: Key Questions on the Hereafter* (Grand Rapids, MI: Baker, 1989). Two other helpful volumes are Peter Toon, *Heaven and Hell: A Biblical and Theological Overview* (Nashville: Thomas Nelson, 1986) and Harry Blamires, *Knowing the Truth About Heaven and Hell: Our Choices and Where They Lead Us* (Ann Arbor, MI: Servant, 1988). Two of the older classics include D.L. Moody, *Heaven and How to Get There* (Chicago: Moody, n.d.) and Edward M. Bounds, *Heaven: A Place, A City, A Home* (Grand Rapids, MI: Baker, 1975).

14. Gilmore, *Probing Heaven,* chap. 4, especially pp. 91–92, 103–105. Cf. David

Winter's statement: "Heaven is *where* God is, *when* God is" (italics his). *(Hereafter: What Happens After Death?* [Wheaton, IL: Harold Shaw, 1972], p. 77.) Blamires agrees: "Heaven is where God dwells" (*Knowing the Truth About Heaven and Hell*, p. 108). Toon says, "Heaven is the place and sphere where God is wholly and specially known" (*Heaven and Hell*, pp. 24–25).

15. Toon, *Heaven and Hell*, p. 157.

16. But some will wonder why the angels fell. On the first scenario, their natures did not prevent them from sinning, as ours will. On the second option, our states and conditions differ. Either way, the angels' circumstances and natures are not the same as ours. Further, their prefallen state might more closely have approximated the prefallen condition of human beings, rather than their glorified state, and sin *was* possible for both. Last, there are no revelational assurances that angels can no longer sin, so we don't have that final knowledge.

17. For some additional thoughts see Charles Ferguson Ball, *Heaven* (Wheaton, IL: Victor, 1981), chap. 6.

18. Bernard Williams, "The Makropulos Case: Reflections on the Tedium of Immortality," *Problems of the Self* (Cambridge: Cambridge University, 1973), pp. 82–100. Williams suggests that "an endless life would be a meaningless one" because we would simply be living our finite number of possible experiences over and over, requiring that one "lose oneself" in the process in an attempt to find meaning (pp. 89–90, 96). Charles Hartshorne, *Omnipotence and Other Theological Mistakes* (Albany, NY: State University of New York, 1984), pp. 32–37. Hartshorne argues that those who desire immortality "either want to be bored to death, so to speak, or to be God" (p. 35).

19. Kreeft, *Everything You Ever Wanted to Know About Heaven*, p. 62. Cf. Kreeft's more detailed treatment in *Heaven*, pp. 50–58.

20. Gilmore, *Probing Heaven*, pp. 169–170.

21. So argues Kreeft, *Everything You Ever Wanted to Know About Heaven*, pp. 64–65; Gilmore, *Probing Heaven*, chap. 13; C.S. Lewis, *Miracles: A Preliminary Study* (New York: Macmillan, 1947), pp. 165–166.

22. Concerning the related matter of the existence of husband-wife companionship in heaven, or families living together, it should be noted that many commentators point out that this passage does not deny such. George Buttrick states that: "Here Christ does not break the bonds of human love: he strengthens them. He says that hereafter the bonds shall be of finer texture, and that love shall have truer and holier instrumentalities." "Matthew" (exposition), *The Interpreter's Bible*, vol. 7, p. 522. Kent agrees: "Nor does this passage imply that the dearest of earthly relationships will be forgotten in the life to come. Just how these relationships will be affected by the possession of glorified bodies is not explained, but all Scripture supports the view that the resurrected state is one of blessedness and perfect fellowship." (Homer A. Kent, "Matthew," *The Wycliffe Bible Commentary*, Charles F. Pfeiffer and Everett F. Harrison, eds. [Nashville: Southwestern, 1962], p. 969.)

23. C.S. Lewis seems to leave it as a rather open issue, although he thinks that if animals are in heaven it will be due to their subordination to man, hence they may receive a possible "derivative immortality." *(The Problem of Pain*, pp. 136–143.)

Kreeft argues in favor of animal immortality, including that of the same pets we owned on earth. "Why Not?" he asks. *(Everything You Ever Wanted to Know About Heaven*, pp. 45–46.)

Gilmore thinks we should take a "wait and see" attitude on this issue, but he also notes that nowhere does Scripture say that animals have immortal souls (Gilmore, *Hereafter*, pp. 130–133). Lewis, on the other hand, thinks that if animals are immortal, Scripture would still probably not have addressed the subject either one way or the other (Lewis, *The Problem of Pain*, p. 137).

Interestingly and somewhat unconventionally, John Zoller argues that there will be plenty of fish in heaven and that they can be caught and eaten *(Heaven: Will You Be There?* [Windsor: Babington, 1965], pp. 220–223.)!

24. Gilmore, *Probing Heaven,* chap. 8.

25. Kreeft, *Everything You Ever Wanted to Know About Heaven,* pp. 17–18; cf. Gilmore, p. 157. Blamires reminds us of some of the elements of earth-bound time that will no longer plague us (pp. 114–119).

26. David Winter argues that both time and space are "quite irrelevant to heaven" and that all normal categories are apparently meaningless *(Hereafter,* pp. 75–76). Granted, it is difficult to know exactly just what he means here, but it is also difficult to know how both time and space are irrelevant. Further, in what sense can we point to Jesus' resurrection body as an example of the believer's, as Winter does, since it definitely occupied space (chap. 4)?

27. Kreeft, *Everything You Ever Wanted to Know About Heaven,* pp. 37–40.

28. See Matt. 5:12, 6:19–21; 1 Cor. 9:24–27; Phil. 4:17; Col. 3:23–24; 1 Thess. 2:19; 1 Tim. 6:18–19; 2 Tim. 4:8; James 1:12; 1 Peter 5:4; Rev. 2:10, 3:11.

29. See Matt. 16:27; 1 Cor. 3:8, 12–15; Rev. 21:12.

30. Such as Matt. 6:19–21; 1 Cor. 9:25–27; Col. 3:23–24; 1 Tim. 6:17–19. See further discussion of this subject in Chap. 12.

31. Blamires proclaims: "In short, . . . heaven is what Christianity is all about" *(Knowing the Truth About Heaven and Hell,* p. 110).

32. Zoller, *Heaven: Will You Be There?* p. 81.

33. Herbert Vander Lugt, *Light in the Valley: A Christian View of Death and Dying* (Wheaton, IL: Victor Books, 1976), pp. 79–80.

34. Joseph Bayly, *The View from a Hearse: A Christian View of Death* (Elgin, IL: Cook, 1969), p. 20. We do not mean to imply by these last two statements that death is not an enemy or that death is "rosy," but only that it is the road to heaven whether we fear it or not. We address this entire topic in Chap. 12.

35. Schaeffer, *Art and the Bible,* p. 61.

Chapter 11   Hell: The Horrible Choice

1. George H. Smith, *Atheism: The Case Against God* (Buffalo, NY: Prometheus, 1979), p. 299.

2. B.C. Johnson, *The Atheist Debater's Handbook* (Buffalo, NY: Prometheus, 1981), p. 116.

3. Morton Kelsey, *Afterlife: The Other Side of Dying* (New York: Paulist, 1979), p. 237.

4. The Old Testament clearly affirms life after death, but the notion was not as central as it is in the New Testament. The main reason for this is the fact that Old Testament religion focused on corporate national life (note that the main form of worship is corporate, not individual), blessings and judgments on the nation, and temporal life in the land of promise.

Furthermore, biblical revelation is progressive—that is, a revealed topic gets clearer and more detailed as time goes on. This applies to the progress of revelation about life after death.

Finally, some people have cited Bible texts that seem to favor the idea that the Old Testament denies life after death. The book most often cited is Ecclesiastes (cf. 3:16–22, 9:5, 6). However, Ecclesiastes is written from a point of view "under the sun" or "under heaven"—from a skeptical perspective. The writer attempts to make sense of life without reference to God or a transcendent realm, hence he declares agnosticism regarding human immortality. Other verses that have been cited (e.g., Ps. 88:11–13; Isa. 38:18–19) refer to one's inability upon death to praise and worship with God's people in the sanctuary. Another text, Job 7:21, can be understood as focusing on existence worth living in this realm (cf. Job 7:7–10) or worth being seen again (cf. Job 23:8; Ps. 37:36) rather than with the existence or nonexistence of an afterlife.

5. Some scientists and philosophers talk about parallel universes—space-time worlds that are equally real to the one we are in but with which we cannot interact. This multiple-world ensemble is thought to be necessary to make sense out of certain quantum phenomena.

We do not agree with this view and we do not embrace the existence of such an ensemble of parallel universes. But, if hell is spatial in some sense, then it would need to be a type of space different from and inaccessible to our own spatial dimensions. Even though we disagree with the parallel-universe view in science, nevertheless, if such talk is at least intelligible, then it does provide an alternative to our view of hell as a nonspatial mode of existence.

But perhaps this view still does not need to be embraced in regard to hell either. If people become disembodied at death, there is no need for space, as we have seen. Hence, we do not need to rely at all on a view that argues for parallel *space*-time universes.

For more on the nature and rationality of hell from a conservative Catholic perspective, see Germain Grisez, *The Way of the Lord Jesus, Volume One: Christian Moral Principles* (Chicago: Franciscan Herald, 1983), pp. 435–52, 814–16.

6. For treatments of purgatory, see Grisez, *The Way of the Lord Jesus, Volume One: Christian Moral Principles,* pp. 765–787; Morton T. Kelsey, *Afterlife: The Other Side of Dying* (New York: Paulist, 1979), pp. 242–252; Loraine Boettner, *Immortality* (Philadelphia: Presbyterian & Reformed, 1956), pp. 124–137.

7. Boettner, *Immortality,* p. 124.

8. Kelsey, *Afterlife,* p. 247.

9. For more on this, see Boettner, *Immortality,* pp. 124–137.

10. Richard Swinburne, *Faith and Reason* (Oxford: Clarendon, 1981), pp. 143–172; *Responsibility and Atonement* (Oxford: Clarendon, 1989), pp. 179–200; "A Theodicy of Heaven and Hell," in *The Existence & Nature of God,* ed. by Alfred J. Freddoso (Notre Dame, IN: University of Notre Dame, 1983), pp. 37–54.

11. Eugene Fontinell, *Self, God, and Immortality* (Philadelphia: Temple University, 1986), p. 217. Cf. a review of this work by J.P. Moreland, *International Philosophical Quarterly* 29 (Dec. 1989), pp. 480–483.

12. For more on this, see Stanley Hauerwas, *Suffering Presence: Theological Reflections on Medicine, the Mentally Handicapped, and the Church* (Notre Dame, IN: University of Notre Dame, 1986); Daniel Callahan, "Minimalistic Ethics," *Hastings Center Report* 11 (Oct. 1983), pp. 19–25; J.P. Moreland and Norman L. Geisler, *The Life and Death Debate: Moral Issues of Our Time* (Westport, CT: Praeger, 1990).

13. See Roderick Chisholm, *Brentano and Intrinsic Value* (Cambridge: Cambridge University, 1986), pp. 76–87; "The Defeat of Good and Evil," in *The Problem of Evil,* ed. by Marilyn McCord Adams and Robert Merrihew Adams (Oxford: Oxford University, 1990), pp. 53–68.

14. Morton Kelsey, *Afterlife,* p. 251.

15. John Hick, *Evil and the God of Love* (New York: Harper & Row, 1978), p. 342; cf. *Death and Eternal Life* (San Francisco: Harper & Row, 1980), pp. 242–261.

16. C.S. Lewis, *The Problem of Pain* (New York: Macmillan, 1962), pp. 106ff.

17. As we pointed out earlier, Morton Kelsey believes that even though people can have a second chance in purgatory, nevertheless, there are ways for people to guarantee they will stay in hell by continuing to align themselves with evil and hatred, by worshipping the devil, by continuing to believe they must earn their way to heaven, by continuing to refuse to believe in a heaven of grace and love, and by refusing to face the prospect of death and resurrection. See Kelsey, *Afterlife,* pp. 248–250.

18. See John Stott, "Taking a Closer Look at Eternal Torture," *World Christian* (May

1989), pp. 31–37; Clark Pinnock, "The Destruction of the Finally Impenitent," *Criswell Theological Review* 4 (Spring 1990), pp. 243–259; Stephen Travis, *Christian Hope and the Future* (Downers Grove, IL: InterVarsity, 1980), pp. 133–36; John W. Wenham, *The Goodness of God* (Downers Grove, IL: InterVarsity, 1974), pp. 34–41; Edward Fudge, *The Fire that Consumes* (Houston: Providential, 1982); P.E. Hughes, *The True Image: The Origin and Destiny of Man in Christ* (Grand Rapids, MI: Eerdmans, 1989), chap. 37; "Universalism: Will Everyone Be Saved?" *Christianity Today* (20 Mar. 1987), pp. 31–45.

19. For more on this, see Robert A. Morey, *Death and the Afterlife* (Minneapolis: Bethany, 1984), pp. 94–170, 199–222; Rene Pache, *The Future Life* (Chicago: Moody, 1962), pp. 290–95; Alan W. Gomes, "Evangelicals and the Annihilation of Hell, Part I" *Christian Research Journal* 13 (Spring 1991), pp. 15–19.

20. David F. Wells, "Everlasting Punishment," *Christianity Today* (20 Mar. 1987), p. 42.

21. Some claim that the current evangelical interest in annihilationism is due to an extrabiblical concept of justice coupled with a liberal, secular sentimentalism. But this claim does not seem to be a fair representation of evangelical annihilationism. First, Pinnock and others appeal to a biblical concept of justice as part of their defense. Second, it is not wrong to use extrabiblical intuitions about justice in an argument, if one believes in natural law. Amos 1 and 2 and Genesis 18 would appear to be examples of using a concept of justice, taken from general revelation, and applying it to God or pagan nations. Annihilationism may not be ultimately defensible, but it does no good to caricature those who argue for it.

22. It is sometimes argued that an infinite payment is just for rejecting an infinite God and his offer. But this argument seems to be a bad one because it equivocates on the word *infinite*. God is infinite, not in a quantitative way, but in a qualitative way: He is a maximally perfect being—that is, he is pure actuality, there is no possible world where a being could exist with more greatness than God. The infinity of the afterlife is a quantitative, potential infinite, and as such, it is actually finite. The future is a potential infinite and it will increase a day at a time forever while always remaining finite and never reaching an actual infinite duration. Thus, this argument from infinity is a poor one and rests on an equivocation. We prefer to use a different term to avoid this confusion, namely *ultimate*.

23. Alan Gomes, "Evangelicals and the Annihilation of Hell, Part II," *Christian Research Journal* 13 (Summer 1991), pp. 8–13.

24. For more on this, see J.P. Moreland and Norman L. Geisler, *The Life and Death Debate*. See also J.P. Moreland, "Ethical Issues at the End of Life," *Eldercare for the Christian Family,* by Timothy S. Smick, James W. Duncan, J.P. Moreland, and Jeffrey A. Watson, (Dallas: Word, 1990), pp. 182–198.

25. Grisez, *The Way of the Lord Jesus,* p. 448.

26. See Robert Lightner, *Heaven For Those Who Can't Believe* (Schaumburg, IL: Regular Baptist, 1977).

27. Leon Morris, "The Dreadful Harvest," *Christianity Today,* vol. 25, no. 6 (27 May 1991), pp. 34–38.

28. See William Lane Craig, " 'No Other Name': A Middle Knowledge Perspective on the Exclusivity of Salvation Through Christ," *Faith and Philosophy* 6 (Apr. 1989), pp. 172–188; *The Only Wise God* (Grand Rapids, MI: Baker, 1987), pp. 127–152; *No Easy Answers* (Chicago: Moody, 1990), pp. 105–116.

29. It may be that Craig is offering his solution as a defense only and not a theodicy, the former merely being an attempt to show that the traditional view of hell is logically consistent with classic Christian theology or other true premises, the latter being an attempt to show that the traditional view of hell is not just possibly true but rationally justifiable. We suspect that Craig believes his solution is also a theodicy and not merely a defense, but in any case, that is how we are appropriating it, namely as a defense.

30. See Craig, "'No Other Name,'" p. 182.

31. Someone could say that this argument turns God into a utilitarian, but we believe it does no such thing. Roughly, a utilitarian justification of some action or rule appeals solely to the nonmoral utility produced in the results of that action or the rule under which it falls. An alternative, and in our view, more adequate view, is a deontological framework. Here, some rules are right because of their intrinsic value. According to deontological theories, factual results do not make something my duty, but they can tell me which of two alternatives is the best way to fulfill what already is my duty intrinsically. God's desire to create a world with an optimal balance of saved vs. unsaved may be thought of as a deontological duty (or it may be that, strictly speaking, a necessarily good being has no duties). For more on this, see J.P. Moreland and Norman L. Geisler, *The Life and Death Debate,* chaps. 1, 8; Thomas V. Morris, *Our Idea of God* (Downers Grove, IL: InterVarsity, 1991), pp. 47–64.

Chapter 12   Becoming Heavenly Minded

1. There are at least two reasons that show this is Jesus' dominant thought here instead of merely being an aside. The portion on the subject of worry also begins by pointing out that life is more important than our daily concerns about it (v. 25b). Further, the key verse in 6:33 makes the top-down perspective central to the entire discourse.

2. Note that we are discussing the *depth* of one's commitment, *not* using this as a test for salvation.

3. It might be said that this passage ends with a brief summary statement in 6:33–34. While our primary goal is to seek God and his kingdom (v. 33a, like vv. 19–25), our daily needs will still be met by God (v. 33b, like vv. 26, 28–32). Besides, anxiety about life's concerns avails nothing, anyway (v. 34, like v. 27).

4. As we will mention in the next chapter, we perhaps cannot remove all sources of concern from our daily affairs. Indeed, even Jesus himself was troubled at the death of his friend, Lazarus (John 11:33–36).

5. This passage raises several theological issues that we cannot go into here. But for an introduction to a few of these questions, see F.F. Bruce, *The Hard Sayings of Jesus* (Downers Grove, IL: InterVarsity, 1983), pp. 166–168.

6. Perhaps it should be noted here that my use of the term *radical* in this context is a very positive one. I choose such a term to emphasize that Jesus not only taught commitment to God and man, but that such a commitment was costly. Several other passages teach this "radical" form of commitment as well (see Matt. 10:37–39; Luke 9:57–62, 12:33, 14:25–35).

7. Quite popular in some contemporary theological circles is the view that what Jesus really indicated by his twofold command was that, by being committed to others, we are actually fulfilling our love of God. Said another way, instead of the "top-down" perspective that we have delineated, we are told that Jesus actually encouraged a "bottom-up" arrangement instead. Thus, some would say that one's salvation is not an act of faith in Jesus, per se, but one's active involvement in the lives of others, which actually is faith in God.

Whether this is a major motivation or not, such an interpretation appears to generalize Jesus' teachings, making them compatible with instruction in other religious traditions. It also contains several pitfalls. Besides essentially finding in Jesus' teachings a type of works-righteousness, it also noticeably ignores Jesus' many injunctions concerning the prerequisite of personal faith in him. This teaching is found throughout the gospel tradition (Matt. 10:37; 18:3, 6; Mark 10:29–30; Luke 24:47; John 1:12; 6:47) in light of his message of salvation (Mark 10:45; Matt. 26:28; John 3:15–17). So we conclude that this interpretation is reductionistic and tends to minimize Jesus' unique claims about himself.

8. There is much debate concerning this passage, such as the issue of whether Paul is addressing the nature of the intermediate or the final, eternal state. However, that he is

speaking on the topic of eternal life is generally acknowledged. See Robert H. Gundry, *Soma in Biblical Theology: With Emphasis on Pauline Anthropology* (Cambridge: Cambridge University, 1976; Grand Rapids, MI: Zondervan, 1989), pp. 149–154.

9. The progress of *"aphthartos* [perish]. . . *amiantos* [spoil]. . . *amarantos* [fade]" in 1:4 strongly emphasizes the sterling qualities of our heavenly existence, as shown by Peter's usage of all three terms in combination.

10. This is a common theme in John's writings. See John 3:36, 5:24, 6:47; 1 John 5:13; cf. Eph. 1:13–14; 2 Thess. 2:13–17.

11. See Ola Elizabeth Winslow, *Jonathan Edwards: Basic Writings* (New York: New American Library, 1966), p. 142. Interestingly enough, Edwards's text for this message was Hebrews 11:13–14 (p. 135).

12. It should be remembered that Revelation 4:10–11 portrays the 24 heavenly elders laying down their own crowns before God's throne so that he might receive the honor, praise, and glory.

13. It is simply imperative that Christians *carefully* check the organizations to which they are interested in sending funds. Whenever possible, visits or phone calls (or letters, as a secondary resort) to administrative officials of the prospective ministries serve as ways to check important aspects, such as the overall philosophy, their major goals in their perceived order of priority, the exact use of the funds (including how much of each dollar is spent for overhead and administrative costs and how much goes directly to the particular need being addressed). This is not as difficult as it may sound. Most ministries are used to these sorts of questions and are quite willing to provide answers.

It is also helpful to probe a bit deeper. What do they *really* mean when they say that a certain percentage always goes to the need? What is included in this figure? Can gifts be designated? Do these ministries exercise controls to assure that their goals, as well as the gift designations, are, indeed, being properly handled? Also, it is wise to ask for an audited statement; again, most groups are very willing to provide a copy.

There are frequently massive differences between various ministries, especially regarding their spiritual priorities and the amount of each dollar that makes it to the desired goal. Over a period of time, a level of trust can certainly be built up, as well as friendships, so that we may be relatively sure how the funds are being used.

Lastly, having done about all that we reasonably can do, we need to pray concerning which ministries we ought to personally support and for our gifts to be utilized in the best possible way, as well as praying that other believers may be convicted in a biblical manner.

14. It would appear that texts such as those examined above establish priorities with which to compare the ideas of Christian ministry, whether our own or another. Jesus' twofold command to love God first and others next (see Matt. 22:34–40, for an example) would seem to present a good basis for the conclusion that introducing others to the gospel takes priority over meeting other sorts of needs. Yet, these two commands might be viewed as the two most crucial priorities for ministry, always in this order, and, as our Lord taught us, we ought to be radically involved in both. This is a helpful rule for either one's own ministry or when considering the issue of giving.

15. David Gill suggests that two radical methods of arranging our financial priorities are either to live in a more simplified manner, work as much as we can, and use as many of our resources as possible for the Lord's work, or to work as few hours as we need to in order to live simply, committing our extra time to the Lord. See David Gill, "Radical Christian: Rethinking Our Financial Priorities," *Right On,* vol. 7, no. 6, Feb.–Mar. 1976, p. 12.

16. Such is variously described either as a command (Matt. 6:20–21; cf. Luke 12:33–34) or as the consequence of what are commanded (1 Tim. 6:18–19) or commended activities (Phil. 4:15–17; Heb. 10:34–35).

17. Our exercise here is adapted from the summary by Peter J. Kreeft, who explains

that the original supposition comes from Augustine. See Kreeft's volume, *Heaven: The Heart's Deepest Longing* (San Francisco: Harper & Row, 1980), p. 27.

18. The same methods presented in Chap. 13 are also *directly* applicable to some of the other subjects we have pursued in this chapter. We hope you will apply those suggestions in a retrospective manner to your personal thinking on the topics here, such as witnessing, personal finances, helping others, pain and suffering, and worry.

Chapter 13   Overcoming the Fear of Death

1. For several examples from the Old Testament poetic writings alone, see Job 5:26, 30:20–23; Ps. 6:3–5, 48:14, 55:4–8, 89:46–48; Prov. 13:14, 14:27. Other passages, especially from the New Testament, will be discussed later.

2. Paul hints at a different aspect of focusing our attention on eternal values in Phil. 1:21–26. Here, in a discussion of life and death, he concentrates not only on eternal life, but also on his earthly ministry—more specifically, on the particular needs of those in the Christian community to whom he was writing. This suggests that we also seek to invest our lives in others, even in times of stress occasioned by various aspects of the subject of death. And even so, this reflects a different angle on the eternal aspect spoken of here, for Paul's efforts on behalf of these Philippian believers are for the ultimate purpose of their own growth in the faith (vv. 25–26), including their progress toward heavenly rewards (4:17).

3. This subject is broad and has many details. Many different topics could be mentioned here, such as an in-depth study of the pertinent passage in Philippians 4:6–9, an analysis of other relevant texts such as Romans 12:2 and Colossians 3:1–4, the psychological grounding for this concept, case studies of actual applications of this methodology, as well as a number of other related subjects. For details on each of these, see Gary R. Habermas, *Dealing with Doubt* (Chicago: Moody, 1990), especially chap. 4, and endnote 5 below.

4. In spite of our language throughout this chapter about the surety of death, we wish to emphasize that the Lord could return at any time, meaning that many believers would not have to face the prospect of dying. This possibility is one of the truths we can tell ourselves in the face of fear. At any rate, Christians need to keep this doctrine in mind, living in the light of its possible reality within our own lifetimes.

5. For important details, see William Backus and Marie Chapian, *Telling Yourself the Truth* (Minneapolis: Bethany, 1980), especially chaps. 1–3.

6. This is neither a pie-in-the-sky statement or a positive-thinking scheme. For more details, especially concerning the actual application of these particulars and examples of how they can work, see Habermas, *Dealing with Doubt,* especially chaps. 4–5.

7. We do not claim that this is the only biblical method nor pattern, or even that there is something inherently necessary about these three steps. We would encourage you to study the subject for yourself and even develop a biblical pattern that may better meet your specific needs. A number of additional ideas are listed in Habermas, *Dealing with Doubt.*

8. In the discussion with Martha and Mary, the focus is on Jesus as the resurrection, not directly on the raising of Lazarus (cf. John 11:25–26). In fact, Jesus presumably dealt with the subject of immortality and resurrection before the sisters even knew that he intended to raise their brother from the dead. With his disciples, the emphasis on his resurrection as the cure for grieving, doubt, and fear is even clearer (see John 20:19–29; Luke 24:36–46). For other New Testament passages that also emphasize Jesus' resurrection in the context of discussions on death, see 1 Cor. 15:45–57; 2 Cor. 4:7–18; 1 Thess. 4:13–18; cf. Heb. 2:14–15; 1 Peter 1:3–4.

Chapter 14   Dealing with Abortion, Infanticide, and Euthanasia

1. See Alan Johnson, "Is There a Biblical Warrant for Natural-Law Theories?" *Journal of the Evangelical Theological Society* 25 (June 1982), pp. 185–99.

2. Cf. Norman Geisler, "A Premillenial View of Law and Government," *Bibliotheca Sacra* 142 (July-Sept. 1985), pp. 250–266.

3. See J.P. Moreland, "Tough Decisions: Cultivating the Art of Ethical Decision-Making," in *Eldercare for the Christian Family* by Tim Smick, James Duncan, J.P. Moreland, and Jeff Watson (Dallas: Word, 1990), pp. 163–181; J.P. Moreland and Norman Geisler, *The Life and Death Debate: Moral Issues of Our Time* (Westport, CT: Praeger, 1990), chap. 1.

4. Another main purpose of ethical theory is to clarify the good life, the virtuous person, and how to develop character. These facets are all part of what is called virtue theory in ethics. Virtue theory can be harmonized easily with a deontological approach to ethics, but not with utilitarianism. Since we are discussing issues in this chapter, we have chosen to focus directly on moral rules and principles, but this should not be taken to imply that we do not value the insights of virtue ethics. For more on virtue theory, see Peter A. French, Theodore E. Uehling, Jr., and Howard K. Wettstein, eds., *Midwest Studies in Philosophy: Studies in the Philosophy of Mind*, (Notre Dame, IN: University of Notre Dame, 1988), vol. 13.

5. Some philosophers distinguish rules from principles, the latter being more basic and serving to justify the former. For example, the principle "respect persons" could be used to justify the rule "don't lie". We have not bothered to make such a distinction and will use the two notions interchangeably. For more on this, see Tom Beauchamp, James Childress, *Principles of Biomedical Ethics,* 2nd edition, (New York: Oxford University, 1983), pp. 3–8.

6. See J.P. Moreland and Norman L. Geisler, *The Life and Death Debate,* chap. 1; Tom Beauchamp, *Philosophical Ethics* (New York: Oxford University, 1989); Louis Pojman, *Ethics: Discovering Right and Wrong* (Belmont, CA: Wadsworth, 1990).

7. Actually rules do not produce consequences in the real world, only actions do. So when utilitarians talk about the utility produced by a rule, they mean something like the utility produced if most or all people conform to the rule as opposed to conforming to an alternative rule.

8. See W.D. Ross, *The Right and the Good* (Oxford: Clarendon, 1930).

9. See the sources cited in note six above for an evaluation of utilitarianism and deontological theories.

10. James F. Childress, *Who Should Decide? Paternalism in Health Care* (New York: Oxford University, 1982), pp. 28–76, 157–85.

11. For a critique of the idea that autonomous choices always override other considerations, see Edmund D. Pellegrino and David C. Thomasma, *For the Patient's Good: The Restoration of Beneficence in Health Care* (New York: Oxford University, 1988).

12. For an articulate defense of the radical view, see James Rachels, *The End of Life* (Oxford: Oxford University, 1986). For a critique of Rachels, see J.P. Moreland, "James Rachels and the Active Euthanasia Debate," *Journal of the Evangelical Theological Society* 31 (Mar. 1988), pp. 81–90, or see the review of *The End of Life* by J.P. Moreland in *The Thomist* 53 (Oct. 1989), pp. 714–722.

13. We do not agree with foregoing artificial food and water because (1) they are not treatments, much less extraordinary ones, but basic means of sustaining life; (2) when extraordinary means are withdrawn the disease itself takes life, but when food and water are withdrawn, the withdrawal itself creates the circumstances that take life directly and intentionally; (3) decisions to forego food and water are reached by comparing ordinary and extraordinary persons, not ordinary and extraordinary treatments, and such judgments are not appropriate.

14. See J.P. Moreland and Norman L. Geisler, *The Life and Death Debate,* chap. 3; Robert Weir, *Selective Nontreatment of Handicapped Newborns* (New York: Oxford University, 1984).

15. In this regard, one must distinguish macroallocation issues vs. microallocation issues. The former focus on distributing society's medical and economic resources to types of individuals, diseases, and research programs. Given that resources are scarce, economic considerations are appropriate. The latter focus on distributing resources to specific individuals and accepts patient advocacy as an appropriate stance. Economic considerations are not appropriate here. For a defense of a modified *third-party-harms* view, see John Hardwig, "What About the Family?" *Hastings Center Report* 20 (Mar./Apr. 1990), pp. 5–10.

16. For more on this, see J.P. Moreland and Norman L. Geisler, *The Life and Death Debate*, pp. 49–55.

17. The same can be said for suicide because it is a case of active euthanasia administered by a person against himself. Further, while there is a long and respectable tradition within the church of pacificism and rejection of capital punishment, in our view, a just war and capital punishment are both justifiable. In each case life is taken according to the principle of justice (a life for a capital offense or to preserve life and justice) and the state, not an individual per se, has the right to take life in war and capital punishment. These topics are covered in J.P. Moreland and Norman L. Geisler, *The Life and Death Debate*, chaps. 6 and 7. Two further treatments of war are found in Robert G. Clouse, ed., *War: Four Christian Views* (Downers Grove, IL: InterVarsity, 1981); Vernon Grounds, ed., *Nuclear Arms: Two Views on World Peace* (Waco, TX: Word, 1987).

18. We have argued in Chap. 10 that all infants go to heaven if they die. We will not rehearse those arguments here, but it must be admitted that the notion of middle knowledge opens up the possibility that not all infants will go to heaven if they die. Why? It could be argued that God knows what they would have done had they had a chance to grow up and hear the gospel, and he judges them in light of what that choice would have been. This argument may well be correct, but one thing should be kept in mind. God should be trusted to be just and merciful in these cases, and we may have to leave our hope in that. Either way—all infants who die go to heaven, or God will deal with them based on how they would have chosen had they had the chance to grow up—when all is said and done, the love, mercy, and justice of God will be vindicated.

19. Germain Grisez, *The Way of the Lord Jesus, Volume One: Christian Moral Principles* (Chicago: Franciscan Herald, 1983), pp. 448–451. He says, "Although the damned abuse their freedom, their reality and their freedom remain great goods," p. 448.

20. The same thing could be said about suicide. See Stanley Hauerwas, *Suffering Presence: Theological Reflections on Medicine, the Mentally Handicapped, and the Church* (Notre Dame, IN: University of Notre Dame, 1986), pp. 100–113.

Eternity in the Balance

1. Although we "tabled" establishing the validity of theism, we believe another strong argument for life after death could be developed if theism was first established. We did not have adequate space to do this, but we would refer you to J.P. Moreland's *Scaling the Secular City* (Grand Rapids, MI: Baker, 1987), chaps. 1–4, for a well-formed case for theism.

About the Authors

Gary R. Habermas is the Chairman of the Department of Philosophy and Theology and professor of apologetics and philosophy at Liberty University, Lynchburg, Virginia. He has written numerous books on life-after-death issues, including *The Resurrection of Jesus: An Apologetic, Did Jesus Rise from the Dead?* (a debate with Antony Flew), *Verdict on the Shroud, The Verdict of History, The Shroud and the Controversy,* and *Dealing with Doubt.*

He has published numerous scholarly and popular articles in such periodicals as *Religious Studies, Faith and Philosophy, Christianity Today, Catholic Digest, New Covenant, Christian Scholar's Review, Bibliotheca Sacra, Saturday Evening Post,* and *Journal of the Evangelical Theological Society.* He received a B.R.E. from William Tyndale College, a M.A. in religious studies from the University of Detroit, and a Ph.D. in history and philosophy of religion from Michigan State University.

Habermas lives in Lynchburg, Virginia, with his wife, Debbie, and their four children: Robbie, Michelle, Holly, and Kevin. In addition to teaching and writing, he also coaches Liberty University's club ice hockey team.

J.P. Moreland is professor of philosophy of religion at Talbot School of Theology, Biola University, La Mirada, California, and serves as director of Talbot's M.A. program in philosophy and ethics. His articles have been published in such professional journals as *The Australasian Journal of Philosophy, The American Philosophical Quarterly, Philosophy and Phenomenological Research, Journal of the Evangelical Theological Society, The Thomist,* and *Process Studies.*

Among his books are *Christianity and the Nature of Science, Scaling the Secular City, Does God Exist?* (a debate with Kai Nielsen), *The Life and Death Debate,* and *Eldercare for the Christian Family.* He has earned four academic degrees: a B.S. in chemistry from the University of Missouri, a Th.M. in theology from Dallas Theological Seminary, a M.A. in philosophy from the University of California at Riverside, and a Ph.D. in philosophy from the University of Southern California.

Moreland's wife, Hope, is a preschool teacher and they have two daughters, Ashley and Allison. His hobbies are jogging and classical music (in that order)!